M000248167

Garden History of Georgia

1733 ~ 1933

Compiled by LORAINE M. COONEY

Edited by HATTIE C. RAINWATER

GEORGIA'S EARLY GARDENS

Author, FLORENCE MARYE

Illustrator, P. THORNTON MARYE, A.I.A.

THE UNIVERSITY OF GEORGIA PRESS

ATHENS

This publication is made possible in part through a grant
from the Mildred Miller Fort Foundation, Inc.

© 2018 by the University of Georgia Press
Athens, Georgia 30602
www.ugapress.org
© 1933 by the Peachtree Garden Club
© 1976 by the Garden Club of Georgia, Inc.
All rights reserved
Illustrations by Dixie Engraving Co., Savannah
Printed and bound by Thomson-Shore, Inc.
The paper in this book meets the guidelines for
permanence and durability of the Committee on
Production Guidelines for Book Longevity of the
Council on Library Resources.

Most University of Georgia Press titles are
available from popular e-book vendors.

Printed in the United States of America
18 19 20 21 22 C 5 4 3 2 1

Library of Congress Cataloging-in-Publication Data
Names: Cooney, Loraine M. (Loraine Meeks), compiler. | Rainwater, Hattie C., editor. | Marye, Florence, author. | Marye, P. Thornton (Philip Thornton), 1872–1935, illustrator. | Marye, Florence. Georgia's early gardens.
Title: Garden history of Georgia, 1733–1933 / compiled by Loraine M. Cooney ; edited by Hattie C. Rainwater. Georgia's early gardens / author, Florence Marye ; illustrator, P. Thornton Marye.
Description: Athens, Georgia : University of Georgia Press, 2018. | "This book was originally published in 1933 by the Peachtree Garden Club. Reprinted in 1976 by the Garden Club of Georgia, Inc." | Includes bibliographical references.
Identifiers: LCCN 2017044581 | ISBN 9780820353012 (hardcover : alk. paper)
Subjects: LCSH: Gardens—Georgia—History. | Architecture, Domestic—Georgia.
Classification: LCC SB466.U62 G43 2018 | DDC 712.09758—dc23
LC record available at https://lccn.loc.gov/2017044581

This book was originally published in 1933 by the Peachtree Garden Club.
Reprinted in 1976 by the Garden Club of Georgia, Inc.

Acknowledgments

THE chairman and the editor desire to thank the following friends who have made lighter the task of preparing for publication the material of *Garden History of Georgia:*

The individual writers who have contributed descriptions of their own gardens or the gardens of friends.

Miss Irene Davis, Thomasville; Mrs. Wymberley DeRenne, Savannah; Mrs. Nelle Womack Hines, Milledgeville; Mrs. M. C. Jarnagin, Athens, and Mrs. Lansing Lee, Augusta, for assistance in collecting material.

Dr. Woolford B. Baker of Emory University for his articles on the flora of Okefenokee Swamp and of Stone Mountain.

Dr. T. H. McHatton of the University of Georgia for his articles entitled "Gardening in Georgia," "The Campuses of the University of Georgia," and for many valuable suggestions.

The Atlanta Journal for photographs.

Mrs. Jesse Draper, Mrs. DeWitt Norton, Mrs. Albert Thornton and Mrs. Arthur Tufts for their invaluable assistance in editing.

A Message from the

Georgia Bicentennial Commission

Nineteen thirty-three will live long in the minds of Georgians as the year in which was held their State-wide celebration commemorating the two-hundredth anniversary of the founding of the Georgia colony and honoring her sons and daughters who have, during the two hundred years, made distinct contribution toward the upbuilding of the State and Nation.

The activities of the celebration extended over a period of ten months, beginning formally at Savannah on Georgia Day, February 12th, and closing on Thanksgiving Day. All Georgia entered into the spirit of the celebration and to it the world was invited. Over three thousand five hundred Bicentennial exercises, meetings and events were held in its one hundred and fifty-nine counties, and in many of the public schools of the United States a review of the history of Georgia had a prominent place in the study program.

One of the most important and useful functions of the Georgia Bicentennial Commission—appointed by Governor Russell and later on added to by Governor Talmadge, and placed in charge of organization and promotion of Bicentennial exercises and events, and State and Nation-wide publicity of the Celebration—was that of collecting and disseminating correct, reliable and interesting information concerning Georgia, past and present.

Working toward this end, the Commission requested Mrs. Robert L. Cooney of Atlanta, Honorary President of the Garden Club of Georgia and President of the Peachtree Garden Club of Atlanta, to act as Chairman of a Committee to be selected by herself, to compile and publish the *Garden History of Georgia.*

The suggestion for the compiling and publication of the *Garden Book* received the endorsement of the Garden Club of Georgia.

As the Commission had no appropriation from the State, nor other funds for this important work, Mrs. Cooney secured the cooperation of the Peachtree Garden Club to sponsor, finance and publish the book.

The Commission recommended as editor Miss Hattie C. Rainwater, Supervisor of Nature Study and Gardening of the Atlanta Public Schools, and offered the services of Dr. Albert R. Rogers, their Director of Celebration, to cooperate with Mrs. Cooney and the Garden Book Committee as business manager.

Complying with the request of the Commission, and working in harmony with their own inclinations, the Garden Book Committee has endeavored to make this a most comprehensive record of gardening in Georgia from Oglethorpe's day, 1733, to the most modern garden of 1933. Through the cooperation of all, the publishers are enabled to sell this splendid and carefully compiled book at a remarkably reasonable price.

The appearance of a living memorial of Georgia's Garden History and of the beautiful gardens of 1933 is one of the outstanding accomplishments of the Georgia Bicentennial Celebration, and the Commission desires thus publicly to express to Mrs. Cooney and her Committee, to Miss Rainwater, to the Peachtree Garden Club, to Mr. and Mrs. P. Thornton Marye, to the Walter W. Brown Publishing Company and their President, Mr. Walter W. Brown, and to the Dixie Engraving Company and their representative, Mr. Harris Hurst, their appreciation for their interest and cooperation, and to express also their appreciation of the generous contributions of time and thought of all who have had a part in making this splendid history of Georgia's Gardens possible.

Sincerely,

PLEASANT A. STOVALL, *President,*
Savannah, Ga.

WILLIS A. SUTTON,
Chairman, Executive Committee,
Atlanta, Ga.

Book Committee

Mrs. Robert L. Cooney, Chairman
Mrs. C. C. Case, Treasurer
Mrs. Clarence Anderson
Mrs. Randolph Jacques
Mrs. Geo. Burrus
Mrs. M. C. Jarnagin
Mrs. Phinizy Calhoun
Mrs. P. Thornton Marye
Mrs. Rodney Cohen
Dr. T. H. McHatton
Miss Irene Davis
Mrs. Cooper Newton
Mrs. Wymberley DeRenne
Mrs. DeWitt Norton
Mrs. Jesse Draper
Mrs. Albert Thornton
Mrs. Bruce Hall
Mrs. Jas. D. Robinson
Mrs. Nelle Womack Hines
Mrs. Geo. Street
Mrs. Jas. Edgar Paullin
Mrs. Arthur Tufts

Subscribers

Agnes Scott College
Mrs. Frank Adair
Mrs. William Akers
James Alexander
Mrs. H. D. Allen
Mrs. T. P. Allen
Mrs. Robert Alston
Mrs. Clarence G. Anderson
W. Montgomery Anderson
J. Randolph Anderson
Elizabeth Arden
Mrs. Preston Arkwright
Mrs. Elizabeth Stewart Armstrong
Mrs. Reuben Arnold
Mrs. H. M. Atkinson
Miss Elizabeth Ball
Mrs. Lucius B. Barbour
Mrs. Craig Barrow
Mrs. Frank E. Beane
Mrs. Frank E. Beane, Jr.
Mrs. Martha K. Beatty
Mrs. Miller S. Bell
Mrs. Thad C. Bell
Miss Martha Berry
Mrs. Thos. W. Berry
Ruth Blair
Mrs. Alfred S. Bourne
Mrs. Valeria Langloth Bonham
Mrs. O. K. Bovard
Mrs. Robert T. Bowman
Mrs. William Bradshaw
Bremen Garden Club
Miriam Brooks
Mrs. O. R. Brooks
Mrs. Shepard Bryan
Mrs. Howard Bucknell
Kate Robinson Butler
Norman Butts
Mrs. Cobb Caldwell
Mrs. Howell Caldwell
Mr. and Mrs. James Hope Caldwell
Mrs. A. W. Calhoun
Mrs. Andrew Calhoun
Mrs. Phinizy Calhoun
Mrs. Cason Callaway
Mrs. Fuller Callaway
Mrs. Fuller Callaway, Jr.
Mrs. J. Bulow Campbell
Lord Cardross
Mrs. Chas. C. Case
Camellia Garden Club, Columbus
Mrs. Howard Candler
Carnegie Library, Atlanta
Carnegie Library, Rome
Mrs. Harry L. Chafee
Eleanor McC. Chalfont

Subscribers

Mrs. Charles M. Chapin
William E. Chapin
Mrs. E. Y. Chapin
Cherokee Garden Club, Atlanta
Mrs. Hunt Chipley
Clarkston Garden Club, Clarkston
Mrs. W. H. Cocke
Mrs. C. Henry Cohen
Mrs. Rodney S. Cohen
Commerce Garden Club
Mrs. Chas. A. Conklin
Mrs. W. Spencer Connerat
Mrs. George W. Connors
Dr. and Mrs. Thos. Connor
Mrs. L. Neil Conrad
Mrs. Robert L. Cooney
Samuel Inman Cooper
Coweta Garden Club, Newnan
Mrs. Dudley R. Cowles
Mrs. Mack W. Cresap
Mr. and Mrs. Francis M. Croft
Henry P. Crowell
Mrs. Fletcher Pearson Crown
Mrs. Duncan Curry
Mrs. L. M. Dabney
Mrs. L. G. Daingerfield
Mrs. Chas. Anderson Dana
Minnie J. Daniel
Mrs. Wymberley W. DeRenne
Mrs. Jackson Dick
Edwin S. Dodge
Mrs. E. Griffith Dodson
Cam D. Dorsey
Mrs. Cam D. Dorsey
Mrs. Hugh Dorsey
Mrs. Rufus Dorsey
Jesse Draper
Constance K. Draper
Mrs. Dan C. Elkin
Mrs. Blanche I. Elrod
Mrs. Jno. O. Enders
Mrs. Thomas C. Erwin
Mrs. G. C. Estill
Mrs. Kelly Evans
Faith School, Atlanta
Mrs. R. W. Fender
Mrs. David Ferguson
Mrs. B. E. Finucane
Mrs. Samuel H. Fisher
Miss Louise Fitten
Mrs. Malcolm Fleming
Mrs. W. A. Flinn
Mrs. Frank Foley
Mrs. J. A. Foster
Donald Edward Frederick
Myron Freeman
J. Herbert Gailey
Garden Club of Nashville
Mrs. W. T. Garrard, Sr.
Mrs. W. F. Garth
General Federation of Woman's Clubs
Georgia Library Commission
Georgia State College for Women Library
Mrs. John H. Gibbons
Mrs. Price Gilbert
Mrs. Thomas K. Glenn
Mrs. John N. Goddard
Mrs. J. J. Goodrum
Mrs. Frances Gordon-Smith
Mrs. John W. Grant
Mrs. Inman Gray
Col. E. A. Greene
Mrs. E. B. Greene
Mrs. Robert Gregg
Miss Nellie Griswold
Mrs. John R. Guilliams
Mrs. J. L. Hand
Mrs. Howard M. Hanna
Mrs. Edward S. Harkness
Mrs. Marion Harper
Anne H. Harris
Mrs. Arthur Harris
Mrs. P. W. Harvey
Mrs. G. H. Haskell
Mrs. Chas. P. Hatcher
Mrs. Clarence Haverty
Miss May Haverty
Mrs. Frank Hawkins
Mrs. B. T. Haynes
Mrs. William Heard
Frances Connally Hentz
Mrs. Arnold A. Hepp
Mrs. Olivia R. Herbert
Mrs. Ada A. Hickey
Miss Nellie Hightower
Mrs. William P. Hill
Mrs. W. H. R. Hilliard
Mrs. Nelle Womack Hines
Mrs. Thomas P. Hinman
Geo. F. Hoffman
Mrs. H. Willis Hogg
Hoke Smith Junior High School, Atlanta
Miss Mary Holder
Mrs. Frank E. Howald

Subscribers

David T. Howard School, Atlanta
Albert Howell, Jr.
Mrs. Clark Howell
Mrs. Clark Howell, Jr.
Katherine Mitchell Howell
Mrs. Roy Arthur Hunt
Mrs. John S. Hurt
Mrs. Palmer Hutcheson
Mrs. Edward W. Hutchins
Mrs. C. L. Hutchinson
Mrs. Jno. A. Hynds
Arthur Crew Inman
Mrs. Edward H. Inman
Frank M. Inman
Henry A. Inman
Mildred McPheeters Inman
Iris Garden Club, Atlanta
Miss Louise Irwin
Mrs. C. Oliver Iselin
Mrs. S. Randolph Jacques
Mrs. Walter B. James
James River Garden Club
Mrs. Allen F. Johnson
Mrs. David C. Johnson
Mrs. Edwin Johnson
Isabel T. Johnston
Pamela Johnston
Mrs. Richard W. Johnston
Mrs. L. W. Johnston
Mrs. B. F. Jones, Jr.
Miss Elizabeth Jones
Major H. Seaver Jones
Mrs. R. C. Jordan
Mrs. M. E. Judd
Esther Green Judkins
Mrs. Alfred G. Kay
Mrs. Frederick R. Kellog
Eugenia Oglesby Kilpatrick
Mrs. Walter E. King
Miss Lula L. Kingsbery
Miss Mary Kingsbery
Mrs. William H. Kiser
Mrs. William J. Knapp
Mrs. John L. Kuser
Mrs. Ethel Toy Lamar
Mrs. Walter R. Lamb
Mrs. J. M. Lang
Mrs. George M. Laughlin, Jr.
Mrs. John W. Lawrence
Alexander R. Lawton, Jr.
Mrs. Willaford Ransom Leach
Mrs. Blewett Lee
F. E. Lee
Mrs. Lansing B. Lee
Mrs. Philip F. L'Engle
Mrs. M. L. Lively
Mrs. Horatio Gates Lloyd
Edwin S. Lodge
Mrs. William Bladen Lowndes
Mr. and Mrs. Baxter Maddox
Miss Laura Maddox
Mrs. Robert F. Maddox
Mr. and Mrs. Robert F. Maddox, Jr.
Mrs. Clifford Mallory
Marguerite Garden Club, Columbus
Percy MacLean Marshall
Miss Helen M. Marshall
Maj. and Mrs. P. Thornton Marye
Mrs. R. G. McAliley
Mr. and Mrs. E. P. McBurney
Mrs. Philip McDuffie
Dr. Thos. H. McHatton
Mrs. William Jay McKenna
Isabelle Nash McPheeters
Irene Palm Morey
Mrs. James S. Metcalfe
Mrs. Brooks Morgan
Mrs. L. G. Morris
Francis Dillon Moss
William Murphy
Mrs. William M. Nichols
J. L. Nisbet
Marieanne Nisbet
A. J. Nitzschke
Mrs. Vaughn Nixon
Mrs. M. DeWitt Norton
Mrs. Henry F. Noyes
Susan Calhoun Oglesby
Willie D. O'Kelly
Mrs. J. H. O'Neill
Miss Leni O'Neill
Mrs. J. D. Osborne
Mrs. Oscar Palmour
Mrs. Mildred Parris
Mrs. Z. C. Patten
Harold Patterson
Edna Frederick Paullin
Peony Garden Club, Atlanta
Perennial Garden Club, Atlanta
Mazie Thompson Perham
Mrs. Hunter Perry
Mrs. J. L. Perry
Miss Mary Lou Phinizy

Subscribers

Mrs. Ferdinand Phinizy
Mrs. Henry A. Platt
Mrs. Lucy B. Pomeroy
Mrs. W. A. Ponder
Alice Steel Powers
Mrs. Geo. L. Pratt
Mrs. W. R. Prescott
Mrs. Mary B. Pritchett
Brown Rainwater
Crawford Rainwater
Mr. and Mrs. E. M. Rainwater
Miss Hattie Rainwater
Miss Josephine Rainwater
Lupton Rainwater
Mr. and Mrs. Paul E. Rainwater
Mr. and Mrs. Veazy Rainwater
Veazy Rainwater, Jr.
Mrs. Gaston C. Raoul
Ben S. Read
Mrs. Isaac W. Read
Mrs. S. M. Page Rees
Walton Reeves
Mrs. Jno. W. Reid
Maude A. Rhodes
Mrs. Hugh Richardson
Mrs. Grant Ridgway
Mr. and Mrs. James D. Robinson
Major Thomas L. Robinson
Albert R. Rogers
Mr. and Mrs. Archie A. Rogers
Mr. and Mrs. Clarence B. Rogers
Mrs. W. C. Ross
Rose Garden Club
Mrs. G. W. Rowbotham
Sarah Rupp
Mr. and Mrs. D. A. Russell
Marie L. Russell
Sandersville Public Library
Mrs. Alfred Sanford
Mrs. Bolling Hall Sasnett
Savannah Public School Library
Seaboard Air Line Free Traveling Library
Sea Island Co.
Mrs. Henry B. Scott
Mrs. Trammell Scott
Mrs. F. B. Screven
Mrs. J. B. Selman
Mrs. Raphael T. Semmes
Sophie M. Shonnard
Mrs. Charles A. Sisson
Mrs. John M. Slaton
Mrs. Alex Smith, Jr.
Mrs. C. T. Smith
Mrs. E. D. Smith
Mrs. Benjamin O. Sprague
Mrs. Rix Stafford
Mrs. H. W. Stephenson
Mr. and Mrs. Pleasant A. Stovall
Mrs. Geo. P. Street
Mrs. Joel Swift
Teacher's Reference Library, Atlanta
Mrs. Geo. D. Thomas
Thomasville Garden Club
Mrs. Albert E. Thornton
Mr. and Mrs. Edward Allison Thornwell
Dr. and Mrs. E. A. Tigner
G. I. Tolson
Mrs. H. N. Torrey
Trustees Garden Club, Savannah
Mrs. Jennie W. Tufts
Mrs. Samuel Yoer Tupper
Mrs. Elizabeth B. Turner
Misses Esther and Emily Upson
United Garden Clubs, Columbus
Mrs. Henry G. Vaughn
Vidalia Garden Club
Jno. Donald Wade
Mrs. J. Carter Walker
Mrs. Fielding Wallace
Gertrude S. Wardlaw
Mrs. Stephen H. Watts
Waycross Rose Society
J. Prince Webster
Mrs. Gordon Wells
Annie E. Wheeler
Mrs. Julia A. White
Mrs. W. B. White
Mrs. Payne Whitney
Mrs. Richard H. Wilmer
Mrs. Jno. G. Williams
Mrs. F. B. Willingham
Marian E. Woodward
Mrs. Jno. J. Woodriff
Cator Woolford
T. G. Woolford
Richardson Wright
Mrs. Wallace Wright
Mrs. James O. Wynn
Mrs. Kenyon B. Zahner
Mrs. Paul Zolotas

CONTENTS

Garden History of Georgia

Part One

GEORGIA'S EARLY GARDENS

A Genealogy of Georgia Gardens 1

Chatham County

Trustees' Garden 15

Wormsloe 18

Savannah 21

Richardson-Maxwell-Owens-Thomas House . 23

Batersby-Hartridge-Wilder-Anderson House . 24

Low House 27

Whitehall Plantation 28

Lebanon 29

Hermitage 30

Avon Hall 33

Glynn County

St. Simons Island 34

Hopeton 46

Altama 48

Elizafield Plantation 50

Camden County

Twin Plantations, Bellevue and Fairfield . . 52

Richmond County

Augusta 54

Carnes-Howard-Thomas-Chafee Place . . 56

Cumming-Langdon Place 59

Rosemary Cottage 60

Fruitlands 62

Elbert County

Rose Hill Plantation 64

Greene County

Greenesboro 66

Oglethorpe County

Upson-Howard Place 70

Clark County

Athens 72

Camak Place 73

Bishop Cottage 75

Thomas House 76

Grant-Hill-White-Bradshaw Place . . . 78

Baldwin County

Williams-Ferguson Place 81

Westover 82

Morgan County

Bonar Hall 84

Kolb-Pou-Newton Place 86

Bibb County

Cowles-Bond-Coleman-Cabaniss-O'Neal Place 88

Thomas County

Greenwood Plantation 90

Carroll County

Oak Lawn 92

Troup County

Ferrell Gardens 94

Muscogee County

Columbus 98

St. Elmo 100

The Elms 102

Esquiline Hill 104

Coweta County

Rosemary 106

Bartow County

Barnsley Gardens 108

Valley View 110

Cobb County

Barrington Hall and Bulloch Hall . . . 112

Mimosa Hall 114

Oakton 116

Fulton County

The Terraces 118

Part Two

MODERN GARDENS

Transition Gardens 123

(1) Casulon Plantation, Walton County . . 124

(2) Veazey Plantation, Greene County . . 127

Gardening in Georgia—*Dr. T. H. McHatton, University of Georgia* 130

Modern Gardens

Albany

Davant, Miss Jane 140

Myer, Mrs. Joe A. 141

Whitehead, Miss Cena J. 143

Ashland Farm 144

Athens

Introduction. The Gardens of Athens . . 147

Hodgson, Mr. and Mrs. E. R. 148

Lumpkin, Mrs. E. K. 149

S. A. E. House 151

Park, Mrs. R. E. 153

Reid, Mrs. Henry 154

Rowland, Mr. and Mrs. C. A. 155

Rucker, Mr. and Mrs. Lamar C. 157

Sasnett, Mr. and Mrs. Bolling Hall . . . 159

Upson, Misses 161

Atlanta

Arkwright, Mr. and Mrs. Preston S. . . . 165

Atkinson, Mr. and Mrs. Henry M. . . . 167

Caldwell, Mr. and Mrs. Cobb 171

Calhoun, Mr. and Mrs. Andrew 177

Calhoun, Dr. and Mrs. Phinizy 181

Campbell, Mr. and Mrs. J. Bulow . . . 184

Candler, Mr. and Mrs. Howard 188

Cooney, Mr. and Mrs. R. L. 191

Dorsey, Mr. and Mrs. Cam 194

Erwin, Mr. and Mrs. Thomas C. . . . 197

Fleming, Mr. and Mrs. Frank 200

Floyd, Mr. and Mrs. James S. 202

Gilbert, Judge and Mrs. Price 207

Goodrum, Mrs. J. J. 209

Harris, Mr. and Mrs. Arthur 213

Harrison, Mr. Z. D. 217

Haverty, Mr. J. J. 221

Hill, Mrs. William P. 223

Howell, Mr. and Mrs. Clark 225

Inman, Mrs. Edward 228

Johnston, Mrs. R. W. 232

Kiser, Mr. and Mrs. William H. 235

Maddox, Mr. and Mrs. R. F. 240

McBurney, Mr. and Mrs. Edgar Poe . . . 244

McRae, Dr. and Mrs. Floyd 248

Rainwater, Mr. and Mrs. C. V. 251

Richardson, Mr. and Mrs. Hugh 255

Rowbotham, Mr. and Mrs. G. W. 259
Slaton, Mr. and Mrs. John M. 262
Selman, Mr. and Mrs. J. T. 265
Stephenson, Mr. and Mrs. H. W. . . . 266
Tompkins, Mr. and Mrs. Henry B. . . . 269
Tufts, Mrs. Arthur 272
Woolford, Mr. Cator 275
Zahner, Mr. and Mrs. Kenyon B. . . . 278

Augusta

Albright, Mrs. Harry 282
Bourne, Mrs. Alfred S. 284
Chafee, Mrs. Harry 288
Cohen, Mrs. C. Henry 291
Cohen, Mr. and Mrs. Rodney S. . . . 294
Crowell, Mr. H. P. 297
Herbert, Mr. and Mrs. John W. . . . 300
Speer, Mr. and Mrs. Joseph McK. . . . 303
Reese, Mrs. Robert G. 306
White, Mr. and Mrs. Wm. B. 308

Cedartown

Campbell, Mr. and Mrs. Robert 311

Columbus

Bradley, Mr. and Mrs. W. C. 313
Jordan, Mr. and Mrs. R. C. 316
McKinnon, Mrs. J. M. and Miss Alsobrook . 318
Woodruff, Mr. and Mrs. J. W. 319

Dalton

Judd, Mrs. M. E. 322

Decatur

Hall, Mrs. Bruce 326
Nichols, Mrs. Wm. 329

LaGrange

Callaway, Mrs. F. E. 330

Macon

Porter, Mr. and Mrs. James 333
Stewart, Mr. and Mrs. T. J. 334

Marietta

McNeel, Mr. and Mrs. Morgan, Sr. . . . 336

Milledgeville

Hines, Judge and Mrs. E. R. 339
Bell, Mr. and Mrs. Miller S. 343

Newnan

Sewell, Mr. and Mrs. Wayne P. 346

Ossabaw Island

Torrey, Dr. and Mrs. H. N. 349

Rock City

Carter, Mr. and Mrs. Garnett 354

Rome

Berry, Mr. and Mrs. Thomas 358

Roswell

Reid, Mrs. John 361

Sapelo Island

Coffin, Mr. Howard 365

Savannah

Notes From W. W. DeRenne Library . . 368
DeRenne, Mr. and Mrs. W. W. 370
Hilton, Mrs. Thomas 374
McLean, Mrs. Malcolm 375
Trosdal, Miss Lucy 378

St. Simons

Lewis, Mr. and Mrs. Eugene W. 380

Thomasville

Chapin, Mrs. Charles Merril 385
Ely, Mr. and Mrs. J. Morse 388
Hanna, Mr. and Mrs. Howard M. . . . 390
Harvey, Mrs. Perry W. 393
Haskell, Mrs. Coburn 396
Lively, Mr. and Mrs. M. L. 399
Wade, J. H. Family 401
Whitney, Mrs. Payne 405

Natural Gardens of Georgia
—*Dr. Woolford B. Baker, Emory University*

Stone Mountain 408
Okefenokee Swamp 409

Part Three

GARDEN CLUB PROJECTS
INSTITUTIONAL GARDENS
SCHOOL GARDENS AND CAMPUSES

Garden Club Projects

Cherokee Garden Club—Atlanta

Egleston Memorial Garden 413

Druid Hills Garden Club—Atlanta

Municipal Rose Garden 417

Iris Garden Club—Atlanta

Iris Garden 419

Lullwater Garden Club—Atlanta .

Lullwater Creek Conservation Project . 421

Sand Hills Garden Club—Augusta

Old Medical College 423

Junior League Garden Club—Savannah

Savannah Female Orphanage . . . 424

Transylvania Garden Club—Sandersville

Sandersville Library 426

Institutional Gardens

Bonaventure, Savannah 426

Spring Hill, Atlanta 428

West View, Atlanta 430

School Gardens and Campuses

Atlanta Public Schools 433

Chatham County Public Schools . . . 442

Old Oglethorpe 444

New Oglethorpe 445

Shorter College 446

Rome High School 446

Martha Berry School 447

Oak Hill

House o' Dreams

University of Georgia Campuses . . . 453

Foreword and Dedication

IT has been the occasion of some surprise that in current garden literature, Georgia is so casually dismissed with a slight bow of recognition and a pleasant smile. A question arises as to whether this originates from a lack of interest or, indeed, from a lack of knowledge, for while Georgians appreciate the better known gardens of other sections, they concede to none of the thirteen original colonies a more interesting or a more romantic garden history.

The gardens in Georgia have been precious to Georgians, but little known elsewhere. As a matter of fact, they, both large and small, have a very distinct flavor and appeal of their own, and a *raison d'etre* better understood at home than abroad.

While for many years the gardens were neglected, bereft as they were of that type of labor to which they had become accustomed, the owners rather quickly adjusted themselves and they now believe that in restoring some of the old gardens and in planning and planting the new, Georgia may occupy that place in the garden interest of the country which is its natural heritage.

Probably the most important work now being accomplished for the improvement of gardens in the State is the training given to the school children. Their knowledge and love of gardening will be infinitely greater than ours, and their lives made richer by the nature study that is part of their education.

To have a small share in recording the gardens that were, and are, and will be, has been a pleasure, and this volume, a Georgia product, is dedicated to gardeners of all climes, with the hope of a wider appreciation of Georgia gardens.

LORAINE MEEKS COONEY.

Part One

EARLY GARDENS

Georgia's Early Gardens

1566 – 1865

BY

FLORENCE MARYE

WITH PEN AND INK ILLUSTRATIONS

BY

P. THORNTON MARYE, A.I.A.

"Ah! spicy border of our clove pinks,
Of fragrant memory that fondly links
Us to the past, I linger here with thee;
And other gardens, other faces see."
—Frank Harwell

Preface

THIS group of early Georgia gardens is the fruit of a difficult selection from a wide field of choice. Their mission is to tell the story of the early development of gardening within the Commonwealth. The twenty-one garden drawings are true to scale. They delineate their subjects as they appeared in the year 1863. The technique used was thought appropriate to that period. Needless to say what value they may have is dependent on accuracy, and to secure this no effort has been spared.

The lists available of trees and shrubs are reasonably adequate; those of bulbs and tubers less so. Of roses, annuals and perennials, there could have been no lack, as the climate and soil of Georgia are favorable to their cultivation, but they have died out and few authentic lists of them have come down to us.

In describing the grounds and gardens, there has been employed the simple nomenclature in familiar use by their owners, who only gave botanical designations to strange or rare specimens. For instance, box was dubbed dwarf or tree, though many varieties of that aristocrat of ancient lineage such as Buxus sempervirens, vars.—arborescens—suffruticosa, and Buxus balearica, plus the variants and sports of each and all, were and still are found throughout Georgia, also other species privately imported and not officially credited to this section.

Botany, an honored course in the curriculum of the innumerable Female Colleges of the State, produced many lady botanists who went about panoplied in Latin and armed with instruments for dissecting plants and flowers. No doubt they had their uses but it was seldom as makers of gardens. The patterns of old Georgia gardens were elaborate, but gardening was taken as a simple pleasure.

The sequence in which they appear was determined by the date of the settling of the district where the gardens were found.

Acknowledgment

IT is a pleasure to acknowledge the gracious and generous assistance rendered us in compiling the data for this work by the descendants of those who planned and planted these gardens and by their present owners.

Valuable help was given us by many Georgians interested in the preservation of a record of the State's early gardens.

The Reference Department of the Carnegie Library of Atlanta and the State Library also rendered valuable assistance.

1572

A fragment of the tabby ruins of Santo Domingo at Talaje, a Spanish mission and casa fuerte or presidio, still standing at Elizafield Plantation on the Altamaha River. This settlement, established by Franciscan monks, was surrounded by tilled fields, orchards, olive and citrus groves and vegetable gardens.

A Genealogy of Georgia Gardens

PICTURES of homes and gardens interest and fascinate us because they are sincere portraits of the people who built and lived in them.

Georgia's gallery covers a span of three hundred and sixty odd years and is distinguished by its variety. Here we see depicted the missions and barracks of Spain's soldiers of cross and crown; the simple, thrifty homes of the unfortunate and persecuted come to seek a new life in a new land; the ample homes of town and city; the mansions of great land owners and the humble cabins of their slaves; the often comfortable dwellings of Creek and Cherokee braves; the wayside or village cottage; the log house of the mountaineer; each set in a garden, true index of the spirit of the dwellers within.

The youngest of our Thirteen Original States, Georgia has a gardening record that perhaps antedates that of any of her sisters, for in 1566 the Adalantado Menendez de Aviles, Spanish governor at St. Augustine, established a permanent settlement, a mission, and a protecting casa fuerte on an

Map of Georgia Country in Spanish Days

By permission of Herbert E. Bolton

island just south of the estuaries of the Savannah River. They called it Santa Catalina. The Yemassee Indians who inhabited this coast were dwellers in villages and tillers of the soil, and on the mainland and islands considerable areas had been cleared, and planted by them in corn, beans, pumpkins and melons. The Fathers extended and gave improved cultivation to these fields. The missionary monks sent out by Spain came from monasteries which were the centers of husbandry and horticulture in that country, or from well established missions in the New World modeled after their mother institutions, and were well fitted to develop the agricultural possibilities of this fertile land.

The year 1572 saw twenty Spanish farmers settled on Santa Catalina.* Two years later a traveler, Dr. Carceres, reported the cultivation of corn at Santa Helena Island just north of the Savannah River, and tells us that "in the gardens of the houses and huts they plant lettuce, radishes, cabbage, pumpkins and seed, etc."** In 1580 three hundred acres were under cultivation on Santa Catalina.*** Almost simultaneously with the founding of this settlement, numerous Spanish missions and their protecting presidios had sprung up along the Georgia coast, to which the name of Guale was given. The map shows how closely linked a chain they formed. The churches, schools and barracks were built of tabby, a form of concrete made from crushed oyster shells, sand and lime from burnt oyster shells. The forts and huts were more often of heavy live oak timbers.

These communities had tilled fields and vegetable gardens. In time olives, dates, figs, pomegranates, peaches, oranges and lemons were set out. We can hope that for their comfort in a strange land, the Fathers had flowers reminiscent of their childhood to place upon the altars for which they fought. It is claimed by some authorities that the Cherokee rose, a native of Asia, was brought to this country by them. At least we know that they did not lack for candles to light their sanctuaries, as myrtle wax from the berries of the Myrica cerefera, so prolific along this coast, was being exported to Europe to illuminate castle and cathedral.****

By the end of the seventeenth century England had pushed Spain south of the St. Marys River.

* The Spanish Period of Georgia and South Carolina History, 1566-1702.—Johnson.

** Original manuscript belongs to Mary Ross, authoress of The Debatable Land.

*** History of Roman Catholic Church.—Dickinson.

**** Horticultural History of the Georgia Coast.—George D. Lowe.

Surviving the ensuing period when this coast became a kind of No Man's Land inhabited by pirates, the cleared fields and remnants of orchards, citrus and olive groves served to form a basis for the cultivation of the land by Oglethorpe's second body of colonists who arrived in Georgia in February, 1736, among whom portions of it were parcelled out.

Three years earlier, February 12, 1733, the first band of colonists brought over by him had been settled on Yamacraw Bluff, some seventeen miles up the Savannah River, and the city of Savannah founded. Agriculture and gardening were immediately initiated under Oglethorpe's fostering care. In the South Carolina Gazette of March 22, 1733, a South Carolina gentleman who had been visiting him, tells us "He (Mr. Oglethorpe) has plowed up some Land, part of which is sowed with Wheat which is come up and looks promising. He has two or three Gardens which he has sowed with diverse Sorts and Seeds and planted Thyme with other sorts of Potherbs, Sage, Leeks, Skellions, Celeri, Liquorice, etc., and several sorts of Fruit trees." Evidently the colonists liked their food highly seasoned.

It was in the spring of 1733 that Oglethorpe laid out what became known as the Trustees' Garden. It covered ten acres just east of the town. Charles C. Jones, Jr., in his History of Georgia, tells us that "A public garden was laid out and a servant detailed at the charge of the trust to cultivate it. This was to serve as a nursery whence might be procured fruit trees, vines, plants, and vegetables for the private orchards and gardens of the inhabitants. It was also largely devoted to the propagation of the white mulberry, from the general cultivation of which as food for the silk worm great benefit was anticipated." There seems to be no record of this famous garden's existence after the War for Independence.

Raw silk and wine were to be the basic products of the colony. This first industry, fostered by subsidies and aided by the easy cultivation of the white mulberry, indigenous to the region, attained considerable proportions. The Saltzburgers at New Ebenezer, founded in 1736, were preeminent in the cultivation of the mulberry tree and in the operation of filatures. Early in its history this thrifty community had many charming small gardens of formal pattern which survive until today.

Of the proposed wine industry we hear very little. In 1737 Mr. Lyon, a Portugese Jew, had what is described as "an improvement of vines."* We

* Col. William Stephens, Journal of Proceedings in Georgia, London MD.CCCXLM, Vol. I, P. 48.

1741-1758

A Map of the County of Savannah

On July 7, 1733, Oglethorpe laid out the City of Savannah and its environs. Each male inhabitant of full age participating in the allotment of land became possessed of a town lot sixty by ninety feet, a garden lot embracing five acres, and a farm containing forty-four acres and one hundred and forty-one poles; fifty acres in all. More extensive grants were made to individuals by the Trustees and later by the Crown when in 1752 Georgia became a Crown Colony. The plan and plot made in 1733 was lost. However, the above map of a later date gives a clear picture of land grants made by the Trustees. On the fifteenth of April, 1741, the Trustees divided the province of Georgia into two counties, Savannah and Frederica. On the seventeenth of March, 1758, the General Assembly approved an act dividing the several districts of the province into eight parishes. On the fifth of February, 1777, the constitutional convention of Georgia abolished the parishes and erected counties in their stead.

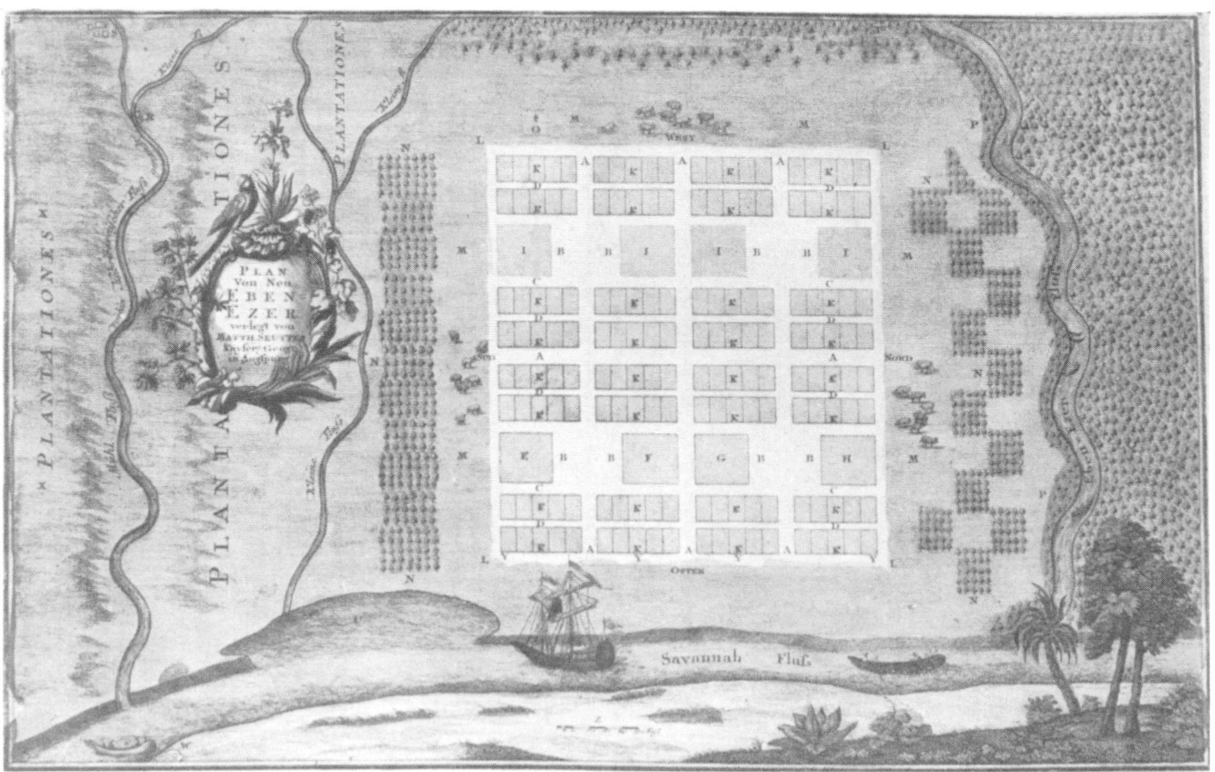

By permission of the Wymberley Jones DeRenne Georgia Library

1736

A Plan of New Ebenezer Showing the Groves of White Mulberries Cultivated for the Silk Worm Industry

New Ebenezer came into being when old Ebenezer, settled by the Saltzburgers in 1733, was abandoned for a more healthful situation.

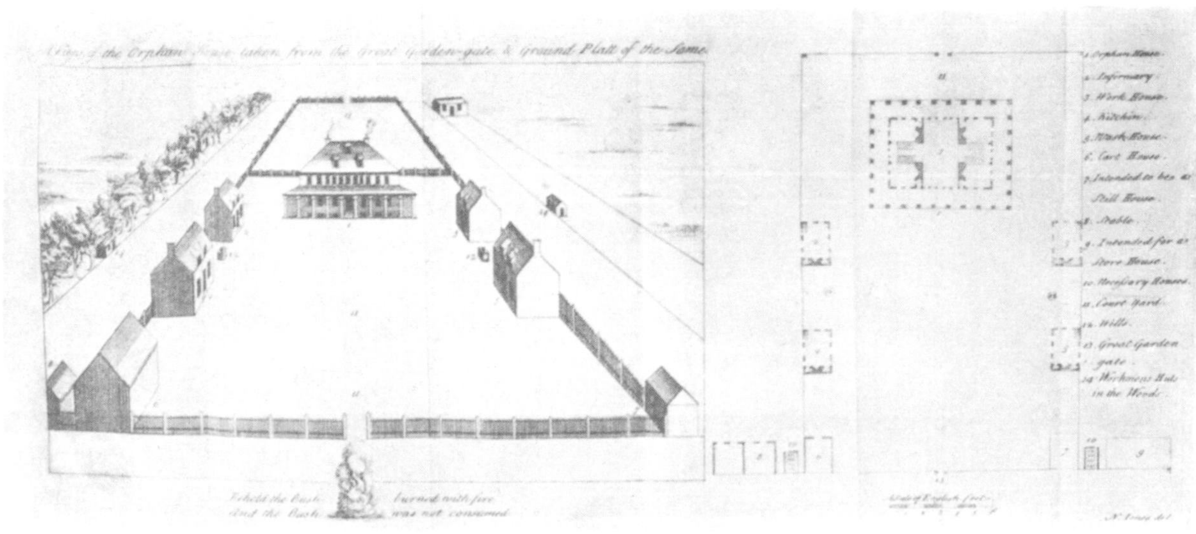

By permission of the Wymberley Jones DeRenne Georgia Library

1739

A Plan of the Bethesda Orphan House on the Isle of Hope, Near Savannah

Established in 1739 by the Reverend George Whitfield, to this day it remains a House of Mercy and is America's oldest surviving charitable institution of that character. Whitfield's garden is no more and the original buildings have several times been replaced, but the old fields and orchards are still under cultivation.

1818

For twelve years the home of Archibald Bullock, and the residence of Robert Habersham and his descendants until demolished in 1899. Very beautiful enclosures dignified Savannah's little front gardens. Wrought iron fencing of delicate design was extensively used for this purpose prior to 1830, when cast iron came into vogue. High tabby or brick walls gave privacy to the side and back gardens.

Liveoaks veiled in the gray of Spanish moss and festooned in flowering vines give a note of poetic beauty to the coast country.

1850

The Very English Savannah Home of Charles Green, an Englishman. For Many Years Past the Residence of Judge Peter Meldrim.

The parterre is developed as a side garden, though the general plan of the place is the conventional one for Trust Lots, adhered to from the town's earliest days until after the Civil War. The very fine cast iron work of the garden fence and verandas is characteristic of the middle of the nineteenth century. Palmettos, so appropriate to Savannah, were not planted within the city until 1880.

know that at General Oglethorpe's villa, Orange Hall, near Frederica, grapes were cultivated.* The Rev. George Whitfield, founder of Bethesda Orphanage, writes from there March 21, 1745, "If the vines hit, we may expect two or three hogsheads of wine out of the vineyard."** The wine made by the colonists was doubtless a source of comfort and pleasure, but it never became a commercial asset.

On July 7, 1733, Oglethorpe had a plan and plot drawn of Savannah, and land allotments were made to the colonists. Each male inhabitant of full age participating in the allotments became possessed of a town lot sixty feet in front, ninety feet in depth, a garden lot embracing five acres, and a farm containing forty-four acres and one hundred and forty-one poles, fifty acres in all, as had been ordered by the Trustees. It was required that each grantee plant one hundred white mulberry trees to be supplied them by the Trustees.***

* History of Georgia, Charles C. Jones, Vol. I, P. 337.

** Historical Collections of Georgia, Rev. George White, P. 329.

*** History of Georgia, Charles C. Jones, Chapter 10, PP. 157 and 159.

At first the little gardens of the town were devoted to the raising of foodstuffs. In a few years the five-acre garden lots were cultivated for this purpose and flower gardens came into being in the city. Comfortable homes of brick, wood or tabby, simple, dignified and very English, were built. A great similarity of plan prevailed. When an important residence occupied one of the four trust lots facing each public square, the mansion was set back from the street; a strip of formal planting or a small formal garden enclosed by a wrought or cast iron fence or a balustraded wall, occupied this space. Between the residence and the carriage house and servants' quarters at the rear lay another garden. Enclosed by high brick or tabby walls, it was generally planted in flowering shrubs, figs and citrus trees. Here also an herb garden would be found. An arbor covered with grapes or roses frequently shaded the path leading from one building to another. The same class of house occupying a corner often had an extra sixty feet laid out as a side garden. It was secluded behind a high wall or iron fence. Between the house and service build-

1765

Button Gwinnett, a signer of the Declaration of Independence, built this pink tabby cottage on St. Catherine's Island, purchased by him in 1765 after the death of Mary Musgrove Bosomworth, Oglethorpe's halfbreed agent, to whom the Island was deeded by the English Crown for her services to the colony. There were large gardens between the house and the bluff. The walks and paths were of crushed oyster shells, as was customary on the coast. For sixty years the house was used as bachelor quarters and gun room by the Rauers family, the owners of the Island.

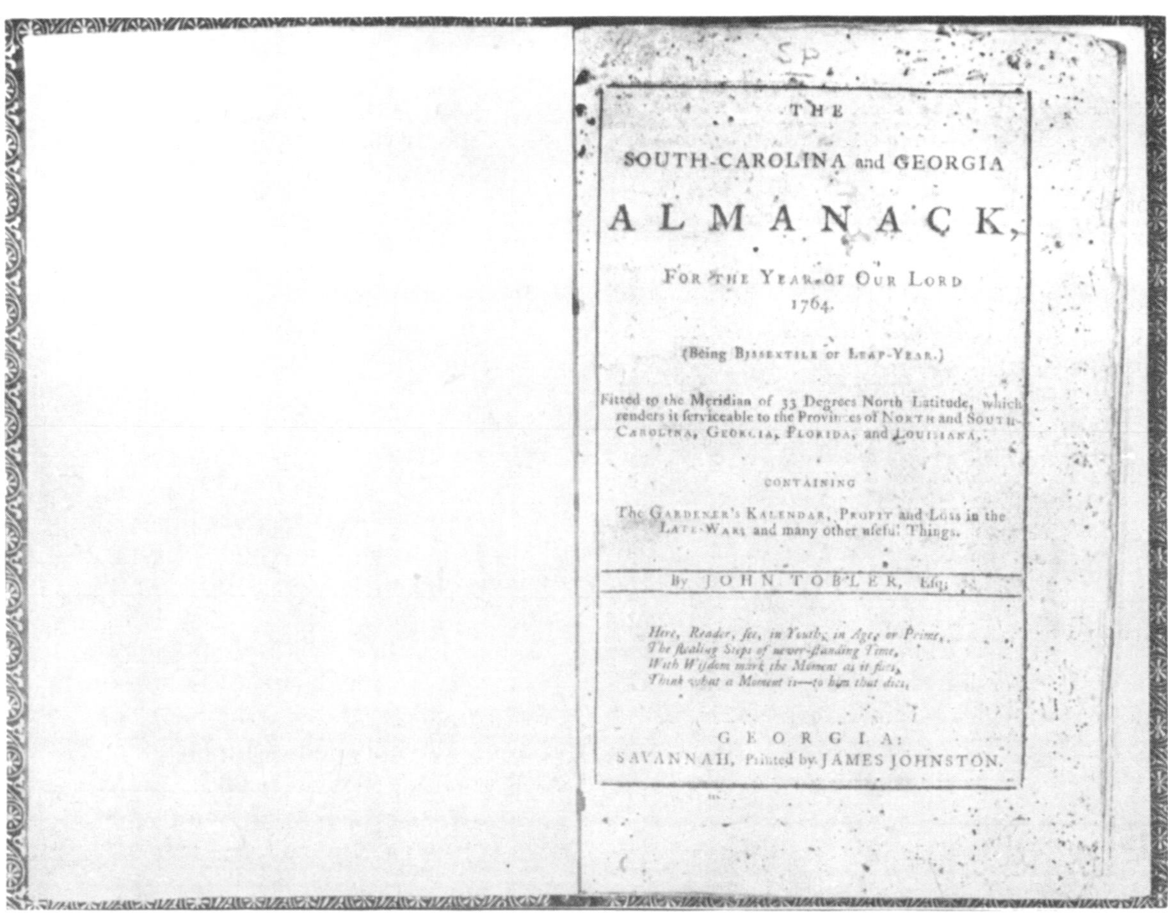

THE

SOUTH-CAROLINA and GEORGIA

ALMANACK,

FOR THE YEAR OF OUR LORD
1764.

(Being BISSEXTILE or LEAP-YEAR.)

Fitted to the Meridian of 33 Degrees North Latitude, which renders it ſerviceable to the Provinces of NORTH and SOUTH-CAROLINA, GEORGIA, FLORIDA, and LOUISIANA.

CONTAINING

The GARDENER'S KALENDAR, PROFIT and LOSS in the LATE WARS and many other uſeful Things.

By JOHN TOBLER, Eſq;

Here, Reader, ſee, in Youth, in Age, or Prime,
The ſtealing Steps of never-ſtanding Time,
With Wiſdom mark the Moment as it flies,
Think what a Moment is—to him that dies.

GEORGIA:
SAVANNAH, Printed by JAMES JOHNSTON.

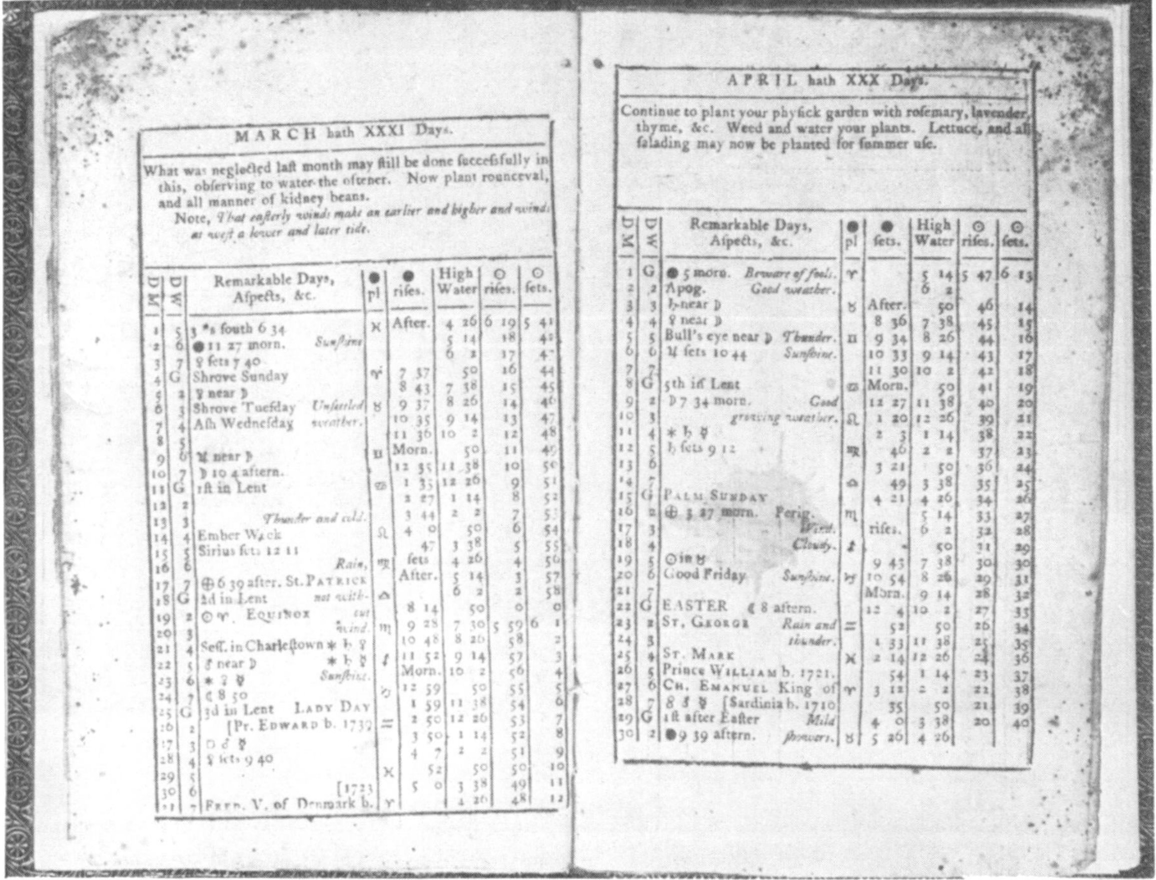

MARCH hath XXXI Days.

What was neglected laſt month may ſtill be done ſucceſsfully in this, obſerving to water the oftener. Now plant rounceval, and all manner of kidney beans.

Note, *That eaſterly winds make an earlier and higher and winds at weſt a lower and later tide.*

D M	D W	Remarkable Days, Aſpects, &c.	☾ pl	☾ riſes.	High Water	☉ riſes.	☉ ſets.
1	5	3 *s ſouth 6 34	♓	After.	4 26	6 19	5 41
2	6	● 11 27 morn. *Sunſhine*			5 14	18	42
3	7	♀ ſets 7 40			6 2	17	43
4	G	Shrove Sunday	♈	7 37	50	16	44
5	2	☿ near ☽		8 43	7 38	15	45
6	3	Shrove Tueſday *Unſettled*	♉	9 37	8 26	14	46
7	4	Aſh Wedneſday *weather.*		10 35	9 14	13	47
8	5			11 36	10 2	12	48
9	6	♅ near ☽	♊	Morn.	50	11	49
10	7	☽ 10 4 aftern.		12 35	11 38	10	50
11	G	1ſt in Lent	♋	1 35	12 26	9	51
12	2			2 27	1 14	8	52
13	3	*Thunder and cold.*		3 44	2 2	7	53
14	4	Ember Week	♌	4 0	50	6	54
15	5	Sirius ſets 12 11		47	3 38	5	55
16	6	*Rain,*	♍	ſets	4 26	4	56
17	7	⊕ 6 39 after. St. PATRICK		After.	5 14	3	57
18	G	2d in Lent *not with-*	♎		6 2	2	58
19	2	☉ ♈. EQUINOX *out*		8 14	50	0	0
20	3	*wind.*	♏	9 28	7 30	5 59	6 1
21	4	Seſſ. in Charleſtown ✱ ♄ ♀		10 48	8 26	58	2
22	5	♂ near ☽ ✱ ♄ ☿	♐	11 52	9 14	57	3
23	6	✱ ♀ ☿ *Sunſhine.*		Morn.	10 2	56	4
24	7	☾ 8 50	♑	12 59	50	55	5
25	G	3d in Lent LADY DAY		1 59	11 38	54	6
26	2	[Pr. EDWARD b. 1739	♒	2 50	12 26	53	7
27	3	□ ♂ ☿		3 50	1 14	52	8
28	4	☿ ſets 9 40		4 7	2 2	51	9
29	5		♓	52	50	50	10
30	6	[1723		5 0	3 38	49	11
31	7	FRED. V. of Denmark b.	♈		4 26	48	12

APRIL hath XXX Days.

Continue to plant your phyſick garden with roſemary, lavender, thyme, &c. Weed and water your plants. Lettuce, and all ſalading may now be planted for ſummer uſe.

D M	D W	Remarkable Days, Aſpects, &c.	☾ pl	☾ ſets.	High Water	☉ riſes.	☉ ſets.
1	G	● 5 morn. *Beware of fools.*	♈		5 14	5 47	6 13
2	2	Apog. *Good weather.*			6 2		
3	3	♄ near ☽	♉	After.	50	46	14
4	4	♀ near ☽		8 36	7 38	45	15
5	5	Bull's eye near ☽ *Thunder.*	♊	9 34	8 26	44	16
6	6	♃ ſets 10 44 *Sunſhine.*		10 33	9 14	43	17
7	7			11 30	10 2	42	18
8	G	5th in Lent	♋	Morn.	50	41	19
9	2	☽ 7 34 morn. *Good*		12 27	11 38	40	20
10	3	*growing weather.*	♌	1 20	12 26	39	21
11	4	✱ ♄ ☿		2 3	1 14	38	22
12	5	♄ ſets 9 12	♍	46	2 2	37	23
13	6			3 21	50	36	24
14	7		♎	49	3 38	35	25
15	G	PALM SUNDAY		4 21	4 26	34	26
16	2	⊕ 3 27 morn. Perig.	♏		5 14	33	27
17	3	*Wind.*		riſes.	6 2	32	28
18	4	*Cloudy.*	♐		50	31	29
19	5	☉ in ♉		9 43	7 38	30	30
20	6	Good Friday *Sunſhine.*	♑	10 54	8 26	29	31
21	7			Morn.	9 14	28	32
22	G	EASTER ☾ 8 aftern.		12 4	10 2	27	33
23	2	ST. GEORGE *Rain and*	♒	52	50	26	34
24	3	*thunder.*		1 33	11 38	25	35
25	4	ST. MARK	♓	2 14	12 26	24	36
26	5	Prince WILLIAM b. 1721.		54	1 14	23	37
27	6	CH. EMANUEL King of	♈	3 12	2 2	22	38
28	7	♂ ♂ ☿ [Sardinia b. 1710		35	50	21	39
29	G	1ſt after Eaſter *Mild*		4 0	3 38	20	40
30	2	● 9 39 aftern. *ſhowers.*	♉	5 26	4 26		

The First Book Published in Georgia

By permission of the Wymberley Jones DeRenne Georgia Library

ings were fruit trees and herb gardens. In the interest of neatness Savannah back yards were partially paved in brick or flag stones, but even in the tiniest of her walled back yards, a fig tree and a climbing rose would be found.

As a large majority of Savannahans owned plantations, also extensive summer homes on the adjacent salt river bluffs, they were not irked by the smallness of their city gardens. All were laid out in intricate geometric patterns, edged with English brick or scalloped tile, bordered with snowdrops, violets and jonquils, or occasionally with a very dwarf box. They displayed camellias, tea olives, azaleas, oleanders, crape myrtles, sago palms, tea plants, banana trees and roses. Garden walls and verandas were festooned with begonias, rhynchospermum, roses and wistaria. These little beauty spots remained intact until the eighties, when the introduction of a carpet grass that remained green in that climate summer and winter, filled the Savannah soul with an ambition to have lawns. Old gardens were dug up and their treasures cast away. Of the old gardens only a handful still retain their original form and planting, and none date earlier than 1838. Now Savannah has lovely modern gardens.

Around Savannah, along the coast and on the sea islands, with some notable exceptions, the original grants were small. Agriculture and gardening were practised by all. General Oglethorpe set a good example at Orange Hall near Frederica on St. Simon's Island. This fifty-acre farm was the only land in Georgia ever owned by him and was Georgia's first governor's mansion. Sev-

1812

By permission of Mrs. Kate McKinley Treanor

From an Old Charcoal Drawing by Carlisle McKinley

South-End House, the Sapelo Island home of Thomas Spalding, stood in an immense liveoak grove. The planting interest consisted of a rose garden three hundred yards from the house, and vegetable gardens, orchards and citrus groves five hundred feet to the rear. This relation of gardens to house was unusual. Sapelo is now the property of Howard E. Coffin.

1790

A house on Telfair Street that is a happy example of the dignity of Augusta's early homes and the beauty of their surroundings. Here Washington was entertained on his visit to the city. Erected in 1790, the wings were added in 1810. The central portion was used for a few years as a county court house. A garden in the rear is of an early date. This property has been owned by the Fitzsimmons, Stovall, Gregg and Murphy families.

eral of his officers built homes near by. Harrington Hall, the home of Captain Raymond Demere, seems to have been the most notable of these estates. This place was surrounded by a hedge of cassena, which enclosed extensive and elaborate grounds and gardens, laid out in a formal design. Harrington Hall was built in the seventeen forties and may well have had the first formal garden in this section of Georgia.

Toward the end of the eighteenth century men of birth, breeding and fortune from the other colonies, as well as from the British Isles and the Continent, moved to Georgia. They welded the small original grants into great plantations. Silk culture having proved a failure, flax, indigo and sugar cane were tried out as staple crops, only to be abandoned for long staple cotton and rice.

Long avenues of live oaks festooned with Spanish moss led up to the plantation houses surrounded by vast groves and set in gardens of luxuriant growth. Tropical plants vied with japonicas, roses, lilies, bulbs and whatever garden flowers would thrive in that climate. As a setting, indigenous flowering trees and shrubs were used freely and with considerable taste and skill. The citrus groves gave an added note of color. Many types of architecture were seen in these homes. They ranged from simple raised cottages to Italian villas, and were built of wood, tabby and brick.

Little is left of all this loveliness. The outcome of the Civil War doomed these plantations to an isolated desolation. Their garden patterns bordered in snowdrops and violets were wiped out by the hand of time. The fertile soil and moist climate made a jungle of flowering shrubs and trees. To console us, in recent years many beautiful new gardens have sprung up to take their place.

Augusta, founded in 1735-6 as a trading post, had a rapid and prosperous development. Her early town houses were dignified and commodious; the grounds and gardens of varied type were both larger and more elaborate than those of Savannah and Ebenezer. Most of them have been destroyed by the march of commerce and a disastrous fire; truly an irreparable loss. Her summer homes were built a few miles out from the city. Here a charming informal architecture was developed; planting was naturalistic or formal at will. On the Sand Hills, Augusta's most famous suburb, the Carnes-Howard-Thomas-Chafee place still possesses, intact as to pattern and character of planting, a beautiful formal bulb garden laid out in the circle, squares and rectangles so dear to the Dutch heart. It dates back to about 1784. The patterns of a few other formal gardens survive, but their planting, alas, is all but gone.

Fruitlands, one of Georgia's earliest commercial nurseries, founded in 1858 by Prosper Jules Alphonse Berckmans, encouraged a continuous horticultural activity in Augusta, whose gardens both old and new have a peculiar charm and grace. Here incense cedars, cypress cedars and cherry laurel grow to great size, as do camellias.

In Georgia the first years of the nineteenth century saw Eli Whitney's gin in operation. Cotton planting received an enormous impetus. People began moving from the coast to the middle and northern sections of the State. There was a general exodus from communities within the fertile but malarial swamp regions; thus came into being many of the strange "Dead Cities of Georgia," deserted by their inhabitants for the healthier sections of the State.

Men of position and fortune from the Carolinas, Virginia, Pennsylvania and New England bought huge acreages from the State and from the Indians, for the planting of short staple cotton. The red clay of Georgia proved a gold mine for those who worked it with plow and hoe. Large fortunes were made and the development of the whole State was extraordinarily rapid. "King Cotton" began his reign. The removal beyond the Mississippi of the Creek and Cherokee Nations opened up vast tracts for settlement.

From the beginning of the century formal gardens became general in Georgia. Its third decade saw the era of Greek Revival architecture in full swing. Classic temples sprang up all over the State, here and there happily relieved by a throwback to the more graceful spirit of the Georgian period. Homes so formal, firmly established a similar taste in gardens. Even the humble wayside cottage had a bordered path from gate to doorstep, flanked by symmetrical planting. Through the twenties garden patterns consisted of circles and rectangles. Later individuality of design became the vogue.

Columbus, Georgia, sprang into being like Athene from the brow of Zeus. In 1827 the site of the city at the head of navigation on the Chattahoo-

1823

Home at Indian Springs, Butts County, of General William McIntosh, halfbreed chief of the Lower Creek Indians. The signing at this house in 1825 of a treaty with the United States for the removal of his people beyond the Mississippi, a few months later, cost him his life. During the first quarter of the nineteenth century, many chiefs of the Creek and Cherokee Nations lived in commodious dwellings, surrounded by fields, orchards and vegetable gardens.

chee River was surveyed and laid out. History tells us that from the 10th to the 23rd of July, '28, auctioning of lots was held until four hundred and twenty-eight building lots and forty-five gardening lots inside the city were sold. The houses built at that time were of mansion type, surrounded by large and beautifully developed grounds. They have remained the finest homes in Columbus. A mile of them lay along the river bank. At Rose Hill outside the city was an important group of plantation homes. At Wynnton, a suburb of Columbus, a number of country homes were built. Southeast Georgia, with Greenwood at Thomasville as its brightest jewel, more or less followed Columbus in its gardening characteristics. Though form was the keynote of the gardens in this section, considerable individuality was shown in their planning. Its planting list was perhaps the most varied in the State. Again the melancholy story of loveliness that is past and gone must be told. Only a few garden patterns survive. Today the people of Columbus, as flower loving as their ancestors, can still claim for the town the title of a "City of Gardens."

From 1825 on the middle and northern sections of Georgia showed a uniformity of plan and planting which held firm until after the Civil War. In town, village and on the plantation the columned mansion or latticed cottage stood in a grove of original growth. Naturalistic plantings of flowering trees and the larger shrubs served as a frame for the house and for the formal box bordered garden lying immediately in front or to one side of the dwelling. This garden, frequently walled by Euonymus japonica, always intricate and individual, strengthened in design by carefully considered plantings of magnolia, laurel, tree box and conifers, carried a bright pattern of flowers and flowering shrubs. It resembled a lovely Persian carpet flung down for the pleasure of the passer-by. Summer houses, tea houses, and pavilion-like greenhouses, these latter used for the winter housing of tropical plants and japonicas, were placed so as to accent the symmetry of the whole. Generally a picket fence formed a dividing line between this part of the grounds and that at the rear of the house, where were found kitchen, smokehouse, dairy and servants' quarters. Beyond these again was the kitchen garden, often box bordered, always embellished by fruit trees, grape arbors, and beds of bulbs and flowers. Within its confines were the herbs, valued equally for seasoning and for medicinal use. The scuppernong arbors because of their vast size were often found in other parts of the grounds. On plantations and at the homes of doctors and lawyers small detached buildings served as offices. The whole group was enclosed within a picket or barred fence, or occasionally one of balustraded form. Outside the house grounds were the carriage house, stables, barns, orchards and fodder fields. On plantations, the quarters for the field hands were situated just beyond. There was always a family burial ground and sometimes one for the slaves.

1855
The Dean Place in White County, Now the Home of James Franklin Miller. The Blooming of a Swept Clay Yard.

In these distinctive developments harmony and convenience were achieved. House and garden were not only contiguous but closely related in form and spirit. The buildings necessary to the varied activities of such self-contained establishments were logically grouped and placed, the whole a symbol of the social philosophy of a period and of a people.

In antebellum Georgia, homes and gardens were strongly influenced by England, and through England by Italy, France and Holland of the renaissance. Possibly even stronger was the architectural influence of ancient Greece, for as we have seen, the State's period of greatest prosperity and building activity coincided with the backwash of a European-wide taste for the purely classic. Yet through the alchemy of climate, soil, racial traits, political trends and social conditions, each section of the State showed an individual development in which the house and garden were always integral and harmonious.

All Georgia shared a problem that definitely influenced its landscaping and garden development. To grow grass was difficult. In early times only two kinds of lawn grass were planted, blue grass that burns up at the first blast of summer heat, and Bermuda that is only green in summer and does not prosper in the shade so necessary to comfort in this section. Where lawns are as costly as Aubusson carpets, they are sparingly used and only by the well-to-do. The swept sand or clay yards of simpler dwellings are as logical in Georgia as the verdant settings of similar homes in grass-growing states. That at the first breath of spring these arid, desolate-looking spots put forth masses of bloom seems as great a miracle as the blossoming of Aaron's rod.

1839

A Greek Revival mansion in Athens built by Gazaway Lamar and shortly after acquired by Dr. Franklin. Since 1870 it has been the home of the Upson family. The original garden is gone but stately old trees and shrub plantings remain.

Because of this difficulty in growing grass and a climatic need of shade, Georgia had few bowling greens within her gardens and not many examples of the English parterre, a flower or tree framed design in beds of grass. When they do occur, they are a very simple type and because of formal or casual shrub plantings within their frame seldom remain entirely characteristic. Her gardens generally were formed of a parterre of cut-work, a type thus described in The Theory and Practice of Gardening, an English translation made in 1712 by John James, of Greenwich, from the French of Dezallier d'Argenville: "Parterres of Cut-work, tho' not so fashionable at present, are however not unworthy of our Regard. They differ from the others, in that all the Parts which compose them should be cut with Symmetry, and that they admit neither of Grass nor Embroidery, but only Borders edged with Box, that serve to raise Flowers in: and by means of a Path of convenient Breadth that runs round each Piece, you may walk through the whole Parterre without hurting anything: All these Paths should be sanded."

It is quite obvious that as a rule Georgia's formal gardens more closely resembled those of the Continent than the garden forms indigenous to England, though the informal frame in which they were set was English in feeling. The planting of Magnolia grandiflora, hollies and wide-based conifers in the beds of cut-work parterres, if not peculiar to Georgia, is certainly characteristic of certain regions of the State. They brought the gardens into balance with the massive columned homes of the Greek Revival period. Though the area of these parterres was not great, dignity was their keynote.

Today Georgia is a greener place to live in, but lawns remain a thorn in the flesh of her gardening sons and daughters.

In early days garden ornaments were little used in Georgia. Shortly before the outbreak of the Civil War an incipient vogue for marble and cast iron urns and statuary showed itself, but fountains were still rare.

There was no space for seats along the narrow paths of the garden but for those wishing to sit within its confines, arbors and summer or tea houses offered protection from the sun considered so injurious to the complexions of the ladies, and from the dews thought dangerous to health.

Porch furniture consisted of wooden chairs, settees and tables in the simplest type of Sheraton; they, as a rule, were painted white. Split bottom ladder back chairs were seen in the less sophisticated establishments. This porch furniture was moved out under the trees for the post prandial naps of the gentlemen, or for julep-cheered masculine conclaves.

In the near-by grove were wooden benches and swings. Here the children played under the careful guardianship of their mammies, maumas or das (as the nurses were variously called) whose picka-ninnies often joined in the games.

About 1830-1840 cast iron furniture made its debut. In the earlier forms it was often beautiful but at no period was it comfortable. White, green and black were the favored paint colors. Being heavy and weather-proof, this furniture remained outdoors. Cast iron chairs, settees, tables and racks were also used on the verandas. The sometimes amusing, but frequently hideous, cast iron garden ornaments of the 70's and 80's should not be confused with these earlier examples.

We hear of landscape architects having been employed and there are traditions of this or that place being laid out by English or Italian gardeners; however, the grounds and gardens of many homes were planned by their owners and planted under their supervision. As architects were scarce and the newly-settled districts isolated, often the head of the family designed the home. Crudities were inevitable but everywhere a striving for the best was found. These homes and gardens had dignified beauty and served as a fitting background for a refined and gentle family life, and a kindly and generous hospitality.

Coast gardens had little chance against a loose soil, hurricanes and an encroaching vegetation, but with their patterns preserved and punctuated by hardy box rooted in a stubborn soil, the gardens of middle and north Georgia under happier circumstances would have survived for our pleasure. The fatal eighties and nineties spoke the beginning of their doom. By then under changed economic conditions these gardens had begun to deteriorate. Keeping box borders properly trimmed required a constant care that could not be given. Neglected they had become lumpy in spots, scraggly in others, unsightly in general. To use the plow seemed the simplest solution. Hundreds of gardens were destroyed in this manner, the precious evergreen thrown aside to die. Thus Georgia lost much of the treasure of her unique garden patterns. All over the State the digging up of box gardens, large and small, still goes on. Happily the cloud has a silver lining, for no longer is this aristocrat of the garden cast aside, but transplanted to where it receives all honor and loving care, it continues to fulfill its mission of sturdy beauty. At best, this persistent destruction of gardens so peculiarly Georgia's own, leaves one with a sense of sadness and regret.

In Georgia after the Civil War gardening ceased to be a cult except to the chosen few. Yet Athens has the honor of having established what is claimed to be the first garden club in the United States. In 1890 the Ladies' Garden Club, later known as the Athens Garden Club, was formed. The Garden Club of America, founded in Philadelphia in 1913, started a movement that has swept every state in the Union. The Peachtree Garden Club, one of its affiliated members, was organized in Atlanta in 1923, and brought to Georgia a renewed garden consciousness which led to the establishment in 1928 by them of the Garden Club of Georgia, with its hundred branches. When in 1932 the Garden Club of America met in Augusta and Atlanta, as the guests of the Sand Hills and Peachtree Garden Clubs, Georgia did not need to hang her head.

Trustees Garden

The County of Savannah — Christ Church Parish — Chatham County

Trustees' Seal, 1733-1752

THE TRUSTEES' GARDEN in Savannah was Georgia's first formally laid out garden and her first experiment station. Charles C. Jones, Jr., in his History of Georgia, tells us that by order of James Oglethorpe in the spring of 1733: "A public garden was laid out and a servant detailed, at the charge of the trust, to cultivate it. This was to serve as a nursery whence might be procured fruit trees, vines, plants, and vegetables for the private orchards and gardens of the inhabitants. It was also largely devoted to the propagation of the white mulberry, from the general cultivation of which, as food for the silkworm, great benefit was anticipated."*

Mr. Commissary VonReck, temporal leader of the Saltzburgers, gives us a very accurate description of this undertaking as it appeared in 1734: "There is laid out near the Town, by Order of the Trustees, a Garden for making Experiments for the Improving Botany and Agriculture; it contains 10 Acres and lies upon the River; and it is cleared and brought into such Order that there is already a fine Nursery of Oranges, Olives, white Mulberries, Figs, Peaches, and many curious Herbs: besides which there are Cabbages, Peas, and other European Pulse and Plants which all thrive. Within the Garden there is an artificial Hill, said by the Indians to be raised over the Body of one of their ancient Emperors."** Much seems to have been accomplished in a single year.

Mr. Francis Moore, who greatly assisted General Oglethorpe in the preparations for his return voyage to Georgia, 1735-36, and who was appointed by the trustees as keeper of the stores, has left an even more detailed account of this admirable public enterprise: "There is near the Town to the East, a Garden belonging to the Trustees, consisting of 10 Acres; the situation is delightful, one-half of it is upon the Top of a Hill, the Foot of which the River Savannah washes, and from it you see the Woody Islands in the Sea. The Remainder of the Garden is the Side and some plain low Ground at the Foot of the Hill where several fine Springs break out. In the Garden is variety of Soils; the Top is sandy and dry, the Sides of the Hill are Clay, and the bottom is a black rich Garden Mould, well watered. On the North-part of the Garden is left standing a Grove of Part of the old Wood as it was before the arrival of the Colony there. The Trees in the Grove are mostly Bay, Sassafras, Evergreen Oak, Pellitory, Hickary, American Ash, and the Laurel Tulip. This last is looked upon as one of the most beautiful Trees in the World; it grows Straight-bodied to 40 or 50 Foot high; the Bark smooth and whitish, the Top spreads regular like an Orange-tree in English Gardens, only larger; the Leaf is like that of a common Laurel, but bigger, and the under-side of a greenish Brown: It blooms about the Month of June; the Flowers are white, fragrant like the Orange, and perfume all the Air around it; the Flower is round, 8 or 10 Inches diameter, thick like the Orange-Flower, and a little yellow near the Heart: As the Flowers drop, the Fruit, which is a Cone with red Berries, succeeds them. There are also some Bay-trees that have Flowers like the Laurel, only less.

"The Garden is laid out with Cross-walks planted with Orange-trees, but the last Winter a good deal of Snow having fallen, had killed those upon the Top of the Hill down to their Roots, but they being cut down, sprouted again, as I saw when I returned to Savannah. In the Squares between the Walks were vast Quantities of Mulberry-trees, this being a Nursery for all the Province, and every Planter that desires it, has young Trees given him gratis from this Nursery. These white Mulberry-trees were planted in order to raise Silk, for which Purpose several Italians were brought, at the Trustees' Expence, from Piedmont by Mr. Amatis; they have fed Worms and wound Silk to as great Per-

* History of Georgia, Charles C. Jones, Vol. I, P. 129.

** An Extract of the Journals of Mr. Commissary VonReck and of the Rev. Mr. Bolzius, PP. 12-15, London, 1734.

A

Compendious Account

Of the whole ART of

BREEDING, NURSING,

AND

The RIGHT ORDERING

OF THE

SILK-WORM.

Illuſtrated with Figures engraven on COPPER: Whereon is curiouſly exhibited the whole Management of this PROFITABLE INSECT.

LONDON:

Printed for JOHN WORRALL, at the *Dove* in *Bell-Yard*, near *Lincolns-Inn*; OLIVE PAYNE, in *Round Court* in the *Strand*; THOMAS BOREMAN, on *Ludgate-Hill*, near the Gate; and THOMAS GAMT, at the *Bible* facing the Eaſt End of the New Church in the *Strand*; Bookſellers.

M.DCC.XXXIII.

TO

The Right Honourable

The Lord Viſcount PERCIVAL,

The Right Honourable

The Lord CARPENTER;

AND TO

The reſt of the Honourable GENTLEMEN,

The Truſtees for Eſtabliſhing the Colony of *Georgia* in *America*:

This TREATISE,

On the Management of the SILK-WORM,

Is with all Humility humbly Inſcribed to your Honours,

BY

Your Honours Moſt Humble, and

Moſt Obedient Servant,

T. B.

In this Draught is ſhewn how you are to range your Scaffold and Shelves to place your Worms, and Leaves to feed them.

fection as any that ever came out of Italy; but the Italians falling out, one of them stole away the Machines for winding, broke the Coppers and spoiled all the Eggs which he could not steal and fled to South Carolina. The others, who continued faithful, had saved but a few Eggs, when Mr. Oglethorpe arrived, therefore he forbade any Silk should be wound, but that all the Worms should be suffered to eat through their Balls in order to have more Eggs against next Year. The Italian Women are obliged to take English Girls Apprentices, whom they teach to wind and feed; and the Men have taught our English Gardeners to tend the Mulberry-trees, and our Joyners have learned how to make the Machines for winding. As the Mulberry-trees increase, there will be a great Quantity of Silk made here.

"Beside the Mulberry-trees there are in some of the Quarters in the coldest part of the Garden, all kinds of Fruit-trees usual in England, such as Apples, Pears, &c. In another Quarter are Olives, Figs, Vines, Pomegranates, and such Fruits as are natural to the warmest Parts of Europe. At the bottom of the Hill, well-sheltered from the North-wind, and in the warmest part of the Garden, there was a Collection of West-India Plants and Trees, some Coffee, some Cocoa-Nuts, Cotton, Palma-Christi, and several West Indian physical Plants, some sent up by Mr. Eveliegh, a publick-spirited Merchant at Charles-Town, and some by Dr. Houstoun from the Spanish West Indies, where he was sent at the Expence of a Collection raised by that curious Physician, Sir Hans Sloan, for to collect and send them to Georgia where the Climate was capable of making a Garden which might contain all kinds of Plants; to which Design his Grace the Duke of Richmond, the Earl of Derby, the Lord Peters, and the Apothecary's Company contributed very generously, as did Sir Hans himself. The Quarrels among the Italians proved fatal to most of these Plants, and they were labouring to repair that loss when I was there, Mr. Miller being employ'd in the room of Dr. Houstoun, who died in Jamaica. We heard he had wrote an Account of his having obtain'd the Plant from whence the true Balsamum Capivi is drawn; and that he was in hopes of getting that from whence the Jesuit's Bark is taken, he designing for that Purpose to send to the Spanish West Indies.

"There is a plant of Bamboo Cane brought from the East Indies, and sent over by Mr. Towers, which thrives well. There was also some Tea seeds which came from the same Place; but the latter, though great Care was taken, did not grow."*

The Trustees' Garden was of incalculable help and benefit to the Colony during its first fifty years. By then the silk worm industry had proved itself only profitable when subsidized. As the Garden's most important function was the propagation of mulberry trees for its development, the interest in it then began to decline. The exact date of its abandonment as a public institution is unknown, but it must have occurred during or soon after the Revolutionary War.

* Moore's Voyage to Georgia, PP. 23-33, Published in London, 1744.

1733

Twenty-five volumes of this work were sent to Georgia by the Trustees for the guidance of the colonists in silk worm culture. It was ordered that a copy be given the Rev. Bolzius, spiritual leader of the Salzburgers at Ebenezer.

Cuts on opposite page used by permission of the Wymberley Jones DeRenne Georgia Library.

Wormsloe

On Skiddoway Narrows

The County of Savannah — Christ Church Parish — Chatham County

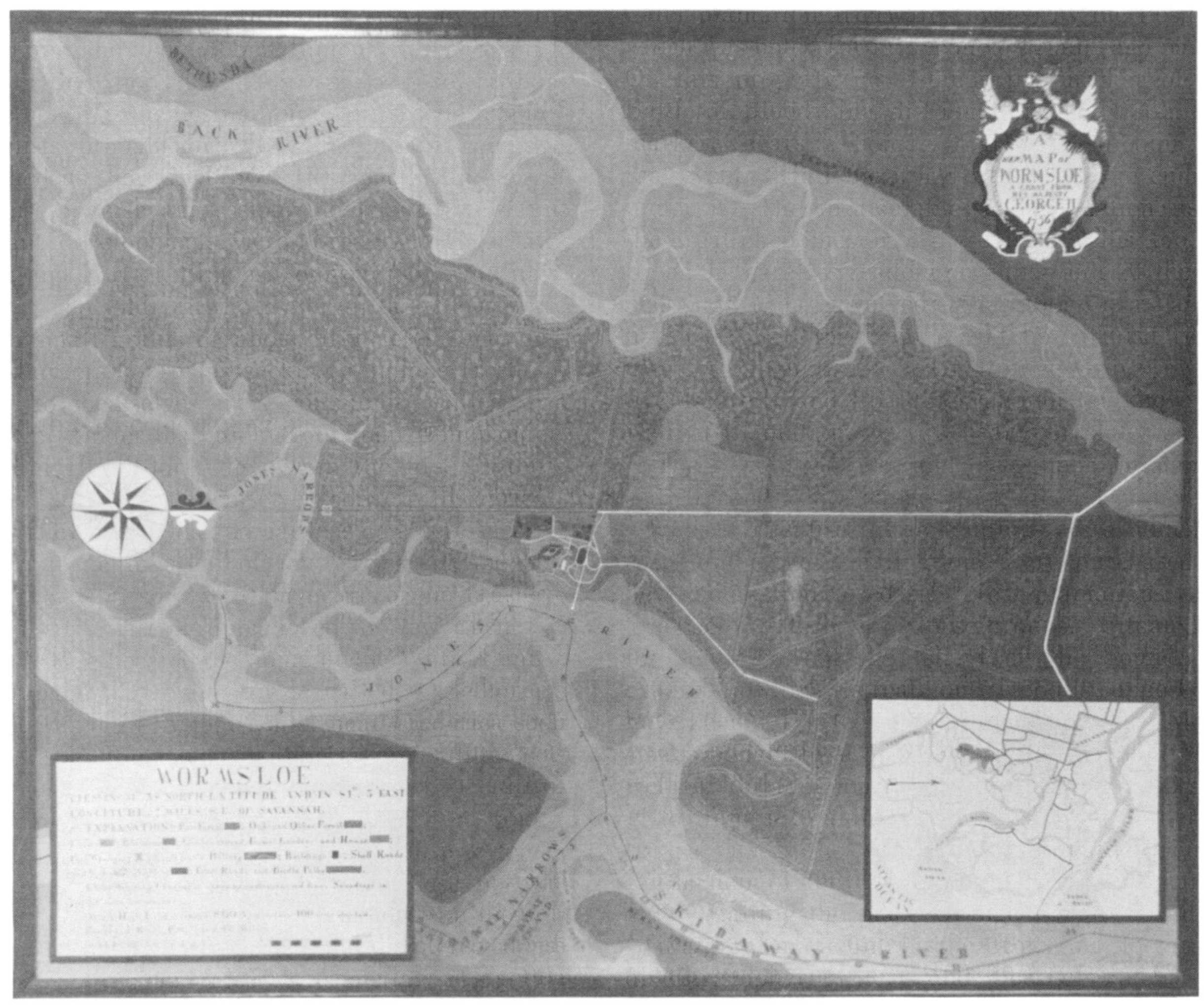

1733

A plan of Wormsloe, the eight hundred acre Trustees' Grant made to Captain Noble Jones in 1733. The property has been continuously held by his descendants.

NOBLE JONES, friend of General Oglethorpe and a member of his first body of colonists, who later became senior judge of the General Court and acting Chief Justice of the Province of Georgia, for twenty years member and sometimes president of His Majesty's Council, and Colonel of the First Georgia Regiment; in 1733 received a grant of eight hundred acres from the Trustees on the Isle of Hope about seven miles from Savannah. He called it Wormsloe.

For the defense of Skiddoway Narrows, a Manchecolas Fort was erected and garrisoned by detachments from Captain Noble Jones' company of marines quartered near his residence. The ground around Fort Wymberley, as it was known, was leased by him, and planted in trees and shrubs both ornamental and useful, among them mulberries to provide food for silk worms.

In 1743 a traveler visiting Wormsloe wrote as follows in the London Magazine, November 1745: "It is the settlement of Mr. Jones, 10 miles S. E. of Savannah and we could not help observing as we passed several very pretty Plantations. Wormsloe is one of the most agreeable spots I ever saw

1833

Ruins of Fort Wymberley on Skiddoway Narrows commanded by Captain Noble Jones. He planted a mulberry grove in its vicinity.

Wormsloe

Bright-hued Azaleas Mirrored in a Clear Brown Pool

and the improvements of that ingenious Man are very extraordinary. He commands a Company of Marines, who are quartered in Huts near his House, which is also a tolerable defensible Place with small arms. From the House there is a vista near three miles through the woods to Mr. Whitfield's Orphan House, which was a fine effect on the sight. The route from Wormsloe to Mr. Whitfield's Orphan House is extremely agreeable, mostly through Pine Groves."

A good example in forest conservation was set by this same gentleman. On December 19, 1750, James Habersham wrote to Benj. Martyn, Esq. "As Ranger and agent for the Indians Noble Jones had published the following proclamation on 'July ye 3rd, 1735': 'This is to give Notice that if any Person Whomsoever after the publication hereof Shall Cutt Down, Deface or Destroy any of the Trees or Committ any Trespass . . ' (on the lands of Tomochi King of Yamacraw) . . 'they will be prosecuted for the Same with the Utmost Severity.' " And again " . . . Or if any person Shall presume on any Pretense to Cut Down, Deface or Destroy any Tree or Shrub anywhere about the Spring or make any Fires there or make it a place to wash Cloaths they will have their Tubs, Potts &ca broke and be Also Prosecuted for the Same." And another: "Whereas by an Cypress Order of the Honble the Trustees for Establishing this Colony, no Person Whomsoever is to Cut Down, Deface or Destroy in any part or parts of this province, on Land not yet granted . . . This is to give notice that if any Person shall presume to act contrary to this their said Order they will be prosecuted for the same with the Utmost Severity."*

In 1765 the Georgia Gazette carried the following piece of news: "Numbers of people have gone recently to the Plantation of Hon. Noble Jones, Esq., seven miles from town to see an Agave plant now in blossom which is said to be 27 and a half feet high and has 33 branches which contain a vast number of blossoms."

The two succeeding owners of Wormsloe, Dr. Noble Wymberley Jones and Dr. George Jones, were men of great distinction who took so active a part in the affairs of the State and Nation that little of their time was spent at Wormsloe. The fourth owner, George Wymberley Jones, left a number of diaries showing his interest in gardening. On December 6, 1855, he notes that the yellow jessamine is in bloom and on the following April 6th "still in bloom," evidently one of Savannah's warm winters. In the 70's he "Marked out an enlargement of garden at Wormsloe," "sent a large single red camellia to Wormsloe," and records that in '77 he planted fourteen camellias and eighteen aloes.

* Colonial Documents Board of Trade, Vol. IV, London.

1733

White Mulberry Planted by Captain Noble Jones

His son, Wymberley Jones DeRenne, did much to enlarge and beautify the gardens. Masses of azalea reflected in clear brown pools are overhung by live oaks draped in moss, wistaria and Cherokee roses. Algerian ivy hangs in incredible festoons from the highest limbs of giant trees and is used as a ground cover under the shade of the live oak grove surrounding the house, a four-story wooden structure, parts of which date back to the eighteenth century but which has been so incessantly added to that no particular style is dominant. A mile long avenue of live oaks was planted at the birth of his son, Wymberley W. DeRenne, the present owner, whose wife, Augusta Floyd DeRenne, designed and planted the enchanting new garden described further on in this volume.

At Wormsloe, a beautiful modern building of classical design houses the Wymberley Jones DeRenne Georgia Library, containing the world's most famous collection of Georgianna.

In describing this plantation it is almost impossible to separate the old from the new, as the informality of its plan and planting has admitted of a constant intermingling of the two. In every phase it is a record of the development of coastal Georgia.

Savannah

The County of Savannah — Christ Church Parish — Chatham County

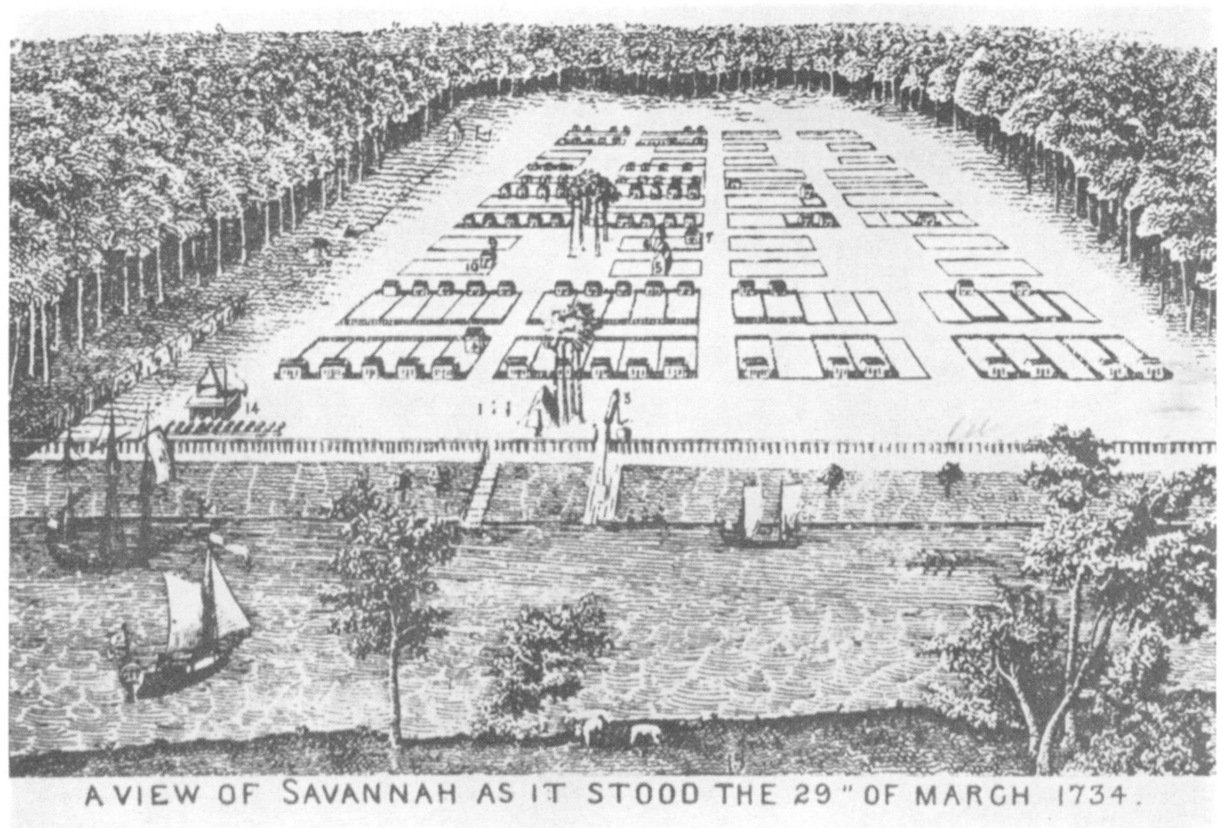

A Drawing by Peter Gordon — By permission of the Wymberley Jones DeRenne Georgia Library

The four Trust Lots facing each square were later occupied by public buildings or by important residences.

SAVANNAH as laid out by Oglethorpe had building lots sixty by ninety feet, and her garden development had to conform to their narrow limits. The earliest map of the city shows the wooden palisades which enclosed them. First food stuffs and shortly afterwards flowers were planted. Turned fences were the next step, but from a very early date these flower gardens were walled and of formal pattern. Semi-tropical plantings mingled with roses and flowers reminiscent of the English homes of the colonists.

Typical of the important early developments of the town was a simple but beautiful Georgian house built in 1765 on a corner lot facing Reynolds Square by John Houston, son of Sir Patrick Houston (Bart.) who took an active part in the settlement of the Colony. John Houston was twice Governor of Georgia, Chief Justice, and Savannah's first Mayor.

On the front portion of the adjoining lot, enclosed by a brick wall, he developed a formal garden planted with tea olives, camellias, banana trees, roses, bulbs and violets. Separating the garden from a bricked back yard was a latticed brick wall pierced by a wrought iron gate and topped with wrought iron trellises veiled by bignonias and Marechal Niel, cloth of gold and Devoniensis roses.

Within the garden was a one-story wine house with a deep cellar used for the storing of the world's finest vintages.

Some time prior to the Civil War this place became the property of Colonel John Scriven, a wealthy rice planter and a scholar of distinction. The house and garden were done away with about 1920 and no reproducible photographs of them seem to have been kept.

Though as a rule more limited in area, gardens of similar character were attached to most Savannah homes and maintained until recent years when they gave way to new fashions in gardening.

1815

Richardson—Maxwell—Owens—Thomas House

Savannah

ONE of Georgia's best examples of Georgian architecture is the residence designed about 1815 by Jay, an English architect, for a Mr. Richardson. It is built of tabby and occupies the northeast Trust Lot on Oglethorpe Square. When General LaFayette was a guest of the City of Savannah he stayed in this house, which by then had passed into the hands of Mrs. Maxwell. George W. Owens bought it five years later from the Bank of Philadelphia and his family and descendants have lived there ever since.

The usual Trust Lot layout is found here. The narrow garden space lying between the front of the house and a fine balustraded wall which encloses it was originally planted in pomegranates, japonicas, oleanders and white crepe myrtle, of which only the last remains. The back garden enclosed on both sides by high tabby walls, each pierced by a solid wooden gate, contained figs and several varieties of orange trees, altheas, four-o'clocks, spider lilies, calicanthus shrub, wistaria and an herb bed. A flagged walk leading to the carriage house and servants' quarters was shaded by a grape covered arbor. The planting of this area has been changed, leaving very little of its original character.

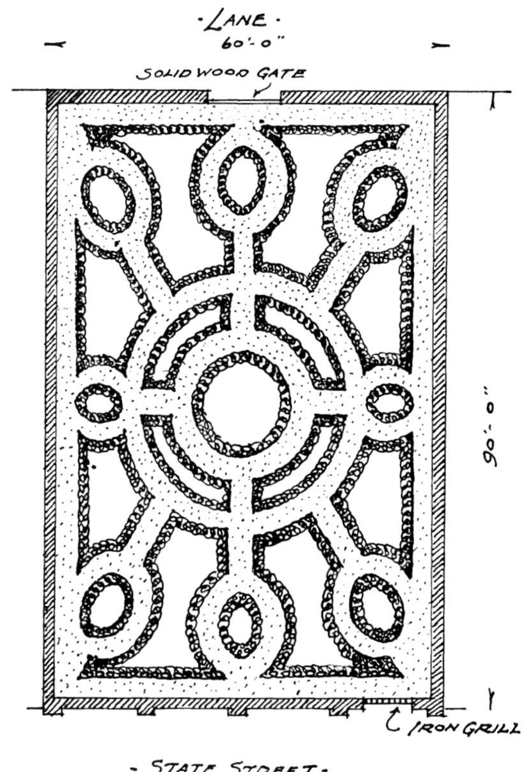

A Plan of the State Street Garden

At a much later date an additional garden was developed. It occupied a sixty by ninety lot on State Street immediately opposite the north garden gate of the house, the street intervening. This garden was laid out by M. M. Kollock, Esq. It was enclosed on all four sides by a high brick wall topped by broken glass bottles to discourage marauders. There was a grilled iron gate on the State Street side and a solid wooden wagon gate at rear on the lane. It presented a pattern of oval and odd shaped beds edged in very dwarf box, and contained Don Kaleare, Ocse Luca, Mutabelis and other varieties of japonicas, banana shrub, sweet oleo, purple and white wistaria, rhynchospermum, English jasmine, ivy, syringa, Guernsey lilies, blue bells, white and blue flags, Roman hyacinths, narcissus, snow drops, Dutch hyacinths, ixias, anemones, asters, pansies, violets, larkspur, and many roses among which were Malmaison, Paul Neyron, cloth of gold, Marie Van Houtte, Maman Cochet and Devoniensis. This list is a fairly complete index of what was to be found in Savannah gardens in the first half of the nineteenth century. Unfortunately an apartment house now occupies the site of this garden.

Batersby—Hartridge—Wilder—Anderson House

Savannah

IN 1837 the City of Savannah passed an ordinance laying off as "Lafayette Ward" a part of the City Commons. A block of this property, facing Lafayette Square, was bought at auction by Andrew Low, ninety feet of which became the property of William Batersby, a cotton merchant born at Lyme Hall, near Liverpool.

This gentleman built a handsome brick home of simple design, with the side porch entrance frequently seen in The Barbadoes. A walled garden lies to the east. It has the distinction of being the oldest surviving Savannah garden retaining its original plan and planting. The oddly shaped beds outlined by double scalloped tiles were edged by violets and snowdrops, now replaced by ivy. The pride of this garden still is the original planting of camellias of the following varieties: Don Kaleare, Camellia reticulata, Lady Hume's blush, the Ella Drayton, Legeman, Abby Wilder, alba plena, and a large, bold red and white variegated, catalogued as "unnamed." A double white variety with fringed petals has died out. A tea plant, then a rarity, imported at the same time as the camellias, grew to great size. Other surviving planting is Pyrus japonica, tea olive, Devoniensis and Gen. Jacqueminot roses, and the lilac begonia which completely covers the walls.

After Mr. Batersby's death, the house was occupied by the Julian Hartridges, until purchased in the eighteen eighties by Joseph John Wilder. To Mrs. Wilder we owe the preservation of this interesting garden, now cherished by her daughter, Mrs. Jefferson Randolph Anderson.

1838

A Corner of the Garden Planted by Mrs. Batersby

1838-1863

The walled side garden of the Batersby-Hartridge-Wilder-Anderson house retains its original form and planting. We see here one of Savannah's brick paved back yards.

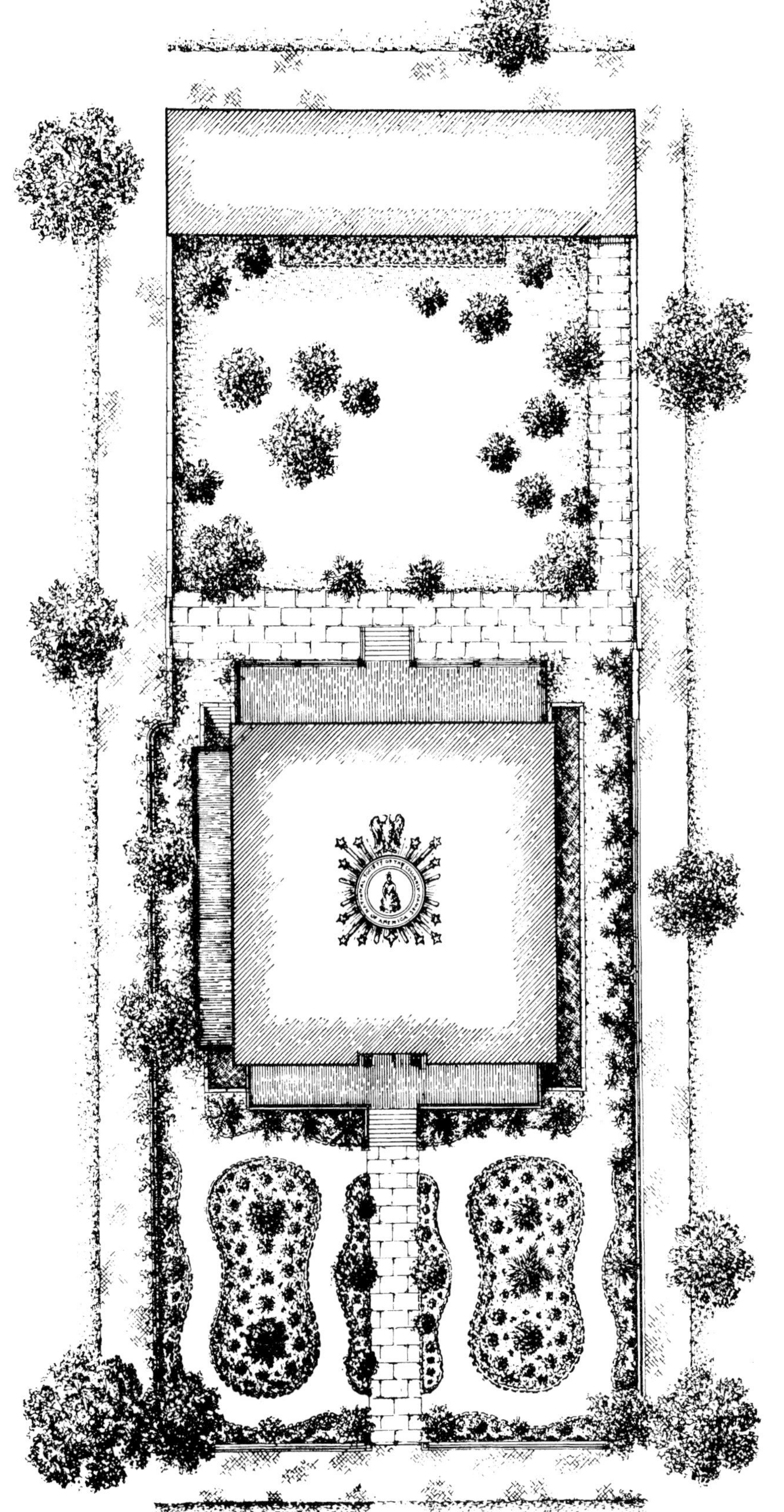

1848-1863

The Low house, now the home of the Georgia Society of the Colonial Dames of America, is a typical Trust Lot development. In Savannah walks were often paved with flags brought as ballast from England.

Low House

Savannah

1847-1848

Many Savannah homes bear the stamp of direct and continuous English influence.

THE area occupied by Lafayette Square was until 1847 the yard attached to the city jail. Savannah's growth made it advisable to move that institution and make this valuable property available for residential purposes. A square and Trust Lots were laid out. One of these was purchased by Andrew Low, an English cotton merchant, and on it he built a home of beauty and dignity, its entrance guarded by the British lions in stone. William Makepeace Thackeray was twice a guest of Mr. Low, then British Consul. Here he wrote "A Leaf Out of a Sketch Book." General Robert E. Lee's last visit to Savannah, in 1870, was spent in this home. Andrew Low's son, William Low of Lemmington, England, was only occasionally in Savannah. His widow, Juliette Gordon Low, founder of the Girl Scouts, occupied this house from 1886 to 1927. At her death it became the property of the Georgia Society of the Colonial Dames of America.

The Low House is a typical Trust Lot development. The front garden retains its form and a portion of the original planting. The garden lying between residence and carriage house has been somewhat altered. It is fortunate that, as Georgia's Colonial Dames House, this fine mid-nineteenth century mansion will be preserved.

Whitehall Plantation

On the Savannah River

Christ Church Parish — Chatham County

ALONG the Savannah and the Big and Little Ogeechee Rivers were the rich rice plantations owned by Savannahans. Here were long avenues of moss hung live oaks and the general character of the gardens resembled those on the Georgia coast. The climate and soil are peculiarly suited to the cultivation of camellias, which are brought to unusual perfection in this swamp section of the State.

This Plantation on the Savannah River six miles above the city of Savannah was a grant from George III to Joseph Gibbons, who moved there from the Barbadoes. Here he and his descendants cultivated rice for a hundred and fifty years.

As Joseph Gibbons was a Tory, his lands were confiscated after the Revolution. Fortunately he had sufficient influence to regain possession and to assist many others in a similar plight.

No records survive describing the house built by Joseph Gibbons which was destroyed during the occupation of Savannah by General Sherman and replaced after the Civil War by a frame dwelling still the home of his descendants. It stands above the river in a twenty-five acre primeval grove of giant live oaks under the shade of which bloom camellias and azaleas.

1770

Here peace and beauty dwell.

Lebanon Plantation

On the Little Ogeechee

Chatham County

1804

Lebanon was built and the garden laid out by James Habersham, Jr.

THE land on which Lebanon stands was a five hundred acre Crown Grant made in 1756 by George II to James Deveaux. This Grant, after passing through several hands, in 1804 became the property of James Habersham and in 1806 was purchased by George Anderson, who developed it into a successful cotton plantation. In an old deed there is found a list of eighty Lebanon slaves containing these quaint names: Syer, Christiana, Isiah, Portland, Titus, Binah, Monimia, Suckey, Bounapart, Polydore, Rolen, Annelia, Clarinda, Christmas, Monday, Nero, Georgia, Anthony, Sannip, Butter, and Price.

It is of interest that the home occupied by James Habersham and George Anderson, both notable in the affairs of Savannah and of the State, stands today. In recent years it has been remodeled and enlarged. In its original form, a commodious two-story frame structure on a high brick basement, it was surrounded by double tiered verandas. The land approach was by a long avenue of live oaks and cedars, sections of which remain. A grove of fine old trees made a setting for the house, in front of which was a rose garden with narcissus bordered beds. Of the roses, only a Madame Lambard still wreaths the veranda to a height of fifteen feet, but thousands of old bulbs bloom each spring and two giant dark red crape myrtles have guarded the steps for more than a century. Of the fringe of flowering trees and shrubs that encircled the house and garden, there survive a banana shrub, Chinese magnolias, and a few camellias such as aeta plena, Lady Hume's Blush and Kurmii.

For many years Lebanon has been the country home of Mr. and Mrs. Mills B. Lane. Mrs. Lane has a distinguished collection of camellias, to which rare varieties are constantly added. Under her care the grounds have become a park with lawns sweeping down to the clear brown waters of the Little Ogeechee River.

The Hermitage

On the Savannah River

Chatham County

OF these river plantations, none is more beautiful and interesting than The Hermitage on the Savannah River, a few miles above the city. It was developed by Henry McAlpin, a young Scotch architect of distinguished ability who also proved himself a good business man. Its acreage was acquired through a series of purchases begun in 1814. On the plot where the mansion stands had been the home of M. Montilet, a French Huguenot, who called it his hermitage. Mr. McAlpin retained the name for the plantation. Another section had been Glebe lands, granted by George III to Christ Church, Georgia's first house of worship.

The Hermitage has never been occupied as a residence since it was sacked by Sherman's soldiers. It remains, however, one of the few early nineteenth century plantations of this district retaining practically all its original features. Only the breed stables and race course have entirely disappeared.

A wooden dwelling was replaced in 1820 by the present mansion designed and erected by Mr. McAlpin. It is an exquisite neo-classic structure. A high basement supports a single story, with duplicate columned porticoes reached by double, curved flights of steps. It and the commodious, well-constructed plantation buildings grouped about it are of brick made on the place, where is found a substrata of clay.

Between the mansion and the river was a sunken garden, a type rarely seen in old Georgia. The retaining walls are of brick and the flight of steps leading down to it of white marble. Square beds were separated by irrigation ditches, spanned by rustic bridges, their flooding controlled by the rise and fall of the river tide. In this garden tropical and semi-tropical plants were featured. The roses, many imported from Europe, were planted in rice field mud and reached a high state of perfection. Of this garden, the retaining walls and steps remain. The old house is bowered in flowering shrubs and camellias, relics of the fenced-in garden that surrounded it.

The descendants of the slaves for whom they were built, still occupy the quarters. These form two hollow squares, one on each side of the majestic live oak avenue leading from the road to the house. The little gardens of each cabin date back to antebellum days when the negroes were encouraged to raise flowers, vegetables and poultry. When they had a surplus it was purchased at market prices by the master. This was the general practice on well conducted plantations.

The Hermitage has been continuously owned by the McAlpin family.

1814-1820

The Hermitage on the Savannah is a jewel in a perfect setting.

1820

At the Hermitage the descendants of the McAlpin slaves still occupy the quarters and cultivate the little gardens attached to each cabin.

1800-1810
Bowered in giant camellias, Avon Hall stands on the banks of the Vernon River at White Bluff.

Avon Hall

White Bluff

Christ Church Parish—Chatham County

SOUTH of the Savannah River, winding and twisting through the salt marshes are estuaries of the sea. Above these so-called rivers high bluffs occasionally occur. Always beautifully wooded, they have from earliest days been prized as ideal building sites for individual estates or for small communities of summer homes.

One of the oldest and loveliest of these is White Bluff on the Vernon River. Here is Avon Hall, built well over a hundred years ago by Dr. Burroughs, a Presbyterian minister, who conducted a boarding school for boys. Standing on a high latticed basement, surrounded by a double tier of piazzas and surmounted by a high pitched roof, Avon Hall is the best type of coast summer home of that early period. The view across river, marsh and hammock is one of peaceful beauty. The shade of live oaks and magnolias is deep and cool.

The first garden was filled with roses and flowering shrubs; of orange trees there was an abundance. In 1865 the property was bought by William Neyle Habersham for a country home. He at once began the planting of cassena hedges, also of camellias imported from France. Of these, twenty-one varieties still bloom from November to April, many having reached the unusual height of twenty feet. Additions to this collection are constantly being made by Mrs. Crisfield, Mr. Habersham's granddaughter, who makes Avon Hall her home.

St. Simons Island

The County of Frederica—St. James' Parish—Glynn County

Some of its vanished gardens

ST. SIMONS ISLAND, called Asoa by the Indians and named San Simon by the Spanish who settled there about 1566-67, was selected by Oglethorpe as the destination of the second band of colonists brought over by him. This company reached its shore in 1736. Designed as an outpost against Spanish aggression, the Island's most important developments were Frederica Town and Fort, and Fort St. Simons, connected by a military road. The soldiers who made up the colony were given small grants of about fifty acres each. The Saltzburgers, Germans seeking religious freedom, lived to themselves in a community called The Village. Under the guidance of their Commander, Captain Hermsdorf, they were the first of these settlers to support themselves entirely by agriculture. They had fields and gardens and were successful in the cultivation of mulberries for the silk worm industry so dear to the hearts of the Trustees. When this thrifty group moved to New Ebenezer, The Village became the home of the Wylly family.

Orange Hall, sometimes called Oglethorpe's Villa, was built by that leader near Frederica soon after its establishment. It was a pretty little cottage standing in fifty acres under perfect cultivation. Here were a garden, figs, orange trees and a vineyard. It served as a model and inspiration to the holders of small grants. This modest spot was the only property owned by Oglethorpe in the colony he founded. It bespeaks the disinterestedness of his motives and also the sometimes forgotten fact that the establishment of the Colony of Georgia was only an incident, though a very important one, in the career of this many sided and distinguished man.

Orange Hall was occupied for some years by James Spalding, President of the Island. After the Revolution, the house meanwhile having been destroyed, the property was sold.

Gascoine Bluff (Hamilton Point) was built by Captain Gascoine of the Hawk, convoy to the vessels on which the colonists came over. Among other important holdings of this early settlement and pre-Revolutionary period were Captain Raymond Demere's home, Harrington Hall, with its formal gardens probably laid out in the seventeen-forties, Mulberry Grove, another Demere estate, and of somewhat later date, Kelwyn Grove, the Cater plantation afterwards owned by the Postells, which was noted for its avenue of giant sago palms. On this property now stands the marker of the Battle of Bloody Marsh fought July 7, 1742. This marker bears Thomas Carlyle's dictum on that event: "Half the world was hidden in embryo under it—The incalculable Yankee nation itself, the great phenomenon of these ages. This, too, little as the careless readers on either side of the sea now know it, lay involved: Shall there be a Yankee nation? Shall the New World be Spanish type? Shall it be English?"* Of Orange Grove, owned by Maxwells and Spaldings and better known as Retreat Plantation, we will hear more later on.

The Revolution over and the country in a more settled condition, changes took place on the Sea Islands. The first large holdings were added to and numbers of small grants were purchased by new comers and fused into great plantations. Retreat belongs to both of these groups. Situated on the south end of the Island on the Sound, the ground on which Retreat house stood is supposed to have been a Trustee's Grant to a man called Moor. It was bought by a Maxwell, son of William Maxwell of Philadelphia, who in turn about 1760 sold it to James Spalding, famous Indian trader, a Scotchman, of the Ashantilly Spaldings of County Perth, heir of the Estate and Barony of Ashantilly.** Calling the place Orange Grove, he added to it a grant made him by the Crown and the grants of Christopher Hillery and George Chubb. On these eight hundred acres were old Indian mounds and cleared fields. A scattered growth of orange, pomegranate and fig trees survived from the Spanish period, for San Bonaventura, the most important of the Island's three Franciscan missions, with its fort and village, is supposed to have been situated at no great distance.

Though Sir James, as he was called by his compatriots, was then occupying Oglethorpe's Villa, he planted a mile long avenue of live oaks on his newly acquired property. In 1774 William Bartram, the celebrated botanist, while wandering over the Island in search of specimens, was informally entertained here by James Spalding's overseer. He

* Carlyle, History of Frederick, the Great, V. 4: 184-5 (Centenary Edition, 1898).

**Register of Sassine County, Perth, 1743.

1760-1765

A remnant of the mile-long liveoak avenue at Retreat Plantation set out by James Spalding. The estate at that time was called Orange Grove.

writes: "This delightful habitation was situated in the midst of a spacious grove of live oak and palms near the strand of the bay, commanding a view of the inlet. A cool area surrounded the low but convenient buildings, from whence, through the groves, was a spacious avenue into the island, terminated by a large savanna; each side of the avenue was lined with bee hives to the number of fifty or sixty;"* He mentions no garden but speaks of the perfume of the yellow jessamine, Lonicera, Andromeda and sweet azalea.

Orange Grove was also visited by Andre Michaux, the French botanist and horticulturist, who was sent to this country in 1785 to select trees and plants for the French Government. He mentions in his Journal that he visited Saint Simon's Island on Sunday, first of June, 1788, and "dined with my son at Mr. Spalding's where there were some ladies of General McIntosh's family and several distinguished persons." He is equally silent about a garden.

* The Travels of William Bartram, New Edition, Part 1, Chapter V, P. 72.

One judges that the Spalding men were never lovers of flowers. The paucity of gardens at beautiful South-End House, Thomas Spalding's home on Sapelo, attests to this.

This distinguished man, James's son, inheriting Orange Grove at his father's death, built in 1793 a story and a half cottage framed in live oak timbers. The chimney of the detached, double kitchen was of unusual size. On each side was a niche built into the brick-work, one for the reception of a cask of Madeira wine, the other for a thirty-gallon puncheon of brandy. This house faced the Sound five hundred feet distant from the site of the house described by Bartram, which seems by then to have disappeared. Thus two groups were formed, one

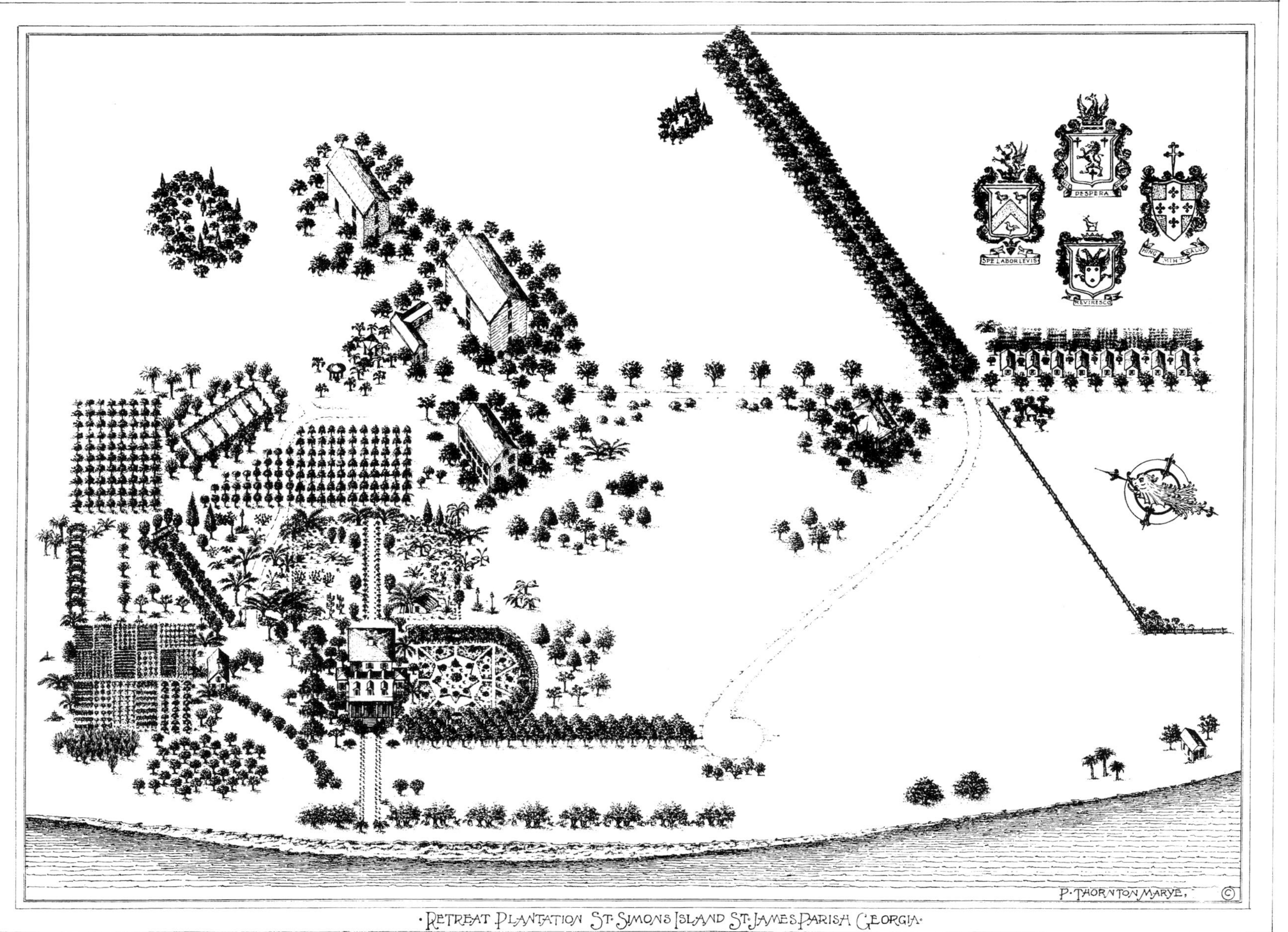

1755-1863

Retreat Plantation on St. Simons Island, known during the eighteenth century as Orange Grove.

consisting of plantation buildings in line with the Great Avenue, and the other set true to the Sound, giving the whole layout an odd cant. Thomas built this house for his bride but abandoned the plan in favor of the more interesting one of spending five years in Europe with her.

In 1798 Major William Page, originally of Page's Point, Prince William Parish, South Carolina, then living on Ottasee, his plantation on the Ogeechee River,* with his wife was paying a visit to his close friend, Major Pierce Butler, a fine Irish gentleman, newly settled at his home, Hampton Point, on the north end of St. Simons Island. Major Butler had brought with him from South Carolina a thousand slaves who built for him a great house with seven chimneys.

In those days year-end rather than week-end visits were the fashion and it is no surprise to learn that during their stay at Hampton Point, a little daughter, Anna Matilda, was born to the Pages. This couple had lost all their many former babies in the then malarial climate of Bryan County. Finding that the new infant throve on St. Simons, they decided to make it their home. Orange Grove, the Spalding property, was selected. The formal contract to buy was not made until 1802, but records show that the Pages were occupying it in 1799. From then on the plantation was known as Retreat.

For reasons best known to himself James Spalding had cut down the live oak grove between the Avenue and the Sound. Major Page immediately started planting trees. The Short Avenue at right angles to the house was planted. It was of water oaks, as were the plantings for shade encircling every building on the place. Cedars and Spanish bayonets edged the bluff. This ground work completed, not only native trees were set out but those from other sections of the States and in time many rare specimens were imported, especially in later years by Mrs. King, the little Anna Matilda, better known as "Sweet Ann Page." Thus was formed a noted arboretum. The extensive citrus grove belonged to the Spalding-Page period. Major Page planted the olive grove near the Sound. (Two years ago a ripe olive was picked from the one tree that still lives). Black walnuts shaded the quarters of the house servants, to each of which was attached a small garden. Mulberry trees surrounded the enormous chicken yard; the peach and pear orchard was just beyond, as was the grape arbor. Out in the fields was the tree shaded burial ground of their slaves whose descendants continued to be buried there and near the Great Avenue was the family cemetery. The pecan and fig trees edging the road to the plantation buildings were planted at a later period. At Retreat all roads, walks and paths are "hard shell;" that is, of crushed oyster shells.

In 1799 Mrs. Page began the planting of her garden which lay between the rear of the house and the slave hospital. The three hundred foot walk through its center was bordered with pink daily roses and edged with snowdrops, in memory of a similar one at Page's Point, their South Carolina home destroyed during the Revolution. In the many changes that took place in this garden as years went on, this feature remained. Mrs. Page built the large tabby hothouse which was later enlarged by her daughter. It seems to have been the only one on the Island. There is no record of what it contained. Imagination fills it, and the big square garden, with plants both lovely and curious, for tropical rarities were already in vogue. Certainly there were plenty of roses, and we know that here were the beds of herbs and simples, and many small bulbs which after a hundred years still defined the garden's outlines. The little, wild Florida lilies, a favorite of Mrs. Page's, today bloom here and there, as do the small bulbs with which she bordered the walk between the veranda and the bluff. To this period also belongs the vast vegetable garden behind the kitchen, where were planted white, blue, Celeste, Turkey and black figs.

The three-story wooden cotton barn, the tabby corn barn, in part of which were stabled the saddle horses, and the lovely commodious tabby slave hospital were built by Major Page. Additional tracts of land were acquired, including New Field Plantation, where tabby quarters for the field hands were built. One still stands. Thus Retreat Plantation became one of the four largest estates on the Island. Anna Matilda, the Page's only surviving child, showed as a young girl the executive gifts that were to make her Georgia's most noted woman agriculturist. After her mother's death, she persuaded her father to spend the summer at Saratoga Springs, and single-handed took entire charge of these two plantations, driving over them each day in a buckboard, of course accompanied by a female relative, a species then never lacking in any household. Daily reports were made out and sent to her father and to Hugh Ross, his factor or business manager. In 1825 she married Thomas Butler King of Kingston, now Palmer, Massachusetts, and Wilkes-Barre, Pennsylvania. Two years later, after her father's death, she inherited Retreat and

* —later New Hope Plantation.

New Field, designated in his will as her dower. Much of Major Page's fortune was invested by the Kings in two great rice plantations on the mainland: Waverly on the Satilla River in Camden County, and Monticello in Wayne County. As at this period the Kings spent most of their time on these plantations and at their summer place at Newport, Rhode Island, Retreat being only occasionally visited, no notable garden developments were undertaken.

Audubon, the great ornithologist, gives his impression of Retreat in 1831. He was on his way to "the Floridas" in the Schooner Agnes, when he was compelled because of a storm to put in at the south end of St. Simons: "I made for the shore, met a gentleman on the beach, presented him my card and was immediately invited to dinner. I visited his gardens, got into such agreeable conversation and quarters, that I was fain to think that I had landed on some one of those fairy islands said to have existed in the Golden Age. But this was not all; the owner of this hospitable mansion pressed me to stay a month with him and subscribed to my Birds of America in the most gentlemanly manner. This was T. B. K., Esq. (Mr. Thomas Butler King of Retreat Plantation, St. Simons Island, Georgia.)"*

Thomas Butler King was a member of Congress for sixteen years. His prolonged absences from home threw the care of four plantations and from twelve to thirteen hundred slaves on his wife's shoulders. In 1842 heavy financial reverses deprived the Kings of their mainland plantations and of a thousand slaves. From then on Retreat was continuously occupied as their home. The original cottage had been given a two-story addition and a small house near the Great Avenue was occupied by the young men of the family. The house at Retreat was never a large or fine residence, and just before the Civil War its replacement by something more appropriate was under contemplation.

1802

Greenhouse at Retreat built by Mrs. Page and enlarged by Mrs. King. It appears to have been the only one on the island.

The development of the gardens became Mrs. King's pleasure and solace. The high peaked roof of the cotton barn served as a landmark by which vessels steered through St. Simons Sound. Grateful sea captains brought Mrs. King rare specimens of trees, shrubs and flowers from the four quarters of the earth. Sometimes plants in tubs that

* Audubon, the Naturalist, by Francis Hobart Herrick, Vol. II, Chapter XXVI, PP. 11 and 12.

had been two years in transit found their final home in her garden. These tropical plants and many specimens from Europe and later from San Francisco, where Mr. King established the Customs House and was the first Collector of Port, were gathered together in Mrs. Page's square garden and soon overlapped its boundaries. We have a description of it by Thomas Wentworth Higginson: " . . . When we afterwards landed the air had that peculiar Mediterranean translucency which southern islands wear and the plantation we visited had the loveliest tropical garden, though tangled and desolate, which I have ever seen in the South . . . The deserted house was embowered in great blossoming shrubs and filled with hyacinthean oders, among which predominated that of the little Chickasaw roses which everywhere bloomed and trailed around. There were Fig Trees and Date Palms, Crepe Myrtles and Wax Myrtles, Mexican Agaves and English Ivies, Japonicas, Bananas, Oranges, Lemons, Oleanders, Jonquils, Great Cactuses and wild Florida Lilies."* This was in 1863. The family were refugeeing on their plantation in Ware County.

Neither her rare collection of trees nor this exotic spot, but her Rose Garden was Mrs. King's special pride. It lay to the left of the house, and measured one hundred and forty by ninety feet. It was horseshoe in shape and was surrounded by a windbreak of Osage oranges trimmed like a mammoth hedge. Within this was a planting of crape myrtle and oleanders sheltering the three latticed summer houses symmetrically placed. The formal beds were edged with snowdrops, the central bed having the form of an eight-pointed star, from which the garden took its name. William Audley Couper, her son-in-law and son of John Couper of Cannon's Point, designed and laid out this garden for Mrs. King. It contained ninety-six varieties of roses and many flowers of European type. Mrs. King writes of it in a letter to her son, Henry Lord Page King, then at The School of Law at Cambridge: "Retreat, 17th April '54 . . . I want everyone to see my Garden in its beauty. I have now 92 different kinds of roses in bloom forming I may say *thousands* of flowers—the Honeysuckles, Honeyflowers, Verbenas, Phlox, Nasturtiums and many others the names forgotten form a perfect blaze of beauty . . . " So powerful was the perfume from this garden that it was enjoyed by passing mariners.

---

* Army Life in a Black Regiment, Chapter 3, P. 91, Thomas Wentworth Higginson.

That Mrs. King continued to add to her garden we know from the following portion of a letter from Mrs. William Audley Couper to her Mother written from Savannah, April 23rd, 1857, giving a list of the contents of a box of plants she was sending her:

". . . . one box of plants containing

6 Japonica	$1.00
1 Rose	.50
3 Fuchsia	.25
1 Cactus	.25 . . . ."

Daddy Quamina, a trusted and esteemed slave, was head gardener at Retreat for thirty years. In a record kept by Mrs. King of the births and deaths on the plantation, the following is found: "Quamina—most honest and true—a faithful servant and good man, after a short illness of twenty-four hours, departed this life, 20th of March, 1860."

During the period when Mrs. King operated Retreat and New Field Plantations she perfected the "Retreat Brand" of Sea Island cotton to such a point that it brought seven cents a pound more on the London and Liverpool markets than any other long staple cotton.

Retreat Plantation was confiscated at the end of the Civil War and was occupied for four years by Mr. Eaton of the Freedman's Bureau. In 1866 a Federal sloop carried off its most valuable trees, plants and flowers which were distributed somewhere north of the Mason and Dixon Line. Later, the King family having regained possession of Retreat, Mr. Eaton as a farewell gesture cut down all the orange and lemon trees.

The place was only occasionally occupied during the next fifty or sixty years. It became the main base of supplies in that section for flowers, shrubs and plants. The people of the Island carried off wagon loads. Those of the neighboring islands and the mainland arrived in yawls, loaded them up and sailed away. The great storm of 1893 blew down the Short Avenue and what remained of the arboretum. In 1906 Retreat house burned down.

In 1927 Mr. Howard E. Coffin bought the property and laid out the links of the Sea Island Beach Golf Club, adjacent to where the house and gardens had been. The tabby corn barn became the Club House.

The following list of planting at Retreat does so little justice to what was there when its development was at its prime, that one hesitates to

By permission of Miss Margie Stiles

1793

The painting, by John Lord Couper, of Cannon's Point on St. Simons Island, is the only contemporary picture we have of an antebellum Sea Island home and garden. It presents a kindly and pleasant scene, and shows the luxuriant, informal planting characteristic of the coast.

present it. However, as far as it goes its authenticity can be vouched for:

Live Oaks	Cherry Laurel
Water Oaks	Sweet Bay
Silver Leafed Aspins	Myrtle (Sand, Sea Wax and European)
Mulberries	
Mock Mulberries	Crape Myrtle
Flowering Locust (black)	Mock Oranges
Catalpa	Ilex (Cassine)
Cedars	Japanese Magnolias
Tree Heath (Erica arborea)	Pittosporum
Magnolia grandiflora	Figs
Black Walnut	Oleanders
Honey Locust	Oppoponacks
Ironwood	Cape Jasmine
Eucalyptus	Pomegranate
Prickly Ash	Japanese Quince
Osage Orange	Spireas
Pecans	Date Palms
Mimosa	Sago Palms
Oranges (sweet and sour)	Century Plant
Lemon	Aloes
Banana	Cactus (several types)
Naka or Heavenbush	Agaves
Olive	

It would be futile to attempt to give a garden list.

At Retreat today one sees a short remnant of the Great Avenue, scattered oleanders and crape myrtle, many old-time bulbs, one fig and one olive tree. Though stripped of its beauty, the fame of its gardens still lives.

John Couper and James Hamilton of Renfrushire, Scotland, having been involved in a boyish scrape, ran away and shipped for America. St. Augustine was the scene of the first of their many mutual business ventures. Its success enabled them in 1793 to move to St. Simons Island, where James acquired Gascoine Bluff, calling it Hamilton's Point, and John purchased on the north end of the Island a three hundred and fifty acre Crown Grant made to Nicholas Nelson in 1760 by George II.

John Couper's first home was the typical story and a half cottage of that region. It stood on a high bluff above the Hampton River, really an arm of the sea. This was the modest nucleus of a huge plantation which in its final development reached five miles inland. With the increase of his family and fortune a very large three-story frame house on high tabby foundations was erected, the original cottage serving as a wing. John Lord Couper's painting of his grandfather's house is the only contemporary pictorial delineation that we have of one of these Sea Island homes and gardens. As can be seen, the planting about the house was luxuriant and informal. The children's garden was laid out in beds edged in snowdrops. John Couper's vegetable garden was as famous as it was extensive.

The noted actress, Fanny Kemble, wife of Pierce Butler, writes in 1839 from Hampton Point, her husband's plantation lying a quarter of a mile just across an arm of the Hampton River: "Mr. C's house is a roomy, comfortable, handsomely laid out mansion, to which he received me with very cordial kindness . . . He showed me his garden, from whence came the beautiful vegetables he had more than once supplied me with." And her journal notes: "A call on dear old Mr. C., whose nursery and kitchen garden are a real refreshment to me."*

Cannon's Point deserves the title of Georgia's first private experimental station. In the nursery spoken of by Fanny Kemble many horticultural experiments were conducted, first by John Couper and later by his distinguished son, James Hamilton Couper. John Couper in 1825 imported two hundred olive trees from France, from which he obtained two to three hundred bottles of oil annually. His long staple cotton was of very high quality and he is credited with having introduced Bermuda grass into this country. James Hamilton Couper conceived the idea of making commercial use of cotton seed oil, but the time was not yet ripe for its acceptance.

Sir Charles Lyell, the celebrated naturalist, describes the fifteen-mile boat trip from Hopeton on the Altamaha where he and his wife were visiting Mr. James Hamilton Couper, to Cannon's Point, which was made in "a long canoe hollowed out of the trunk of a single cypress, rowed by six negroes, who were singing loudly and keeping time to the stroke of their oars." Arriving at Cannon's Point he continues: "We found Mr. Couper's villa, near the water's edge, shaded by a veranda and by a sago tree. There were also many lemon trees, a fine grove of olive trees and five date palms which bear fruit. These were brought from Bussora, Persia."** He is intensely interested in an immense mound left by the Indians which covered ten acres at Cannon's Point, and was elevated to an average of five feet, composed of shells with flint, arrow heads, stone axes and pottery throughout the mass.

After the construction of Hopeton on the Altamaha, a joint enterprise of John Couper and James Hamilton and later run by James Hamilton Couper as James Hamilton's executor, it was used as a winter home by both families and their St. Simons plantations only occupied during the summer.

* Journal of a Residence on a Georgia Plantation, 1838-1839, by Frances Anne Kemble, PP. 284-5.

** Second Visit to the United States, by Sir Charles Lyell.

Hamilton Point, one of the finest estates on the Island, was more noted for its vegetable gardens than for its flowers, though Fanny Kemble admired a hedge of Spanish bayonets seen here.

Our next picture of Cannon's Point is filled with pathos. The Honorable James Leigh of Stoneley Abbey, and later Dean of Hereford, England, in 1873, writing from Butler's Island, his wife's plantation inherited from her father, Pierce Butler, says: "I made an excursion to St. Simons in the company of Mr. James Couper whose father once had a fine house and large plantation there before the War. At Cannon's Point stands what once must have been a very fine three-story mansion with a veranda running all around, and having a large portico on each side of it, while surrounding it were vestiges of pretty grounds and gardens which had been tastefully laid out. Stately date palms reared their heads above the portico and oleanders and other flowering shrubs were dotted about. My companion had not been to his old home for sixteen years—What a change it must have seemed to him from the days when that home was the scene of unbounded hospitality and full of merry children. There among the tall grass and reeds he could still make out the little garden which was the children's own, and from which he was able to dig up some roses and bulbs to carry away as a memento. There on the old oak tree near the house used to hang the swing on which the young ones were wont to amuse themselves, and there actually was the old negro woman who had been a faithful servant in the family,—old Rina: and was she not delighted to see Massa Jimmy once more, and would she not do everything she could to make us comfortable in the old deserted house, even though it had not a scrap of furniture in it, and did she not send 'a heap of howdy' to all the members of his family?"*

Today visiting Cannon's Point one passes through the gate into a great forest of primeval oaks veiled in grey moss. The long live oak avenue at its end leads to the ruins of plantation buildings, quarters, kitchen and the tabby foundations

* Ten Years on a Rice Plantation, by the Honorable Mrs. Leigh.

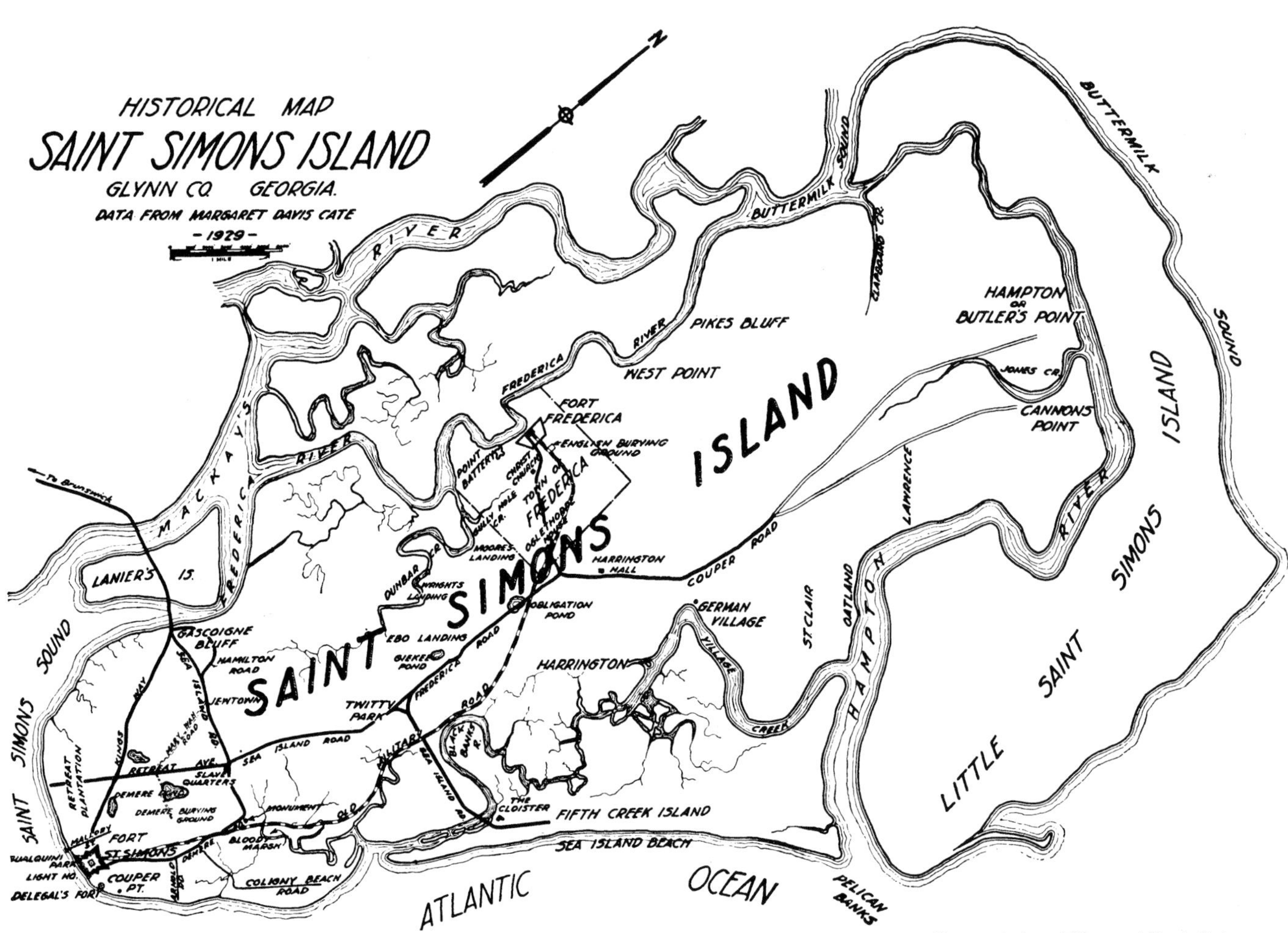

By permission of Margaret Davis Cate

of the house, standing in a jungle of giant cedars, chinaberries, crape myrtles and oleanders. A forty-foot Bussora date palm dominates the scene. There is a thicket of olive trees, and iris and snowdrops still bloom in the children's garden. The stump of the live oak from which the stern post of the Frigate Constitution, "Old Ironsides," was made is seen near, all that remains of Mr. Couper's villa at Cannon's Point.

Major Pierce Butler, son of Sir Pierce Butler of the House of Ormond, an Irishman but an officer

Ruins of South and West Walls Enclosing a Service Yard at Hampton Point, Erroneously Called Fanny Kemble's Sunken Garden

in the British Army, married and settled in South Carolina. During the Revolution he sided with America, thus losing his title and estates. In 1795 he moved to St. Simons Island, having purchased from Mr. Ladson of Charleston a property on the north end of the Island and the adjacent MacIntosh tract. Bringing with him a thousand slaves, he was assisted in the move by his friend, Major William Page. On a high bluff above an arm of the sea, from then on called Hampton River, he built what was known as the "Big House," a very large structure of wood and tabby, noted for its seven chimneys. Between it and the bluff was an orange grove.* As Mrs. Butler was a Middleton, we may be sure that the gardens were of the best.

It was here that Aaron Burr, seeking seclusion after his fatal duel with Alexander Hamilton, spent the summer and fall of 1804. Major Pierce Butler and his family were according to custom summering at Butler Place in Chestnut Hill, Pennsylvania. Notwithstanding this, the Vice-President seems to have made himself thoroughly at home in the comfortable quarters and circumstances provided by his absent host. In a letter to his adored daughter, Theodosia, Mrs. Joseph Alston, of South Carolina, he writes from St. Simons, August 31, 1804: "I am now quite settled. My establishment consists of a housekeeper, cook, and chambermaid, seamstress, and two footmen. There are, besides, two fishermen and four bargemen always at command. The department of laundress is done abroad. The plantation affords plenty of milk, cream, and butter; turkeys, fowls, kids, pigs, geese and mutton; fish, of course in abundance. Of figs, peaches and melons there are yet a few. Oranges and pomegranates just begin to be eatable. The house affords Madeira wine, brandy, and porter. Yesterday my neighbor, Mr. Couper, sent me an assortment of French wines, consisting of Claret, Sauterne, and Champagne, all excellent; and at least a twelve months' supply of orange shrub, which makes a most delicious punch. Madame Couper added sweetmeats and pickles."

Doubtless he enjoyed many wild turkeys, as St. Simons Island seemed to have been to an extraordinary degree their natural habitat. Old chronicles reveal that in 1575 a French fleet of sixty sails came to a roadstead off St. Simons Island and traded with Indians of Guale for turkeys, sassafras and pelts of deer and beaver. More than ten thousand turkeys were shipped to France in one year. The Indians caught the turkeys on this island and its neighbors—Jekyl and Sapelo. Spain owned the islands but France got the birds. The French king ate his first turkey in 1575 and the fowl be-

Low East Wall of the Same Service Yard

No definite date can be found for the two tabby houses to which it is attached.

* Journal of a Residence on a Georgia Plantation, 1838-1839, by Frances Anne Kemble, P. 244.

came a royal bird because only a few persons could afford the price of one.

How different a picture of Hampton Point is presented to us by Fanny Kemble, wife of Pierce Butler, the Major's grandson and heir, who on acquiring these properties had dispensed with the services of Roswell and Barrington King, for so many years managers of Butler's Island and Hampton Point for their absentee owners, who from 1815 on spent not only their summers but their winters at Butler Place. However, 1838-39 found brilliant, beautiful Fanny living on these plantations. Boiling with abolitionist prejudice and indignation, her life there was a combination of mental anguish and physical discomfort. On Butler's Island, acquired in 1800 and never intended to be used as a residential plantation, Mr. Butler, herself and their two daughters occupied a tiny overseer's cottage. The plantation's only claim to beauty, a double row of orange trees encircling the Island, had been killed by frost two years earlier. At Hampton Point they lived in a barrack-like tabby house, unoccupied and fallen into dilapidation since the departure of the Kings for whom it was built in 1825. The Big House half a mile distant had been partially destroyed years before by storms and the orange grove and gardens swept into the river, into which the house itself ultimately tumbled.

A close study of the journal of the great actress dealing with this unhappy period of her life reveals her love of all growing things and the exquisite pleasure given her by the natural beauties of the Island. That she planted gardens either on Butler or St. Simons Island is a myth. She describes the modest garden she found around the cottage at Butler's Island and notes the fact* that one afternoon she amused herself by having some bulbs moved within its confines.

At Hampton Point she records that near the house is a "would-be garden, a plot of ground with one or two peach trees in full bloom, tufts of silver narcissus and jonquils, and a quantity of violets, and an exquisite myrtle bush; wherefore I said my prayers with especial gratitude."** She made no effort at planting here, as at this time a very large house was being constructed about two miles inland which was to serve as a residence for the incumbent overseer and for the Butler family during their stays on the plantation. Shortly before her departure, never to return, she superintended the clearing of the ground around this house, intending to lay out a garden, but the closest inspection of the land around its ruins reveals no trace of there ever having been any flower or shrub planting. She probably was responsible for the setting out of the strange windbreak of giant water oaks enclosing a quadralateral of three hundred by six hundred feet, in the midst of which the house stood.

The walled enclosures called by many Fanny Kemble's sunken and walled gardens are in reality something quite different. Several hundred feet inland from the Roswell King house there stand two two-story residential buildings only a few feet apart, built of tabby, connected by a tabby wall and with a tabby wall enclosing an oblong yard at their rear. It measures possibly one hundred and fifty by three hundred and fifty feet. Its west wall, which has fallen down, is about ten feet high, as is the south wall; the east wall is only two feet high. The enclosed area is about one foot lower than the foundations of the wall, and is bare of all vegetation. This is the so-called "Fanny Kemble Sunken Garden." The unequal height of the walls is a matter of puzzlement, but when one remembers that a part of Fort Frederica, built of tabby, was sawed up and used for the building of the first lighthouse on St. Simons Island, and that many tabby buildings on the Island were pulled down, the tabby put through crushers and used to make roads, it does not seem improbable that originally this wall was all of one height. The place would seem to have been a service yard in connection with plantation activities, adjacent to a sub-overseer's house, and possibly bachelors' quarters so frequently found on Southern plantations.

Even further inland there is again a tabby building, spoken of by some as Fanny Kemble's hothouse. It is without windows, has a gabled roof and is attached to a large walled enclosure. The building is quite obviously a carriage and wagon shed, as it has only back and side walls and the adjoining enclosure was the stable yard.

Major Butler came of the great land-owning class of the British Isles, on whose estates walled enclosures of every kind were the rule. Those of Hampton Point being unique on the sea islands, their purpose has been easily misunderstood.

Had these supposed magnificent gardening developments been undertaken and carried through by flower-loving Fanny Kemble, she would surely have mentioned them in her carefully-kept journal.

* Journal of a Residence on a Georgia Plantation in 1838-1839, by Frances Anne Kemble, P. 144.

** Journal of a Residence on a Georgia Plantation in 1838-1839, by Frances Anne Kemble, P. 160.

The planting described by her at Hampton Point survived the burning of the place by Federalist troops. Her daughter, Fanny, later the Honorable Mrs. Leigh, writing from Hampton Point, May 5, 1868, says: "I long to cut and trim, lay out, and take up making the place as beautiful as it is capable of being made."* Her husband, the Honorable James Leigh, wrote in the 70's describing peach, wild plum and orange trees still in abundance.

This vast property has remained intact, though it has passed into other hands. It is seven miles from the entrance gate to the ruins still standing on the bluff above Hampton River, where rosy blooms of flowering shrubs gleam through grey veils of moss, softening a scene of desolation.

* Ten Years on a Rice Plantation, by the Honorable Mrs. Leigh.

Hopeton

On the Altamaha

Glynn County

AT the beginning of the nineteenth century, John Couper of Cannon's Point and James Hamilton of Hamilton Point, the Damon and Pythias of St. Simons Island, undertook a mutual agriculture enterprise on the mainland. In 1805 they purchased Wright's Island from the estates of Laurens, Middleton and Deds of South Carolina, and Carr's Island from Dr. Proctor of Savannah, about two thousand acres in all. These properties were on the Altamaha River, five miles above Darien. The plantation was called Hopeton, for their friend and banker, William Hopeton.

Practically none of the land had been cleared. While this was being done and the residence constructed, nine hundred slaves were moved over to the property. First cotton, then sugar and ultimately rice were planted. By 1816 one thousand two hundred acres of rice fields, banked and ditched, were under cultivation. James Hamilton Couper, son of John Couper, was made manager of the estate. Under his care the rice acreage was greatly increased, four to five hundred slaves being required to work this vast development. At James Hamilton's death, James Hamilton Couper was appointed the sole executor and trustee for his estate, and continued in charge of these properties until the majority of Richard Corbin in 1857 relieved him of his duties.

The mansion, built of tabby, was distinctly Latin in type. Standing on a bluff above the Altamaha River, it was surrounded by wide Bermuda lawns, a feature peculiar to all Couper places. The land approach was by an avenue of sixty live oaks; a canal a quarter of a mile long cut through the rice fields formed the water approach. The Couper and Hamilton families used Hopeton only as a winter residence; therefore no formal garden was laid out. There was, however, an elaborate use of flowering shrubs about the lawn and houses, brought from the gardens at Cannon's Point.

James Hamilton Couper was a great agriculturist, leading conchologist, and a microscopist of note who made many discoveries in the then new field of germ life. His famous library was housed at Hopeton, where he was visited by men and women of distinction from all over the world, among whom were Captain Basil Hall, Sir Charles and Lady Lyell, and the Honorable Amelia Murray, daughter of Lord George Murray, Bishop of St. Davids, and Lady in Waiting to Queen Victoria. She later lost her place at Court because of the publication of her letters in which she gave a favorable account of the treatment of slaves in the South.

In a letter dated Darien, Georgia, February 9, 1855, the Hon. Amelia gives us a pleasing picture of Hopeton: "A four-oared canoe-like boat, of Mr. Hamilton Couper's, had come down from his plantation on the Altamaha, upon some business. Dr. Turner insured our being taken up with him; we met Mr. Couper also by accident, and after a very pleasant row of about five miles, he brought us to his English-like house (as respects the interior) and interesting home, my first resident introduction to plantation life. A happy attached negro population surrounds this abode; I never saw servants in any old English family more comfortable, or more devoted; it is quite a relief to see anything so patriarchal, after the apparently uncomfortable relations of masters and servants in the Northern States. I should much prefer being a 'slave' here, to a grumbling saucy 'help' there; but everyone to their tastes. We left the river about a quarter of a mile from the house, and came up a narrow canal, between rice plantations, almost to the door; we passed two or three large flat boats, laden with rice; and Mr. Couper took me to see the threshing machine which was at work in a barn; the women putting in the rice just as we do our grain; they were more comfortably dressed than our peasantry, and looked happier; otherwise (except the complexions) the scene was much of the same kind as that at a threshing-barn in England."*

From Hopeton, February 14, 1855,* she again writes: "I cannot find myself dull with this pleasant family; yesterday we did all sorts of things, just as I should have done among my own belongings in England. We cooked, and drew, and studied natural history."

For fifty years Hopeton has been a jungle-surrounded ruin.

* Letters from the United States, Cuba and Canada, PP. 218 and 224.

From an old painting by John Lord Couper

1806

Hopeton, the Winter Home of the Hamiltons and Coupers

By permission of James Maxwell Couper

Altama

On the Altamaha

Glynn County

IN 1855 James Hamilton Couper, contemplating retirement from his executorship of the estate of James Hamilton, and desiring a mainland winter home of his own which might serve ultimately as a dower house for his wife, purchased from James Hamilton's heirs, to whom Hopeton now belonged, a considerable acreage of that plantation. A commodious tabby house was built after plans drawn by himself, resembling Hopeton in type, but smaller and of lighter design. Erected where an Indian village once stood surrounded by cleared fields, it occupied the crest of a large knoll, a feature unusual in the topography of this section. All around were rice fields except on one side where there was a stretch of pine barren, and a thicket of live oaks, magnolias and palmettos. A wide lawn of Bermuda grass lay in front of the house, at one side of which was a long, narrow garden of simple design enclosed by a picket fence. A fine wisteria vine grew over the porch, which was shaded by a mispilla plum. In the garden were roses, cape jasmine, crepe myrtle, oleanders, snowdrops, narcissus and violets; orange trees grew near by. Here as well as at Hopeton were large vegetable gardens, and in the quarters each family had their own garden patch.

Altama still stands in its original grove, though its old garden is gone and the house modernized. It is used as a hunting lodge by Cator Woolford, the present owner.

1856-1863

Altama on the Altamaha still stands within its ancient grove. In the Indian tongue Altama meant "the way to Tama," an Indian town at the junction of the Oconee and Ocmulgee. Up country tribes canoed down this river, afterwards known as the Altamaha, to the coast for the fishing seasons. It is said that they took back peach stones from the Spanish missions to plant in their own orchards.

Elizafield Plantation

On the Altamaha

Glynn County

WHEN Dr. Robert Grant of Leigh, Scotland, came to America in 1781 he made his home in Charleston. After serving as surgeon with Marion in the War of 1812 he moved to Georgia and developed two rice plantations on the Altamaha River—Evelyn and Grantley. Purchasing in 1825 a large tract adjacent to Hopeton, the Couper-Hamilton Estate, he gave this plantation to his son, Hugh Frazer Grant, who called it Elizafield.

Building and the laying out of the grounds were at once started. At right angles to an avenue, in a fine grove of live oaks and magnolias, rose a commodious two-story frame dwelling graced by Corinthian columned porticos, of which a school house to the left was a miniature one-story replica. Here tutors held classes for the Grant children and for those of neighbors within driving or boating distance.

On each side of the entrance were beds of flowers, and at the rear of the house curved hedges of oleander, crape myrtle, mock orange, dogwood, holly and cassina formed a frame enclosing a semicircular Bermuda lawn bisected by a narrow oyster shell walk flanked by beds of roses, small shrubs and plantings of silver leaf poplar, flowering locust, catalpa, flowering wild olive, mock mulberry, sago palm, sweet bay, trembling aspen and opoponacks.

A large formal garden enclosed in a picket fence lay at the end of the right hand lawn. Roses were its pride. Here were the usual tropical plants always seen in this section; also spirea, cape jasmine, white and purple flags, gladioli, fuchias, verbenas and several kinds of lilies. The beds were outlined by narcissus, snowdrops and violets which still bloom with the coming of spring.

Opposite this garden were the quarters of the house servants, beyond which stood the carriage house, stables and vegetable garden. A grape arbor, orchard and citrus grove masked a fenced enclosure containing wagon sheds and team stables. Here close to the rice field bank, and approached by a canal, was the rice mill.

Near the formal garden was the family burying ground enclosed by a tabby wall. A flight of steps ascended to the top and another flight descended into the interior. In the corner of this wall is cut the date "1830." The burying ground is all that remains of Elizafield, now the property of Cator Woolford, who uses it as a hunting preserve in conjunction with Hopeton and Altama. On Elizafield Plantation still stand the ruins of Santo Domingo at Talaje, one of the missions built by Franciscan monks during the last quarter of the sixteenth century not long after this coast was settled by Spain.

1825-1863

Opposite is a plan of Elizafield, Hugh Frazer Grant's home on the Altamaha River. It illustrates how self-contained were many of the coast plantations.

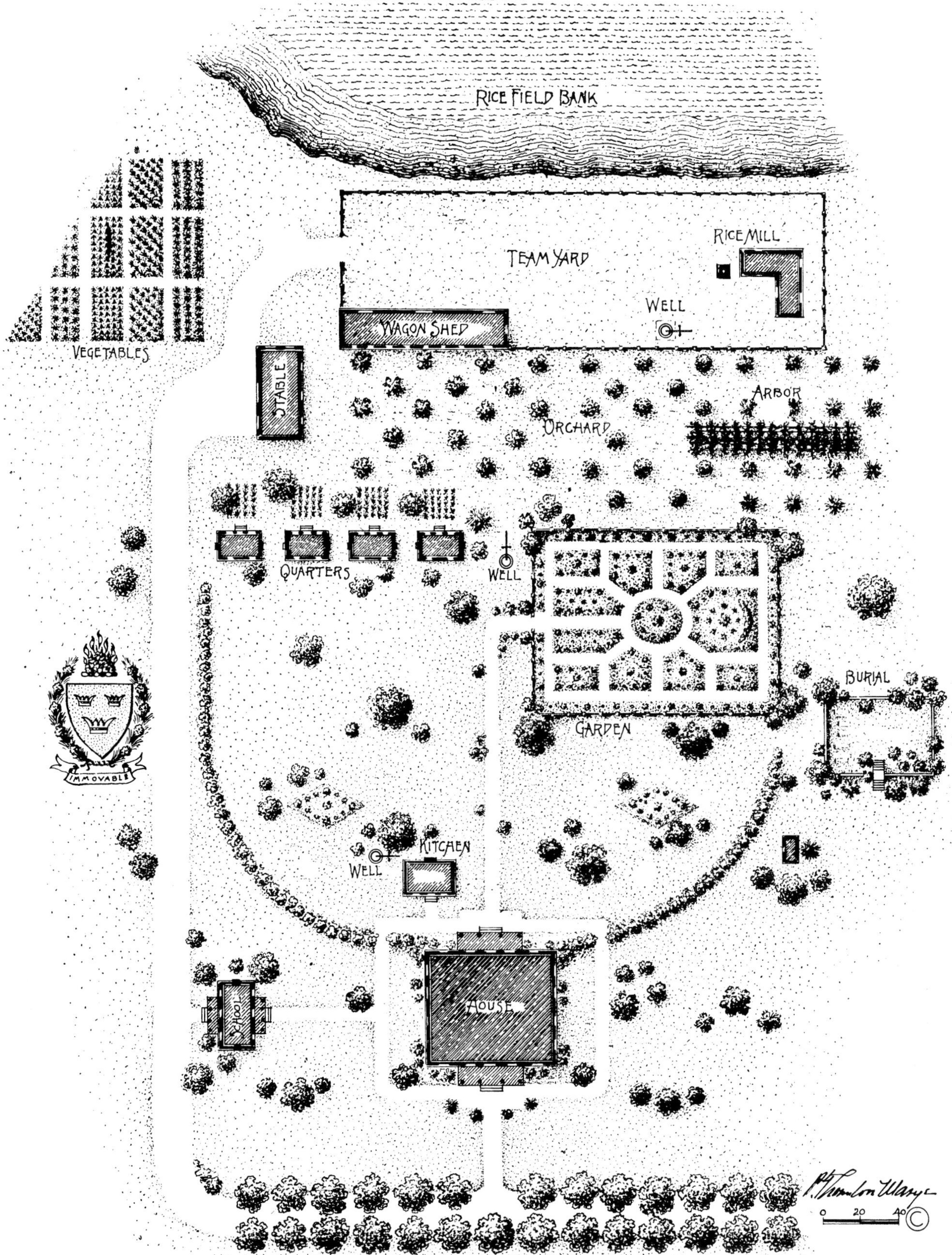

RICE FIELD BANK
TEAM YARD
RICE MILL
WELL
WAGON SHED
VEGETABLES
STABLE
ARBOR
ORCHARD
QUARTERS
WELL
GARDEN
BURIAL
IMMOVABLE
KITCHEN
WELL
HOUSE
SCHOOL
0 20 40

Bellevue and Fairfield, The Twin Plantations

On the Satilla

Camden County

COLONEL CHARLES FLOYD, a native of Northampton County, Virginia, settled on St. Helena, South Carolina, and took an active part in the Revolutionary War as leader of the St. Helena Guards. His home on that Island having been destroyed by the British, he moved first to McIntosh and then to Camden County, where he commanded a fort protecting the border against the Spanish in Florida.

In 1800 he purchased eight hundred adjacent acres consisting largely of lands cleared and cultivated first by the Indians and later by their Spanish conquerors.

Two handsome homes were erected. Bellevue for the Colonel, and a mile away, Fairfield, for his son, John. An avenue of live oaks and cedars bordered the connecting road. Under its shade was a hedge-like planting of myrtle imported from Germany, edged with thousands of bulbs. Both houses had formally laid out gardens set in lawns graced by shrubs and flowering trees. Half an acre of roses framed the great semi-circular drawing room at Bellevue, known from its plan as the Anchor House. When these garden developments were undertaken, one of Colonel Floyd's vessels constructed at his own ship yard in McIntosh County brought a full cargo of tropical and semi-tropical plants from the West Indies.

General John Floyd, and his brother, General Charles R. Floyd, both distinguished soldiers and successful agriculturists, extended and beautified the grounds and gardens of these extensive plantations, where first indigo and then cotton were successfully cultivated.

Surviving the devastation of the eighteen sixties, when both houses were burned, there can be found on the sites of the gardens of Bellevue and Fairfield silver maples, pecans, crepe myrtles, sweet and sour oranges, figs, quinces, plums, peaches, pears, ribbon grass, roses, jonquils, snowdrops and violets.

The outline of the Avenue can still be seen and there are long stretches where the limbs of great cedars meet overhead. The "Parade Ground" used by the garrison, about two hundred acres that was kept in turf, is covered with low brush but no trees have grown on it. The tabby foundations of the houses remain and the family burial ground with its dignified monuments is still cared for. These properties form a part of the Sea Island Shooting Preserve.

1800

Snowflakes at the foot of an ancient white mulberry. These little flowers bravely survive in all coast gardens.

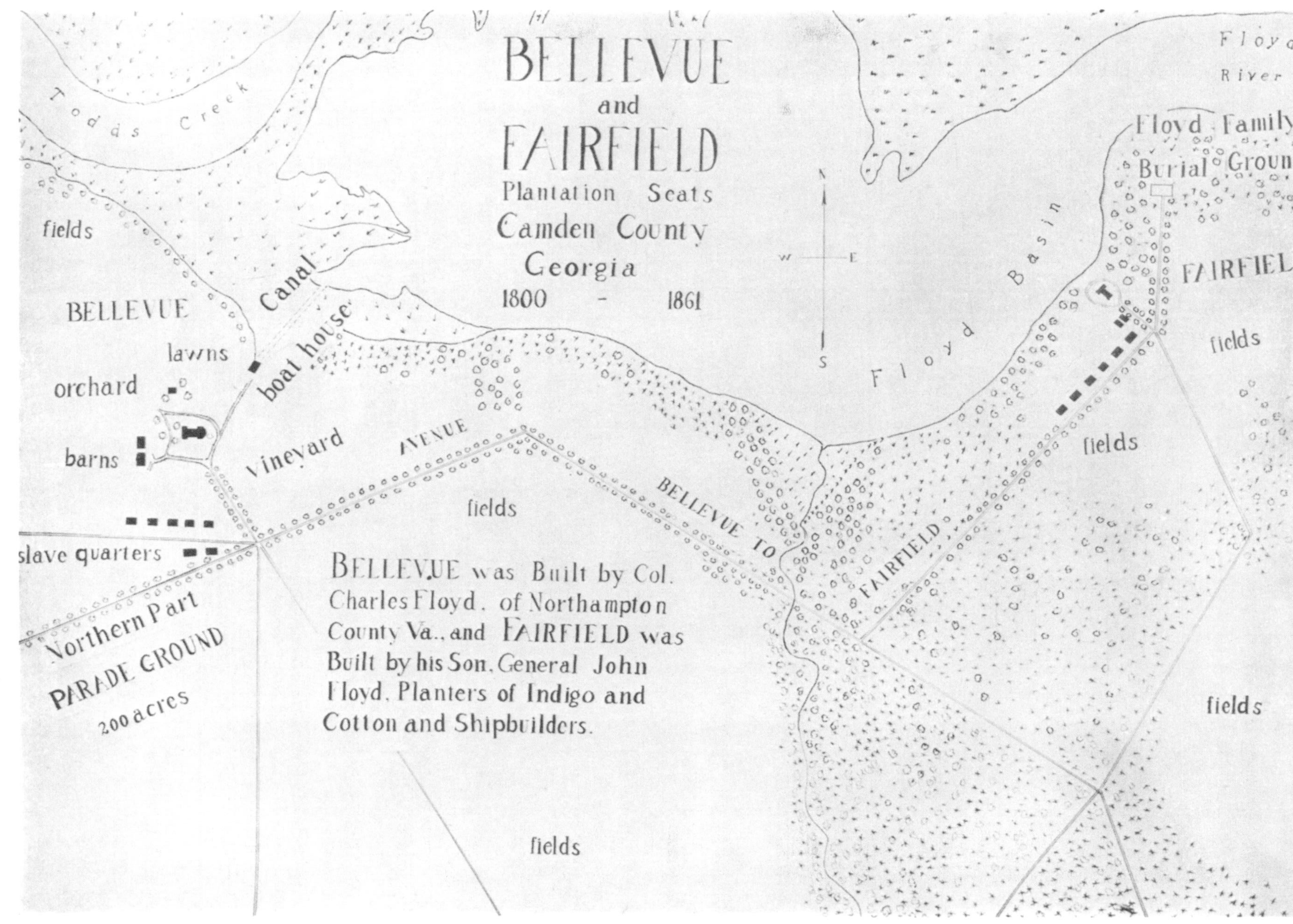

By permission of Augusta Floyd DeRenne

Augusta

The County of Savannah—St. Paul's Parish—Richmond County

OGLETHORPE, having established Savannah, Ebenezer and a number of forts for the protection of the Colony's southern borders, turned his energies to the development of a strong trading center higher up the Savannah River. In 1735 the town of Augusta was laid out and the following year a garrison was detailed for its defense. So advantageous was its situation that the town became the leading mart for Indian trade in Georgia and South Carolina. A road capable of being traveled on horseback was opened to Savannah and the growth of this prosperous community went steadily forward.

The city's earliest homes and gardens were along the river front, where recently levees have been raised as flood protection. Those of a somewhat later date, and Augusta's handsomest residences and gardens, were largely destroyed by fire. A few still stand along beautiful Green and Telfair Streets, but for better preserved early gardens we must turn to the small adjacent communities where Augusta's wealth and fashion spent the summer months. Of these the most important was The Sand Hills, or The Hill as it is now known.

1807

The Ware-Silbey-Clark House is one of the fine old residences that still stand along Telfair Street. The narrow space between the wrought iron fence and the double front steps is laid out in little formal beds with an original planting of camellias and wistaria. In the walled side garden are old shrubs and bulbs.

1806

The Howard-Gardner-Hadry-Wallace Place on The Sand Hills

Augusta's suburban cottages and villas often had naturalistic settings. Here native and cultivated shrubs lend beauty to a stretch of woodland that for a hundred summer days is made radiant by the bloom of pink crape myrtle.

Carnes-Howard-Thomas-Chafee Place

The Sand Hills

Augusta

IN the last quarter of the eighteenth century Peter Carnes had erected a pretty cottage on a five and a half acre plot on Milledge Road. Prior to his death in 1784 he sold this property to Mrs. Howard who enlarged the house to its present dimensions. It is of a cottage type developed around Augusta, modeled after the first homes erected by the Colonists, of which variants are found in all the older sections of the State.

Mrs. Howard's Dutch bulb garden has the honor of being Georgia's only eighteenth century formal garden to retain both its pattern and original character of planting. The seventeen beds of which it is comprised were formerly edged in spice pinks. These, worn out by blooming, have been replaced by narrow copings. The bands of old fashioned blue hyacinths which outline all the beds are those set out by Mrs. Howard, as are the butter and eggs daffodils filling some of them. Unquestionably there were tulips in this garden but they have disappeared. The color scheme is now blue and yellow. A handful of feathery lilac Roman hyacinths, a very old variety, still survive. This garden lay at one end of a picket enclosed pleasance, where were found stretches of lawn planted in trees and shrubs, generously proportioned vegetable and herb beds, fig trees and a fine strawberry patch. It was entered through an arbor shaded gate. The lovely Banksia roses covering it belong to the garden's earliest period.

Some years later Mrs. John Howard made a rose garden just outside this gate. Consisting of six very long, narrow beds, it was surrounded on three sides by tree and shrub plantings, whose encroachment proved its doom. Some of the pink dailies now form a horseshoe planting where a part of this garden lay. The little seven sister roses have been transplanted to a replica of the old rose garden that now occupies a part of the vegetable garden. Mrs. Harry Chafee, Mrs. Howard's great great granddaughter, has made a little paradise of her ancestral home. The grounds are beautifully developed and under perfect cultivation, the old and the new being delightfully blended. The lovely flowering cherry laurel, seen in such perfection in and about Augusta, forms group plantings, screens and close cut hedges. Splendid California incense cedars (Liborcerrus decurrens) flank the entrance of the house, near which is a giant larch. Oaks, hackberries, black locust, deodars, crepe myrtle, chinaberries, wild plum, ilex, grand-daddy gray beard, crabapple, Judas trees, dogwood, Mahonia, Spanish bayonet, spirea, and philadelphus are of the old planting, as are Chandeleri, Hermese and alba plina camellias. On tree and trellis, jessamine and Cherokee roses have twined and wreathed for a hundred years. A very interesting and unusual eighteenth century molded brick edging defines the walks, along which it is a delight to wander. A charming and more personal article on Mrs. Chafee's home may be found in the modern section of this volume.

1780-1863

On the following page is shown Mistress Hannah Howard's square Dutch bulb garden, at her summer home on the Sand Hills, laid out by her in 1784. Its seventeen beds retain much of their original planting. The nearby vegetable beds cheerfully bordered in herbs and flowers have in recent years become a rose garden, the duplicate of the one planted by Mrs. John Howard early in the nineteenth century and shown on this drawing.

MALE MORA QUAM FOEDORI
0 10 20 ©

1800

Three Oaks was an early development on The Sand Hills. It has been owned successively by the Fluernoys, Carmichaels, Johnsons, Courtenays and Heards. Distinguished as an arboretum, it possesses twin giant Cypress cedars (Cypressus pyramidolis horizontalis) two hundred years old and seventy-seven feet high, perhaps the finest of this species in the United States. These trees, like other horticultural rarities, were imported from Italy during Augusta's early and very prosperous days.

1806

Nowhere in Georgia did flowering shrubs and trees grow to greater beauty than on The Sand Hills at Augusta. Fine specimens of both are seen at the Langdon place on Milledge Road. The outlines of the original garden laid out by Thomas Gardener in 1806 are still discernible. The present house was built in 1854.

Cumming-Langdon Place

The Sand Hills

Augusta

IN 1826, following the then prevailing fashion, Thomas Cumming built a summer home on The Sand Hills. To the northwest of the large, comfortable dwelling his wife, Ann, laid out a formal garden of simple design. Rectangular in shape, surrounded by a picket fence pierced by two gates, it has a round central bed, four rectangular beds and a border bed just within the fence line. The shrubs in this last are about all that remain of the planting, though the garden form can be easily followed. Flowering trees and shrubs surround both house and garden.

There is a second formal garden to the west designed for Miss Sarah Cumming by Ignaze A. Pilate, a Hungarian landscape gardener, who came to Augusta with Frederick Law Olmstead, and was later associated with him and Calvert Vaux in laying out Central Park in New York. Ignaze claimed descent from Pontius Pilate. Of this garden's intricate pattern only the central bed remains. Miss Nan Langdon, who with her brother owns the property, has Pilate's original drawing and his bill for making it.

These gardens are excellent examples of the two distinct types of formal gardens found in Georgia.

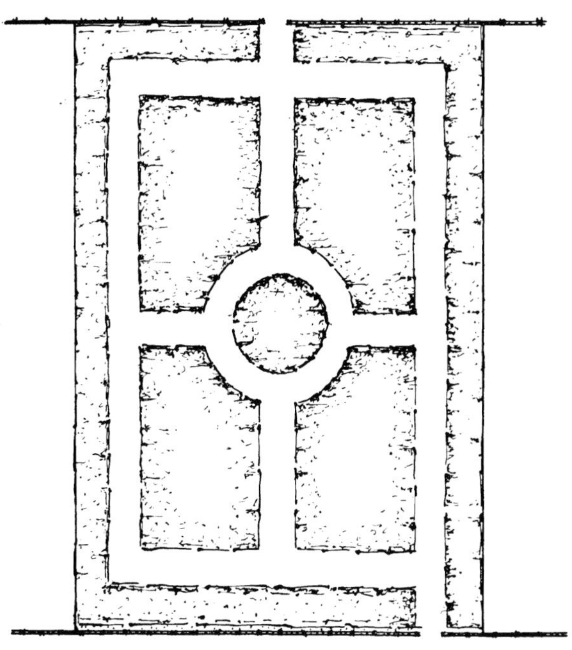

1826

A Plan of Mrs. Thomas Cumming's Garden on The Sand Hills

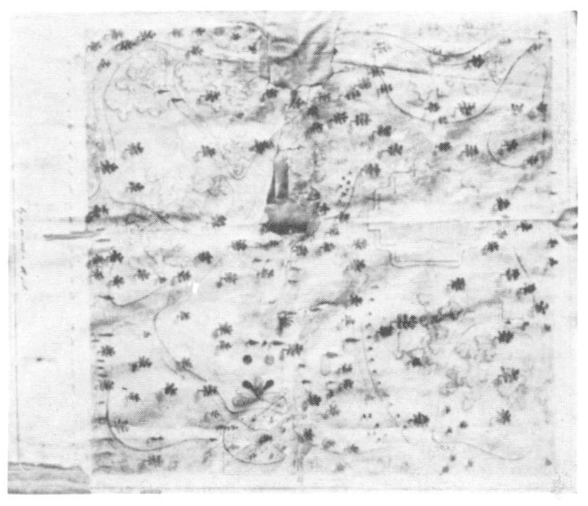

1856

A Fragment of the Garden Plan Drawn by Ignaze A. Pilate for Miss Sarah Cumming

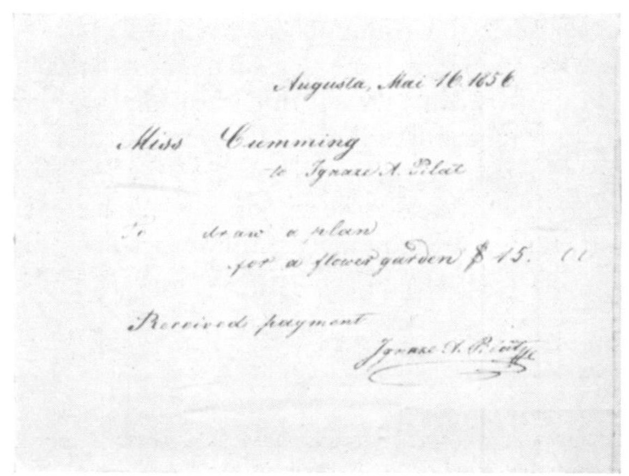

Augusta, Mai 16 1856

Miss Cumming
to Ignaze A. Pilat

To draw a plan
for a flower garden $ 15. 00

Received payment
Ignaze A. Pilat

The Bill Rendered by Pilate

Rosemary Cottage

Harrisonville

Augusta

IN 1829 Samuel Hale, a Northern gentleman, built an attractive story and a half cottage just outside of Augusta, on a forty-three-acre plot on Carnes Road (now the Jefferson Davis Highway). The house stood well back from the road in a setting of giant oaks, holly and crape myrtle. In the rear yard were the kitchen, servant quarters, overseer's house, smokehouse and well; beyond were the barns and stables. The Hales had their extensive grounds laid off by a Northern landscape gardener. They were said to have resembled the famous gardens attached to the Niblo Theatre in New York City. The central feature, a formal garden, was flanked by cultivated areas, one planted in small fruits and fruit trees, the other as a kitchen garden. Scuppernong arbors, each one hundred and twenty-five feet long, stretched from the house to the outer boundary of these units. In the middle of each arbor was a summer house. The other three sides of these sections were bordered by handsome euonymus bushes, the whole framed in oaks.

In the center of the formal garden was a large oval bowling green bordered by handsome trees. Its character as such was marred by a central planting of euonymus. Surrounding it were beds in a variety of shapes, with strong magnolia and cedar plantings. At Rosemary Cottage is found a very interesting character of edging: bricks eighteen inches long have one end so molded that when two are set in the ground together they form a scallop. These bricks came to Savannah as ballast on an English sailing vessel and were hauled by oxcarts to Augusta over the old Tobacco Road. Within this edging the lawn and four circular beds were bordered in dwarf arborvitae; all other beds in dwarf box. Within this again were spice pinks, violets, and a variety of bulbs. The beds were filled with dogwood, other native shrubs, crape myrtle in shades of pink, lavender and purple, lilacs, altheas, pomegranates, wild olive, flowering almonds, tea olive, and roses of many varieties. English ivy, wistaria, star jasmine and Lady Banksias festooned trees and arbors.

A picket fence ran along the road for many hundred feet. It curved gracefully on each side of the carriage gate whose posts carried iron watch dogs. The posts of the two picket gates and those marking the confines of the central garden were topped by American eagles holding United States shields in their claws, these also in cast iron, as were the large urns in front of the house.

In 1855 Rosemary Cottage was purchased by William Sterling Roberts. By that time a few prominent families had built homes in the neighborhood, forming a community called Harrisonville, and it still bears this name, though it has become a part of Augusta. Mr. Roberts lived continuously at Rosemary until his death in 1912, and his daughter, Mrs. Frank Eastman Beane, still makes it her home. The house shows only minor additions and the lovely old garden keeps its form and character, although the setting out many years ago of additional shade trees has changed some of the flower beds into fancifully shaped bits of green sward. Banksia roses bloom and one huge scuppernong arbor still provides grapes for the making of delicious wine. Here, as all over Georgia, the euonymous was destroyed by a pest. The planted areas they enclosed have been put to other uses. At Rosemary Cottage the charm of the past has been preserved, as the place has always been loved and well cared for.

1829-1863

At Rosemary Cottage in old Harrisonville the formal garden, orchard, kitchen garden and scuppernong arbors were developed in a single harmonious scheme.

Fruitlands

Bedford, now The Hill

Augusta

BECAUSE of its mild and equable climate, Prosper Jules Alphonse Berckmans fixed on Augusta as the site of one of Georgia's first commercial nurseries. This distinguished scholar, botanist, horticulturist, landscape architect and nurseryman, was a Belgian of noble birth. In 1857-58 he and his father bought Dennis Redmond's estate, Fruitlands, and an additional fifty acres of land at a settlement known as Bedford, now included in The Hill. He completed the large, concrete house which had been commenced four years earlier by Redmond. With its double tier of encircling piazzas it is reminiscent of Mississippi and Louisiana. The approach is by an avenue of magnolias grown from seed sent to Mr. Berckmans from two trees in Athens about 1858 or 1859. Here are seen various forms, for magnolias, when grown from seed, do not always follow the character of the parent tree. Rare and lovely plants grow in the park-like grounds. Among those planted during the first twenty-five years after Fruitlands was developed, are a Darlington Oak, a Spanish cork oak, Japanese persimmons, Chinese pine, Chinese holly, Japanese trailing juniper, holly-leaved tea olive, a hardy lemon hedge (Citrus trifoliata) from Japan, an Amur privet hedge (Ligustrum Amurense), called the "Mother Hedge" for from its ten original plants imported from France in 1860 have come all the privet hedges of the South. There are many camellias from France, Germany, Japan and Belgium; azaleas, forty varieties of which were imported prior to 1861; an Elliottia racemosa, now practically extinct; and a Rhodophyllum Macropodon, a very rare broad-leaved evergreen imported from Japan about sixty years ago.

Mr. Berckmans originated, introduced and disseminated many fruits and shrubs. Those originated by him are Peen-to Peach, Biota Aurea Nana, Biota Aureau Conspicua, Biota Pyramidalis, Juniperus Communis Glauca, Elaeagnus Fruitlandi, Climbing Clothilde Soupert Rose and several Althoeas. In Mr. Berckmans' catalogue of 1861, he says that his test grounds contain upwards of 1,300 varieties of pears, 900 of apples, 300 of grapes, 300 of peaches and over 100 each of azaleas and camellias.

In recognition of Mr. Berckmans' work in horticulture, he was honored by many societies in Europe and America. The University of Georgia conferred upon him the degree of Master of Science. He was likewise honored by the Society of Horticulture and Natural History of Montpelier, France; the Pomological Society of France, the Horticultural Society of Bordeaux and a number of others. In 1876 he founded the Georgia State Horticultural Society, over which he presided until the date of his death. In 1883-4 he went to Europe for the United States Government to collect horticultural exhibits for the New Orleans Exposition. In 1887 he was elected President of the American Pomological Society. In 1893 he presided over the Horticultural Congress in Chicago. He was Chairman of the Jury of Awards at the Jamestown Exposition in 1907, and was the only American to act as judge at the Centennial of the Royal Agricultural Society in Ghent in 1908.

Fruitlands is now the home of the Augusta National Golf Club, with its Bobby Jones Course, and the house and grounds remain unchanged.

1857
The house at Fruitlands is surrounded by rare trees and shrubs imported prior to 1865.

1859
Magnolia Avenue, one-third of a mile long, leading to the residence of the late Prosper Jules Alphonse Berckmans. These trees were grown from seed secured in Athens, Georgia. It is said to be the oldest Magnolia Avenue in the South. The picture was taken in 1885, showing the rapid growth of these giant flowering trees.

Rose Hill Plantation

Wilkes County—Elbert County

IN 1740 Stephen Heard was born in Hancock County, Virginia. His father, John Heard, belonged to a wealthy English family who owned estates in England and Ireland. He came to Virginia in 1720 and with his son moved to Georgia in 1769. They settled in the ceded lands in that section which in 1777 became Wilkes County. Here Stephen Heard built Heard's Fort, later known as Washington, and in 1780 while Governor of Georgia he moved the State capital from Augusta to this place.

At the close of the Revolution, he moved from this strongly fortified home to a plantation eight miles distant, known as Heardmont. Several years were required for the completion of his fine new house surrounded by gardens. The cottage occupied by the family during that period was moved to Rose Hill, a thousand-acre plantation some miles from the future site of Elberton, the seat of Elbert County which was created in 1790 out of a part of Wilkes.

It was at Rose Hill that Thomas Jefferson, Stephen's son, made his home. 1810 saw the cottage that was moved to Heardmont incorporated in a charming and commodious dwelling, having the two-storied porch so frequently used on Georgia plantation houses of that period. An academic balance and simplicity characterized the grounds and gardens. Originally a public road divided the property, but to accommodate the Heards it was diverted and this section became a private or plantation road. Along it Thomas's wife, Nancy Middleton, planted an avenue of elms. With the exception of one splendid red oak, within the house grounds of old Rose Hill, the trees were exclusively elms and cedars. A picket fence divided the gardens from the elm shaded road, and these were screened from it by a twelve-foot cedar hedge. A wide walk leading from the gate to the porch was bordered by alternate plantings of crape myrtle trees and plinth-like forms of euonymus. Similar euonymus plantings outlined a simple interpretation of English parterres. These lay between the cedar hedge and the box garden which had circular and squared beds of Dutch simplicity. It not only lay along the facade of the house, but to each side of it. Twin elms shaded the front porch, and cedars, cherry laurel, hollies and mimosa made the heavy planting. Shrubs, roses, little honeysweet jonquils, blue hyacinths and Jacob's ladders (gladioli) filled the beds.

To the west of the dwelling were smokehouse and well; beyond them the stables, carriage house and plantation buildings. They were approached by an avenue of elms and cedars which continued towards the house. These service buildings were completely screened by another twelve-foot cedar hedge.

To the east was a vast vegetable, herb and small fruit garden with plantings of fruit trees. At its north boundary was a scuppernong arbor. Beyond this garden was a vineyard, with a brick wine cellar in its center. Between the vineyard and the road were the quarters hidden by giant cedars. Across the road were apple orchards. An avenue of crepe myrtle led through them from just opposite the entrance gate down to the big spring.

Though many changes have taken place, Rose Hill has retained its essential character and spirit. The euonymus is gone but most of the box and cedar hedges remain. Elms, cedars and the flowering trees are now gigantic. The roses planted by Nancy Middleton Heard have been moved to a lovely terraced garden banded by iris. In her memory they are affectionately called "Grandmother Roses." They are of three varieties—May, daily and little seven sisters.

The vegetable and fruit garden has become a sweep of lawn, its paths edged with iris. A beautiful peony garden surrounds a sun dial. To the old house two wide wings have been added. The three sections are called respectively "Middlesex," "Essex" and "Wessex;" their porches "Welcome," "Contentment" and "Recreation." The property is owned by Eugene Bernard Heard, whose wife was a noted gardener, as is his daughter, Mrs. James Young Swift, under whose care Rose Hill's twenty-five acres of park and gardens bloom and flourish.

1787-1810-1863

The gardens at Rose Hill Plantation were planted in 1810, when the original cottage built by Governor Stephen Heard was incorporated in a larger dwelling. Giant cedar hedges and plinths of euonymus gave them individuality.

Greensboro

Greene County

GREENE, one of Georgia's earlier counties, was created in 1786 out of a part of Washington and in turn portions of Greene went to form Hancock, Oglethorpe, Clarke, Oconee, Taliaferro and Baldwin Counties.

1797
Old Planting in the North Garden of the Lewis-Davis-Rice Place in Greensboro

One of the older houses in Greensboro, the county seat, was erected in 1797 by Nicholas Lewis within the boundaries of the hundred-acre tract which in 1786 was surveyed as the proposed site of the State College. The Commission had agreed on its selection but reconsidered their action at the request of the member from Greensboro, who, apparently valuing his own fruits above those of learning, objected on the ground that the students might steal his apples. In 1832 the Lewis home passed into the hands of Samuel Davis; it occupied most of the block bounded by East, South and Main Streets. The house which through frequent remodeling has lost its original character is built close to the street and has a setting of shade, fruit and flowering trees.

The acre of garden at the rear of the house was one of the friendly spots where generous vegetable beds were bordered by flags, narcissus, daffodils, jonquils and hyacinths. The scuppernong arbor shaded the central walk. An herb border, the length of one side of the garden, held sage, tansy, thyme, lavender, rosemary, boneset, pennyroyal, etc. Raspberries, currants and other small fruits extended along another boundary, and one of the large square beds was full of roses and fig trees.

In 1875 this section of the property was sold and

1800
The Cobb-Dawson-Clayton-Townsend Place in Greensboro

1800
Massed Planting in the Garden of the Cobb-Dawson-Clayton-Townsend Place in Greensboro

the flowers having been reserved, a duplicate of the garden was planted at the north side of the house. There, still bloom many bulbs and roses from the original garden.

The property has been continuously owned by the descendants of Samuel Davis and is now occupied by his granddaughter, Mrs. Thaddeus Brockett Rice.

Diagonally across East Street is a fine old Georgian house built in 1800 by United States Senator Judge Thomas Willis Cobb, one of the many Virginia gentlemen who moved to this section. At his death, in 1835, it was purchased by William Crosby Dawson and later by Philip Clayton, Minister to Peru, whose granddaughter, Miss Maud Townsend, makes it her home. This house also stands close to the street and has a back garden. Its original pattern has been replaced by a luxuriant informality. Flowering trees, flowering shrubs and vine-covered trellises are clustered about by lilies, roses, perennials, bulbs and annuals, largely survivals from the past.

Many big cotton plantations were developed near Greensboro. Among them was Oak Hill, about five miles from the town, built some time prior to 1820 by Judge Thomas Stocks whose parents also had moved to Georgia from Virginia.

The house, a fine two-story frame structure with colonnaded facade, stood on a hill well studded in oak, hickory, magnolia and mimosa.

1830
A Remnant of the Box Edged Cedar Avenue at the Poullain Place Near Greensboro

In former years pink roses festooned its giant trees to their topmost branches.

The very extensive gardens at Oak Hill showed three distinct developments. The oldest of these lay between the front lawn and the house. Here a brick wall enclosed a box garden of the simple, early, circle-within-a-square pattern. A giant magnolia stood in the centers of the twin circular beds. To the west of the mansion was a second box garden of later date and much more intricate design. Here was topiary work executed in euonymus. Both gardens were planted in roses, perennials, annuals and flowering shrubs. Beyond this west garden were the vegetable gardens, orchards and scuppernong arbor.

To the east was a small, box bordered bulb garden, below which spread terraces planted in cape jasmine, crape myrtle, roses and dahlias. A gate led to a terraced lawn terminating in a stretch of woodland.

Many years ago Oak Hill passed out of the hands of the Stocks family and its gardens have vanished.

About 1830 Dr. Thomas Poullain built a beautiful home just outside of Greensboro. The house, Greek Revival in type, was approached through triple gates and by an eight hundred foot avenue of giant cedars garlanded in pink roses. Within the line of cedars were alternate sections of dwarf and tree box and the avenue was flanked by walkways hedged in English hawthorn. A fine grove shaded the front lawn, while near the house were groups of rare trees, among them California incense cedars. Gardens were on both sides of the house, the beds edged in box. Summer houses were bowered in Banksias and trellises wreathed in coral vine. Heavy clumps of Spanish bayonets made a picturesque feature.

The north garden was planted in bulbs and flowering shrubs such as Erythina crista galli, lauristimus, euonymous, deutzia, spirea, pyrus japonica, pyracantha, syringa, viburnam and vitex. Here also were magnolias.

1845-1850

A double row of stately, ivy-clad cedars leads to the entrance of the Johnson-Story-Merrit House in Greensboro.

The south garden was devoted to the cultivation of roses; the giant of battles, Solfaterra and Malmaisons are remembered varieties. The property is in alien hands, the Poullain house replaced by a modern structure and of the gardens nothing is left. A small section of the avenue stands, as do a few ornamental trees, magnolias, a splendid holly of great height and a privet pruned to an umbrella shape that has grown to shade tree size.

Upson-Howard Place

Lexington

Oglethorpe County

LEXINGTON, founded the end of the eighteenth century, though small, was of definite importance because of the distinguished men who made it their home. Among these were Judge Cobb, Stevens Thomas, Governor Gilmer, Governor Lumpkin and William Harris Crawford, United States Senator, Minister to France and candidate for the Presidency.

In 1808 Stephen Upson came to Lexington which, though the county seat, was rather a group of gentlemen's homes than a town. A native of Connecticut, a man of good birth, and a recent graduate of Yale University, he brought letters to Crawford and was soon reading law in his office. He became a person of importance in his community and in the State.

Not long before his untimely death in 1825 he purchased five and a half acres in Lexington and built a simple though attractive home which was occupied by his family and descendants until in 1903 when it passed into the hands of William King Howard.

The whole place bears a New England stamp. The stone wall of semi-dressed blocks enclosing the entire property is unique in Georgia. The usual box garden did not occupy the space between the house and street; instead there were two panels of shrub planted lawn enclosed by euonymous hedges and divided by an elaborately designed box bordered path. The terraced kitchen garden with its grape arbor, fruit trees, rose and lily beds bordered by iris and bulbs, and vegetable beds edged with herbs and small flowers were immediately left of the house. A drive shaded by red cedars led to the house, then past kitchen and quarters and continued to the barns and stables through a fine grove of oaks. In common with these extensive town and village establishments, not only food for the humans but fodder for the livestock was raised.

Some additions have been made to the house; the garden, alas, is no more, and the euonymus was killed by the pest that all over the State destroyed the high hedges of this broad-leafed shrub so universally used as a garden and lawn frame in Georgia's early days.

Mr. and Mrs. Howard are giving every care to the preservation of what is left of old planting at this charming and very individual spot.

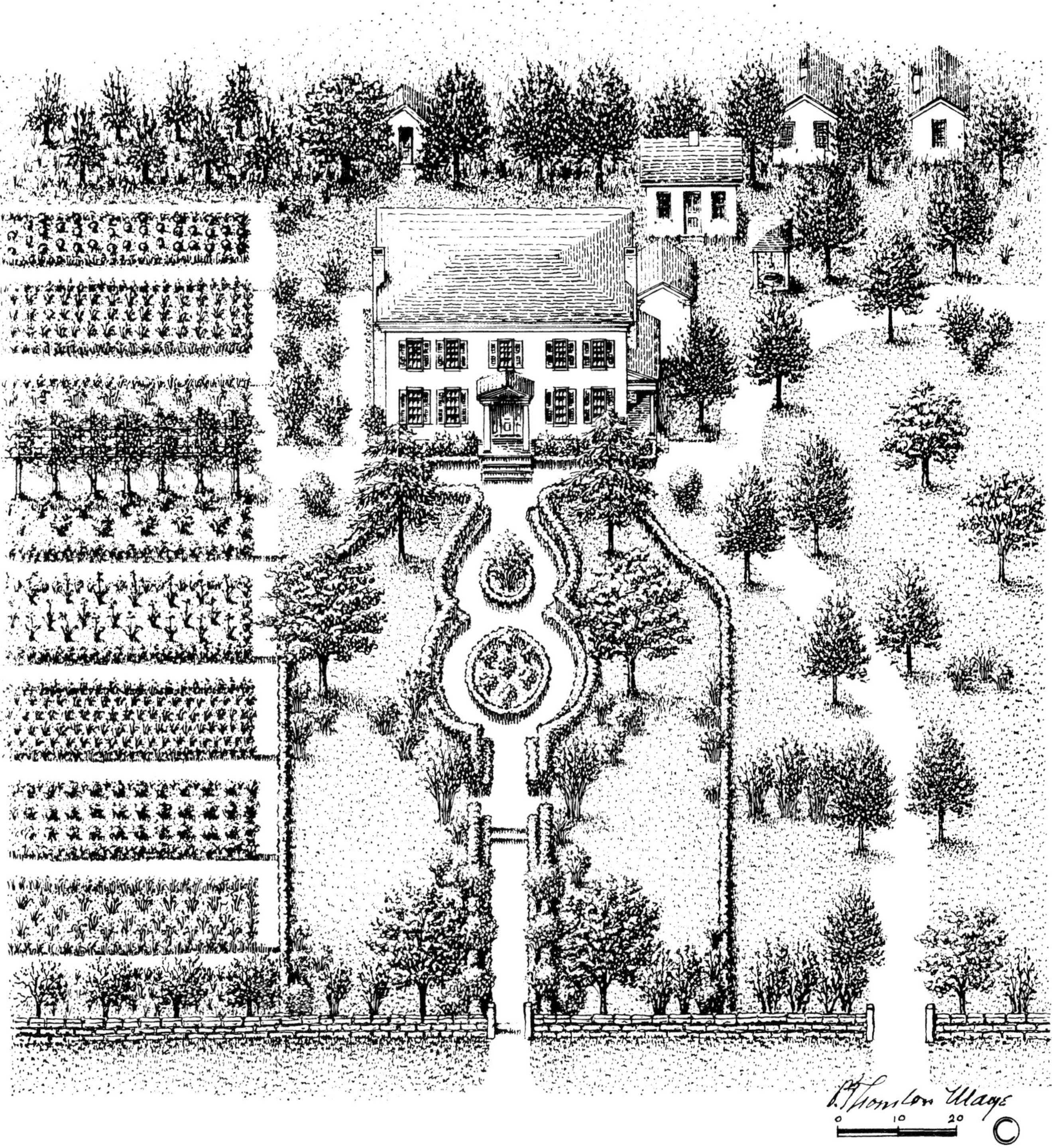

1822-1863

The encircling stone wall of this old Lexington place is a unique feature in Georgia. It was built by the Upsons in affectionate memory of their New England home. Here in place of a formal garden, we have hedge framed grass panels divided by an elaborate box bordered walk. This walk and the garden paths were of tan bark.

Athens

Clark County

IN July, 1783, Governor Lyman Hall recommended a state university. The following year the Legislature, sitting at Louisville, voted the establishment of Washington and Franklin Counties, providing in that act for a grant of forty thousand acres of land to be used as an endowment for "a college or seminary of learning," also trustees were named. January 27, 1785, saw a charter granted for the University of Georgia, and the Senatus Acadimicus of the University of Georgia was appointed for its general regulation. For fourteen years its location was discussed and fought over. In 1801 the question was settled: John Milledge donated six hundred and thirty acres of land where the city of Athens now stands, with the understanding that the University be located there. That year Josiah Meigs, LL.D., was made President of Franklin College, the nucleus of the University. The first classes were held under a giant oak tree, and the first graduating class of ten students received their diplomas in "an arbor formed of branches of trees."

Notwithstanding many setbacks and discouragements, through the ensuing twenty years or more the University grew and developed. The same can be said of the town surrounding it. Athens' first house was built in 1801; streets were laid out in 1804. In this period a number of substantial homes were erected. The Athens of these first twenty years had to face all the problems and difficulties of any frontier town set on the edge of a wilderness. Indians were not lacking. The town was within the Cherokee Nation until its removal west in 1838. Young braves were often students at the University.

Georgia's tremendous prosperity beginning in the late 1820's was reflected in both University and Town.

In 1833 through the efforts of Malthus A. Ward, Professor of Natural History, a botanical garden was developed. The person directly in charge of it was John Bishop, a native of England. This garden was in a depression through which flowed too small converging brooks forming an artificial lake in which fish and an alligator were kept. Two thousand plants and shrubs were collected from every corner of the globe. A sprig of the weeping willow from the grave of Napoleon on St. Helena found its way here, as did also sprigs from the Washington Elm on Boston Commons and from the Charter Oak at Sunbury. Two naval officers presented the garden with plants from the Cape of Good Hope.

For a time the Trustees of the University took a considerable interest in the garden and appropriated each year for its upkeep six hundred dollars, but by 1844 they found it too great a strain on their finances and cut the sum to three hundred dollars, and finally in 1856 they sold it for a thousand dollars. Today the garden is a memory.

Athens, named for the Goddess of Wisdom and having come into being as a seat of learning, has yet a third claim to the title of "The Classic City." Nowhere else in America are seen so many examples of Greek Revival architecture. In the town itself and in Cobbham, a district of residences, magnificent columned homes were built; others equally charming were in a transition or modified Georgian style. All had acres of grounds and gardens. These homes still grace its streets, but in common with the rest of the State, most of the old gardens have been replaced by modern landscaping.

Camak Place

Athens

TODAY finds the Camak Place, on Meigs Street, built in 1830 and occupied by five generations of that family, still standing in its original four acres of park-like planting. Here the traditional formal garden is lacking but not missed.

The house, a simple, dignified brick structure, with lacy iron work on steps and gallery, has beauty and individuality. Of all spots in Athens, this is the least changed. Erected by James Camak, first Professor of Mathematics at the University of Georgia, first President of the Georgia Railroad, Trustee of the University of Georgia, and Commissioner for the State of Georgia to establish the boundary lines between Georgia and the territories of Tennessee, Alabama and Florida, it now is the residence of James deXavier Camak V, the last of his line.

1830

The passing of a hundred years has left the Camak Place unchanged. It was the first white man's home built in Clark County outside the town limits of Athens and stood for eight years within the boundaries of the Cherokee Nation.

The Bishop Cottage

Athens

WHEN spring comes, in all Athens there is no more lovely spot than Miss Lucy Bishop's garden. It extends across the front and falls away in terraces on either side of a cottage of excellent neo-classic design built about 1840 by her grandfather, Thomas Jefferson Bishop, a native of St. Johnsbury, Vermont.

The property originally consisted of a number of acres. Although on Jackson Street and immediately adjacent to the University, it like many other old Athens homes resembled a miniature farm, and contained a carriage house and stables, a barn for cows, and one for storing cotton, a smoke house for the curing of meat, an ash house for the making of soap, quarters, corn fields, pastures and vegetable gardens.

New England elms shade the street, from which the property is separated by a picket fence. The box bordered walk from gate to porch is paved in square brick. When originally designed, a box garden was placed on both sides. These are gone but the tree box defining their outer borders remain. Box guards the steps leading from the front walk down to the garden terrace level and edges this terrace along the facade of the house.

To the left of the house three terraces are planted in fruit trees, shrubs and flowers. One for many years had in its center an elm, a scion from the tree in Cambridge under which Washington stood when he took command of the Continental Army; another has a curved boundary line of box.

To the immediate right of the house is a terraced bulb garden, defined by box and shaded by large flowering shrubs and a very lovely weeping box, trimmed to resemble a fringed parasol. Across a walk running along it from the street to the rear of the house, these terraces, now quite shallow, are set out in fruit trees. The fourth and final terrace is entirely given over to utilitarian planting.

The charm of the Bishop garden lies in the well considered use of a broken terrain, unified by a closely woven carpet of flowers. That from time to time it has been patched here and added to there has only meant an increase of beauty.

1840

The garden of the Bishop Cottage is a riot of bloom against a background of boxwood.

Stevens Thomas Place

Athens

IN 1848 Colonel Stevens Thomas, a gentleman of Welsh descent, and son of the Stevens Thomas who in its earliest days came to Athens from nearby Lexington, bought a piece of ground on Hancock Street and began construction of a handsome residence.

John Bishop, an English landscape gardener in charge of the University's Botanical Garden, was entrusted with the laying out of the grounds. This was done with intelligence and good taste. Oaks shaded a lawn that framed a box garden resembling two oriental rugs in a palm and crescent design, accented by Magnolia grandiflora, Japanese magnolias and cape jasmine. Between it and the front fence were rose trellises and flowering shrubs. The house was surrounded by a luxuriance of vines, shrubs and flowers, and the service yard masked by high plantings. Carriage house and stables, fruit trees and a vegetable garden with flower bordered beds occupied the rear of the lot.

This property was bought by the Y. M. C. A. many years ago, the house moved, and their club building erected on the site of the garden. Happily a drawing of that charming spot was obtainable, also what is possibly the most complete list of mid-century North Georgia planting.

SHRUBS
Cherry Laurel
Spirea, Double and Single
  Bridal Wreath
Forsythia
Kerria, Yellow Balls
Scotch Broom
Pyrus Japonica
Burning Bush, Red
Sweet Syringa
Deutzia
Lilacs, Persian and European
Crape Myrtle
Japanese Magnolia
Chaste Plant
Pittosporum
Tea Olive
Holly
Euonymus
Tea Plants
Mimosa
Tree Box
Pink Spirea
Snow Balls
Pomegranate
Night Blooming Cereus

FLOWERS
Hollyhocks
Double Hollyhocks,
  Sulphur Colored
Wallflowers
Candytuft
Sweet Allyssum
Sweet Williams
Portulacca
House Leek
Lantana
China Aster
Geraniums, Lemon Stag, etc.
Primrose
Spice Pinks
Lemon Verbena

ROSES
Louis Phillippe
Paul Neyron
Madame Pactole
Musk Cluster
Malmaison
Damask Rose, very sweet
Moss
Wild Rose
Devoniensis
Harrison Rose, Yellow
Lady Banksia
Marechal Niel
Woodland Climber
Margaret Rose

BULBS AND TUBERS
Flags, White and Purple
Narcissus
Jonquils
Snowdrops
Star of Bethlehem
Blue Bottles
Hyacinths, Blue and White
Lilies of the Valley
Tube Roses
Crocus
Jacob's Ladders (Gladioli)

VINES
Honeysuckle
Star Jasmine
Eglantine
Ivy
Rhynchospermum
Madeira Vine
Wandering Jew
Wistaria
Grand Duke Jasmine

FRUITS
Figs, Blue Celeste
Pears, Bartlett and Seckle
Strawberries

1848-1863

On the opposite page is shown the home of Colonel Stevens Thomas. The box garden has an unusual oriental pattern.

Grant-Hill-White-Bradshaw Place

Old Cobbham

Athens

ABOUT 1700 Thomas Grant of Inverness, Scotland, settled in Virginia and was made Landgraf of eleven hundred acres in Hanover County. His descendants moved first to North Carolina, then to Wilkes County, Georgia. Thomas Grant, the great great grandson of the Landgraf, lived in Walton County. A few years before the outbreak of the Civil War he moved to Athens and purchased seven acres on Prince Avenue. A pretty little cottage which had stood on this property for twenty years was moved and a splendid house in the later Greek Revival mode was built. The large box garden has a particularly dignified design carrying heavy plantings of magnolia, cedar of Lebanon, cherry laurel and tree box.

Filling the beds are cape jasmine, evergreen bush (euonymus), Mahonia aquifolia, winter jasmine, yucca, cassinas, pittosporum, tea and tea olive, flowering quince, Persian and European lilac, forsythia, althea, weigela, sweet syringa, sweet shrub, snow ball, bridal wreath spirea, ribbon grass, roses and bulbs. A screen of cherry laurel and crape myrtle secures privacy from the passer-by.

Arched openings through cedar hedges lead to tree planted lawns on each side of the house. They and the formal garden were hedged by euonymous. The fenced-off service yard contains well, kitchen and the original cottage used as a servants' house.

This very complete development is enclosed in a picket fence. A few changes have been made in the lawn sections, but practically all plantings here and in the garden are original or are careful replacements. The remaining acreage used by the Grants for orchards, vegetable garden and pasturage, and where stood the usual barn, carriage house and stable buildings, have been developed by the present owner into a beautiful stretch of lawn and garden.

Sold in 1869 to Georgia's distinguished statesman, Ben Hill, after his death it was owned for a short period by Josiah T. Leonard. In '88 it became the home of Captain James White and now belongs to his daughter, Mrs. William Francis Bradshaw.

1855-1863

This Athens home built by John Thomas Grant has much dignity. The garden is an excellent example of cut work.

In Athens is an ancient tree that owns itself. A marble slab at its foot bears this inscription: "For and in consideration of the love I bear this tree and the great desire I have for its protection, for all time I convey to it entire possession of itself and all land within eight feet of the tree on all sides. William Jackson."

The Williams-Ferguson Place

Milledgeville

Baldwin County

DURING the governorship of John Milledge it was decided to remove the capital of the State from Louisville. A site on the banks of the Oconee in Baldwin County was selected and in 1803 a plan was drawn according to which the town was laid out. Needless to say, where the State government went, many followed.

Among those making an early move to Milledgeville was Peter J. Williams, who in 1818 built there a fine home in a transition style between Georgian and Greek Revival often seen in houses belonging to the first quarter of the nineteenth century.

His lovely young wife, Lucinda, laid out the grounds. The box garden lies on either side of the front walk and consists of circles enclosed in rectangles. There are formal box tree plantings, and groups of Pyrus japonica, pomegranates, crepe myrtle, sweet syringa, German myrtle and vitex, both blue and pink, the latter a rare specimen. On each side of the house, leading from the garden toward the rear, is a wide box bordered walk forty feet long. Handsome red cedars encompass the garden, those on the west carrying a glorious mantle of wistaria, the growth of one hundred and twenty years.

Lucinda's granddaughter, Mrs. David Ferguson, to whom this charming old place belongs, makes it her pride to keep it unchanged.

1818

The Box Garden and Wistaria Planted in 1820 by Mistress Lucinda Park Williams

Westover

Near Milledgeville on the old Eatonton Road

Baldwin County

COLONEL BEN JORDAN, a man of wide political power, established himself in 1822 on an extensive plantation four miles out from Milledgeville on the old Eatonton Road. It served as a convenient meeting place for the discussion of public affairs. Designed by Elam Alexander, the house is a handsome frame mansion, with two-storied columned porch. It was remodeled and enlarged in 1852 when a magnificent banqueting hall was added.

All the planting seen at Westover dates before the Civil War. The grounds lying before the house measure three hundred and fifty by two hundred feet, and are divided into three distinct sections, all enclosed by a spearhead picket fence. The central portion is bisected by a very wide walkway bordered in a hedge of dwarf box flanked by a tree box planting and a row of crepe myrtles. A double circular drive shaded by an avenue of elms, magnolias and cedars leads from the gate to the base of the formal garden in front of the house. It consists of two rectangular and two circular beds edged with dwarf box, as is this whole central division, which contains a formal planting of cedars, crape myrtle, pomegranate, tea olive and Cape jasmine.

The left section is laid out in odd sized rectangular, box bordered beds, interspersed with crape myrtle, tree box, Grecian laurel, cherry laurel, Japanese magnolia, photinia, English dogwood, Ligustrum japonica and cedars. In its center stands one of the pavilion-like greenhouses characteristic of Georgia. Here in winter tubbed camellias were housed. Perhaps in summer they reposed within the odd shaped box plantings surrounding it.

On the right is a grove of cedars, cherry laurel, mimosa and tea olives, bordered on each side by tree box. Down its center runs a line of small box edged beds. In its middle we see a one-room office building, a replica of the green house, except for the fenstration. They give balance to the design. There is a tradition of topiary work at Westover, but no evidence of it can be found. A double row of cedars planted across the highway and similar rows at each end of these gardens formed at one time a windbreak for their protection.

Everything at Westover was in the grand manner. Few places in Georgia had more extensive plantation buildings and quarters. In addition to vegetable gardens and orchards, winter grapes were grown under glass. The estate, for many years occupied by the Jordan family, fell on evil days when it passed into other hands. Happily Dr. L. C. Lindsley, the present owner, is restoring the fine house and grounds, with due regard to the period which they so well represent.

Westover House *1822*

1822-1863

The Interesting Grounds and Gardens at Westover, Built by Colonel Ben Jordan

Bonar Hall

Madison

Morgan County

MADISON is one of the State's most charming old towns. Founded in 1809 it soon became an important point on the Post Road between Charleston and New Orleans, and the center of a rich cotton district. The men who settled there were of Georgia's best. They built themselves fine homes graced by lovely gardens.

Colonel John Byne Walker, moving in 1832 from Burke to Morgan County, became the owner of thousands of acres. On the Post Road just outside of Madison he built a two-story brick home, an excellent example of Georgian architecture. It stands a couple of hundred feet from the road on a hundred acre tract of lawn, garden and orchard development which formerly was enclosed on the front by a brick wall and picket fence, on the rear and sides by an impenetrable hedge of osage orange.

The grounds show careful planning and a classical sense of balance. The lawn was surrounded by a brick wall pierced in a diamond shaped pattern. Bisecting the lawn and encircling the house is an eighteen foot walk edged by a six foot bed of bulbs. Within its borders stands a line of granite posts supporting standards of vines, between which Madonna lilies once were planted. A summer house and an orangery of matching design flank the house. The very fine boxwood garden lies to the left, outside the brick wall. It contained rare shrubs and trees, many of which still live; beyond this was a water garden of which practically nothing remains. The family burying ground, now removed, was box bordered and approached by a long walk edged by the same shrub. The vegetable garden, orchards, slave quarters and plantation buildings as usual lay to the rear.

Mrs. Broughton acquired this fine property from the estate of Colonel John Byne Walker. The alterations shown in the house today were made by her in the eighties. The present owners are Mrs. William Thomas Bacon, Edward Taylor Newton and Miss Theressa Newton.

Much of the original planting survives, and is interesting and extensive enough to be given in list form:

TREES
Red Oaks
White Oaks
Water Oaks
Elms
Hickory
English Walnut
Black Walnut
Pines (three species)
Chinaberry
Cedar
Mimosa
Mock Orange
Cork Oak
Silicium Anisatum
Japanese Yew
English Yew
False Yew
Cryptomeria Lobbi
Cunninghamia
Magnolia Grandiflora
Magnolia Glauca (sweet bay)
Fragrant Cedar
Catalpa

FRUIT TREES
Mulberries
Plums
Peaches
Apples
Cherries
Pears
Figs
Quinces
Quincydonias

SHRUBS
January Jasmine
Crape Myrtle
Grandfather's Beard
Vitex (Chaste Plant)
Spirea (Bridal Wreath)
Altheas
English Dogwood
Cherry Laurel
Japanese Magnolia
Purple and White Lilac
Sweet Syringa
Pyrus Japonica
Buxus Sempervirens vars. Suffruticosa and Arborescens
Weeping and Curly Box, var. Arborescens
Euonymus Japonica
Arborvitae
Grand Duke Jasmine

VINES
Grapes
Wistaria
Small and Large Leaf Ivy
Honeysuckle (two species)
Trumpet Vine

FLOWERS
Roses (three kinds—Red Daily, Marechal Niel and Malmaison)
Day Lilies
Ribbon Grasses
White and Purple Flags

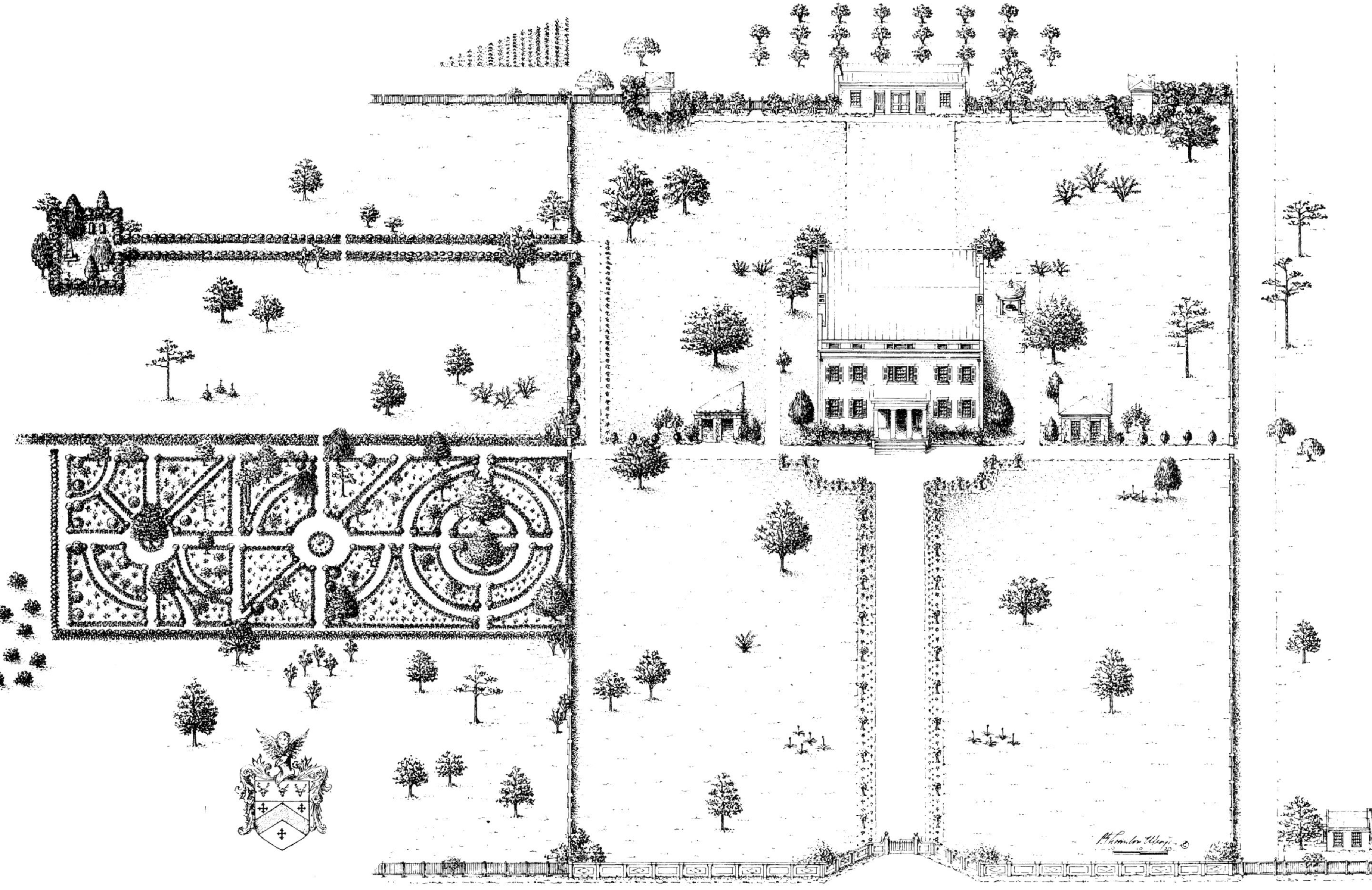

1832-1863

An academic balance is the distinguishing characteristic of the Madison home built by Colonel John Byne Walker.

Kolb-Pou-Newton Place

Madison

Morgan County

IN 1851 at the apex of Georgia's antebellum prosperity Wildes Kolb purchased a block of property in the heart of Madison. On one half of it he built a home for himself; on the other, one for his daughter, Mrs. Spear.

The Kolb house, a severely handsome structure, boasts a rare possession, twin box gardens. Their exquisite geometric patterns are obviously the work of some one thoroughly familiar with and practised in design. The euonymus hedge fringed with crape myrtle that framed them is gone but clipping has preserved the dwarf box borders in excellent condition. Some of the tree box and one of the giant magnolias still stand. It is to be regretted that the coronal plantings of cedar were cut down a few years ago and that, as is so frequently the case, casual shrub and tree plantings of a later date disturb no little the symmetry of the original designs. Some of the old roses and lilies grow in these gardens, as do Pyrus japonica, Japanese magnolia, cherry laurel and January jasmine.

Though a town house, the service yard, which in this case lies to the side, contains not only carriage house and stables but a cow barn as well, and is flanked on one side by a vegetable garden and orchard, and on the other by a pasture. Balancing these is a strip of ground running from street to street still spoken of as the cotton patch. It was also used for the raising of fodder.

This property was purchased in 1861 by Louis Pou, and occupied by his family until 1905 when it passed into the hands of John Thomas Newton whose wife and daughter today make it their home.

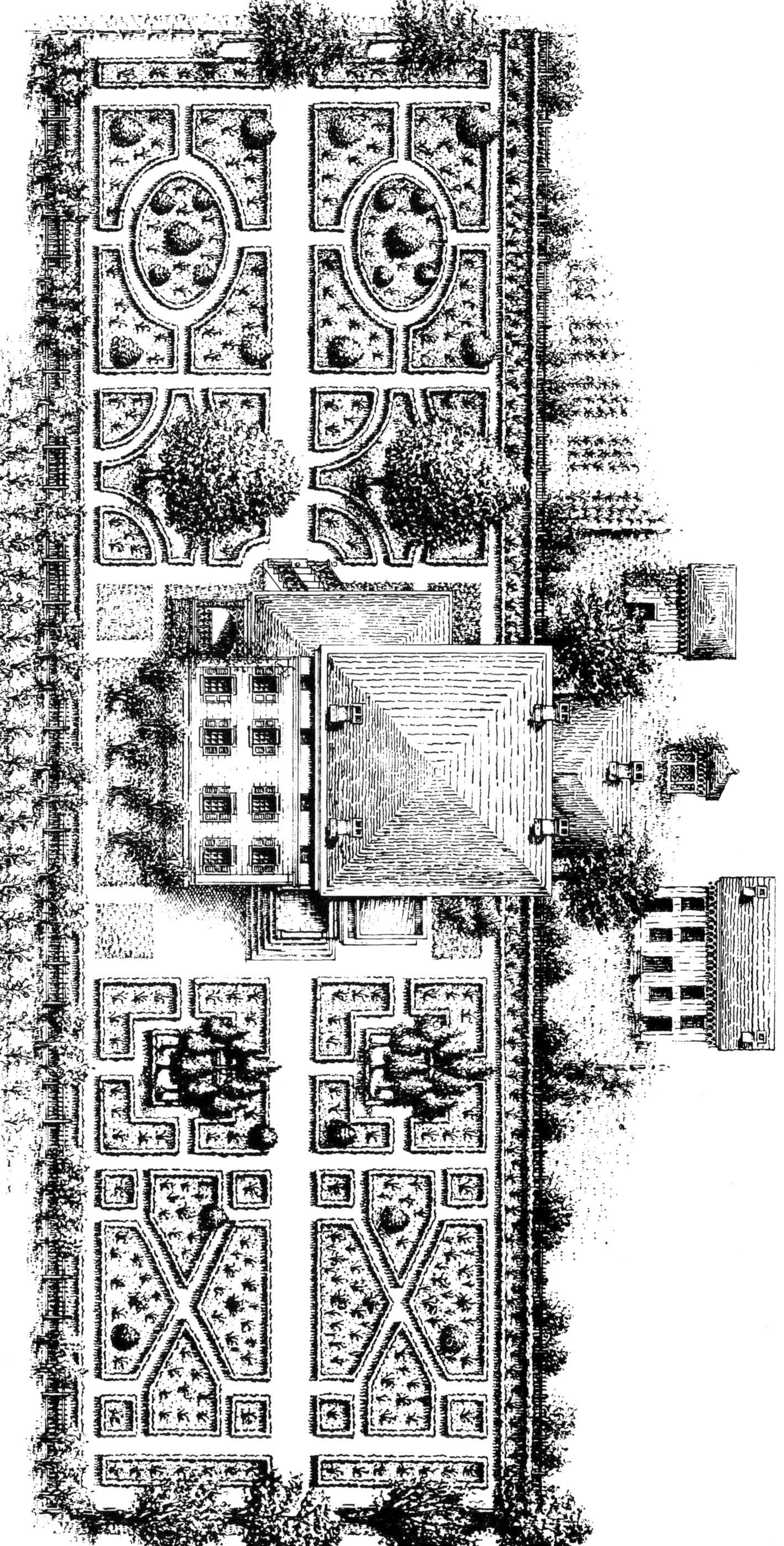

1851-1863

The twin box gardens of the Kolb-Pou-Newton Place display unusual symmetry in design.

Cowles-Bond-Coleman-Cabaniss-O'Neal Place

Macon

Bibb County

ABOUT 1838, Jerry Cowles, a prominent citizen of Macon, with an eye for a fine view, built a magnificent home on what is now known as Murray Street. Designed by Elam Alexander, who called himself a contractor but was through natural gifts an architect of high ability, the house remains an outstanding example of what Georgia gentlemen of that period considered a proper setting for their home life. It boasts eighteen Doric columns and flanking wings, an addition of the 50's, to which period the fantastic tea house also belongs.

The original four acres in which it stood were planted by Mrs. Jerry Cowles in mimosa, cherry laurel, magnolias, cedars and camellias. The principal box garden was in recent years dug up to make a tennis court. In front of the right wing is a small box maze. Part of the grounds including the peach orchard became a public park in 1879, when the handsome iron entrance gates were removed.

This beautiful place has been owned in turn by Jerry Cowles, Joseph Bond, Samuel Taylor Coleman, Warren Cabaniss and B. T. O'Neal.

A Remnant of the Little Box Maze

1838

Home of Jerry Cowles Built Thirteen Years After the Founding of Macon

Of the old planting there survive boxwood, shrubs and flowering trees.

Greenwood Plantation

Near Thomasville

Thomas County

FROM the close of the Revolution to the outbreak of the Civil War every day was moving day in Georgia. Scarcely a year passed without the establishment of a new county with its seat all laid out and ready for an auction sale of building lots. 1825 saw Thomas County and Thomasville come into being on the southwest border of the State.

There were always restless and adventurous spirits ready to move from wherever they were to these newly developed sections. To this company belonged Thomas Jones who in 1827 became a leading citizen of Thomas County.

He was of a Welsh family who seem to have had wanderlust in their blood. Francis Jones, his grandfather, had come to Virginia, thence to North Carolina, thence to Georgia, receiving in 1769 a Royal Grant in St. Georgia's Parish (later Burke and Screven Counties). His son, James, in 1774 received a grant of land in Burke and Jefferson Counties. James' son, Thomas, however, was born in Bullock County.

In those days when a man of substance made such a move, it took on the character of a tribal migration. The ladies and children traveled by carriage, the gentlemen of the family on horseback. Covered wagons drawn by mules or oxen were loaded with furniture, household goods and provisions, or spilled over with the master's "people;" coops of chickens and ducks were fastened on here and everywhere; sheep, hogs and cattle brought

1827-1835

These little flower beds and specimen camellia trees are relics of the old garden at Greenwood.

Noble Trees at Greenwood

up the rear. So closely knit was the upper strata of the State's social structure that at night camp seldom had to be made, for hospitable doors stood open all along the road. Having arrived at their destination, where as a rule the purchase of property had already been consummated, the slaves who were skilled in carpentry quickly built a simple but adequate dwelling for the master's family and shelters for his people. All necessary farm implements and seed having been brought from the old home, the clearing and planting of fields were quickly begun. Virgin soil means bumper crops. Cotton was King, and in a few years a pillared mansion rose where so short a time back, there had been a wilderness. Architects were scarce but every gentleman had enjoyed a classical education and was saturated with a love of beauty and a desire to live among beautiful things. The houses and gardens in these remote districts testify to this.

At Greenwood, Thomas Jones's great plantation near Thomasville, the first buildings were of logs. A provision crop having been made, a two-story frame dwelling was erected. It was 1835 before the construction of the Greek Revival mansion was begun. The Jones's were fortunate in securing the services of John Wind, a well known English architect, graduate of Queen's College. It took nine years for its completion, Mr. Wind himself carving much of the interior woodwork.

This fine home standing in a splendid grove of live oaks, palmettos and magnolias, demanded a garden just as fine. Squares of lawn now stretch where many flower beds once formed the fanciful patterns dear to the hearts of the 1830-40's. The garden must have lain also on each side of the house, for here still are old plantings of camellias, a few of which grow in little beds, relics of the gardens that are now gone. Indigenous trees, shrubs and flowers were successfully used here and in the more informal plantings. The family burying ground entered through a graceful Gothic gate remains unchanged and speaks eloquently of the past.

Since 1889 Greenwood has been successively owned by the VanDuzers, Paynes and Whitneys of New York, and has become a splendid estate where every natural beauty has been developed to the highest degree of perfection. (See Later Gardens Section.)

Oak Lawn

Near Carrollton

Carroll County

IN 1827, only a year after the establishment of Carroll County, Sanford Kingsbery of Derby, Vermont, settled in the brand new village of Carrollton, where a brisk trade with the Cherokee Indians brought quick and substantial profits.

Nine years later he purchased a pretty, four hundred acre farm, just outside the town. Here he interested himself in stock raising and made a success of the venture.

The house at Oak Lawn had the two-storied portico supported by twin columns and the delicately balustraded balcony seen in north Georgia houses, an initial type of the Greek Revival architecture then sweeping the State. Here the Kingsberys, both New Englanders and doubtless homesick for familiar things, did not plant the usual formal garden of the district. On either side of the box bordered, stone flagged walk leading from an arched picket gateway to the doorstep were square lawns bounded by flower-filled borders, rose beds and bands of bulbs. Two rock mounds planted in blue and white periwinkle belonged to the late fifties, giving a solemn Victorian note. Ivy, roses, woodbine and yellow jessamine wreathed the house, which with its garden was girdled by flowering shrubs and fruit trees and shaded by splendid oaks, black walnuts and hickories. From the road a semi-circular drive led to the garden gate, and within the arc of the driveway was an expanse of lawn. Across the road were the vegetable gardens, while below the paddock and through the pastures flowed the Little Tallapoosa River. Recently abandoned Indian trails made bridle paths for the children of the family.

The Kingsberys had come South to found a fortune, not a permanent home. In 1849, having accomplished their objective, they and their three young sons returned to the family farm in Vermont, the journey made in covered wagons requiring forty-eight weary days. However, the ties formed in Georgia could not be broken; within a few years they came back to lovely Oak Lawn, the true home of their hearts.

After the Civil War the property passed by inheritance to Captain Joseph Kingsbery, who in the evening of his life established at Oak Lawn the most noted stock farm in the State. The kindly old house still stands, but the Captain's private race course and his mother's garden are but happy memories.

1836

Oak Lawn

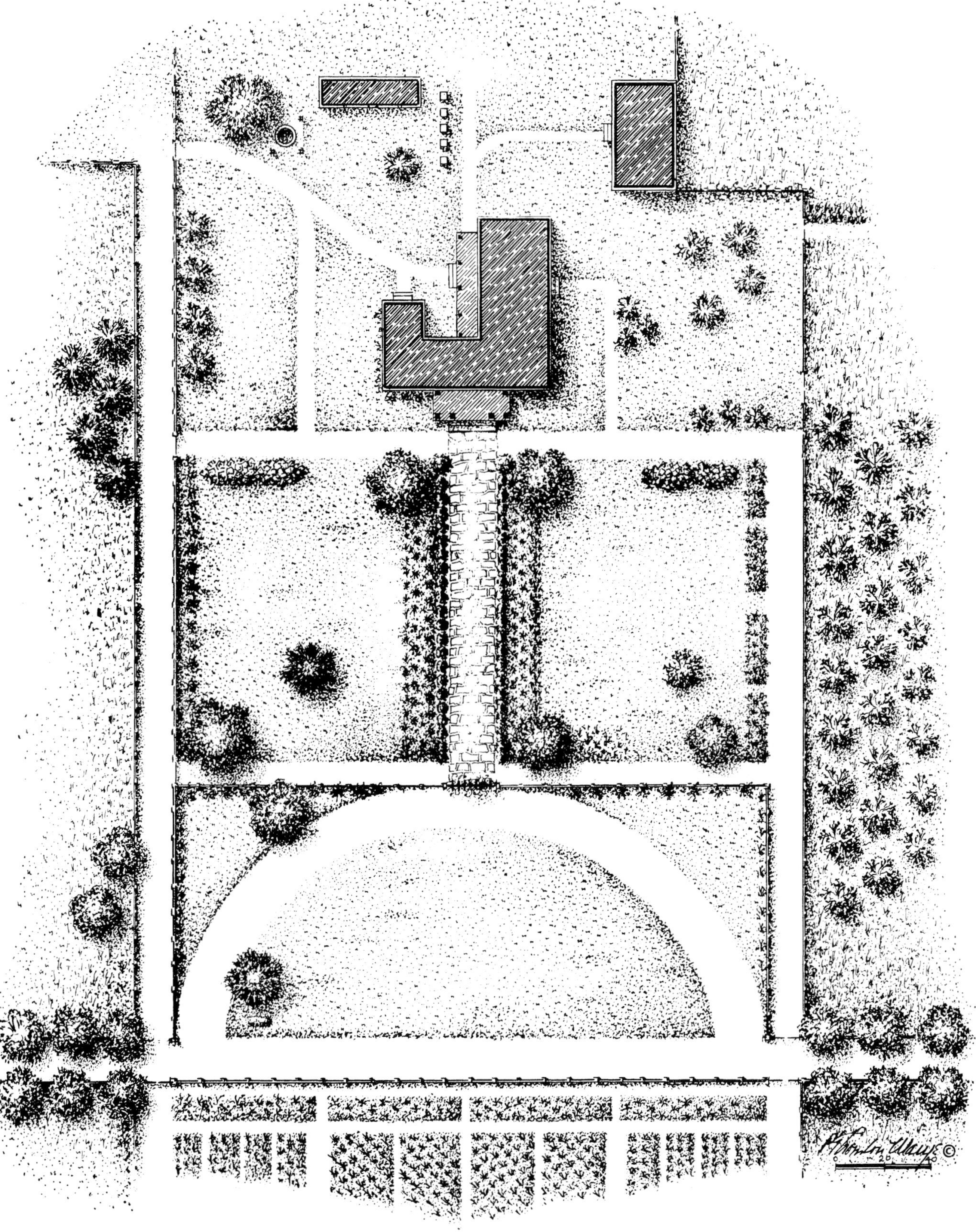

1836-1863

Oak Lawn, laid out by New Englanders, is in its flower bordered lawns reminiscent of old England. Flagged walks such as this were somewhat rare in North Georgia.

Ferrell Gardens

LaGrange

Troup County

THE apotheosis of all Georgia box gardens is found just outside of LaGrange in Troup County. Here Judge and Mrs. Ferrell established a fine estate soon after the town's founding in 1827.

Almost at once Mrs. Ferrell began the development of a remarkable group of gardens, connected by paths and walks equally beautiful and interesting, all all through the gardens, which seem an expression of Mrs. Ferrell's fervent and simple faith.

Proceeding along a high box hedge banded by spirea, the oldest of the gardens is reached. Situated immediately to the south of the house, it shares a wide level with fine trees. Completely walled in by box trees, in this parterre are found

1833
Mrs. Ferrell's favorite motto, "God Is Love," is perpetuated in boxwood.

framed in magnificent tree plantings. Though each of these units is distinctive in motif and came into being successively over a considerable period of years, the plan of what is now known as "Hills and Dales" shows them as an harmonious whole, undisturbed by the addition of the Fuller Callaway's sunken garden and the beautiful mansion built in 1913 when the property came into their hands.

The house is approached by a drive through a fine grove of indigenous trees. A path from the entrance grove leads to the old wrought iron wicket, the east gate of the gardens. Passing through it one comes into an outdoor sanctuary, for at the base of a wall of cherry laurel and crape myrtle is the word "God" in giant letters outlined by a double row of dwarf box. This religious note is dominant mottoes of close clipped dwarf box. On one side is Mrs. Ferrell's "God Is Love," companioned by the Judge's "Fiat Justitia;" opposite are the present owners' "Ora Pro Mi," and "St. Callaway."

To its west is the rose garden, laid out in simple rectangular forms. Dividing it from the original garden and leading down to the Church Garden at its base is the Walk of Sentinel Box. Behind a border of dwarf box stands the row of plinths eighteen feet high of clipped box. It is here that the garden is reminiscent of Italy. The Church or West Garden, though perhaps not the most beautiful, is unquestionably the most individual development on the place. There is a harp shaped bed with gold leafed altenanthera for strings, an organ cut from a thirty foot box tree, a pulpit, a bishop's chair and several mourners' benches, all formed of box. Time has blurred their edges and wreathed them in flowers but they stand a testimony to faith. An immense Cunninghamia gives shade, and tea olives perfume the air.

The east garden is in lighter mood. Formed of scrolls, knots and whimsies in dwarf box, it twists and twines around its center feature, a conventionalized flower, and is nearest in type to the parterre of embroidery. Below the central garden is a long, lovely walk, known as Lovers' Lane, and well patronized for a hundred years.

A level below this romantic spot is a remarkable arboretum. Here are red wood and Virginia cedars, live oaks, maples, mimosas, bay trees, wild olive, anise, dogwood, crape myrtle, magnolias and hemlocks, a glorious yew from Ireland, a hedge of Chinese tea plants, a huge ginkgo from Japan, hawthorns from England, lindens from Germany, and a splendid cedar of Lebanon with twin trunks. A recent addition is a four foot caraab tree raised from seed brought from Jerusalem. A giant Shittah tree from the shores of the Dead Sea, one of the garden's rarest specimens, stands near the house. One feels sure that Sarah Coleman Ferrell was familiar with the nineteenth verse of Chapter XLI of Isaiah which reads, "I will plant in the wilderness the cedar, the Shittah tree and the myrtle, and the oil tree; I will set in the desert the fir tree, and the pine, and the boxwood together." Though no wilderness, this section of Georgia was isolated and sparsely settled when the Ferrell Gardens came into being and this makes all the more remarkable these five acres of perfect design and cultivation.

No mere words can do justice to these gardens, where beauty and individuality of form are softened by an ever changing, many hued mantle of vines and flowers. January jasmine comes in with the

1833

The Walk of Sentinel Box leads to the Church Garden. The box plinths are eighteen feet high and eight feet thick.

One of the Lovely Vistas at the Ferrell Gardens

New Year; so do violets. Daffies and bluebells follow close behind. By March the trees and arbors are draped in wistaria, Confederate and yellow jessamine, Lady Banksia and Multiflora roses. All the flowering shrubs are seen in profusion and early blooming, old fashioned roses are not wanting. The parterres are filled with bulb plantings, violets, pansies and johnny-jump-ups. Early summer brings its riot of bloom; August the pink and lavender of crape myrtle. Mr. and Mrs. Callaway have changed nothing of the old gardens; they have added to them with good taste and understanding. The Italian marbles placed by them in these formal gardens of old Georgia seem quite at home and form a connecting link between them and the architecture of the new house. Mrs. Callaway's interesting and important garden activities are described in a separate article.

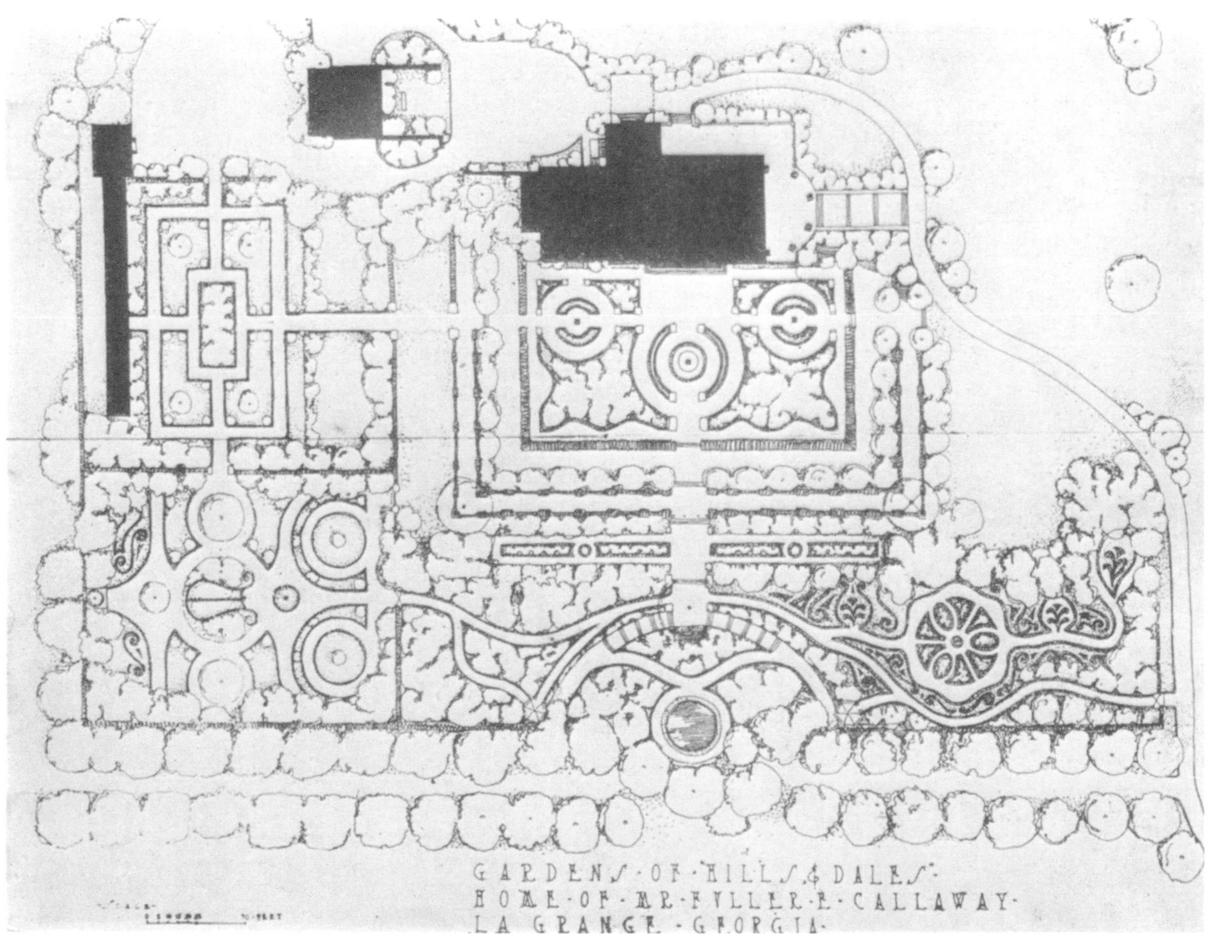

1833-1912

In this plan of Hills and Dales, as the Ferrell Gardens are now called, Mrs. Ferrell's four gardens, her arboretum and the connecting walks and avenues can be easily followed.

Columbus

Muscogee County

THE signing of a treaty between the United States Government and the Creek Indians for their removal beyond the Mississippi opened up a vast region for safe settlement. In this period when all over the State towns and villages were springing up almost over night, Columbus stands out as having had a most rapid and substantial development. 1828-29 not only saw this city come into being, but Rose Hill, the nucleus of a rich plantation settlement, and Wynnton, a community of handsome country homes, both within a few miles of Columbus, were established. The river bank homes which were so long its pride have given way to the city's business development. Here only the Fontaine and Shorter houses stand as reminders of what once was; as does the Redd place with its box garden at Rose Hill, now swallowed up by the growth of the town; Wynnton alone retains something of its original character. It has become a beautiful suburb where side by side are seen charming modern homes and lovely old country houses, part of whose grounds have been laid off in streets.

COLUMBUS HORTICULTURAL LIST, 1828-1838

SHRUBS
Cape Jasmine
Flowering Almond, Pink
Oleander, Pink, Crimson and White
Tea Olive
Camellia Japonica
Chinese Myrtle
Nude Stem Jasmine
Boxwood, Tree and Dwarf
Wild Olive
Euonymus
Service Berry
Smoke Tree
Fringe-Tree
Spikenard
Mock Orange
Snow Ball
Sweet Shrub
Lilac
Banana Shrub
Bush Honeysuckle
Hawthorn
Spirea
Christmas Jasmine
Flowering Quince
Pomegranate
Bay Tree, Dwarf Magnolia
Crab-Apple
Silver Bell
Haw
Red Bud
Dogwood
Yaupon
Cedar

VINES AND CLIMBING ROSES
Wistaria
Trumpet Vine, Bignonia
Clematis Paniculata and Single Purple
Honeysuckle
Yellow Jessamine
Wood Vine
Virginia Creeper
Confederate Jasmine
Potato Vine
Coral Vine
Southern Smilax or Bamboo Vine
Rose, Banksia Noisette
Cherokee Rose, White and Pink
McCartney Rose

FLOWERS
Hollyhock
Poppy
Orange and Rain Lily
Marigold, Sans Souci
Spiced Pinks
Snapdragon
Butter and Eggs
Touch-me-not
Tulips
Heartsease
Violets
Hyacinths
Periwinkle
Corn Flower
Larkspur, Single Blue
Blue Scilla
Coreopsis, Bronze Heart
Garden Sage
Plumbago
Moss Rose

In walled pits were grown all sorts of plants imported by our grandparents, such as geranium, wax vine, heliotrope, lilies and hibiscus.

1828

The home of the Honorable John Fontaine, first Mayor of Columbus, is still occupied by his descendants. Terraced gardens extended to the banks of the Chattahoochee. Homes and gardens stretched for a mile along the river bank.

St. Elmo

Columbus

A FEW miles out of Columbus, on the old coach road between Savannah and Mobile, St. Elmo stands in its fifteen-acre park. The house, said to have been built in Revolutionary days near a settlement clustering around the southmost ford of the Chattahoochee, in time became the property of John Howard and in 1832 was remodeled in the Greek Revival manner by his son-in-law, Seaborn Jones. In its palmy days giant tropical plants were housed in a conservatory, there was a square box garden in front of the house, and additional formal gardens with statue guarded walks lay on each side. Today gardens and statuary are gone, as is the marble basin into which flowed a spring so copious that for many years it served as the water supply of the neighboring community. A blazing hedge of Pyrus japonica, giant wistaria looped from tree to tree, and a three hundred foot scuppernong arbor leading down to an enchanting lake, speak eloquently of the past and give pleasure today.

Augusta Evans Wilson was John Howard's granddaughter, and was frequently the guest of her aunt, Mrs. Jones, in whose home she completed her novel, St. Elmo. In her honor it was given the name of St. Elmo by Major Jeremiah Slade, who purchased the property in 1878. Up to that time it was known as the Jones Place. Miss Florence Slade, his daughter and the present owner, has made it a shrine to the memory of this Georgia authoress.

1832

Lovely St. Elmo dreams of a romantic past when Augusta Evans Wilson paced its statue-guarded walks.

1832

Ancient cedars encircle St. Elmo's lily-padded lake. With the coming of spring, its banks and the little island are starred and wreathed with old-fashioned blossoms and flowering vines.

The Elms

Columbus

ON Buena Vista Road we find The Elms. Built as a country home in '32 by Hanson Scott Estes of Columbus, it stood on many acres, some of which have gone to the development of a modern suburb. Around it this gentleman set out the trees from which it took its name. The central portion of the house built by him is an exquisite Greek Revival cottage. It is oddly companioned by bow window shaped wings added by Lloyd Guyton Bowers of Bowers' Shore, Massachusetts, who purchased the property in the 50's. Yet another note is struck by the delightful butterfly design of the box garden. Its form was preserved by brick edgings, as the box borders were dug up a number of years ago. Now they have been replaced, as has been much of the shrub planting. The parterre formerly filled with roses is in grass. The giant magnolia which dominates house and garden was not a part of the original scheme. At The Elms the picket fence carried pineapple finials across its front section and enclosed the service yard and buildings. In recent years the Lloyd Bowers have developed wide stretches of lawn and garden. The Elms as we see it today is made up of seemingly inconsistent elements molded into a charming whole.

1832-1863

The Bowers' butterfly garden at The Elms has a charm and grace all its own.

Esquiline Hill

Near Columbus

THE fifteen years prior to the Civil War was a period of growing prosperity in middle and north Georgia. Fortunes were made and spent. Many handsome homes were built and many gardens planted. In 1849 Major Raphael Moses of Columbus selected as the site for his home a high plateau some five miles from that city. Here was a fine natural growth of timber, several springs and a lovely view of the surrounding country. With the building of his house completed, Major Moses turned his attention to the grounds and gardens. Berckmans of Augusta was given carte blanche. He in turn sent to England for Kidd, a noted landscape gardener, who demanded a free hand and three years in which to develop the estate.

In 1860 the task was finished. An avenue of crape myrtle one and a half miles long led from the road to the house. For the formal garden a design of circles and semi-circles was employed. The large beds were hedged in cherry laurel; the small beds bordered by box. In addition there was a mystic maze. The rose garden contained almost every variety then known, bulbs and garden flowers were in profusion, and rare plants

1849-1858

A Fragment of the Formal Garden at Esquiline Hill

To the left is seen part of the mile-and-a-half-long avenue of crape myrtle that led from the entrance gate to the house.

were cared for in a hothouse. Near the dwelling a circular summer house formed of cherry laurel and climbing roses still affords a charming setting for the weddings of the Major's great granddaughters.

The climate of Columbus is favorable to the growth of magnolias, tea olives and camellias. At Esquiline Hill these flowering trees have reached a mammoth size. A camellia forty feet in height is almost matched by a tea olive. Cedars and holly also grew in the formal garden, beyond which three cork oaks sent to Major Moses from Spain still proudly rear their heads amidst huge pecan and walnut trees.

At the rear of the house a walk bordered by Cherokee roses led to the quarters. A great vegetable garden was near by, also wide orchards planted in pears, peaches, apples, apricots and figs. The cultivation of white and purple grapes was undertaken and a pergola half a mile long supported the vines. A mile of pear trees with alternate plantings of red and white roses was named Benning Avenue for an admired friend. In 1918 at the instance of Major Moses' daughter, Mrs. Lionel Levy, the neighboring war-time training camp was called after "Old Oak" General Benning. Now as Fort Benning, it is approached by a road which cuts through Esquiline Hill.

The classical taste and the kindly customs of the day combined to give to this estate its name. Mr. Forsyth in thanking his friend Major Moses for a basket of choice fruit and flowers, compared him to Roman Maecenas whose Villa on the Esquiline was famed equally for hospitality and the beauty of its orchards and gardens. He suggested calling the plantation Esquiline Hill.

The devastations of war and the following disastrous economic conditions destroyed much of what has been described. However, enough remains to make Esquiline Hill one of Georgia's interesting survivals of a vanished past. It is pleasant to know that the Levy family, descendants of Major Moses, make the lovely old place their home.

Rosemary

Newnan

Coweta County

BERCKMANS, the distinguished Belgian landscape gardener, seems to have been in a playful mood when designing the garden at Rosemary. Dominated by two gigantic, sentinel-like magnolias, one of which is almost smothered in wistaria, its petal shaped beds are outlined by carefully clipped box. There are plantings of clipped tree box and many flowering shrubs. Of these Japanese lime, sweet bay, January jasmine, forsythia, Japanese magnolia and crape myrtle survive. Roses filled the beds. Malmaisons and Louis Phillippes are still seen within wreaths of Madonna, lemon and valley lilies.

The original cottage built by Dr. Joel W. Terrell in 1828 was in turn owned by Andrew J. Berry, Dr. C. L. Redwine, who added to it and in 1859 employed Berckmans to lay out the garden, Captain Tom Jones, Dr. and Mrs. James Stacey and Dr. and Mrs. Thomas Jefferson Jones into whose hands it passed in 1912. A couple of years later they moved the cottage to another part of the property and built a handsome modern home. Mrs. Jones happily preserved the garden, which gives pleasure to all who pass that way. It is the only box garden in Newnan to escape destruction.

1828-1859-1863

At Rosemary high trimmed giant magnolias lend dignity to a whimsical garden pattern.

Barnsley Gardens

Cass County—Bartow County

GODFREY BARNSLEY, of the English group of Savannah cotton merchants, showed imagination and enterprise when selecting a site for the residence on his ten thousand acre North Georgia plantation near Kingston. A high knoll stood in the midst of one of his wide, smiling valleys. On its peak was the house of an Indian chief to whose tribe the land had belonged. In 1833 the Barnsleys moved into this primitive abode for the summer months. A few years later the top of the hill was levelled and a modest frame cottage built to serve as a dwelling while a permanent home was being constructed. Its first unit, a detached brick wing, contains a dining room of banquet proportions, two kitchens and guest rooms. There is an additional guest house for gentlemen below the slope of the hill. During the 50's the erection of the central feature of a planned group of three detached houses was undertaken. It is only a brick shell for work on it was interrupted by the outbreak of the Civil War, and a tornado later having taken off the roof, its completion was abandoned.

The first cottage, which was to have been replaced by yet another brick guest house, and the dining room wing continue to be occupied by Godfrey Barnsley's granddaughter, Mrs. Saylor, and her family.

Shortly after the levelling of the acorn shaped hill on which these buildings stand, the development of an elaborate scheme of landscaping and gardens was undertaken. This work was in the hands of and carried to completion by John Connally, Mr. Barnsley's Irish head gardener. The entrance driveway flanked by rose and shrub plantings, divides to sweep around either side of an exquisite oval box garden, the design of which seems to have been taken from a motif in a Marseilles quilt. In its center is an antique Italian fountain of white marble. Statuary brought from Italy for its adornment was shipped North in '64. Triangular rock gardens fill the spaces between it and the drive across the terrace on which the three dwellings stand. A small box garden lies in front of the left wing; a croquet ground in front of the wing to the right.

In 1859, P. J. Berckmans set out the then rare English and Japanese yews, Cunninghamias, Nordsman's firs, Thuja orientalis, also a magnificent ailanthus. The wide lawns encircling the hill had well placed groups of indigenous trees and a thicket of Mr. Berckmans' favorite cherry laurel. Tropical plants were cared for in extensive greenhouses built on the southern slope of the hill.

The quarters and plantation buildings were in the valley at the rear of the property and were built along the edge of a wide, clear stream.

In the gardens are found every shrub grown fifty to a hundred years ago in North Georgia. The same can be said of bulbs and tubers. Roses abound: daily and moss roses in red, pink and white, green roses, purple roses, Picayune roses, Malmaisons, Louis Phillippes, gold of Ophirs, musk clusters, little seven sisters, Jane Hachettes, red and white tree roses from Germany, General Jaquimenots, cloth of gold, Marechal Niel and Devoniensis. There are many more varieties, their names now forgotten. A veritable Niagara of Cherokee roses, pink, white and double, tumbles down the south fall of the hill. The ruined house is completely veiled in wistaria.

There have been few changes at Barnsley Gardens, and it is of interest that this plantation is said to have been used by Augusta Evans Wilson as a setting for her romantic novel, St. Elmo.

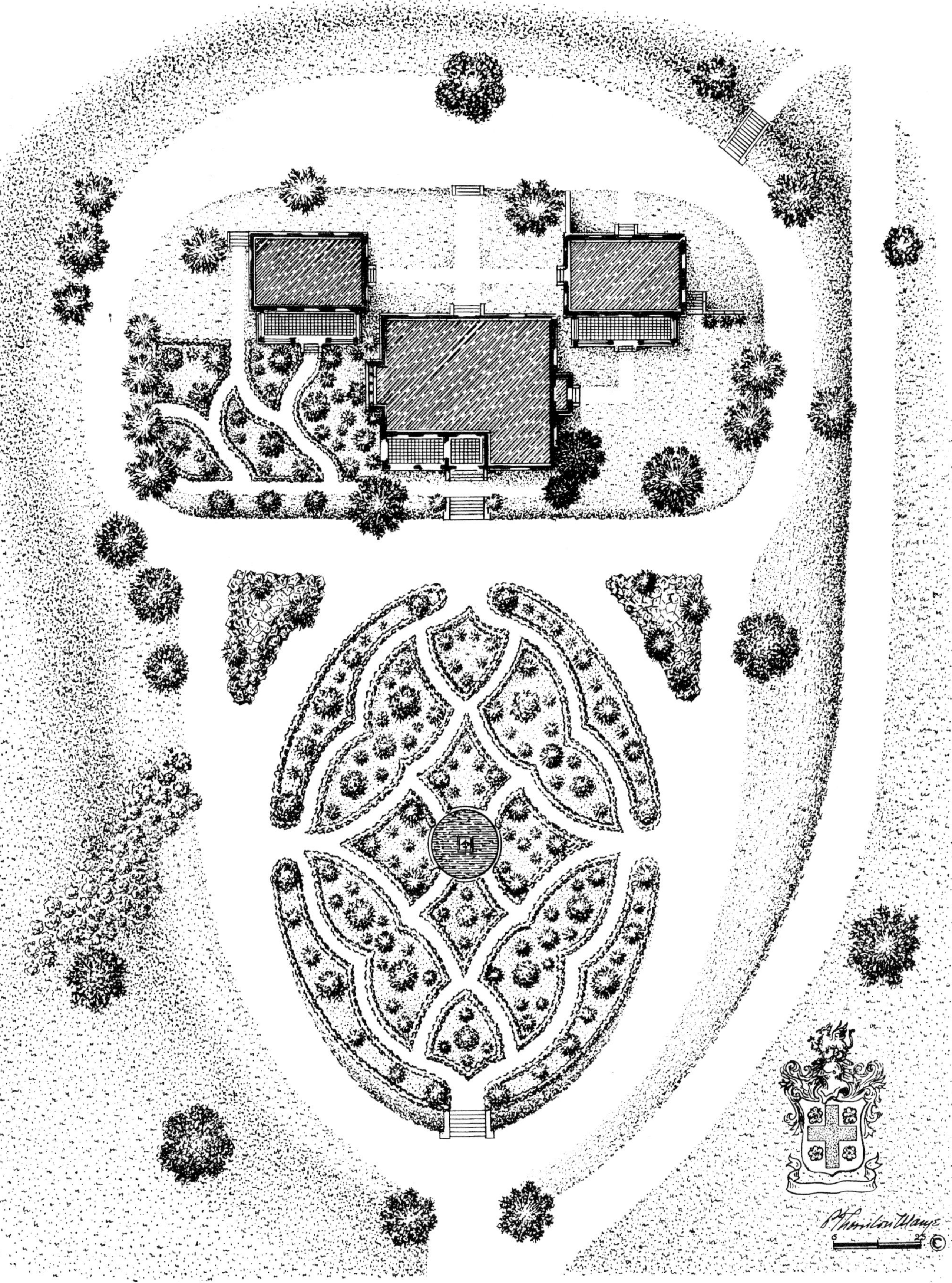

1833-1863

At Barnsley Gardens a levelled hilltop was cleverly developed into an harmonious scheme of buildings and gardens. The oval parterre is a perfect example of cut-work.

Valley View

On the Old Rome-Cartersville Road

Cass County—Bartow County

IN THE late 1840's Colonel James Caldwell Sproull of Abbeyville, South Carolina, moved to Cass County, Georgia, and developed on the road between Cartersville and Rome an extensive cotton plantation. A large brick house was built and a dignified formal garden laid out. Both stand unchanged, although the occupation of the house by Sherman's men left its mark.

Passing the entrance gates one drives through a quarter of a mile of lovely woods before reaching the house, which overlooks a wide valley. The garden's most distinguished feature is triple hedges bordering the central walk, formed of Carolina cherries and box. The garden bounded on one side by Carolina cherry and by bush wistaria on the other, shows original plantings of well trimmed dwarf box borders, tree box, Carolina cherry, English laurel, euonymus, Norway spruce and fir, Persian lilacs, crape myrtle, mock orange, flowering holly, cape jasmine, Pyrus japonica and forsythia. The roses are Maman Cochets, Malmaisons, dailies, both red and pink, moss roses, and a highly valued green rose. Bands of lilies, narcissus and violets flourish. All the box was brought from Cedar Grove, the old Marshall home in Abbeyville.

Locusts and cedars form a frame to the house and garden, and the service yard is shaded by splendid oaks. Next to the smoke house stands an unusual feature, a brick water tower. Vegetable gardens, orchards, plantation buildings and quarters complete the picture of a mid-nineteenth century plantation home, carefully preserved by Colonel Sproull's grandson, Sproull Fouche, the present owner of Valley View.

1848-1863

Valley View on the old road between Cartersville and Rome, home of the Sproulls and Fouches, is one of Georgia's best preserved mid-nineteenth century cotton plantations. Triple hedges of Carolina cherry and box are an interesting feature of its garden. Such herring-bone brick walks were general throughout the State.

Barrington Hall and Bulloch Hall

Roswell

Cobb County

JAMES ROSWELL KING, a native of New England, banker of Darien and manager of the Butler plantations, Butler's Island and Hampton Point on St. Simons, was a man of enterprise. Traveling through the State on horseback in the eighteen thirties, he selected a spot on the Chattahoochee River some twenty miles north of the future city of Atlanta, as the site of a new town planned to serve as the hub of a wide agricultural development. Buying a huge acreage of land from the Indians and State, he invited a number of Darien friends to join him in an enterprise, the management of which he turned over to his son Barrington. As an inducement, each family head was promised a deed to a twelve acre tract within the town, on which they were to build a home. In turn they were to buy a plantation from him. The undertaking proved profitable for all concerned. Within a couple of years a very small community of very big homes was established and called Roswell for its founder. While these first houses were being built, all the families lived in a community dwelling erected by the Kings.

Barrington Hall, the columned home of Barrington King, is surmounted by a whale-walk, showing that a sentiment for New England lingered in their hearts. On the east a little circular box maze is nested in bridal wreath spirea, crape myrtle, Spanish bayonet and tiger lilies; balancing it on the west there is an informal planting of cherry laurel, lilacs, roses and sweet lavender. A heart shaped double driveway similar to that at Mimosa Hall leads through a grove of oaks, hickories and black walnuts. Here we have no modern garden or plantings. Descendants of the Kings still own the place.

1838

Barrington Hall, built by one of the founders of Roswell, has a little box maze nested in tall, flowering shrubs.

Bulloch Hall, built by Major James F. Bulloch of Savannah, belongs to this period and group. It is a Greek Revival structure, and has the same heart shaped approach. The central path was bordered by cedars, of which a few remain. There never was a garden; a scuppernong arbor and an informal planting of flowering shrubs and fruit trees dates back to the 1830's. Bulloch Hall was the summer home of Mittie Bulloch, mother of President Theodore Roosevelt.

1838

Bulloch Hall in Roswell was the girlhood home of the mother of Theodore Roosevelt, who was also the grandmother of Mrs. Franklin Delano Roosevelt, and is visited as an historic shrine.

Mimosa Hall, formerly Phoenix Hall

Roswell

Cobb County

TO celebrate the completion of his fine house, John Dunwoody gave a great entertainment, during which a fire broke out. The wooden edifice was burned to the ground. Undaunted, but having lost his taste for timber, he made bricks on the place and built of them a replica of his destroyed home, calling it Phoenix Hall. A good example of the Greek Revival period, it, as well as most of old Roswell, was designed by a Boston architect, whose name has unfortunately been forgotten. On the twelve acres deeded John Dunwoody is a primeval grove of white and red oaks, hickories, tulip poplars, black locusts, black gum, beeches, holly, dogwood, red bud, chinquapins and black walnuts. To these were added elms. The mimosas which gave the place its later name were brought from Darien. A row of them is planted on each side of the path leading from gate to front door. A formal planting of giant cedars flanks this walk, and mimosa, cedars and Osage oranges are used at other points. To the west of the house there survive five beds of a formal garden. They are edged with stone coping. To the east is a fall of terraces planted with duetzia, syringa, Persian lilacs, flowering quince, daily roses shading from red to pink, and several varieties of old time jonquils. These terraces are partially overgrown with honeysuckle, but in the spring the old planting courageously pushes through. The original double driveway was heart shaped. When evening parties were given it was illumined by pine knot torches stuck into holders five and seven feet in diameter, formed by pierced brick walls two feet high built in a circle, and filled with earth. Here and there old planting is still found: chaste plant, ivy, wistaria, one chinquapin rose and thousands of valley lilies.

The Hansell family occupied Mimosa Hall for a number of years. From them it was bought in 1916 by Neel Reid, a noted architect, who restored the house and developed five acres of landscaping and gardens, in perfect harmony with the period and spirit of the place, of which a description is given in another part of the book. This home is now occupied by his mother, Mrs. John Reid.

1838-1863

A heart-shaped drive, formal garden and fall of terraces made an interesting composition at Mimosa Hall.

Oakton

Near Marietta

Cobb County

MIDWAY between Marietta and the foot of Kennesaw Mountain stands Oakton, a farm of some three hundred fifty acres, for eighty years the summer home of the Wilders and Andersons. It was purchased in 1852 from George Allen by John Randolph Wilder of Savannah, a New Englander by birth.

There is some uncertainty as to when and by whom the original Greek Revival cottage was built. It forms the central portion of the commodious dwelling developed in a later style by the Wilders. Mrs. Wilder, a lover of flowers, employed an Englishman to lay out and care for the grounds and gardens, which remain almost unchanged. These cover an area of some twenty-five acres on a low, ridge-like hill, approximately fifteen hundred feet in length. The face of this hill is divided into three sections; in the center a five acre lawn is shaded by splendid oaks, Norway spruce and cedars, and was originally hedged on three sides by euonymus. A double driveway meets in front of the house, which crowns the hill. To the left there was formerly a well stocked deer park, now a pasture; to the right an orchard. Immediately in front of the house is a lovely little half moon rose and lily garden of simple design, its beds outlined in very dwarf box. Giant yews, clipped and bound to a formal slenderness, flank the walk from the garden to the flower encircled house. An avenue of lilac and crape myrtle leads to the former deer park, and a path bordered by bulbs and Louis Phillippe roses to the orchard. Mrs. Wilder had a garden of tube roses close to the house.

Beyond kitchen, well, smoke house and dairy is an acre and a half of garden enclosed by a picket fence; here we find apple, fig, pear, quince and cherry trees. A grape arbor shades the path leading to an orchard at the rear. The box bordered beds contain small fruits and berries, musk cluster and Malmaison roses, peonies, iris, narcissus, jonquils and snowdrops, a mint bed, long borders of sweet lavender and knotted rows of herbs and seasonings. The seven varieties of vegetables formerly thought necessary to any dinner can still be gathered here. A large flower pit shelters delicate plants during the winter months. The many elms planted by Mrs. Wilder as a reminder of her New England home, frame this delightful spot, one of the few gardens of the type extant in Georgia.

Oakton was inherited in the eighties by Joseph John Wilder; its well preserved grounds and gardens reflect the constant care given them by his wife and by his daughter, Mrs. Jefferson Randolph Anderson, who continues to occupy it as a summer home.

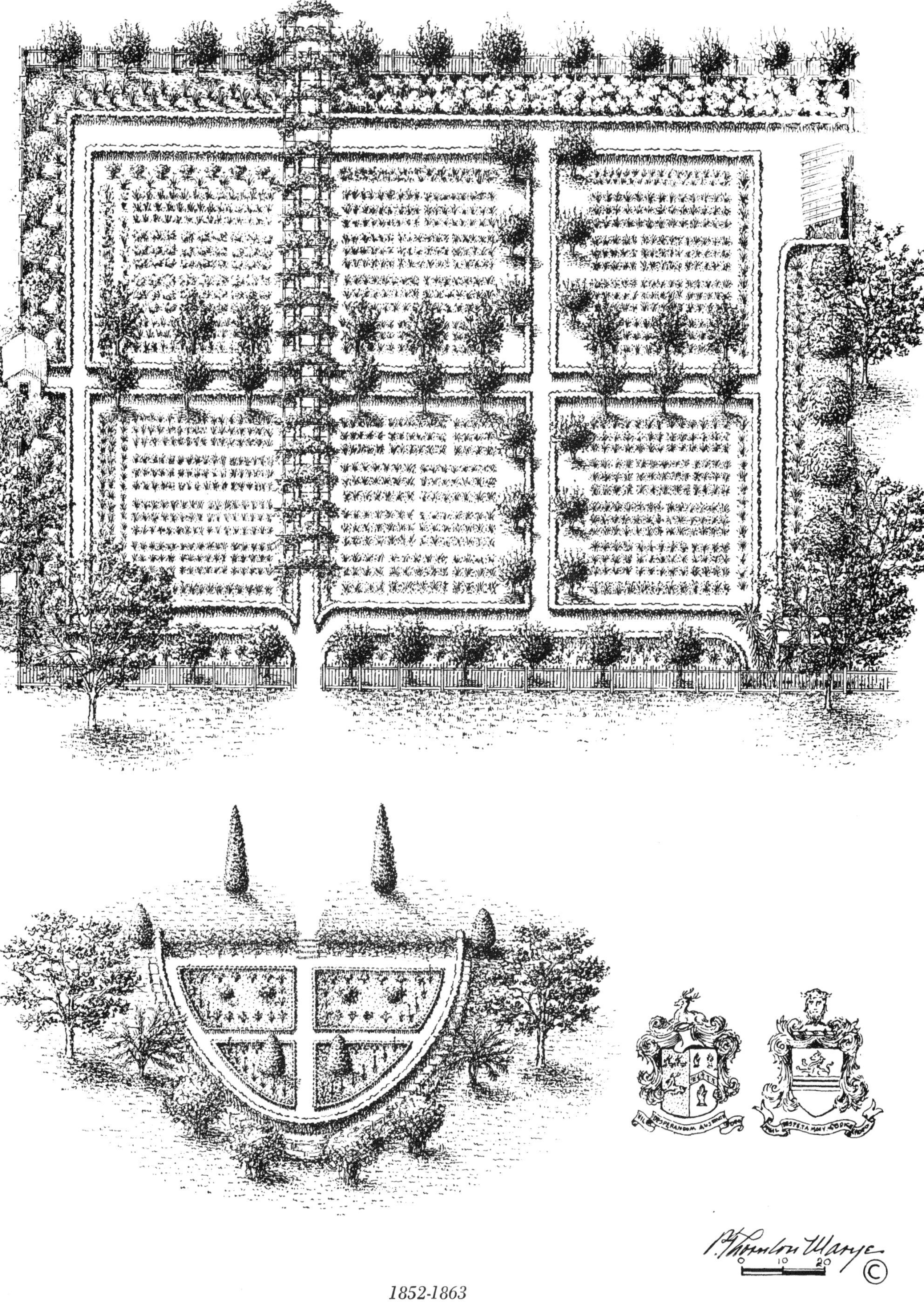

1852-1863

Mrs. John Randolph Wilder developed the grounds at Oakton. The kitchen garden has every feature peculiar to these delightful spots formerly so prevalent in Georgia. Simplicity gives charm to the little box bordered half moon rose and lily garden.

The Terraces

Atlanta
Fulton County

1859

This home was occupied by Federal officers after the fall of Atlanta in 1864 and thus escaped destruction.

THE home of Edward Elijah Rawson was built two years after he moved to Atlanta from Stewart County.

Occupying ten acres on South Pryor Street, it was for many years the show place of the community. The spacious house stood on the crest of a wide spreading and beautiful terraced hill. That these terraces were carpeted the year round in green sod was a triumph for the Scotch gardener who laid out and cared for the grounds. An unusual collection of conifers and topiary work executed in box and euonymus, vied in interest with a well designed box garden.

Until 1886 the Rawson family continued to live on this charming town estate.

Bibliography

Anderson, Jefferson Randolph: The Genesis of Georgia, Georgia Historical Quarterly.

Bartram, William: The Travels of William Bartram.

Bolton, Herbert E.: Spain's Title to Georgia.

Cate, Margaret Davis: Our Todays and Yesterdays.

Carlyle, Frederick: History of Frederick the Great.

Coulter, E. Merton: College Life in the Old South.

Dickinson: History of Roman Catholic Church.

Herrick, Francis H.: Audubon the Naturalist.

Higginson, Thomas Wentworth: Army Life in a Black Regiment.

James, John, of Greenwich: The Theory and Practice of Gardening, from the French of Dezallier d'Argenville.

Johnson: The Spanish Period of Georgia and South Carolina History, 1566-1702.

Jones, Charles C.: History of Georgia.

Journal of Mr. Commissary von Reck and of the Rev. Mr. Bolzius.

Kemble, Frances Anne: Journal of a Residence on a Georgia Plantation, 1838-1839.

Leigh, Hon. Mrs.: Ten Years on a Rice Plantation.

Lowe, George D.: Horticultural History of the Georgia Coast, a Report of the Fifty-fourth Annual Meeting of the Georgia State Horticulturists.

Lyell, Sir Charles: Second Visit to the United States.

Moore, Francis: Voyage to Georgia.

Murray, Hon. Amelia: Letters from Canada, United States and Cuba.

Ross, Mary: The Debatable Land.

Stephens, Col. William: Journal of Proceedings in Georgia.

White, Rev. George: Historical Collections of Georgia.

Wylly, Charles Spalding: The Annals of Glynn.

ERRATA

Date under illustration of ruins of Santo Domingo corrected to 1592-1600.

Page six, 1850 corrected to 1850-1855.

Page thirty-one, 1814-1820 corrected to 1814, 1820.

Page thirty-two, 1800-1810 corrected to 1800-10.

BENEATH this muted conference of oak
Spreading an emerald heaven overhead,
With grey moss hanging like a phantom smoke,
Time counts the timeless hours of the dead.
No spoken word awakes the quiet here,
No footfall, save the darkness and the dawn,
No stir save jasmine breathing on the air,
Dropping their dying petals on each stone.
Deep in our hearts they sleep, these pioneers,
The young, the brave, the beautiful, the old,
Who made an alien shore so wholly theirs!
Down the slow centuries as the years are told
By Time's cold fingers at his crumbling door
They are at peace with earth. They ask no more.

—Daniel Whitehead Hicky,
"*Thirteen Sonnets of Georgia*"

Transition Gardens

AFTER the War Between the States, slave labor in the South was no more, therefore gardening activities were curtailed, and continued only with readjustments. The gardens became smaller, the box plantings less elaborate, and the plant placing not so studied nor symmetrical, perhaps. The work was done by the owners themselves or by freed men who had attached themselves to the old master's family for small pay. Casulon Plantation, the home of the Harris family in Walton County, and the Veazey Plantation in Greene County are given here as examples of transition gardens in Georgia.

Casulon Plantation

Miss Sally Maud Jones

High Shoals

AT High Shoals, not far from Athens, is Casulon Plantation, a particularly interesting example of the ante-bellum cotton planter's establishment, and one of the few to survive, unchanged by the ravages of time, fire, or the aftermath of the war. Additions and alterations made from time to time by four generations of the Harris family who have always owned and lived at Casulon, fortunately have taken from it none of its "before the war" atmosphere—possibly because the life at Casulon today is still very like the days of yore.

The plantation consists of six thousand acres, a great part of it in woods, but enough under cultivation to have produced yearly fourteen hundred bales of cotton before the advent of the boll weevil. Nowadays the farming has been greatly curtailed and the abandoned fields are over run by game and quail—as many as a hundred coveys having been spotted last season. The slave quarters are a thing of the past, yet some of the original slaves and many of their descendants are tenants on the place. Behind the house the old detached kitchen has been replaced by a modern "cook-room," but the smoke house with its meat-cutting bench still stands at one side of the big clean-swept yard shaded by massive trees, where the plantation activities continually go forward.

The earliest part of the "Big House" at Casulon was built in 1825, of timbers cut on the grounds. Porches and wings of a slightly later date keep faith with the classic notions of the day when "leisure, learning, and love of beauty" fitted these fine simple dwellings into settings of natural grace and gardens of a specially suitable type. Lord Bacon's famous statement that man learned to build stately long before he learned to garden well, scarcely holds good here. For the old plantation gardens of intricately patterned boxwood and lustrous evergreens could hardly be improved on as surroundings for the homes of that or any other day.

Approaching the house through pine woods and past broad cotton fields one comes on the hardwood grove which surrounds the house and the garden area. Across the front and enclosed in a white picket fence lies the main garden, re-made in 1865 just after the war, while to the east, connected by a rose arbor, is a modern informal garden with hedges of

Spires of Cherry Laurel and Boxwood on Entrance Walk at Casulon

Box Garden at Casulon Plantation

flowering shrubs, a sun dial in a stretch of open lawn, many beds of flowers, and a summer house; —an interesting contrast in form with the old garden.

Box-edged paths and parterres carry out the formal pattern of the front garden. The verandah looks down over the interwoven masses of pungent boxwood, and on one side of the doorway stands a big elm, covered in vines, on the other a native cedar. Symmetrical in design, the garden picture has the varied high lights of the foliage of the coarser evergreens with the dogwood and the pinkish trunks of many crepe myrtle trees, but the most striking accents in height and shape are two clipped spires of cherry laurel which flank the center walk and which were here long before the garden was.

Probably the oldest wooden plantation house left in this section of Georgia—its hundred years substantiated not by recorded deeds but by family history and dates on the stones of the old burying ground—Casulon is a romantic survival. Its claim to distinction is not for grandeur or glory in the days that were, but more for carrying on into these less glamorous times a picture of a peculiarly American civilization which can never come again.

Veazey Plantation

Greene County

SOMEWHAT different from Casulon Plantation which combined pre-war memories with its "After the War" garden, there grew up over Georgia through the efforts of valiant souls, whose chief asset was a force within themselves to start again at rock-bottom and build anew, homes of a new type. Homes that served as community centers to assist a bewildered and uprooted people again to get their bearings and go forward. The colored "hands" were no longer in quarters but in small tenant houses scattered about the plantation. With their gardens and "patches" these little cabins proved the first training schools for a new citizenry, who had to be taught by degrees independence of thought and action. Here the trustworthy among the detached freemen found homes, encouragement, and training until able to stand alone. The non-trustworthy were controlled through the existence of an organization of determined self-controlled citizens, so quietly operated that no one saw the wheels go round.

A larger type of tenant house was established for the white non-land owner who usually farmed a small acreage on shares, but assisted on the cotton plantation when and where needed. The plantation owner "stood for his supplies" until the crop was made.

An excellent example of this type of "After the War" Southern home was the Veazey plantation in Greene County, not several thousand acres upon many of which the owner had never trod, but a thousand acres every inch of which served a definite purpose in carrying on. Court House records show the ownership of this property to have passed from 1834 through Lewis, Jackson, Moore and Harris families, before its purchase by Mr. E. A. Veazey in 1869. Across the plantation was cut the public road leading from Greensboro to Sparta and at a point on this highway four miles from Greensboro, George Moore had built the house in 1868 at the apex of a gentle slope a quarter mile from the road. A triple row of willow and water oaks changing the six hundred fifty foot lane from house to highway into a double driveway of great beauty was also the work of a former owner, Mr. Pink Harris, but the making of the whole into a successful plantation and a charming home was the work of Mr. and Mrs. Veazey.

Cotton was still the most extensive and most cash-producing crop, but food products for home consumption made the plantation an independent unit, just as had been the greater plantations before the War. The family, the tenants, and the stock were all considered in the plantings, and corn, grains, haying crops, potatoes, peanuts, peas, and garden truck were grown in quantity.

Utilities in the form of cotton gin and press, cane mill, cotton and stock market, circulating threshing machine, and general store were maintained for the convenience of the small land owners for miles around, while at the same time giving required service to tenant farmers and to the plantation itself.

The area of immediate home activities lay within a great oval, enclosed by a series of fruit orchards beginning at the highway and swinging about the oval to the highway again. The first orchard on the right was a mulberry grove—a playground for children and a paradise for birds—the mulberry's soft green contrasting at blossom time with the pastel colors of the fruit trees. Apples, pears, cherries and plums continued around the horseshoe curve and flowered each spring against a native woodland in whose depth a spring and a spring-box not only offered cooling drink but served as the family refrigerator until the wells were made. Farther around the curve a grove of chestnuts waved their June plumes high above the kitchen garden and corral, and in autumn were the scene of picnics for the nut-gatherers. Opposite the mulberry grove on the other side of the oval were the broad acres planted to peach trees whose tops in blossom season made a sea of pink visible not only from the house but for miles along the highway.

Set well back within the curve of the horseshoe of orchards was the house, enclosed by two fences. The outer one of horizontal boards and large gates—a warning fence—like feudal days, saying,

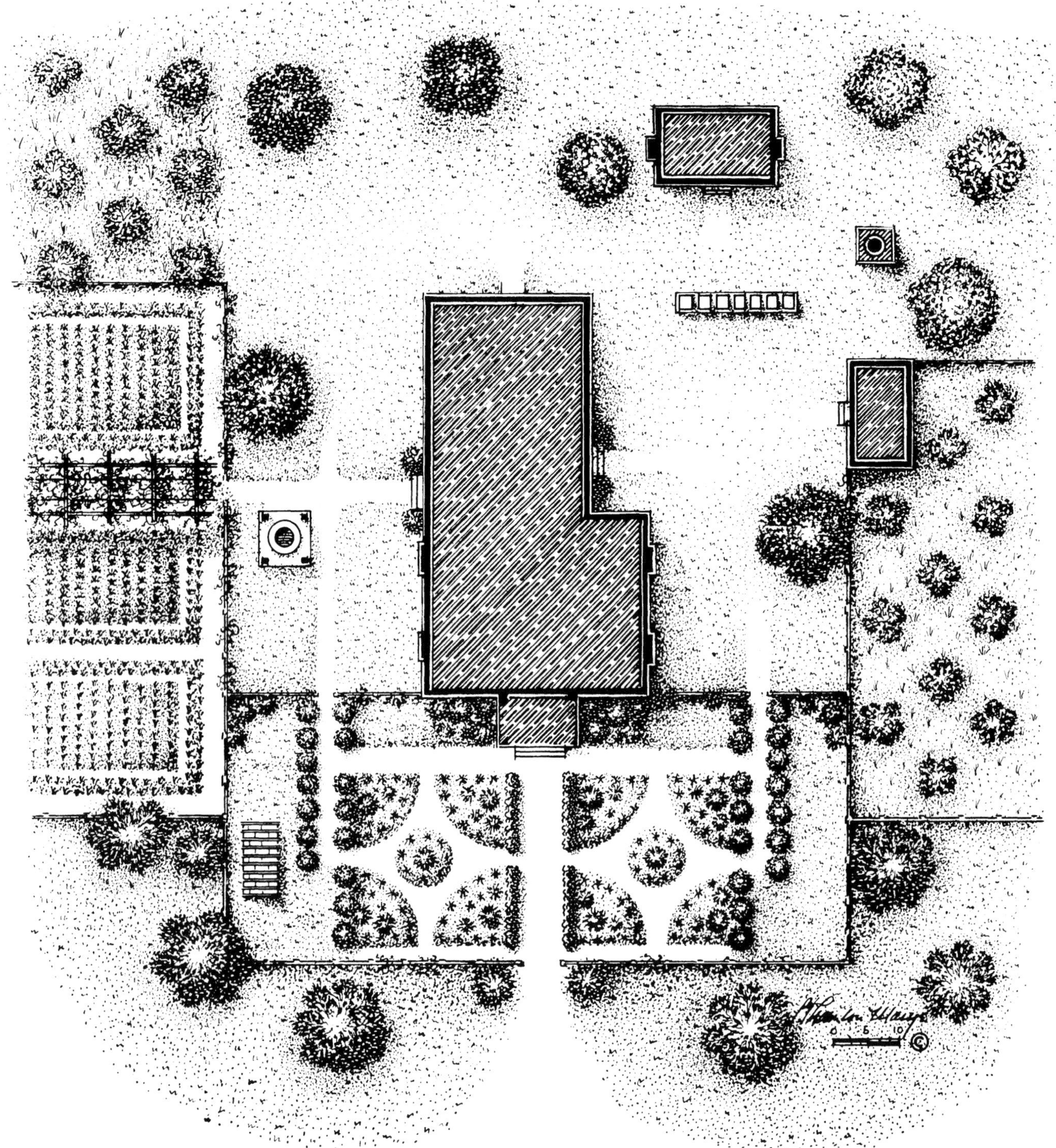

Veazey Plantation

Plan of Flower Garden and Kitchen Garden Around Homestead, 1869

"Only friends enter here." Within this fence, on each side of the swept grounds, was a group of three very large Willow oaks, overshadowing the two carriage houses where guests left their equipages. The inner fence of white pickets enclosed the house and its formal flower garden, laid out and planted by the Veazeys in 1869. Here dwarf box edged the beds, tree box accented the corners, and hedge box bordered the walkway to the steps and mingled with the blossoming shrubs; sweet syringa, lilac, flowering quince and almond, Christmas jasmine, snowball, Cape jasmine, and spirea—along the fences. Euonymous and Cape jasmine softened the lines of the porch, and Lady Banksia roses and yellow jessamine climbed against the columns and wall trellises. Old-fashioned perennials and annuals filled the beds, while potted plants from the "pit" came out with warm weather to increase the flower effect. Large apple trees shaded the gateway that led to the side yard and well. The kitchen garden, with picket fence and scuppernong arbor, was placed close in at the side of the house in the fashion of a former generation.

Some years ago the house burned, but many of the great oaks still stand as monuments to a day that was.

(Greene County gardens of an earlier date are described in another part of the book.)

Willow Oak Lane at Veazey Plantation

Gardening in Georgia

T. H. McHatton

TWO hundred years ago when Oglethorpe and his intrepid band first stepped upon the land which was later to become the State of Georgia, they little realized the magnitude and native wealth of the colony they were establishing. Moving up the bosom of a majestic river, they were surrounded by waving marshes, later to be immortalized by the pen of Lanier; in the hinterland they caught glimpses of verdant forests, accented by the spears of giant palmettos. They were thrilled at what they saw, but had they been able to visualize the sources of that same river as it sprang from the heart of great hills, cascaded over the falls of Tallulah and wound its way through an ever changing, undulating country to the sea, they would have exulted even more in anticipation of the opportunities that were yet to come.

Fifty-nine thousand square miles of territory make Georgia the largest State east of the Mississippi River. From the lower tip of the Okefenokee Swamp, in an air line to the boundaries of North Carolina the distance is approximately four hundred miles, and its greatest breadth, west from the tip of Chatham County, is over three hundred miles. In this vast area, running from sea level to elevations of five thousand feet, are many types of topography, soils and climates—the latter varying as much as sixty days in planting and blooming dates, within the boundaries of the State.

Actually Georgia may be divided into four definite and distinct areas. Naturally along their boundaries these sections merge one into another, but there are many instances where the line of demarcation is most distinct. The coastal section from Savannah to St. Marys constitutes the early historical portion of the State and is made up of six counties, mostly low, level, and largely sandy, as are many tide water areas. In this division lie the famous sea islands, about which so much has found its way into literature. The Coastal Plain starts at a line running east from Columbus, through Macon to Augusta and takes in practically all of the southern section of the State. In the main, this area is level and flat, often poorly drained, but it contains a wealth of botanic interest. The very lowest southeastern corner of Georgia is the Okefenokee Swamp. Out of this there comes the St. Mary's River on one side and the far famed Suwanee River on the other, the former going slowly into the Atlantic Ocean and the other winding its way to the Gulf of Mexico. This particular swamp contains seven hundred thousand acres, handed down to us from early geological times. Nothing else is exactly like it. Within its heart one finds level islands supporting tall pines and other native trees, while all about them, in the coffee-colored water of the swamp, grow giant cypresses festooned with Spanish moss. The area is the haunt of wild and aquatic life of all kinds and should be preserved for future generations but, unfortunately, the march of progress has permitted the removal of a large portion of the big cypress trees.

From the fall-line north, one enters the Piedmont region of the State. This is a broken, rolling area, becoming more rugged and reaching higher elevations as it approaches the mountain sections into which it gradually merges. The upper two or three tiers of counties may be considered the mountain region. Here Rabun-Bald, Brasstown-Bald and Blood mountains reach altitudes of nearly five thousand feet, a rugged and beautiful territory, bringing into Georgia conditions that are usually found much farther north, and forming a natural landscape of remarkable scenic beauty.

Throughout this great diversity of level, rolling, and mountain lands, one finds over four hundred types of soil. Naturally, in each section there is a predominance of one kind and the careful gardener will take this into consideration when practicing the landscape art. The soil of the Coastal Plain is generally light, quite a bit of it is very sandy, yet in this area there are found large quantities of Tifton pebbly lands that adapt themselves magnificently to gardening operations. There are also large amounts and many phases of Greenville and Orangeburg soils that are excellent for plants. These latter types are found mainly in the central coastal area from a few miles south of Macon to Americus and westward to Cuthbert, along the Chattahoochee River.

In the Piedmont region one sees the red hills of Georgia, for which the State is famous. These are made up of the Cecil soils in their various phases with an admixture of the Davidson types. In the mountain territories deep, rich valley lands like the Porters loam are common. It is believed that at one time these mountains were much higher than they are now and that erosion dwarfed their mighty size and builded, in part, from them the Piedmont and Coastal sections of the State. There is no dearth of soils for garden purposes in Georgia, numerous types and conditions, in small areas, permitting the growth of a great variety of plants.

Climates verging from the sub-tropical to the boreal are found within the boundaries of the State. In the southern section, particularly in the coastal regions, oranges and palms will thrive; the summers are long and warm, but are rendered pleasant by breezes from the ocean and the gulf. This is an especially fine climate for certain types of gardening as can be seen from the results obtained both along the coast and at Thomasville, which is considerably more than one hundred miles from the Atlantic. Ample rainfall and moisture are available in this section, and as a rule, are well distributed through the growing season. Piedmont Georgia does not have so long a summer as the south. It is more temperate and, normally, is well supplied with moisture. From the upper Piedmont into the mountains one passes into a section with a season too short for the production of cotton, where often temperatures of forty-five degrees F. are attained during summer nights. In the northeastern portion of this area the rainfall is the heaviest in the State, approximating seventy-five inches annually. So diversified are the climates of Georgia that one finds winter resorts and summer resorts scarcely three hundred miles apart.

Fortunately, the State is well supplied with streams. The sluggish, slow-moving coffee-colored water of the Coastal Plain has a beauty and a charm all its own. The streams are fed by innumerable creeks and never become muddy as they drain great areas of light sandy soils that wash but little. The color comes from their organic content, rising as they often do in swamps and flowing through almost sub-tropical vegetation either to the ocean or the gulf. The red streams start in the mountains as crystal brooks, cold and clear, the home of the speckled trout. The mountains are filled with rills and tiny creeks that soon group themselves together, forming rivers, some of which flow into the Tennessee, and thence into the Ohio and Mississippi, while the others take a southern course, forming the Savannah or the Chattahoochee, the former going into the ocean and the latter into the gulf at Appalachicola. There is a place at Rabun Gap where, close together, two springs have their sources, one flowing into the Little Tennessee and the other into the Savannah. As the south bound rivers work their way through the mountains and red clay hills of the Piedmont, they gather the silt and the clay that gives them the yellow-orange color that they carry to the sea. Gardening is largely dependent upon water and fortunate is the region that possesses the number of rills and brooks and

Magnolia Grandiflora, Athens

streams that are found in Georgia.

The flora of the different regions is indicative of the garden wealth of the State. Those interested would do well to take the travels of William Bartram and follow him through his journeys in this section, read his description of the Gordonia altamaha, see what he has to say about the live oak, the long leaf pine, the cypress, the giant palmetto and its scrubby brother; hear how the yellow jessamine takes the woods and where he found the grand flowered magnolia; how in his wanderings through coastal and southern Georgia he came upon these magnificent plants in their native habitat and natural surroundings. Then follow him through the Piedmont and note how the flora changes, the grand flowered magnolia disappears to be replaced by the tulip tree and other allied species, the live oak gives way to the water oak and the white oak begins to predominate, and the long leaf pine is replaced by the Loblolly. Then again trail him into the mountains where he finds flame azaleas, white pines and hemlocks with rhododendrons and kalmias on hillsides covered with trailing arbutus. What more graphic demonstration is needed to show that between St. Marys and Blood Mountain there is at least two months' difference in the opening of spring, as well as in the beginning of fall.

With such a variety of soils and climates it is no wonder that many introduced plants have found congenial homes within the State. A study of Asa Gray's theory of plant distribution throughout the world, will readily explain why so many of the oriental species have become prominent in our gardens. They have found it more congenial here than on the Pacific coast where many of them were originally introduced; and if we must credit William Bartram for the vision of our State in 1776, we must also give honor to Prosper Julius Berckmans, the owner and originator of the Fruitland Nurseries at Augusta, whose great interest in plants made him the importer and disseminator of more worthy ornamental forms than any other southern horticulturist. To have known him and to have visited his plants with him was to get an insight into the wide possibilities offered by the climates and soils of Georgia. Not only this State, but the entire South should be grateful to Mr. Berckmans for his additions to our flora.

It is only natural that in the various sections of the State different types of gardening predominate—and should predominate—for the soils, climate and flora differ so strongly. In the matter of cultivation South Georgia is not very old, excepting along the coast, for practically the whole area was an unbroken pine forest even into the 1890's, but now the timber has been harvested and in its stead there have sprung up farms and cities and in some sections a great deal of landscaping has been done. Most of this might be said to be of the naturalistically beautiful type. Often the pine forest with its carpet of wire grass has been cleaned up and sweeping roads have been laid through it with judicious planting to accentuate the native growth already present. Advantage has been taken of swampy areas and adjacent uplands to develop a type of landscape peculiar to the country. Where live oaks have been available, these magnificent trees have been extensively utilized, and particularly is this true in the coastal area. Where the gray Spanish moss is common, it adds an inevitable touch of mysterious age and beauty to the landscape and the sluggish dark colored streams with their even banks blend harmoniously into the surroundings. The general motive in this level area is naturalness; the streams, the live oaks and the moss giving a picturesqueness that should be accentuated rather than obliterated. About the homes, palms, magnolias, gardenias, and camellias are planted more formally in pleasing contrast with the prevailing natural forms.

In the Piedmont the flora changes and the rolling topography calls for a more planned type of gardening. Formality characterizes the gardens close to the homes as it did the boxwood plantings of the olden days, but modern gardening in this area more nearly approaches that which has attained prominence in many other sections of our country, and as we go north in the Piedmont this similarity to gardening in the more northern states increases.

In the mountains the land and plants combine to force a rugged naturalness and, in many instances, a definite picturesqueness. The towering hemlocks and the rhododendrons with the arbutus and the rushing mountain streams need little of man's attention to make them startlingly beautiful. Nowhere outside of the mountains of the South does the opportunity for landscape gardening appear so great. Here where the floras of the North and the South mingle, where the white pine can grow side by side with the grand flowered magnolia, where hemlock and spruce, rhododendron and kalmia can flourish with boxwood and azaleas, there is opportunity for the most glorious gardens possible. The verdant hills adapt themselves more gracefully than do the mountains of the Rockies, and though not so gigantic and rough as the western ranges, they are rugged and rocky enough to work harmoniously into superb landscapes.

The South is not blest with a multiplicity of narrow-leaf evergreens. Outside of the mountain sections a majority of them do not do well during the long hot summers or in periods of drouth, but in their place we have a wealth of broadleaf evergreens, both native and introduced. Many gardens are now being builded almost entirely of this type of plant and, fortunately, most of this material, which is deciduous farther north, retains its leaves here during the winter. Many of these broad-leaf evergreens produce fragrant flowers. During the winter the foliage is a deep dark green; in spring fresh growth comes out a brilliant green against the larger darker leaves, and when in bloom their flowers are offset by a lustrous background.

Southern gardeners would do well to use less extensive plantings of deciduous shrubs and to replace them with gardenias and camellias, tea olives and eleagnus, along with yellow jessamine, live oaks and Carolina cherries. Such gardening would be typical of the section and have more individuality and indigenous charm.

There is one problem of the southern gardener which requires real ingenuity and work, and that is the lawn. As a basis of all good landscape work, particularly adjacent to the house, this phase of gardening should receive careful consideration. It is often said that good lawns are impossible in the South. This is far from true. Bermuda grass is adapted to the whole of the State of Georgia and makes an excellent summer lawn. A winter lawn may be had by sowing rye grass or blue grass over the Bermuda; and in the mountains of Georgia blue grass will grow the whole year round, as it does in Kentucky. For the more southern areas St. Augustine grass and carpet grass may be used; and, where shade is dense, the ground can be covered with ivy or vinca, in beautiful effect. Of course the South is blest with an open winter and faces the necessity of maintaining a green lawn the year around. This naturally means more work, but, in the end, more enjoyment.

Prior to the Civil War there were in Georgia numbers of elaborately developed properties. In the coast counties there was found one of the most delightful of American civilizations, the life of the rice planters. The group of people who built their homes on the tide-water streams of the Atlantic lived in a pleasant luxury and elegance. With their multitude of slaves, they dyked out the water of the ocean and established an industry that made them affluent. The loss of the control of their labor along with the subsequent development of rice growing on firmer bottom soils elsewhere brought on the downfall of this picturesque life. These homes and those on the Sea Islands had a distinctive character of their own. The live oaks and cypresses festooned with Spanish moss were mingled with palms, palmettos and sub-tropical plants, flowering broad-leaf evergreens, camellias, gardenias, magnolias and the like. Such plant material, plus an inexhaustible supply of time and la-

Crepe Myrtle Against a Wall of Ivy

bor, created magnificent gardens contiguous to and above the waving marshes of the area. These plantations, famed in song and story, have gone the way of past glories, yet even now there may be found about the old sites wonderful specimens and fragments of old plantings that speak of the golden days that were.

With the spread of agriculture into the hinterland behind the sea, there sprang up the ante-bellum cotton plantations. Following the revival, by Thomas Jefferson, of Grecian architecture, these post-colonial and ante-bellum structures rivaled Greek temples in their beauty. About most of them were planted the formal boxwood gardens, from one to several acres, that fitted so harmoniously with the classical dignity of the residence. Some of the gardens were free in line and design, others intricate and formal and the beds were filled with old-time flowers peculiar to the South. Often crepe myrtles and red cedars made the background or the boundary of the formal development and many a one was encompassed by white picket fences. Occasionally there was a library in the yard where seclusion could be had by the studiously inclined. The boxwood grew and developed under the shade of giant magnolias and the atmosphere was perfumed with the tea olive in spring and fall. Yellow jessamine was rampant in the park which often surrounded the formal enclosure, the parklands adding a touch of English rural life to the Greek Revival. There were numerous Ethiopian gardeners to carry out the slightest whims of the mistress or the master. Mellow moonlit evenings were redolent with gardenia or osmanthus, the air filled with the music of that prince of southern songsters, the mocking bird, as he poured out his heart from the tipmost top of a great magnolia, accompanied by the plaintive chanting of the slaves. A type of gardening distinctively of the American south, to be builded only under such conditions as then existed, when men and women had time to plan and think, and also the means to carry out the cultural ideas that emanated from an ancestry of education and refinement. Such gardens could only develop under the influence of a very salubrious climate, in soils particularly adapted to their making, and under the condition of a completely controlled and inexhaustible labor supply. In almost the twinkling of an eye this typically American art of landscaping which had borrowed but little from the English and less from others, and which flowered under the influence of a Greek revival, was smashed and obliterated and, though we may weep at the loss, we must realize that out of its desecration has sprung a greater nation.

The princes from the rice fields, and the barons from the cotton acres, quite often moved their families to the mountains for the summer. In many places there grew up gardens of entirely different types and made up of different plants; less formal and more natural, to fit into the spirit of vacation. As they were merely transient homes for a few months to escape the lengthy heat of southern summers, they were not elaborate nor as well tended as the others. There are still a few of such gardens left, enough to show that in the past the beauties

Osmanthus Fortunei, West View, Atlanta

of the mountains were appreciated and not neglected.

Thus has the gardening of the past shown us the possibilities of our State. In the new era things are different. The rice planters have gone, but in their stead has come a multiplicity of comparatively small land owners along the coast, building their cities and their homes under modern influence, but using the same old plants effectively. The Sea Islands have changed hands and the very rich of America are now adorning them with an admixture of several types of architecture and landscaping. There may yet emerge a typical garden from this section but the old ante-bellum homes are gone, the rural life has flowed into the city and our modern gardens are much like those of other sections in the country. Somehow the abundant use of broad-leaf evergreens has given place to plants that do as well elsewhere. We have not sensed the opportunities nor exploited the wealth that is ours. A large number of our gardens, lovely though they are, could be seen in almost any other section of the United States. They do not belong to the South, they do not belong to Georgia, they are not ours, but every man's. Naturally the ante-bellum plantations cannot be revived and we must build anew.

Happily the mountains are again becoming of importance in our landscaping, but even here there is a tendency to get away from nature's plans and to use methods, designs and materials because they have proved successful in other sections. The north Georgia mountain area more closely resembles the woods of Maine and Michigan than it does the Piedmont and coastal area of the South, and possibly the gardening that has proved satisfactory in more northern places can be better adapted here than elsewhere in the State. It is to be hoped, however, that the plants of local worth will be accentuated in the designs and that little by little this northernmost portion of our commonwealth will have well planned horticultural beauty in addition to the natural grandeur of scenery.

Mermaid. Garden of F. E. Lee, Atlanta

Ilex Aquifolia Burfordii, West View, Atlanta

There have been few landscape architects in Georgia. The ante-bellum landlord, if the need arose, imported one from England and these, fortunately, appreciated the inherent beauty of the South and, in collaboration with a cultured and garden-loving people, evolved most satisfactory "pleasure grounds." The modern revival of gardening interest and enthusiasm has made clear the fact that within the State every type of garden is possible—from the tropical, with its palms, cacti and yucca, to the boreal with its hemlocks, rhododendrons and arbutus. With this in mind and looking to the future, the University of Georgia, the oldest of state universities, established in 1928 a degree course in Landscape Architecture, the first degree of its kind in the South. From here can go out the youth of our State and of our sister states, imbued with the traditions which are theirs and, with thorough knowledge of our climates, soils and plants, so to build that there may be again a typical Georgia art in gardening that will proclaim her horticultural wealth.

Gardening in Georgia

IT would be well to give a lengthy list of the plants that could be used and are used by Georgia gardeners. The list must, however, be pruned and from the abundance of material at our disposal only a few selected for special mention. It must be understood that the native plants are not only found in Georgia, but are indigenous to other parts of the South as well, and that not only in Georgia but in most of the southern states do the introduced plants succeed, for many of them have a wide distribution and use. However, all of the following group are used extensively in enhancing the beauty of our natural landscape.

Magnolia Soulangeana in Garden of Mrs. Henry Cohen, Augusta

The live oak, Quercus Virginiana, is probably one of the most magnificent trees of the country, attaining giant size in the coastal area of the State, broad and sweeping, powerful and mighty, a good specimen can make a picture by itself; slow of growth, but permanent; a magnificent plant about which to build a garden.

The giant palmetto, or cabbage palmetto, Sabal palmetto, one of the few native palms of the South, is used extensively along the coasts and in the southern coastal plains, producing a tropical effect. Many palms are adapted to growth in Georgia. Even as far north as Eatonton, in the central Piedmont, Dr. Benjamin W. Hunt, a noted horticulturist, who is an authority on palms in the South, grows many introduced species in the open with little or no protection.

The Spanish moss or gray moss, Tillandsia usneoides, festoons the trees in swamps and lowlands along the coastal rivers and further inland; attractive in the sunlight and by moonlight; beautiful when hanging straight in the humid atmosphere or waving like uncontrolled locks under the influence of the wind; a weirdly attractive plant peculiar to certain sections of the South.

The cypress, Taxodium distichum, a deciduous conifer, is adapted to low, wet swampy lands. Its massive buttressed base with tall, straight, magnificent trunk rearing itself out of the water of pond or stream makes a landscape picture all its own. This tree may be grown on high lands, but does not attain the beauty nor the size under such conditions. It is not adaptable north of the central section of the State.

The grand flowered magnolia, Magnolia grandiflora, one of the most splendid native plants, is adapted largely to hammock lands, but can be grown practically throughout the State, though seldom in the mountains and never native; a broadleaf evergreen of slow growth whose large glossy leaves and enormous, heavily perfumed white flowers make one of the finest landscape plants the South possesses; particularly adapted to formality. It seems to belong to the old ante-bellum southern home about which it was so extensively planted.

The long-leaf pine, Pinus palustris, found mainly from central Georgia south, grows on numerous kinds of soils. Forests of long-leaf pine are one of the most characteristic beauties of the State. Large areas have been cut over for lumber but gardeners are using this plant heavily in its native sections; one of the most beautiful of pines, typical of Georgia.

The white pine, Pinus strobus, is found growing native only in the mountains where it attains enor-

Cherokee Rose, Concord

mous size; a beautiful tree, especially along streams, in coves and valleys.

Hemlock, Tsuga canadensis, is native only in the mountains. Tremendous specimens are found particularly beyond the north divide. There is no bit of scenery more attractive than hemlocks growing near the mountain waterfalls. Gardeners in the mountains use this plant extensively for hedges.

The Carolina cherry, Laurocerasus caroliniana; this broad-leaf evergreen is one of the most satisfactory plants to use in southern gardening. Adapted from the upper Piedmont to the coast, it makes excellent specimen plants, good windbreaks and fine hedges.

The yellow jessamine, Gelsemium sempervirens, is an evergreen vine producing fragrant yellow flowers in the early spring. Where grown in quantity, its sweetness pervades the atmosphere; particularly southern and not adapted above the central Piedmont.

The trailing arbutus, Epigaea repens, is found along the banks of some of the water courses having northern exposures as far south as central Piedmont. In the mountains the arbutus makes a rich ground cover for the rugged slopes and along the streams.

Rhododendron, R. species with maximum predominating, is almost too common in certain sections of the United States to need description. The native plants are said to be finer in the mountains of the South than in any other area.

Lotus in Garden of Mr. and Mrs. Inman Gray, Atlanta

The native azaleas, Azalea species. From the central Piedmont north, particularly in the mountain section, the flame azaleas and wild honeysuckles, so called, abound. They are found in a great variety of colors and are being used extensively where conditions permit.

Hawthorn in Lumpkin Garden, Athens

The myrtles, Myrica species, are found in number and variety in the southern and coastal areas. These are excellent broad-leaf evergreen shrubs and are coming rapidly into wider use.

In various sections, we find the kalmia, the silver bell, the haws, the sweetgums, the elms, the hackberry, the tulip tree, several deciduous magnolias, the Loblolly pine, the Slash pine and others, all of which have their adaptations in our State.

Among the most outstanding of the introduced plants is the Camellia japonica. In the South and along the coast these bushes attain enormous size. With protection some of them can be grown in the northern Piedmont, but there they become exotics, while in Thomasville, Brunswick, Savannah and like places they make the foundation of many gardens.

The Gardenia florida, commonly called Cape jasmine, is another introduced shrub that has found a home with us. These magnificent broad-leaf evergreen plants have been grown in quantity since ante-bellum times. A tender greenhouse flower further north, they bloom in Georgia gardens in great profusion over a long period of the summer.

There is no sweeter nor more attractive garden plant than the tea olive, Osmanthus fragrans, and many of its close relatives. It can be grown as far north as the foothills of the mountains if given slight protection.

Eleagnus, in several species, is another broad-leaf evergreen that produces its sweetly perfumed flowers in the late fall. It grows well even up in the hills.

The boxwood, Buxus sempervirens, adapted from the Piedmont areas north, has been the basis of many gardens in Georgia.

Euonymus japonica is one of the earliest of the evergreens introduced in this section. It was widely used during the last half of the nineteenth century. It is unfortunately subject to scales which, however, can be controlled with oils. This broad-leaf evergreen does well up to the mountains.

The Indian azalea, Azalea indica, is becoming especially popular and grows fairly well in the northern Piedmont, but reaches its greatest perfection along the coast.

Crepe myrtle, Lagerstroemia indica, typical of the old South, makes a fine background for boxwood gardens. It is a mid-summer blooming shrub of great beauty.

The banana shrub, Michelia fuscata, closely related to the magnolias, can be grown with protection in the northern Piedmont, but is particularly adapted to the South. It is found extensively about old gardens.

Pittosporum, Pittosporum tobira, another broad-leaf evergreen shrub with fragrant white blossoms, is especially adapted to the southern section of the State.

The tea plant, Thea sinensis, also grows well along the coast and in the middle areas.

The camphor, Cinnamomum camphora, is one of the most attractive small shrubby trees in the lower coastal plain and along the coast, and may be grown with protection in the southern Piedmont. This broad-leaf evergreen, where it will stand the climate, is a valuable adjunct to landscaping.

Golden arborvita, Thuja orientalis conspicua, is a golden tinged arborvita originated and introduced by P. J. Berckmans; one of the best narrow-leaf evergreens for formal southern plantings.

The dwarf golden arborvita, Thuja orientalis aurea nana, also originated and introduced by P. J. Berckmans, is used largely in formal gardening; an excellent narrow-leaf evergreen for this country.

There are many introduced junipers that help fill the lack of narrow-leaf evergreen shrubs for southern use. Of course the red cedar, Juniperus virginiana, does well and is found extensively throughout the State, particularly about old home-sites.

This list, as well as the list of natives, could be greatly increased.

Part Two

MODERN GARDENS

Miss Jane Davant

Albany

IN a pine grove on the edge of town where the streets are unpaved and country still holds sway, is the picturesque garden of the Davants—rising out of native growth and after a bit melting into it again.

A winding path paved with pine needles and bordered with iris and lady slippers leads leisurely to the front door of the house where the angles shelter massed plantings of nandina, junipers, and Azalea formosa. At one side is a border of narcissi, amaryllis, plumbago and petunias to give continuous bloom for many months. On the other side the lawn stretches away into a shrubbery which merges into the native undergrowth of the fragrant pine woods in the background.

Behind the house the garden starts in twisting borders of annuals and perennials edged with the soft colored local limestone which is also used for stepping stones and for the wall which is one boundary of the garden. Vine-covered fences, a tangle of yellow jessamine, honeysuckle and roses, complete the enclosure of the charmingly informal garden plot. At the farther end is an irregular pool set in narrow rock plantings, and in the pool are lilies, poppies, hyacinths and many underwater plants, all lorded over by the stately lotus whose spicy pink blooms and huge leaf pads show in high relief against the encircling pines. Among the rocks grow creeping phloxes, heartsease, wild violets and bluebottles.

A group of four large pines inside the garden gives shade and shelter to a most colorful arrangement of azaleas—many native as well as imported kinds thriving here. Interplanted with them are wild ferns whose tall fronds appear when the azalea bloom has gone and then spread open to stay cool and green all summer.

Mr. and Mrs. Joseph A. Myer

Albany

PAST the lawns and iris borders which surround the house on the street side, Mrs. Myer has made her flower garden on two ascending levels by terracing the slope immediately to the rear of the house.

Rock steps, flanked by two fine Italian cypresses, lead up through the center of the banks to the two garden levels—the first one planted informally with many kinds of perennials and annuals, the upper one cut through by a flagstone walk ending at a stone bench with a pleasant outlook over the colorful ranks of bloom. The background of the rose garden, on the higher terrace, is a long rustic trellis and against the shrubbery outlines are plantings of brilliant amaryllis.

At the eastern end of the garden another trellis has yellow jessamine, wistaria and woodbine clambering over it in profusion. Evergreen and native shrubs here have underplantings of bulbs and wild flowers, while large beds of azaleas—the native as well as the cultivated—stretch between this higher point and the house.

A picturesque pool features the opposite southwest corner of the garden. Recessed and overhung to look like a natural little grotto, a tiny waterfall splashes into the pool over which a weeping willow droops, and growing from the surrounding rocks are maidenhair and many other varieties of wild ferns.

Evergreens and Rose Arbor, Myer Garden

Pool in Myer Garden

Iris Court

Miss Cena J. Whitehead
Albany

IN 1854 when Judge John Jackson, the grandfather of Miss Whitehead, built the house at Iris Court he also planned and planted the original garden. Many of the fine trees and shrubs set out then by the noted horticulturist, P. J. Berckmans, for Judge Jackson, are living today, increased in size and beauty, and composing a lovely dark evergreen background for the new formal garden, built in 1921 by Mrs. John Randolph Whitehead.

Among the specimen trees of the old garden now adding glamor to the new, are tall cedars—red, Lebanon and incense,—wild olives, hollies, magnolias, pecans and palm trees. The dogwoods have spread wide and into the fig trees a man may climb. There are thickets of the older spireas, big oleanders and pomegranates, and the air is musky when the pittosporum, gardenias and tea olive bloom. With these last three evergreen shrubs in a southern garden there is scarcely a month without some rich fragrance.

The new garden, which suggested the name, Iris Court, is connected with the house by iris paths, and in the formally laid beds are many lilies, iris, phlox, and other perennials to insure a succession of bloom from early spring till late fall.

Ashland Farm

Mrs. Z. C. Patten
Walker County

ALL the natural beauty of the North Georgia woodland has been most carefully preserved and protected at Ashland Farm, picturesquely situated in the foothills of Lookout Mountain. The spacious home, southern colonial in architecture, was constructed in 1904.

To quote Mrs. Patten: "Miss E. A. Andrews, whose 'Botany' is now in use in many public schools throughout the country, started me on my love for wild flowers. She was with me for several weeks the first spring we lived at Ashland Farm, and I think it will be interesting to many that she said our hillside which runs down to the creek contained more wild flowers than she had ever found anywhere in America in a similar area. One of my most cherished possessions is my 'Botany' in which she marked the flowers she found there with both their common and botanical names."

The woodland at Ashland Farm is never so entrancing as when spring contends with winter. Even under the snow the delicate hepatica blooms, wrapped in fuzzy furs against the cold and the pink blossom of trailing arbutus opens among withered leaves of oak and chestnut. Quaker Ladies, sometimes called "Bluettes," are among the first flowers to appear and in a few short weeks the woods are blue with bird's-foot violets.

Shortly before dogwood time Judas trees blossom, soon to be followed by sweet scented wild crabs. At the water's edge near the old mill are great patches of the delicate blue and pink of mertensias (Virginia bluebells) and along the winding pathways wood anemones grow in accordance with the Greek tradition that Anemos, the wind, sends his fragile namesakes to herald his coming in early spring. Next are foam flower, blue and white-eyed grass, and pink wood sorrel. A step farther on one may discover wild geranium, true Solomon's seal, wild delphinium, and trillium. Then a mass of blue phlox, mountain columbine, and white vetch, combine with primroses, jonquils and narcissi, these last adding to the charm of the wildings.

The sweet azalea appears in June, its spicy white flowers opening after the foliage, which in autumn turns to brilliant red. This is the largest of the native azaleas, sometimes attaining a height of twenty feet. Early in June the woods and hillsides are covered with fragrant masses of wild honeysuckles, rhododendron, and swamp azalea. These natives thrive in low, wet spots and are found here in soft tints of buff, sulphur, and primrose shading to orange and apricot, with tinges of vermillion.

Each season, in turn, brings to this woodland paradise fresh loveliness, yet it is perhaps nearest perfection when in April the spreading branches of countless flowering dogwoods whiten the landscape as though an untimely snow-storm had smothered hillside and deep ravine with dazzling white.

Mill at Ashland, Walker County

Ashland, Walker County

Ground Cover of Erythronium at Ashland

ATHENS

ATHENS, the "Classic City" of Georgia, which grew up about the site set apart for the state university in 1785, has changed less with the passing of the years—perhaps because of its quiet, academic mode of life—than most of its sister cities of Georgia. The atmosphere of the Old South still lingers under the spreading shade trees of its four green campuses and pervades its typical southern gardens. It has always been a city of garden lovers. Its old colonial homes stand back from the quiet streets, gleaming white through the green tracery of drooping boughs and tangled shrubbery, beckoning through boxwood-bordered pathways.

In the spring its dooryards offer a succession of flower shows for the delight of the passers-by—first forsythia and Japanese quince, then jonquils and violets, and in turn Cape jasmine, spirea, wistaria, iris, roses, and crepe myrtle. The town has a wealth of these, and many of the homes are notable for their Lady Banksias, weeping cherries, crabapples, and peonies.

Some of the loveliest old places are on hedge-bordered islands of privacy washed by the rising tide of commerce—such as the old Brumby and Gerdine places, still standing in the business section down town. And some, built before the town was laid out in its present form, are off the beaten track—including the Camak home behind the High School and the old Cobb place back of the Episcopal Church. Many are still on the borders of the original University campus, like the W. J. Morton place, home of Chancellor Snelling, the Madison Nicholson place, Miss Lucy Bishop's quaint home, and the old Crawford Long residence. A few are now used as public buildings—such as the Chief Justice Lumpkin home, which is the Athens Woman's Club, and the Governor Lumpkin place on the Agricultural College campus. Still others are chapter houses of the college fraternities. The former home of General T. R. R. Cobb, architecturally unique in its day by reason of its two octagonal wings, is occupied by the Lambda Tau Alphas, and the S. A. E. chapter house is in a beautiful old Greek Revival mansion.

Architecturally there is much of interest. Fine examples of old iron work are presented by the Hunnicutt house, the Barrett Phinizy home and the old Hamilton place, built by slave labor before the "War Between the States" and now owned by E. R. Hodgson, Jr. Varying styles of Greek columns are exemplified on the old Augustus Hull place, now the Darwin residence; the Henry Grady place, now the property of O. D. Grimes; the handsome old Upson home; the James White place (sometimes known as the Ben Hill place, because it was occupied for a time by Governor Benjamin Harvey Hill), which is now the home of James White's daughter, Mrs. W. F. Bradshaw; and the charming old red brick Dearing place, beloved by artists and sketchers.

This list is by no means complete. It would be difficult to name all the fine old southern colonial homes in Athens, and impossible to present in photographs the quality of their ante-bellum charm. Some have been faithfully restored and the best of the new homes conform in architecture to the classic tradition of yesterday, the gardens preserving in their main features the same characteristics of style. The former Lucy Cobb Institute campus, which has now become the property of the University—its buildings serving as girls' dormitories—is still laid out in the design used when that school was founded in 1856. The old Botanical Gardens, in the picturesque hollow at the end of Dearing Street, though fallen into decay, are still a treasure-trove of botanical specimens.

Many of the old homes have surrendered much of their original territory for city lots, but some of them are still surrounded by park-like areas, and every Athens garden is given a deeper meaning by its setting which is hallowed by associations with the historic past.

Mr. and Mrs. E. R. Hodgson, Jr.
Athens

A SPOT altogether typical of the classic atmosphere which is peculiarly Athens' is the garden of Mr. and Mrs. E. R. Hodgson, Jr.

The Hodgsons bought and restored an old house built by the Hamiltons with slave labor before the war, and they have been as careful to preserve the character of the landscaping and planting as of the architecture. This is truly an old garden, for while the original plots were overgrown and fallen into decay, the terracing has been left untouched and most of the shrubs and flowers here now are descendants of the old ones. All of the plants belong to the period which the garden represents, for the owners have been careful to introduce no varieties which did not exist in ante-bellum days.

The ascent to the front of the house from the street is made by a succession of concave crescent-shaped terraces on which, in spring, yellow jonquils bloom row on row by thousands. The house itself is an example of the square cement-covered brick style of architecture with iron grill trim on the front porch. The rear elevation, white-painted like the rest of the house, with low wings, a wide railed veranda and quaint outside staircase, looks over the back garden. Old-fashioned gardens may be imitated, but nothing except the mellowing of time can produce an effect like this old home as seen from the garden, shaded by its magnificent oak trees.

The garden is large, several acres in extent. It drops away from the house in three grassy terraces with steps set into the turf, but so wide are the terraces that the total effect is that of a sweeping level, the last terrace barely visible through the trees.

There is no formal planting. Everywhere the effort has been made to preserve the restful effect of wide stretches of lawn deep in shade. The plantings are all of old-fashioned shrubs—English laurel, wild olive, Japanese quince, flowering crab-apple. Opposite the back porch and in such a position that it can be seen through the front door and down the length of the long central hall when both entrances are open, is a clump of wild olive, whose glossy leaves catch the sunlight, and reflect it from a thousand facets. This planting, originally placed to screen a barn which has long since been torn down, is delightful when viewed on a summer's day, framed between the sidelights of the hospitable colonial doorway and down the cool length of the stately hall.

To the west of the house lies a small formal flower garden with brick paths and low box hedges. It is a spring and fall garden, in spring abloom with daffodils, narcissi, tulips, and delphinium, and in fall with asters and chrysanthemums. Most of these have been propagated from the bulbs and roots of flowers in the original garden.

The whole place is on the scale of life of the more spacious days, and, in the play of light and shade, on grass, trees and sweeping lawns, recalls the dignity of that life which passed with the period of the old South.

Old Grove from Garden Walk

Mrs. E. K. Lumpkin
Athens

TWO views are given of the home of Mrs. E. K. Lumpkin, in Athens, one of the front of the house, which was built in the fifties by a son of Richard D. B. Taylor, a prominent citizen, the other of Mrs. Lumpkin's parlor, where the meeting was held in January, 1891, which resulted in the formation of the Ladies' Garden Club, and the election of the first set of officers of that body.

The Ladies' Garden Club has continued in existence ever since, although the name has been changed to the Garden Club of Athens. On the authority of P. J. Berckmans of Augusta, who was at the zenith of his career as a horticulturist at the time of its organization, this was the first club of its kind to be formed in America, with a president and other officers working on a parliamentary basis.

Mrs. Lamar Cobb was elected president; Mrs. Lumpkin, vice president; Mrs. S. J. Tribble, secretary; and Miss Julia Carleton, treasurer. The other members were Mrs. T. P. Vincent, Mrs. Tinsley Rucker, Mrs. John Gerdine, Mrs. G. C. Thomas, Mrs. Henry West, Mrs. R. D. Mure, and Mrs. W. B. Burnett. Each member pledged herself to a different line of work: Mrs. Cobb, for instance, experimented with strawberries, Mrs. Lumpkin with roses and asparagus, and Miss Julia Carleton with the saving of fine seed that would be acclimated to this section. All the members specialized in something in which they had a common interest.

In 1891 they began staging the flower shows which have been an outstanding feature of the club's activities ever since. At first they held two shows annually, one in the spring and one in the fall, with exhibits of flowers and vegetables grown by club members. For a number of years an annual rose show was staged on the grounds of the old court house, now the site of the Athens High

Parlor where Ladies' Garden Club was organized in 1891

Lumpkin Home

School. During the years of 1917 and 1918 the club concentrated on war knitting, the rolling of bandages and other Red Cross work, but in 1919 flower shows were resumed on a larger scale than formerly. The first flower show in 1891 would have been considered a comical thing in comparison with the elaborate exhibits of today, for Athens is well known for the beauty of its shows, which take high rank among cities of its size anywhere. The ladies in those early years brought their flowers and fruits and vegetables in whatever bowls and baskets the individual household provided, along with all the other potted plants they could muster, and set them about, without any attempt at classification, in the old Y. M. C. A. Hall. After the first one or two shows they called upon Mr. Berckmans to come up from Augusta to help, and he collected the various displays into groups and established some sort of order and made up a set of rules and a premium list. By 1894 the club had a printed premium list and set of rules drawn up by Mr. Berckmans "to prevent any unpleasantness between the members," which might well serve as a guide for staging a flower show today. Several copies of that "Premium List of the Third Annual Chrysanthemum Show and Vegetable Exhibition of the Ladies' Garden Club of Athens, Georgia," are still owned by families of the original members, and one is the property of the Athens Garden Club.

Athens girls who had married and gone elsewhere to live wrote home for copies of Mr. Berckman's rules to use in establishing similar shows in their new homes, and from this requests for copies came in from many other places. It is known that in different sections of the country garden clubs modeled on the Ladies' Garden Club of Athens, were organized wherever these little books found their way, one of them as far north as Maine.

The furnishings of the room as shown in the picture are in general just as they were at the time of the establishment of the first garden club, except that the furniture, which has now been re-covered, was then a set of horsehair chairs and sofa.

Box Garden

S. A. E. Chapter House

Athens

THE accompanying view is of the S. A. E. House in Athens, now used as a chapter house by one of the University of Georgia fraternities. It is one of the oldest homes in Athens. The box garden, a part of which shows in the photograph, was planted by the builder of the house, Mr. Ross Crane, ninety-one years ago and is still very beautiful. It was formerly one of the handsomest in this part of the State. The long walk was bordered on both sides with box from the house to the street. Outside the box borders ran paths of white sand, which were in turn edged with cypress trees and rose bushes. In time the house was sold by its builder and later owners destroyed most of the old time garden. The old magnolias on the lawn, survivors of the original garden, today are magnificent specimens.

Dr. and Mrs. R. E. Park
Athens

HIDDEN away behind the residence of Dr. and Mrs. R. E. Park on quaint old Dearing Street is a garden which is typical of the modern small garden. Two sections have been completed; one semi-formal, the other naturalistic. In the semi-formal garden a path encircles three sides of a space of turf in the center, which is shaded by mimosa and pecan trees. Beyond the path the borders, laid out in serpentine curves, are planted in peonies, geum, Madonna lilies, and flowering crab-apple. At one side is a bird bath surrounded by iris and lilacs, and opposite is a trellis supporting a fine Lady Banksia rose which is flanked by lilacs which are in lavender bloom at the same time the rose is a mass of yellow. Stone seats are placed against a background of spirea and arbor vitae, garden figures are used among the shrubbery and in the center lawn are inviting groups of furniture and gay umbrellas.

At each side the path ends in a flight of brick steps leading down to the level of the rustic garden where a pool lies in the center of a grassy plot. Oblong in shape, the pool has a rim of flat stones and at either end mounds of prone cedar give length to the design. Beyond a pergola fronts a group of Lombardy poplars which overtop a hedge trimmed to rise to its greatest height directly behind the pergola and behind the hedge a magnificent oak completes the banked effect of the background. A rock terrace between the two levels of the garden is planted with ivy, thrift, and phlox subulata.

Of interest in the border plantings is a Florida palm which has so far survived the Georgia winters. The colors are, in the main, in delicate shades and a great deal of Texas bluebonnet is used, but one brilliant splash is afforded by a clump of Scotch broom against a Paul's Scarlet climber on a trellis. Dogwood, azaleas, Persian lilac, and redbud grow in the border, while pansies and candytuft edge it.

Seats have been built around the shade trees, and trellises support the climbing roses. American Beauties and American Pillars meet on the pergola, while two lovely Jacotte roses are trained over the side of the house on the open terrace.

Dr. and Mrs. Henry Reid

Athens

THE garden of Dr. and Mrs. Reid shows a pleasing variation in types, and serves as an outdoor extension for family activities.

On a lower level than the front lawns the gardens are entered by steps sunk between the moss-covered stones of a terrace planted with rock plants —ferns, sedums, forget-me-nots, thrift and various cacti. A flat-rimmed pool, fringed in ivy, is set back in a recess of the bank and is overshadowed by tall English laurel and nandina, while around it maiden hair fern, Japanese iris and other flowers that thrive in moist soil abound.

Beyond the pool the rock garden extends the length of the formally planned portion of the main garden which is divided into two sections connected by a rose hung pergola and flag stone paths under trellises of roses. In the scheme of the two gardens two features add balance to the design. At one end of the enclosure an ornamental gazing globe stands in a curve of shrubbery behind which tall poplar trees are grouped. Opposite this at the far end of the formal planting lies a curved pool holding a fountain figure and flanked by two graceful urns. The flower beds in this section of the garden are patterned around a smooth stretch of lawn and in the boundary plantings of various flowering and evergreen shrubs. Here, too, are Mrs. Reid's extensive collection of iris, and a succession of perennials in color arrangements of pink, blue and white.

On the pergola Silver Moon and Chaplin roses are combined while the trellises bear the old-time favorite Marechal Niel, but a rose garden which lies between the shrubbery and the children's play garden offers the main rose display.

In the rustic garden the planting is informal, the background of evergreens setting off the pink and white flowering shrubs, the borders colorful with pinks and pansies, and the eulalias and pampas grass showing ornamental plumes.

Corner of Informal Garden

Beech Haven

Mr. and Mrs. C. A. Rowland

Athens

MANY years ago Mr. and Mrs. C. A. Rowland, of Athens, purchased a tract of over two hundred acres of wooded land on the banks of the winding Oconee, and in developing it have been careful not to destroy a single feature of the wild grandeur of rock, woodland pool, and tangled solitude. They have preserved the thickly clustered laurel on banks of tumbling streams, the splendid rhododendrons on wooded hillsides and the many twisted vines draped from tree to tree.

From an entrance gate set in a wild hedge a mile of roadway leads through pine forests, follows the bank of "Boulder Creek" and crosses a stone bridge over an irregularly-shaped pool filled with water plants. Before it reaches the house, the road leads past many restful spots overlooking scenes of woodland beauty. A flight of steps leading up to the house from the banks of Boulder Creek is flanked by two rows of stone lanterns built of the natural rock set at intervals along the stairway. Finally the drive winds in a wide semi-circle up three sides of the hill on which the house is placed. Within the curve of the driveway a formal garden is laid out.

In the heart of the woodland stands the rustic home which has served for many years as a summer residence for the family. Opposite the roughhewn stone porch of the main residence a long path cut through the trees and irregularly paved with stepping stones mounts the hill to a tennis court and furnishes a vista somewhat like the pleached allees of more formal gardens.

On a level stretch of ground within easy reach of the house is an outdoor kitchen with stone fireplace and benches for picnic suppers and barbecues.

Between the formal garden and the barn a long scuppernong arbor stretches across one side of a walkway, and at one corner of the barn a narrow path drops off through the woods and down a steep hillside to a spring. At the foot of the hill this woodland path crosses a tiny branch on a camelback bridge built of stone in imitation of the steep arched bridges of Japan. The grassy space around the spring is walled in, with comfortable armed benches built into the rock. From this point rustic signs on the trees point the visitor over the hills by stepping stones to the "Silver Shoals" of the river.

Everywhere throughout the estate flowers have been planted in groupings of a size commensurate with the large area and suitable to this type of garden. From early spring, when the fruit trees and flowering Japanese cherries are in blossom, on through the seasons of wistaria, red-bud and dogwood, laurel, rhododendron and iris, Beech Haven is a center of attraction to the nature-lovers of Athens and the surrounding communities.

Woodland Bridge, Beech Haven

Laurel and Rhododendron along Boulder Creek, Beech Haven

Mr. and Mrs. Lamar Rucker

Athens

THE garden of Mr. and Mrs. Lamar Rucker, although new in the sense that they have had all the joy of creation, is old enough to have the charm of ante-bellum days and the advantage of specimen shade trees planted before the middle of the last century, for Mr. and Mrs. Rucker bought one of the historic places of Athens and have carefully restored it to its original beauty.

The home stands on level ground at the top of a slope that drops sharply to Tanyard Branch, the stream which separates the two sides of the University campus. The house, built in 1829, was the first home on "the other side" of Tanyard Branch. It has belonged to a succession of owners whose names are connected with the early days of the University. Among these was William H. Jackson, son of Governor James Jackson, who so loved a certain spreading oak in the shade of which he was wont to sit and read that he set aside the ground surrounding it as a grant to the tree itself in his will. The "tree that owns itself" stands now on the opposite side of Dearing Street, but still reaches out its branches toward the old home in benediction. Another occupant was Professor Ward who had charge of the Botanical Gardens planted back in the fifties by the Department of Natural History in the University.

Several trees in the garden surrounding the Rucker home have survived the ravages of the War Between the States and the mutations of the lean

Grancy Greybeard and Roses in Garden Background, Rucker Garden

years that followed. Flourishing in the finished beauty of the restored area are a stately ginkgo tree whose leaf, shaped like the maidenhair fern, turns to gold in the winds of autumn; a Kentucky coffee tree; a swamp cypress; a rare buckeye and three varieties of magnolia.

In recent years a small formal garden has been added and on the east side of the house, an uncovered brick terrace bordered with boxwood has been laid. A flight of stone steps leads down to the lower garden. Here is a platform with a rugged fireplace and rock seats. Beside it a winding stream runs from beneath large boulders down the steep hillside, and Japanese iris and wild azaleas grow in profusion through the bog. In an irregular bed hollyhocks, hardy phlox, and other perennials flower before a background of oak-leaf hydrangeas and tall bamboo. A Paul's Scarlet climber blooms on a trellis over the house door which opens onto the terrace, and dwarf boxwood flanks the wide pathway leading up to the front entrance.

At the foot of the hill toward Tanyard Branch is a wall of bamboo with arbor vitae and althea planted in front to form a screen from the street. A feature of the garden is an arbor holding an Emily Gray rose that has grown so huge it is almost a tree. It is covered in spring with a blanket of golden blossoms.

Mrs. Rucker's favorite spot is her "moonlight garden." Lingering here one feels the peace of an old garden haunted by sweet memories.

Mr. and Mrs. Bolling Hall Sasnett

Athens

IN January, 1932, Mrs. Bolling Hall Sasnett undertook the restoration of the gardens about the colonial home after a family absence of fifteen years. Of the original plantings, only the privet hedge that enclosed the back garden and the handsome trees were left. A little cottage at the back of the garden, guarded by a pine which had stood since "before the war" still housed the old negro mammy of the family.

With the house, the trees, the hedge and the cottage as background, Mrs. Sasnett aimed for a blossoming garden by April 22nd, the date of the meeting of the Garden Club of Georgia in Athens.

The house was Southern Colonial, the entrance striking the keynote of the whole—spaciousness, leisurely living, a sense of ampleness and freedom—so the garden was made a place of leisurely enjoyment, a retreat from the noise and hurry of the outside world.

A definite color scheme of pastel tints: cream, pink, blue and yellow, was worked out in the acid soil of shady spots, with brighter tones in the open sunlight. The relation of each mass of color to the whole scheme has been well considered in the placing of plants and the design of the garden is worked out by a fine choice of flowers. The formal planting about the house achieves its color scheme with pink azaleas, blue Phlox divaricata, daphne, and yellow pansies. Spanish and Dutch iris in the open sunlight make gay mantles of color, mixed with fleecy white gypsophila, fragrant lemon lilies and pink pentstemon. Great splashes of vivid pigments were added with German iris.

There is no more effective feature in the planting plan than the naturalistic pool, which, with its irregular, flower-sprinkled outline on one side and its smooth matrix of turf on the other, its black waters mirroring a weeping cherry tree, feathery and delicate as a mist, lies at the foot of the lawn.

By April 22, 1932, the garden was alive with bloom!

A more substantial planting has been worked out since the Garden Club Meeting, and 1933 finds shrubbery background, numerous perennials, and water plants increasing the beauty and assuring the permanency of this garden which was "rushed to the front" in the emergency of 1932.

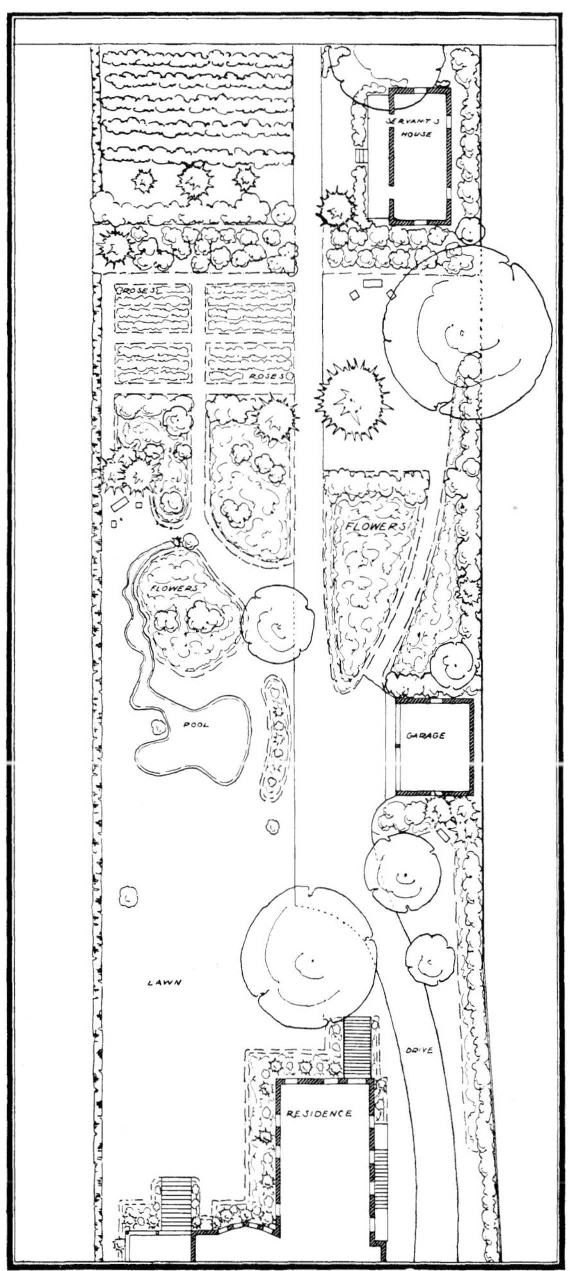

Plan of Sasnett Garden

Lotus in Sasnett Garden

Misses Upson

Athens

THE Upson house* stands on Prince Avenue, half hidden by giant magnolias and hemlocks, a perfect example of the Greek Revival style of architecture. It was built by Gazaway Lamar of Macon, and a boxwood maze was originally in front, but magnolias and hemlocks are today the dominating features of a broad lawn.

The old place was a plantation home when it was bought by the father of the Misses Upson, Stephen Upson, in 1883, and though the gardens are new, many features of the landscaping are survivals of an earlier era. In the vista from the back porch, used by the family as a living room in summer, is an old well, a brick carriage house clothed in climbing roses, and a smoke house. Back of the house flower-bordered lawns stretch away past these landmarks to a fenced vegetable garden.

The house faces south. To the east a formal garden, one of the most elaborate in this part of Georgia, is made on three levels. The upper level is a terrace lying along the wall of the old house and reached by low steps from the end of the high pillared porch. From the north side of the terrace, steps go down to a green garden on the second level, which is oval in shape, of smooth green turf, and planted in Italian cypress, ligustrum, junipers, and Lombardy poplars. Leading through this garden from the terrace above to the flower garden below, is a twelve-foot allee of arbor vitae. At the point where the arbor vitae allee makes an intersection with the hedge about the formal flower garden two Magnolia soulangeanas have been used to give height and accent to the entrance. These trees are an example of the manner in which the old plantings have been utilized in enhancing the beauty of the new gardens. A very

* See early garden section.

old specimen of this magnolia had grown so large that it was easily capable of division and the transplanted trees now spread above the arbor vitae to form tall entrance pillars abloom with purple blossoms in early spring, and add a note of sentiment in their association with the past.

A vista from the terrace through the green garden and into the flower garden is terminated by a statue placed in a semi-circle of the boundary hedge. Steps lead down at each side of the statue one flight to a croquet ground, the other into a cut flower area, from which an interesting pathway leads into a long pleached allee of ligustrum, where stands a second statue.

Eastward the terrace overlooks yet another garden, a small round one centered with a pool and placed where the grass tennis courts of an older generation formerly lay. One side of the circle cuts into the terrace in an arc, where the steps descend. North of the circular garden is a formal planting of Ligustrum amurense, a square measuring sixty feet each way, which has stood since the early days of the old place and is thought to be among the first introduced into Georgia. It has been cleared out below but allowed to grow together in a thick shade overhead to afford a cool and shadowy retreat in summer.

Beyond the circular garden and to the east are the new tennis courts, and northward toward the vegetable garden a rose garden is being developed.

West of the house another and smaller terrace is laid out in formal design and is bound with a low hedge inside of which is a border of iris. The geometric figures of the design are executed in lines of hedge, with Spanish bayonet used to accent the breaks. Behind it the service driveway, cleverly concealed, enters on a lower level, and beyond the drive is a wide rolling lawn with fine specimens of cedar, lilac, Lawson cypress, and flowering quince, many of which are of the original plantings.

ATLANTA

Home of Mr. and Mrs. Henry Heinz

Druid Hills in Spring

April Color in Formal Garden at Pinebloom

Pinebloom

Mr. and Mrs. Preston Arkwright

Dr. and Mrs. Glenville Giddings

Atlanta

THE old home of Mrs. Arkwright's family, the Colquitts of South Georgia, has lent its name "Pinebloom" to this Druid Hills estate. An added sentiment attached to the name comes from a legend of the Georgia countryside that the pine tree blooms so luxuriantly every seven years that the ground beneath the trees is thickly carpeted with yellow pollen and that this exerts a kind of magic to bring happiness and prosperity to a homestead founded, as this one was, in a year of the golden dust!

Not only pines but many other desirable native trees, white oaks, sweet gums with their burgundy foliage in autumn, beeches, hickories, flowering crabs and especially numerous dogwoods of fine size shade the lawns which spread in a gentle rise from the stream on the western boundary up to the plateau on which the house is built. Cherry laurel, grown into sizable trees, combines with the native pines to make evergreen backgrounds for the white clouds of dogwood in spring and for groups of pink English hawthorn.

The house, of English type, its foundation planting of hedges and large specimens of old boxwood, looks out over living-room terraces of grass or flagstones, bound in, too, by hedges of box, towards the gardens which are so placed as to be a part of each day's—even each rainy day's—enjoyment. The formal garden is connected with the south terrace by wide steps of gray stone, and flagstone walkways, bordered in boxwood, outline the beds designed about a circular pool edged with the same stone. The whole pattern is enclosed by graduating lines of box hedges inside a screen of evergreens,

each of the four corners heightened by tall arbor vitae and, towards the lawn, by massed plantings of nandina.

Strips of evergreen grass separate the paths from the four large flower beds where, for spring, the color scheme is blue and yellow, later to change gradually into an all white garden, cool and fragrant for summers of intense sunshine. In April and May a subtle gradation of color, height and texture is achieved by an excellent planting scheme. Spilling over the edges of the beds is a profusion of blue and yellow blossoms: phlox divaricata, alyssum saxatile, forget-me-nots, early lemon gaillardias, dwarf yellow feverfew and violas. Behind these, doranicum, blue chimney bells and stokesia are set off by heuchera and bleeding heart whose rosy hues only intensify the masses of blue and yellow. Perry's Siberian iris, German iris in blues and yellows, groups of pinkish gold tritomas rising from mists of anchusa, give heightening emphasis of foliage and flower, and, repeating the faint notes of rose near the borders, each bed has in its further corners a clump of exquisite single peonies whose gold anthered centres are flowers in themselves. Veronicas, cynoglossum, sweet william and memorial daisies link the spring garden with the later white of hardy phlox, shastas, lilies, verbenas and small white chrysanthemums, set off in high relief by the surrounding evergreens.

From the formal garden an iris walk leads to the rock garden, and other flagged paths approach the terraced cutting garden, the children's playground with its garden and pool, and the cabin where a wide fieldstone paving under old sweet gum trees holds benches and tables made from huge curved slabs of native rock.

A natural terrace marked out by lichen-covered boulders and shaded by some of the largest trees, runs irregularly across the slope above the stream. Winding paths with rough stone steps go through plantations of laurel, native azalea, rhododendrons and tree ferns, and hugging the gray rocks are mats of sedums, vinca, and mosses of many kinds. Seventy-five varieties of native wild flowers thrive here in healthy colonies. Such woodland beauties as bloodroot, lady slipper, bird's bill, trillium, jack-in-the-pulpit, heart leaves, galax and arbutus are tucked in among the rocks and gnarled old tree roots, while in the deepest shade a wide patch of maidenhair fern surrounds a bird bath hollowed out of an old piece of moss covered granite.

Mayfair

Mr. and Mrs. Henry Morrell Atkinson
Mr. and Mrs. Jackson P. Dick
Atlanta

CURVING walls of white brick, topped by wooden railings and delicate colonial urns, outline the Habersham Way boundary of Mayfair, the home of Mr. and Mrs. H. M. Atkinson and Mr. and Mrs. Jackson P. Dick. Along the walls are climbing roses, wistaria and jessamine, while behind them grow thickets of evergreens and red fruited firethorns. Mimosa trees further screen the house from the road but the wide iron gates disclose a view of the tall columns and classic portico of a long brick house shining white from a setting of southern evergreens and emerald lawns. Georgia pines make traceries on the painted white brick, old Virginia red cedars are at either end of the house, and the lustrous greens of magnolias, holly trees, Carolina cherry laurel and Cape jasmine are much in evidence but the dominant feature of the picture is the splendid old boxwood which is so massed it seems an integral part of the architecture.

Two twenty-foot specimens of tree box flank the entrance portico and two enormous pieces of dwarf box, whose trunks measure five inches in diameter, lean towards the main door. The low walls of the fore-court and turn-around are almost hidden by billowing hedges of dwarf box while conical and rounded specimens of the intermediate kind are used as accents on the branching drives to the service courts. In spring Azalea hinodigeri is vivid near the house. Pyracantha yunnanensis, espaliered against the walls between two of the green-shuttered windows, adds a color note in win-

One of Twin Gardens at Mayfair

Entrance, Mayfair

Along the Road to Mayfair

ter but the clear cut composition of white and strong dark greens against the blue Georgia sky is particularly striking when summer brings to the magnolias and Cape jasmine their decoration of white bloom.

On the opposite—southwest—facade is a long high-columned porch opening onto two levels of grass terraces which command woodland views and are shaded by big oak trees. Here, defining the curved retaining wall of the lower level is another fine hedge of dwarf box. The two walled and iron-railed terraces, the width of the verandah, separate two small formal gardens which lie flush with the house at either side of the porch and whose low brick walls extend from the house.

The problem of a home for two families has been successfully solved in the plan of this double house and the balanced scheme is completed in the two "Siamese" gardens with their twin old lead wall founts and almost identical planting. The original designs for the setting of the house and the twin gardens were made by Ellen Shipman in 1929. The later planting is by Constance Draper.

At either side of the steps leading down into the two gardens are matched pieces of dwarf box and their duplicates flank the lead founts facing them across the central panels of turf. Box-edged flower beds are separated from the wide borders by narrow grass paths. The pattern is simple and symmetrical enough to be charming even when there is no bloom. There are two big rounded specimens of holly-leafed tea olive (Osmanthus fortunei) for evergreen emphasis and lower clumps of tea plant (Thea bohea). Cotoneaster horizontalis is trained on the low outer walls while against the house are clipped pyracanthas. For spring, tulips, Spanish iris, and anemones are planted among the permanent old-fashioned perennials and are followed by a succession of lilies, the bulbous kinds combined with hemerocallis and funkias, to bloom till the ginger lilies of late fall add their perfume to the fainter fragrance of the tiny bloom of the osmanthus. The waxy flowers of the tea plant (mother of Camellias) last almost till Christmas and all winter

Estate of
Henry - M - Atkinson
Atlanta - Georgia
Golf Course
Ellen Shipman

the berries of cotoneaster and pyracanthas are colorful against the white walls.

The long veranda and terraces of this side of the house look down a slope of natural woods, full of rhododendron and laurel, towards a stream at the foot of the hill where native azaleas flame in early spring under tall beeches and cucumber trees. From the lower terrace a "rocky Primrose Path" descends through the woods where hepaticas, trilliums, foam-flowers, wood violets, and Siberian squills are in drifts among the primroses. Daffodils and Scilla nutans have been naturalized through the woodlands, and vinca, gound ivy and trailing ranunculus are used as ground covers in the dense shade. Along the stream's edge grow yellow water iris, "hunter's cup" pitcher plants, lady slippers, and zephyr lilies. A cedar footbridge twined with yellow jessamine crosses the stream to the vine hung tennis court on the other side. In the meadow beyond is a small golf course hidden from the high road by a hedge of arbor vitae next the iron fence which is planted in climbing roses. Willows, pecans and white paulownia trees grow on this level greensward.

A pine needle road follows the stream westward past a tiny duck pond and winds through untouched woods to "Sweet-Shrub Shack," the children's log cabin playhouse and barbecue pit. Further on are the barns, stables, kennels and rabbit hutches. Then comes a wide cleared space, the stream and woodland trees in the background, where a cutting garden has been made, its upper boundary a hillside laid in three rock-walled terraces.

A survey discovers forty different varieties of trees growing in this 30 acre tract, dogwoods, Judas, styrax, and crabapples being the most conspicuous of the spring flowering natives. All through the year birds of many kinds and colors dwell in these protected glades, and a complete list of the wild flowers, shrubs and trees would fill many pages. Fortunately they are so cared for that their tribes have increased and the woods of Mayfair are as interesting a feature of the place as the formally planted shrubberies and gardens near the house.

Southlook

Mr. and Mrs. H. Cobb Caldwell
Atlanta

THE home of Mr. and Mrs. H. Cobb Caldwell on Peachtree Road is one of the oldest in the vicinity of Atlanta, the original building having been erected by Mr. House in 1825, on property known at one time as the Luckie place. General Sherman, with his staff, occupied the old house on the afternoon and night of July 20, 1864, two days before the Battle of Atlanta.

Mr. W. T. Ashford, Mrs. Caldwell's father, bought the property in 1903, and later purchased adjoining lands which increased the estate to fifteen hundred acres, the lawns and gardens about the home now covering approximately fourteen acres. Near the main house still stand the kitchens and outbuildings of old hand made red brick, overhung by tremendous chinaberry trees, and the great clumps of yucca and boxwood planted sixty years ago today almost hide the old smoke-house. The "big house" has been added to and a considerable change made in its appearance by a porch with classic columns, and for many years Mrs. Caldwell, by a wise use of distinctively southern material, has planned and planted her gardens faithfully in keeping with the spirit of antebellum days.

Facing the highroad is a large lawn with the many trees and shrubs arranged so as to leave an

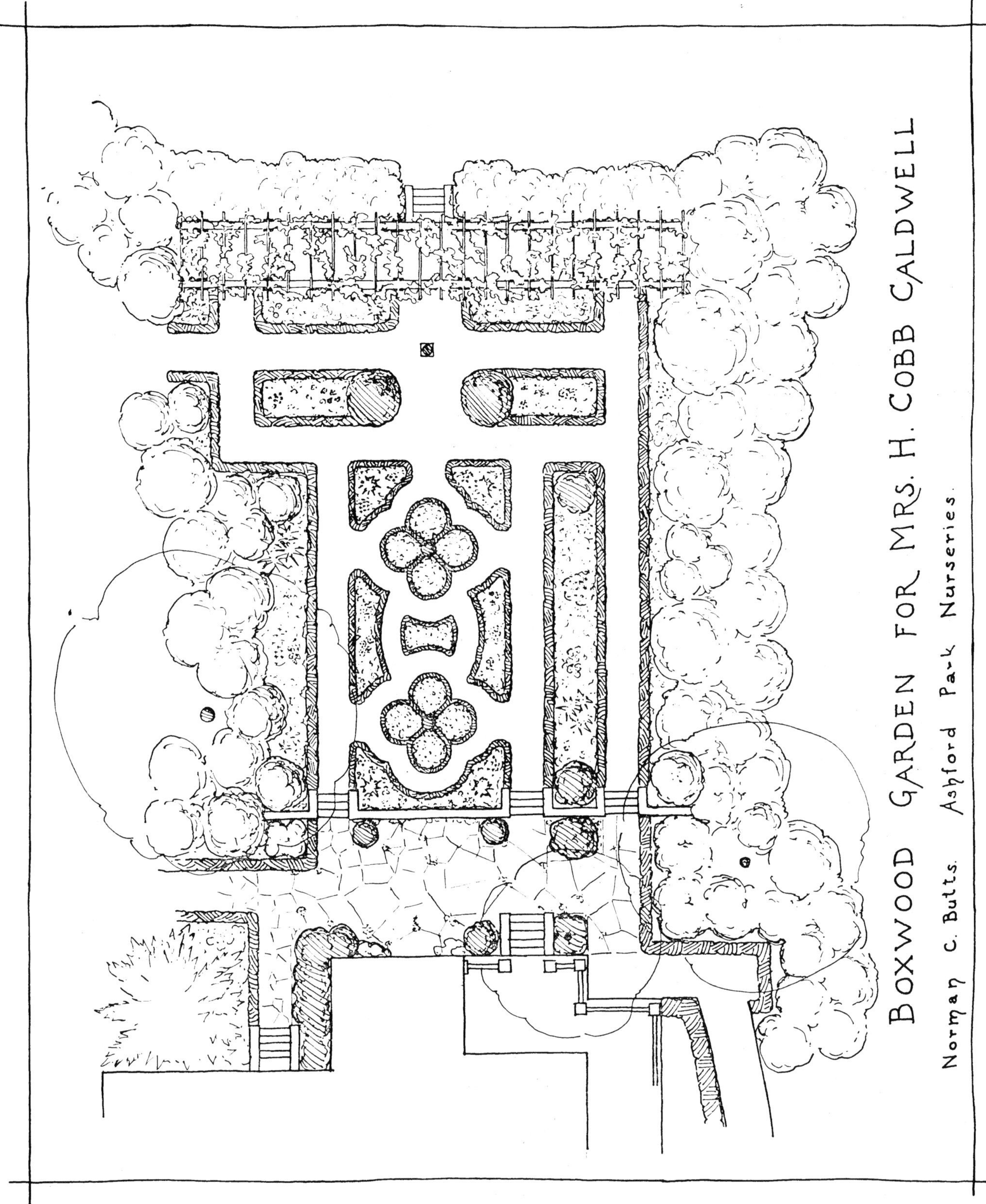
BOXWOOD GARDEN FOR MRS. H. COBB CALDWELL
Norman C. Butts. Ashford Park Nurseries.

Mimosa Walk, Southlook

Rock Garden at Southlook

open oval-shaped space on the west axis of the house. The driveway curves in, past heavy plantings of evergreens, hedges of crepe myrtle and a particularly noticeable white wistaria bush, to a porte cochere on the west side of the house. Here, past the foundation planting of old boxwood lies an informal garden, an irregularly shaped lawn bordered by shrubs, boxwood and bands of lilies and spring bulbs. At the far end and to the right is the entrance to the cutting garden enclosed by a tall privet hedge. The paths through the wide beds of perennials and roses converge on an old time wrought iron summer house which is hung in star jasmine and clematis. Magnolia trees show in the background and old briar roses are at the intersections of the paths, while nepeta, lavender, rosemary and santolina soften the path lines between the perennials.

From this garden a walk cut like a tunnel through thickets of cherry laurel and bordered with snow drops and vinca comes out on the north lawn to the rear of the house where a group of picturesque old red maples, with the daffodils naturalized in the grass, compose a lovely picture in springtime.

Diagonally across the lawn is a small lake overhung by weeping willows, its banks lush with water iris and cattails while water-lilies of many sorts are conspicuous among the other aquatic plants. Around the lake, a series of rock gardens set in the farther woods make this one of the most interesting newer parts of the place, with a great variety of plants, including many rare wild flowers. A paved terrace, shaded by an old sweet gum tree, overlooks the lake and in another secluded corner is a grass plot with garden furniture. Near by is a particularly charming birch shaded pool, while below the lake a series of tiny water-falls end in a brook which wanders between colonies of azaleas, laurel and other natives.

Turning back toward the house, a long walk bordered with perennials and lilies and arched overhead by mimosa trees leads to a flagstone terrace at the east side of the house which overlooks an old fashioned boxwood garden (the plan of which is reproduced.) Along with the boxwood the plants typical of old southern gardens grow —such as crepe myrtle, banana shrub, fragrant tea olive and even a camellia or two, which only occasionally accustom themselves to outdoor conditions in this part of the State. The far boundary of the garden is a white-columned pergola weighted down by wistaria and trumpet vine. The parterres are full of old time annuals and perennials and in summer the background evergreens bring into high relief the fragrant lavender spikes of the chaste trees and the vivid bloom of the great hedges of crepe myrtle behind them.

Here at Southlook can be found an unusually fine collection of southern plant material—in trees, shrubs and flowers—wide in scope and of great interest to the horticulturist.

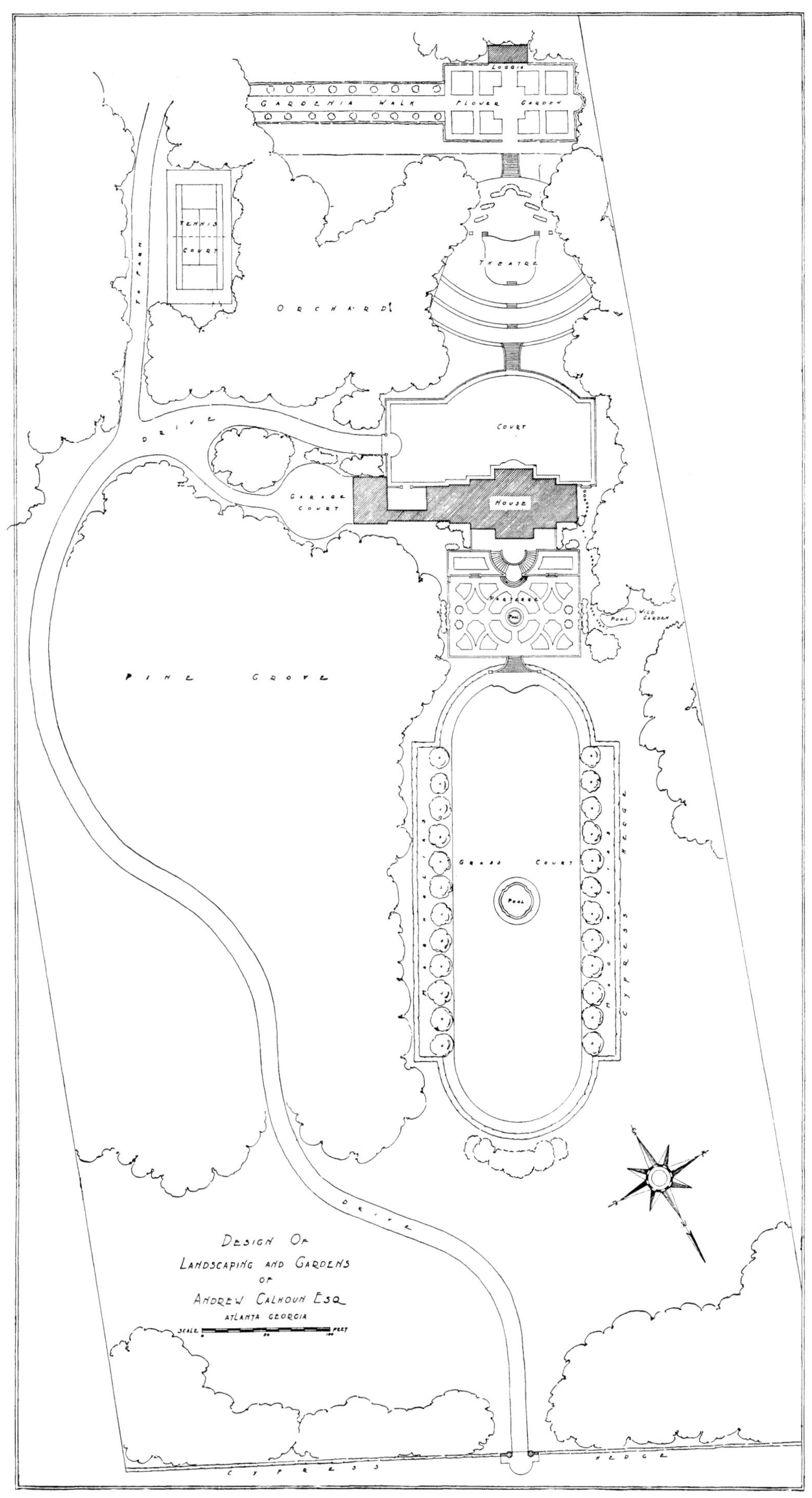
LOGGIA
GARDENIA WALK
FLOWER GARDEN
TENNIS COURT
ORCHARD
THEATRE
DRIVE
COURT
GARAGE COURT
HOUSE
POOL
WILD GARDEN
PINE GROVE
GRASS COURT
POOL
CYPRESS HEDGE
DESIGN OF
LANDSCAPING AND GARDENS
OF
ANDREW CALHOUN ESQ
ATLANTA GEORGIA
SCALE 0 50 100 FEET
CYPRESS HEDGE

Trygveson

Mr. and Mrs. Andrew Calhoun
Atlanta

Photo by F. E. Lee

ITALY in Georgia—this is not as far a cry as it seems—for the Georgia climate offers every aid to reproduce the growth and color characteristic of Italian country places—or villas. The Georgia blue sky, forests of tall pines, luxuriant southern evergreens overgrown by a profusion of climbing roses, great tropical plantings of yucca, allees of magnolias and Cape jasmine—all these as a setting for an Italian house of plaster, colored like the strata of Georgia clay, make a picture which re-creates vividly the atmosphere of the villas of Tuscany.

The late Neel Reid, whose genius as a landscape architect gave such beautiful surroundings to the fine houses he designed, in 1923 planned this villa for Mr. and Mrs. Andrew Calhoun.

On Pace's Ferry Road, where the boundary screen is of cedars and cherry laurel, the rust tinted entrance gates frame a dramatic view of the house and its sunken gardens set far back on a tree-shadowed hill. A drive, traversing wide lawns, winds through pine groves where native azaleas echo the sunset colors of the house, then leads between dense plantings of eleagnus, Spanish bayonet and gardenias to the semi-circular entrance court of the facade opposite the gates. Here wistaria festoons the loggia connecting house and garage, magnolias are espaliered against the faded orange walls, and, as in Italy, there are many pots and tubs containing pomegranates, orange trees, oleanders and geraniums.

The views from the court yard look over the orchards and the distant terraced cutting gardens towards the farm and vineyards which are partly screened by pines, mimosas and thickets of bamboo. The children's playhouse and tennis courts are

Photo by F. E. Lee

Rose Time at Trygveson

View of Formal Garden from Terrace of House, Trygveson

Photo by F. E. Lee

hidden by the eleagnus and honeysuckle which have grown high into the trees surrounding them.

At one side of the walled court, steps descend through fragrant tea-olive and boxwood to a wild garden and tiny frog pool where azaleas, kalmias, and native ferns grow from carpetings of many sorts of violets.

The Baroque style of the house is carried on and completed in the architecture of the formal terraced gardens on the facade facing the road. Curving double stairs, separated by a wall fountain, descend from the high walled terrace of the house to a garden of boxwood and clipped ivy parterres. In the center is a fountain pool with sponge-stone ornamentation, in the side walls are niches with the same elaboration, and there are big terra cotta jars and stone pots holding aloes and azaleas. Over the soft buff-colored walls hang sprays of jessamine and climbing roses which grow from the background of tall tree box and clustered cedars while Paul Scarlet roses twine through the balustrades and around the two Baroque statues at each side of the wide shallow steps down to the lawn.

This long oval stretch of grass is enclosed by a hedge of sheared arbor vitae and bordered by double avenues of magnolias. In the center of the long axis between house and entrance gates is a flat circular basin with a tall jet of water.

From the Villa Cuzzano, near Verona, the Villa Gori at Sienna and the Villa Spada on the Janiculum, came the inspiration for much of the architectural detail used here in house and garden. But the plans show imagination, a spontaneity, and a masterly handling of scale and design which could never be associated with slavish copying, and the result is a splendid example of architectural and landscape art, inspired by Italy but perfectly adapted to Georgia.

Photo by F. E. Lee

Rossdhu

Dr. and Mrs. Phinizy Calhoun

Atlanta

MASSED plantings of evergreen and blossoming shrubs on each side of the broad entrance to Rossdhu, the home of Dr. and Mrs. Phinizy Calhoun, only partially conceal the broad expanse of lawn, and produce a decorative frame effect for the entrance facade of the English house which is set on the crest of a pleasant slope. Among the dogwoods and native trees left about the lawn to give shade and prevent conscious exactness groups of Prunus pissardi have been planted.

Ivy is trained on the walls of the turreted red house, box softens the foundation lines, and near the entrance are hemlock trees and rare specimens of osmanthus with an underplanting of vinca. A terrace of varicolored flagstones surrounds the house on three sides, and is so enclosed by plantings of box as to make three secluded open air sitting rooms. To the north, slightly sunken below the level of the terrace, is a rectangular green and white garden where the variety in broad-leaf evergreen shrub species that outline the grass plot make interesting study. Here are found banana shrub, aucuba, mahonia, Ilex cassine and glabra, photinia, English laurel, cherry laurel, Virginia red cedar, Illicium anisatum, Viburnum tinus, euonymous, pyracantha, and crepe myrtle. White Azalea indica is banked in front of the evergreens and the brick paths are bordered by white violas and liriope. An ivy covered sundial guarded by two old-fashioned iron dogs, forms the center piece of this garden.

From the west terrace a woodland pathway bordered by ferns and colonies of wild flowers shaded by dogwoods, sweet-shrubs, azaleas, rhododendrons, kalmias, and larger woods trees, invites delay on the way to the gardens of bright flowers, the camellia house, and the propagating grounds.

Wide irregular borders of primroses, interspersed with snowdrops and scillas, form the outer edge planting against the shrub enclosure of the flower garden, which consists of a succession of terraces separated by low walls—dry-laid with one exception—overhung with nepeta, Phlox subulata, verbena, and sedum. The first terrace has a formal planting of roses outlined with low box, the paths bordered with spice pinks. Hugonis roses and syringa form the north boundary, while climbing yellow roses hang over the low wall. The second terrace with lateral box-hedges features iris in great variety with interspersed beds of perennials and annuals for later blooming. The third terrace is a study in blossoming herbaceous plants with one border given over entirely to old-fashioned fragrant herbs and on the last level are flowers for cutting. Upright iron standards on all the walls furnish support for climbing roses which are trained to hang in garlands from post to post.

In the camellia house, which is almost hidden by hedges of intermediate box, are propagated seedlings for the spring beds, sub-tropical vines of many species, and pot plants for decorative purposes. Mrs. Calhoun specializes in camellia growing, and her collection contains many fine varieties.

The screen plantings in the rear of the house are of tree box and euonymous while a massive planting of box and another of nandina relieves the severity of the exit drive as it curves from the porte-cochere.

Photo by F. E. Lee

Woodland Path at Rossdhu

Green Garden at Rossdhu

Photo by F. E. Lee

Bellvoir

Mr. and Mrs. J. Bulow Campbell

Atlanta

THE sixteen acre hill which first attracted Mr. and Mrs. Campbell because of its wealth of wild azaleas has been developed into a series of enclosed and connected gardens, each with its distinctive planting and lovely vista. Planned entirely by Mrs. Campbell the gardens make beautiful surroundings for a modern Georgian house.

A little paved terrace at the back of the house is the first vantage point from which stretch out many alluring prospects. In the immediate foreground are old millstones paving the way to a shallow brick stairway where each step is banked in ivy, trained to keep the treads free but to cover each rise with living green. The steps lead to a lawn circled with boxwood and centered by a pool filled with the translucent pink and white of water-lilies. Beyond the pool is a green corridor, the walls of privet and ivy hedges broken by vine-wreathed arches, and stretching in long perspective between the formal gardens on either side.

From the house terrace, one turns to the right to see silhouetted against the green of oaks and pine, Judas and dogwoods, the lace-like iron grills of a summer-house and, in the distance, the white marble forms of Pan and an adoring nymph. Pan is not alone in recalling the Greek myths. Leda and the Swan in bronze form the fountain centre of one of the three pools that lend the grace of sparkling water, and by her side is an old amphora brought from Rome to emphasize the Italian note struck by the marble benches under their canopy of yellow jessamine. The garden is practically never without bloom, for each season in turn takes its place in filling the floral calendar, and the slowly moving hours are marked by a sundial shaped like a Grecian urn.

One spring picture has the happy combination of the simultaneous flowering of white wistaria and Cherokee roses on a stone wall at the end of the main vista. At the back of the wall, against which hollyhocks form a close picket, is a wild garden where azaleas, rhododendrons, laurel, ferns, Indian-pipes, lady-slippers and hepatica grow.

A paved terrace at the rear of the house at Bellvoir leads onto a green enclosure, with beckoning path beyond.

Yellow Jessamine Garlands the Garden Gate at Bellvoir

Vista Through Evergreens, Bellvoir

There are no discords in the wisely planned stretches of lawn, woodland glades and flower-beds, and it is appropriate that the old-world charm of the "sweet garden," filled with heliotrope, lavender and the white pinks our grandmothers loved, should be approached by a path of sunken mill-stones which had their origin near the Georgia plantations where these flowers grew. Steps made of the millstones cut in half climb to one of the formal gardens which in early spring is filled with purple and gold pansies and blue forget-me-nots, and then with crimson poppies, which in turn give way to vari-colored roses and delicately tinted peonies.

The increasing warmth of the July sun brings to perfection zinnias, marigolds, lupines, and celandines which flaunt their vivid colors in the face of midsummer heat and defy for weeks the blight of frost while blending with late autumn's chrysanthemums.

And so the floral calendar moves on, keeping the garden always profligate in its offering of color and fragrance.

Callenwolde

Mr. and Mrs. C. H. Candler
Atlanta

Tulips at Callenwolde Photo by Reeves

BEHIND the tall iron gates of Callenwolde, the lawns sweep back to an irregular wide planting of flowering shrubs and evergreens fringing the woods between house and road. Dogwoods and crabapples grow thick under the taller trees. Narcissi have been scattered among the native pink azaleas and sweet shrubs, and many weeping cherries are planted along the drive.

The house of English type, set back in a park of natural as well as planned growth, was designed for Mr. and Mrs. Candler by Henry Hornbostle of New York. Ivy and Virginia creeper mantle the walls while the base planting is of boxwood and junipers.

The nearest garden is a small formal court garden opening from the house and sheltered by it on three sides. A perfectly symmetrical white dogwood, in relief against the red brick, is the focal point of the picture. Rounded specimens of boxwood flank the dogwood, the ivy and box bound parterres are filled with tulips, and bay trees in tubs stand around the small fountain at the axis of the paths.

Across the driveway from the house is a formal garden of perennials, the beds designed about a sun dial. A pergola hung in grape vines is at the far end and beyond this is the sunken "rose bowl." Hybrid teas of many colors are in the curved beds while climbing roses cover the sloping banks.

A grassy hillside at the right is given over to the orchard and at the summit are the propagating houses and the orchid house. Under the big trees near the glass houses many sedums and other rock plants are tucked into the boulders which once formed part of a Confederate breastworks. From here a wide walkway, bordered on one side by white lilacs, on the other by a fence of espaliered apple trees, approaches the kitchen gardens and small fruit gardens which are laid out in elaborate patterns.

Paths lead through the untouched woodlands to a swimming pool, screened by hedges of flowering shrubs, and to the tennis court which is curtained by wistaria vines.

Court Garden at Callenwolde Photo by Reeves

Shrub Planting Surrounding the Swimming Pool at Callenwolde Photo by Reeves

Coon Hollow

Mr. and Mrs. R. L. Cooney
Atlanta

Rhododendrons on Rock Stairway Photo by Reeves

"COON HOLLOW" lies at the foot of Druid Hills, the natural park which was developed many years ago by the Olmstead Brothers. The property was acquired by R. L. Cooney in 1923, and with the knowledge that "possums" and coons were actually hunted in the surrounding woods, who could resist "Coon Hollow" for the name? The house is unpretentious, its only claim to the attention of passers-by being a well kept lawn with specimen Cedrus deodara, and English laurel. About the property is a clipped hedge of Ligustrum amurense. There is a conspicuous absence of the popular massed planting and the evergreens are set with adequate space for their ultimate perfection. The property has a frontage on Ponce de Leon Avenue of one hundred twenty-five feet and a depth of about eight hundred feet. In the rear the precipitous slopes, falling away to a creek which borders the property, present difficulties that only the most determined would essay.

A natural woodland of white oak, tulip, wild bay, beech, linden, crabapple, and dogwood was the beginning, and, in the shade created by such trees, planting was necessarily limited. Grass itself was difficult, and for that reason ivy has been used in abundance. A collection donated by friends, now includes plants from Kenilworth, Melrose Abbey, Stratford, Blarney Castle, Oxford, Mount Vernon, and the old Pohick Church where George Washington worshipped. Walls of native stone were made to surround the perennial garden. These walls, now covered with ivy, and terraces outlined with box hedges, create a friendly green even in winter.

Near the house a terrace in which a small pool is built, is surrounded by potted plants, including geraniums, begonias, dracaenas, with an occasional orange or lemon tree, hibiscus, and pomegranate, and with water lilies, papyrus, and hyacinths in the pool, it is a comfortable and pleasing spot during the long summers.

From the terrace, a walk leads to a rock stairway between two hills planted with rhododendrons, kalmias and azaleas (calendulaceae) above a variety of ground covers including pachysandra, shortia, creeping ranunculus, vinca, bloodroot and Iris cristata. The hill to the right is terraced and is the nearest approach to formality. Eight levels are box enclosed, and climbing Killarney roses and large gardenias are featured in the center level. A garden house at the foot of the formal garden overlooks the area below, which is bordered by a meandering creek.

The hill to the left of the stairway is planted most informally. Rhododendrons thrive in its acid soil and ferns, Jack-in-the-Pulpits, spiderworts, anemones, hepaticas, and atamasco lilies are scattered through the woodland, with primroses, narcissi and mertensia along the walk. On the brow of the hill is a "lookover," a place to rest and enjoy the scene below where birds love to nest in the

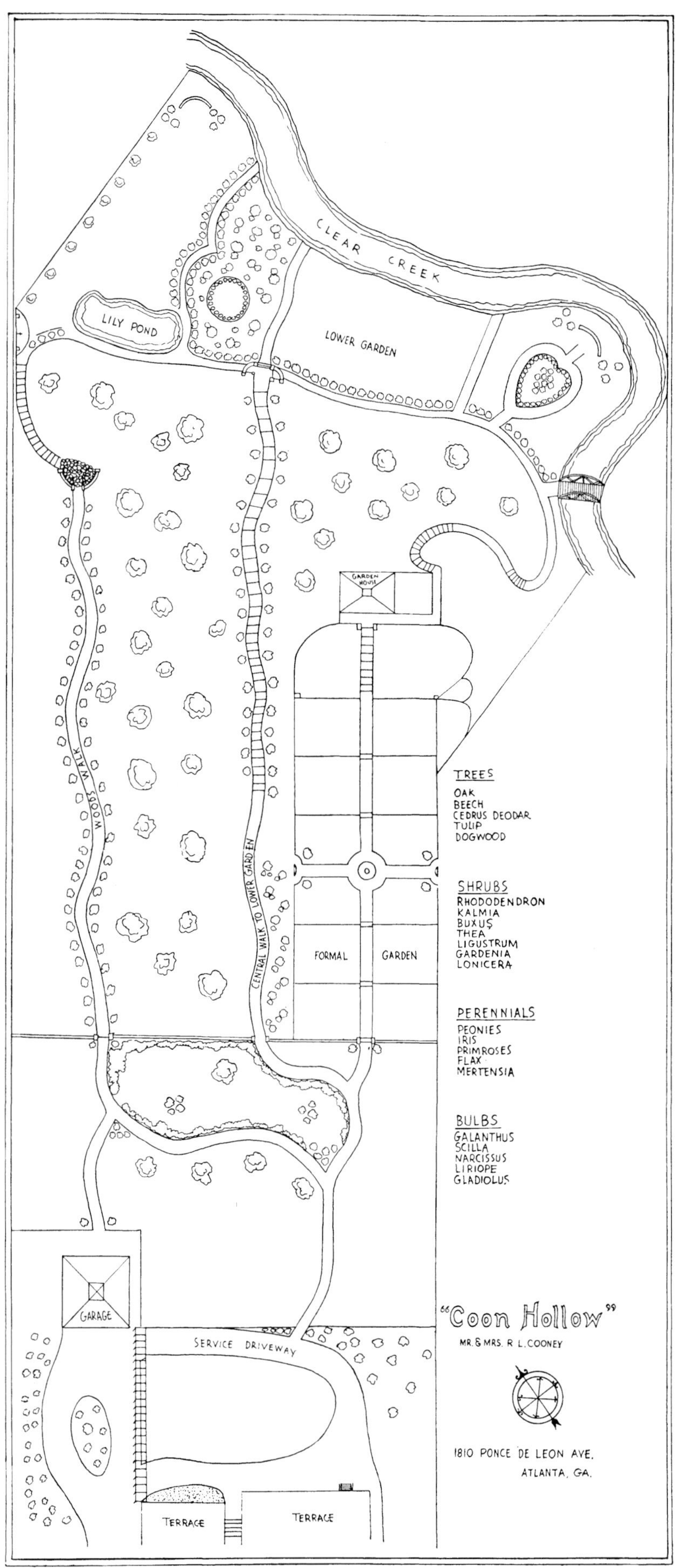
CLEAR CREEK
LILY POND
LOWER GARDEN
GARDEN HOUSE
WOODS WALK
CENTRAL WALK TO LOWER GARDEN
FORMAL GARDEN
TREES
OAK
BEECH
CEDRUS DEODAR
TULIP
DOGWOOD
SHRUBS
RHODODENDRON
KALMIA
BUXUS
THEA
LIGUSTRUM
GARDENIA
LONICERA
PERENNIALS
PEONIES
IRIS
PRIMROSES
FLAX
MERTENSIA
BULBS
GALANTHUS
SCILLA
NARCISSUS
LIRIOPE
GLADIOLUS
GARAGE
SERVICE DRIVEWAY
TERRACE
TERRACE
"Coon Hollow"
MR. & MRS. R. L. COONEY
1810 PONCE DE LEON AVE.
ATLANTA, GA.

At the Foot of the Hill and Across the Meadow at Coon Hollow

Photo by Reeves

natural growth along the stream. With gardenias, roses and butterfly lilies to scent the air, the "look-over" is a favorite retreat. Across the stream is a meadow, and beyond that a long green of pine wood that does not belong to "Coon Hollow," except in the pleasure of the view it affords.

The garden has grown gracefully and naturally. The steep wooded hillsides afford ideal conditions for wild flower planting, but offer scant opportunity for planting in the grand manner.

Lane's End

Mr. and Mrs. Cam D. Dorsey

Atlanta

THE name "Lane's End" comes from the fact that the house is reached by way of a three hundred and fifty foot lane from Vernon Road, so enclosed by shrubbery that the house itself is visible only when the lane's end has been reached. The broad whitewashed brick house, planned by the late Neel Reid, and patterned from the Dorsey family home, "Belmont," near Baltimore, is set

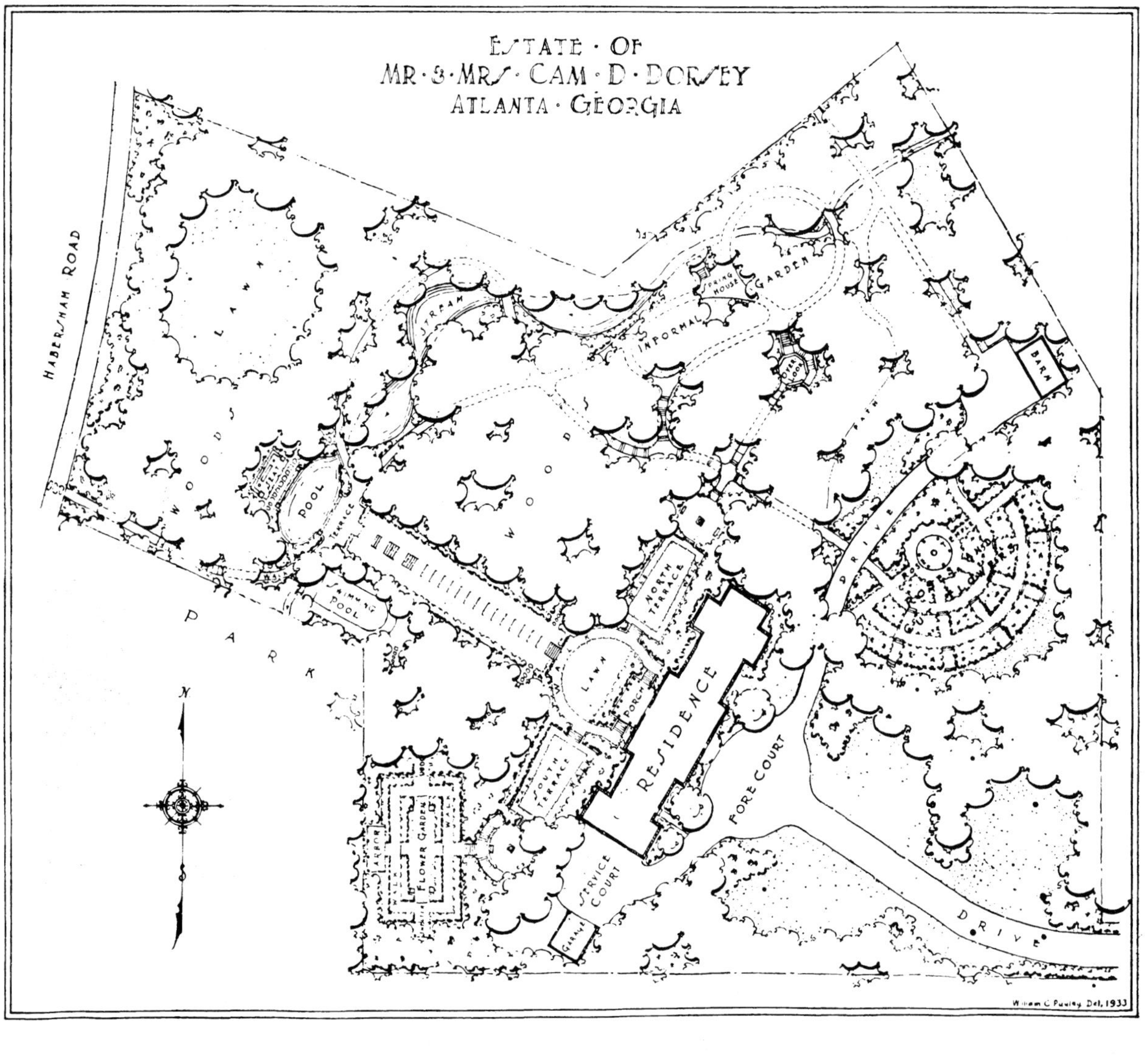

ESTATE · OF
MR · & · MRS · CAM · D · DORSEY
ATLANTA · GEORGIA

William C. Pauley Del. 1933

House at Lane's End in Its Luxuriant Setting, as Seen from Habersham Road

Photo by F. E. Lee

Lane's End Photo by F. E. Lee

upon the brow of a hill overlooking a deep valley and facing Habersham Road. Seven acres of native woodland are included in the Dorsey tract, the native growth consisting of white oaks, water oaks, post oaks, scarlet oaks, Southern red oaks, several varieties of hickories, tulip poplars, sweet gums, sour wood, wild cherries, American beeches, small leaf elms, swamp or red maples, and an occasional great leaf magnolia; while in their shade grow the native small flowering trees and shrubs: dogwood, red bud, hawthorns, azaleas in great variety, sweet shrubs (Calycanthus floridus), viburnums, and "Grancy greybeard" (Chiomanthus virginica). This natural beauty is augmented by the introduction of great numbers of kalmias and rhododendrons.

From the house broad grass steps lead down to the valley where a winding stream runs between plantations of countless varieties of wild flowers, and over banks and hillsides thousands of early spring bulbs have been naturalized to enhance the outlook from the porch.

All the broad leafed southern evergreens—cherry laurel, magnolias, ilexes, gardenia, abelia, ligustrum and photinia—are in massed plantings surrounding the house which is set in the heart of the deciduous wood. Old boxwood is used extensively and English ivy adds its deep green to cover walls, soften steps and border the pathways.

There are two formal gardens at Lane's End, one on the house level, and also an informal rose garden. The lower formal garden, reached by steps from the side of the front terrace, is a square garden of straight line beds planted in annuals and wide bands of iris, the whole enclosed by abelia and spirea. The upper garden is rectangular, hedged in by broad-leaf evergreens, and its parterres outlined with wavy lines of dwarf box are planted informally.

On the right of the house and somewhat back are a series of terraces, the dividing banks covered with pink Phlox subulata, and on the terraces roses of many varieties are grown.

Mr. and Mrs. Thomas C. Erwin
Atlanta

THE garden of Mr. and Mrs. Thomas C. Erwin was planned by its owners and begun about ten years ago. Simple in design, and canopied with the green of oak and beech, its plan and wide variety of plant material give evidence of the skilled gardener.

From the terrace steps, an expanse of lawn spreads out to a group of venerable oaks under whose leafy boughs rhododendron, ferns and laurel are serenely content. Opening from this shady spot a flight of stone steps leads down into a formal garden. A wide flagstone panel divides this area, and on either side lie box-bordered rose beds. Great tubs of oleanders and dwarf lemon trees are used with fine effect. At the far end of the garden is a semi-circular lily pool, spreading out against a luxuriant planting of shrubbery, with groups of Iris pseudacorus introduced at intervals. The coping of the pool is ivy-clad, and for ornament there are two slender-legged bronze herons. Over beyond the roses, to right and left, are wide borders filled with lilies and here, each June, are displayed the magnificent Regale lilies for which the mistress of this garden is famed. All grown by her from seed, some of these specimens attain a height of seven feet and produce as many as thirty blossoms each.

Adjacent to the formal garden, though completely screened from it by a jungle growth of bamboo, are the kennels where the frisky Cairn terriers—ribbon winners many of them—are at home and bestow upon all visitors a boisterous welcome.

From the upper corner of the pool garden, the steps ascend to a spacious out-of-door living room, which is the joy of the family. About the lawn comfortable seats have been arranged, and there is a center-table formed of a giant millstone a century old. Across the upper boundary of this grassy

At the entrance to the Rose Garden, Oleanders and Hydrangeas in bloom

Regal Lilies bloom from seed in sixteen months in the Erwin Garden—

section runs a low rock wall, and along its ledge are displayed pots of ferns and flowering plants, agapanthus, lilies, azaleas, and ivy geraniums. Irregular in outline, a wide border of choice perennials and shrubs hedges this portion of the grounds and here each early spring blossoms a broad band of blue Phlox divaricata, outstanding in its beauty. Next the shrubbery, toward the left, is a dense screen of Japanese bamboo which effectively separates this garden from the greenhouse, trial grounds and propagating beds beyond. Some of this bamboo has reached the astonishing height of fifty feet.

Flagstones lead the way down into the peony and iris garden, which is designed around an old English ivy-covered sundial. Thrusting aside the heavy foliage, the date "1659" is faintly traceable. Here quantities of Phlox subulata outline the beds, and masses of hardy candytuft have been freely used. Peony plants, long undisturbed, have attained enormous size, and there is an excellent collection of iris.

Photo by F. E. Lee

—and Mushrooms, not so beautiful, but as successfully grown.

Farther on lies the informal rose garden, and beyond are long rows of annuals and perennials for cutting; then come the asparagus bed, and the berry and small fruit gardens.

But most interesting of all, at least to a real dirt-digging gardener, is the greenhouse where are carried forward all sorts of experiments in grafting and propagating. Here also are housed numbers of Camellia japonicas, while great colonies of mushrooms thrive in the moist semi-gloom beneath the benches.

Mr. and Mrs. Frank Fleming
Miss Hightower
Atlanta

Photo by F. E. Lee

THE Little Hillside Garden, which specializes in native azaleas and naturalized narcissi, begins with a flagstone terrace filled with white azaleas and gardenias. The next level, reached by circular stone steps entwined with ivy, has an arch of dogwood trees at the base of the steps. From the terrace the natural slope extends west to the rear of the property and is reached by a winding path of stepping stones, bordered with wild violets of several varieties, trillium, snowdrops, and hepaticas, with narcissus grouped between.

On each side of the path is a profusion of native azaleas, tall, medium and low, in shades of pale pink, apricot, orange, red, flame and rose pink, each color blending in the harmony that only nature can achieve. Emphasizing their color are many white dogwood trees overhead. Down this fragrant path one approaches the rockery, and, by a dividing walk, the cutting garden. Leaving the rockery one comes to an open space where the ground is terraced off with beds of English daisies, pansies, phlox divaricata, columbines, peonies, bleeding heart, iris, and tulips. In the terrace above are pink and yellow tulips, with ranunculus growing between the rocks that border the terrace, to add from spring to fall a welcome touch of yellow.

The walk separating the terraces is planted to grass and under the low spreading dogwoods are several inviting benches where one may pause and enjoy the vista toward the hillside where the azaleas weave a pattern of arresting beauty. The upper terraces are divided with walks of grass and stepping stones, and to the left are the rose beds. The last hillside has a background of magnolia trees, dogwood and crab-apple and against this screen are found the most brilliant of the azaleas, cerise and pink, many of them eight and ten feet in height. Narcissus is planted below the azaleas with buttercups, and native ferns are in a border close to the rocks. The walk ends at a circular bench against a mass of rose pink azaleas.

The garden comes into bloom about the first of February with the earliest yellow jonquils, against a background of forsythia, and the hillside is a mass of gold when winter releases its hold. The first of April the garden turns to white with the bloom of various Leedsi narcissi, with white kerrias, spireas, philadelphus, deutzia and dogwoods. At evening, by the brilliance of a full moon, the white blossoms and the perfume of narcissi and azaleas make this an enchanting spot.

The chief distinction of the Little Hillside Garden lies in its native azaleas which have been left where nature herself placed them. The earliest to bloom is the white, followed by the lighter pinks which are the glory of the garden. Most beautiful of all are the watermelon pinks, some of which have attained a height and width of ten and twelve feet. Then come the saffron and yellow tones, succeeded by the flame shades of red, and finally the bright reds growing low to the ground and lasting until early June.

Collection of Native Azaleas in the Little Hillside Garden

Photo by F. E. Lee

Boxwood House

Mr. and Mrs. James S. Floyd

Atlanta

BOXWOOD HOUSE, the home of the James Swann Floyds, stands upon a hillside at the beginning of the Prado, overlooking a woodland. The drive ascends the slope past a low rock retaining wall bordered on the upper side by tall boxwood and brilliant azaleas and on the lower side, by a box hedge, overshadowed by the branches of a row of purple plum trees. Uphill it curves to the east entrance of the rambling white house which was built many years ago but remodeled in more recent years.

Gardens, formal and wild, that are excellent both from the picturesque and horticultural points of view, have gradually been developed. The gardens were planned as a continuation of the house, with each of the three main doors opening into a pleasant outdoor room. As the name denotes, boxwoods are the leading features, along with old lead brought from England and millstones laid in walks.

The east entrance faces a pool built of white quartz rocks, in the center of which is a bronze figure of a kneeling boy holding a fish. Tall cedars banked with azaleas frame the picture. From the north terrace one gazes across the turf to a huge semi-circle of tall massed box that obstructs the view of the street but not of the woods beyond. The lawn is circled by clipped box hedges which are also the borders of the flower beds, the formal layout having its richest expression when columbine, bleeding heart, delphinium, and phlox are in bloom.

The living room doors open on the south terrace and from here one steps into a bit of old England. Two levels of grass are surrounded by a brick wall overhung by flowering trees and screened by boxwood. Lilacs, camellias and cape jasmine are clustered near the house and from the terrace a path of millstones leads to the grass plots, then continues, encircling the middle feature—a round

Photo by F. E. Lee

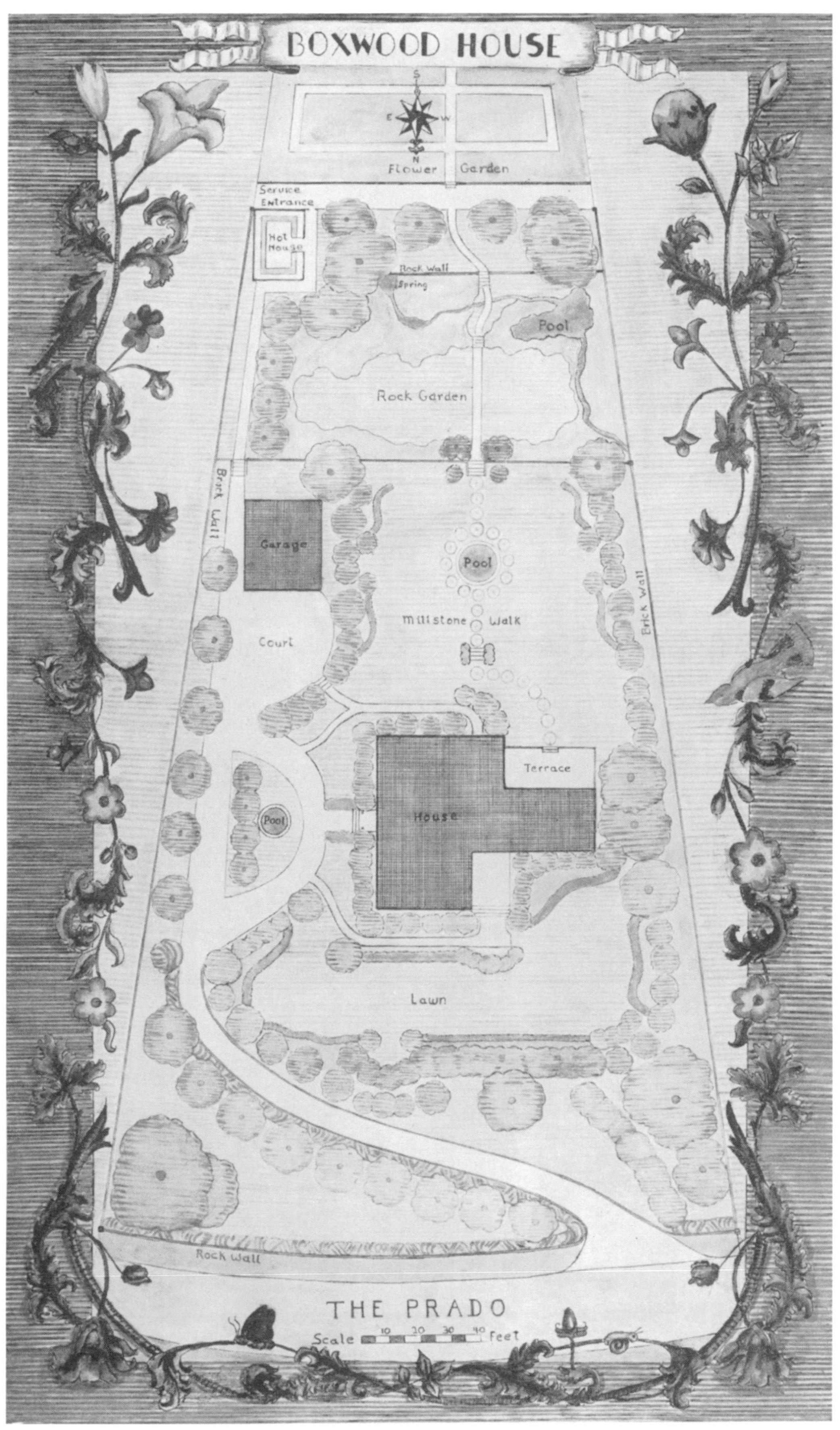
BOXWOOD HOUSE
S
E
W
N
Flower Garden
Service Entrance
Hot House
Rock Wall
Spring
Pool
Rock Garden
Brick Wall
Garage
Pool
Millstone Walk
Brick Wall
Court
Terrace
Pool
House
Lawn
Rock Wall
THE PRADO
Scale 10 20 30 40 Feet

lily pool with a lead fountain of a boy with dolphin. The pool is rimmed in ivy, and tiny mazus flowers grow in the center of each millstone. On either side of the garden, set in boxwood nooks, are iron benches where one may enjoy the shade. Leaden figures—one a hunter, one a reaper—stand in two corners of the garden against backgrounds of massed hawthorns, and upon the ivy-clad wall above are lead peacocks with spreading tails.

Steps between the walls and under an arch of roses lead to a rock-set hillside planted with alpines and enclosed by tall red cedars, hemlock, dogwood, crabapple, and other trees that do not intrude their shade too near. A rough mossy stone path meanders between the miniature stream and the up-crop of bold weathered rock. Half way up the slope is a jagged pool fed by a stream from a spring half hidden under mossy rock and fern and from the pool a waterfall cascades into a stream below banked with rhododendrons and mountain laurel.

From the rock garden the path continues up another level through a gate and into the flower garden. Here roses and cut flowers are grown for the house and young plants and shrubs are started to replenish the other gardens. One corner is occupied by the wistaria-draped pheasant pen.

Rock Plants in Continuous Bloom, Shrubs and Flowering Trees in Floyd Garden Photo by F. E. Lee

Masses of Boxwood Enclosing Green Garden in Floyd Garden

Photo by F. E. Lee

Photo by Reeves

Terraced Garden with Woodland Background at Ihagee

Ihagee

Judge and Mrs. Price Gilbert

Atlanta

MRS. GILBERT'S garden follows the natural line of a crescent shaped hill sloping down from the house. A flat stone walk between rows of large box leads to a series of terraces. Near the house are plantings of flowering shrubs and evergreens on one side, and on the other side beyond a bird bath which centers a bed of hyacinths, snow drops and tulips, is a border of native shrubs. Here are several varieties of azaleas, dogwood, black haw and wahoo, while near by a yellow jessamine climbs into a white oak tree. Around another twines a wild clematis bearing a shower of blossoms in mid-summer and its attractive seed clusters through November.

Below these beds a wall of field stone is gay all summer with pansies, violas, English daisies, thrift, cerastium, and other low-growing plants. And against the wall a broad terrace of grass makes a pleasant setting for afternoon tea.

The garden has three terraces one hundred twenty by twenty feet. The walls supporting the terraces as well as the steps and walkways are of weathered stone, some covered with ivy, others with climbing roses. All the paths are bordered with dwarf box and neat rows of old-fashioned white and blue hyacinths and many varieties of narcissi follow the lines of the boxwood, while beyond are wide bands of iris in some fifty varieties. These beds are permanent and practically uniform, but the space inside varies on each terrace. Perhaps there are more lilies than any other flower, for beginning with valley lilies there is some variety in bloom until late autumn. The display begins with early hemerocallis and continues with fairy lilies, madonnas, regales, rubrums and others. In August appears the crimson Nassau lily and last of all in late autumn the fragrant hedychium.

Below the three terraces lies a rock garden featuring indigenous flowers and shrubs. Here laurel blooms well, and also flame azalea. Eglantine spreads over every available space and the ground is starred with pale blue and yellow woods violets. Into the overhanging trees wistaria and clematis climb, and the red haw with its crimson berries is lovely in autumn. A rock-bordered pool holds gold fish and water lilies.

Pine needle paths lead from this spot through a stone pillared pergola covered in scuppernong grapes to a hedged rose garden. The planting of bush roses shade from white to deep crimson and the climbers trained up on the tree trunks with cables from one tree to another make a proper background.

HABERSHAM ROAD
Brick Wall
Camellia House
Chinese Pavilion
Pool
Bosco
Bosco
Bamboo Walk
Temple
Dogwood Arbor
Flower Garden
Terrace
House
Court
Garage
Theatre
Pool
Porch
Clairvoyee
Service Entrance
Forecourt
Brick Wall
ARDEN ROAD
Lawn
Lawn
PACE'S FERRY ROAD
S
E
W
N
Plan of the Garden of
MRS JAMES J GOODRUM
ATLANTA GEORGIA
Scale Feet

Mrs. James J. Goodrum
Atlanta

Star Pool and Theatre — Photo by F. E. Lee

MRS. GOODRUM'S garden lies within the confines of a serpentine wall whose bricks, lightly washed in yellow, afford a background for beds of tulips, columbine, and Canterbury bells. Down the center of this enclosed garden stretches a miniature bowling green, hedged in with sturdy clumps of true boxwood planted to follow the winding outline of the wall. The bowling green forms the axis, with the face of the garden house at one end and at the other a latticed gazebo of McIntyre design, its graceful dome crowned with a little gilt eagle. In summer the lattice is embowered in the purple stars of Clematis jackmanii, while to right and left are giant gardenia bushes, and across the green, magnolia trees espaliered against the garden house wall, mingle their fragrance with a myriad other scents. Further along are cherry trees pinned fan-like to the yellow-washed bricks, their crimson fruit and glossy leaves thrown into high relief.

Lining the walled garden plot, which is rectangular in shape, is a border raised several inches above the level of the walks by a dry-wall of ledgestone. Between this and the bowling green are long, irregularly-shaped beds designed to fit the space between the straight walks and the wavy lines of boxwood. In some of these are standard roses, with pansies growing thickly about their feet, while the others are planted like the long borders against the wall, in tulips, iris, and perennials. The effect of the borders, serpentine at the back and straight along the walks, with here and there the blue spikes of delphinium showing above the heads of other flowers, and masses of alyssum and phlox divaricata spilling over the flat stones, is indescribably lovely. And as if eager to see and share in all this bloom, fig trees planted in each outer recess of the curving wall grow taller with the seasons, and a group of old apple trees near the garden house scatter fragrant petals. The use of turf

Two Views of Walled Garden, Goodrum Garden

Photos by F. E. Lee

Formal Garden from Gazebo, Goodrum Garden

Photo by F. E. Lee

walks which wind in and out among the beds and tie in with the central grass plot, give an effect of space beyond the actual dimensions.

Delightful is this little garden close, but it by no means has a monopoly on the beauty of Mrs. Goodrum's estate. Connected with it by a lacy wrought-iron gate is a terraced garden, directly against the rear facade of the house. This is a semi-circular stretch of grass, enclosed by an entirely different sort of wall—a dry-wall of small, dark-brown, flat stones. The planting here is limited to a narrow bed at the base of the wall, filled with lilies and peonies. Zinnias and lantanas are used to fill in, while on top of the wall, boxes of geraniums, petunias, and foliage plants are placed at intervals. Coral vine runs over the wall, also.

Below the terrace and surrounding the back of the grounds is a stretch of native woodland. Winding along its edge is a dogwood walk, the trees pruned so that their branches spread laterally to ground level, to shade the valley lilies which grow here. Following along this quiet way one comes, through another iron gate, to a perfect bit of garden architecture. It lies before the living-porch of the house—a small green, centered with a star-shaped lily pool, and back of this a little outdoor stage, its footlights of dwarf box, its backdrop of tree-box—giant specimens. Last of all a row of willows presents a curtain of waving green. Perhaps more than any other feature this little verdant stage ties the house, which is English Regency, to its period, for the Regency in England was a fanciful time, when men treated their houses and their gardens with a lighter touch and learned to make for themselves charming outdoor retreats such as this one.

The boxwood here is a foretaste of the beauty of that which borders the entrance drive and the court. These boxwoods formerly grew in old Georgia gardens and have for company masses of feathery mimosa trees, flowering quince, crabapple, gardenias, and lilacs—familiar and loved friends of every Georgian who has known a garden.

House and plans by Hentz, Adler & Shutze. Planting by J. W. Shannon.

Summer Bloom Along Serpentine Wall, Goodrum Garden Photo by F. E. Lee

Mr. and Mrs. Arthur I. Harris
Atlanta

THE gardens of Mr. and Mrs. Arthur Harris have been designed to include many charming types of planting. Constructed a quarter-century ago, the brick residence, Elizabethan in feeling, has a setting of luxuriant shrubbery: boxwood, ilex and gardenias growing close to the ivy-covered balustrades of the terrace.

The formal garden lying to the rear of the house is connected with it by brick-paved walkways. Dim and cool in the shadow of old trees, this is a sheltered spot filled with bloom throughout the year—from the first splash of early crocus to the purple and gold of fall asters and chrysanthemums. Centering a grass panel is a sixteenth century Venetian well-head of weathered marble, pinkish in tone, and flanking the well are quaint old metal sprinkler pots brought from Dijon.

Toward the left a flight of steps leads down into a little green garden, enclosed by evergreen shrubs, and to a still lower level where a brick-bordered lily pool holds an old Spanish fountain figure. Beyond in a little bay stands a bird bath, and sur-

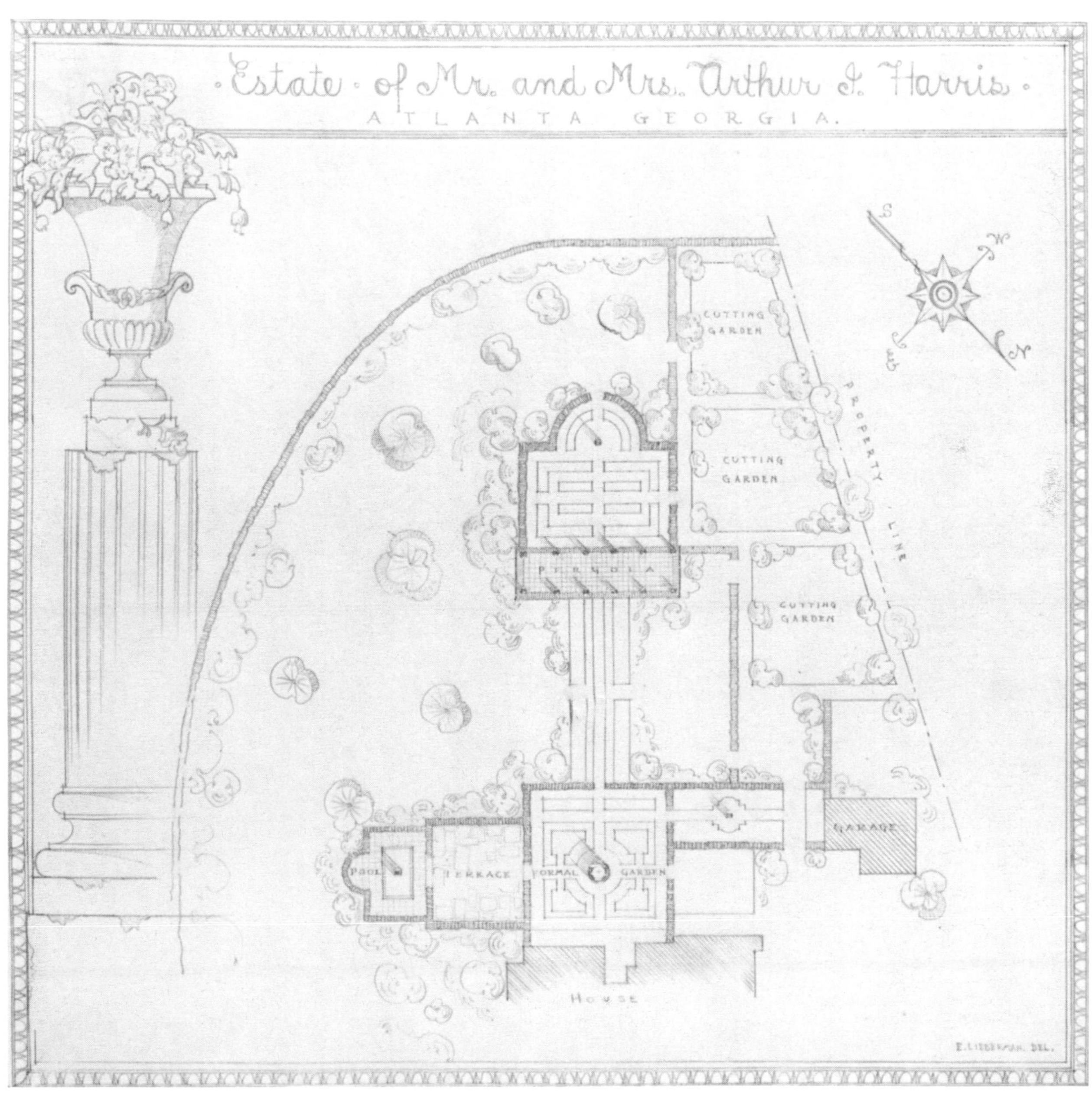

Photo by F. E. Lee

Formal Garden in Early Spring, Harris Garden

rounding this entire garden is a sheared abelia hedge. Grouped about the pool, which is rectangular in shape, are jars of fragrant white Confederate jasmine trained on spiral frames, and a queer wax plant, fifty years old, covered in season with pale pink blossoms.

Back again to the garden-of-the-well, a broad walk leads on through wide flower borders. Here are massed rare perennials, lilies, and iris, with dwarf boxwood edgings and standard roses—Madame Edouard Herriott—introduced for accent. Gradually the planting begins to merge with that of the wild garden where fern and lady-slipper, thalictrum and arbutus intermingle after nature's own fashion. Terminating this section of the grounds is a long pergola covered with euonymous and grape vines, while twining around the pillars are large-flowered Clematis—Ramona, Madame Edouard Andree, Jackmanni, and Henryii.

Beyond the pergola lies the out-of-door living room, an expanse of turf with millstone pathway and two semi-circular rose beds, where various shades of red in bush roses blend with standards of Etoile de Hollande. Through a rose-twined trellis a path leads across the lawn to the iris garden, which has a background of dense shrubbery to mark the property line beyond. Quite as interesting as the more formal areas, is the peony garden near by, its enclosure a picket fence stained a soft woodsy brown. Generous-sized beds of peonies are inter-planted with Japanese iris and edged with Phlox divaricata laphami, and along the fence are climbing roses in shades of orange and yellow. Here, too, is an old pear tree with a tiny bird house.

The design and planting plans for the gardens were prepared in 1921 by Robert C. Cridland, of Philadelphia.

Rose Enclosed Peony Borders, Harris Garden Photo by Reeves

Green Garden and Pool, Harris Garden Photo by Reeves

Fernbank

Z. D. Harrison
Atlanta

Photo by F. E. Lee

FERNBANK, in Druid Hills, the home of Z. D. Harrison, has its garden, of course, its garden with roses, iris, peonies and pinks, but other gardens a-plenty have all of these and more; what Fernbank has that is truly remarkable is its forest.

In the forest the trees grow so dense and tall that walking amid their green silences one gets a sense of being miles from civilization, when, in fact, Atlanta is at its edge, and Five Points, the very heart of the city, is only fifteen minutes away by automobile. How has this miracle come to pass, a miracle of joining together a city and a primitive woodland? By the simple process of development on the one hand and protection on the other. The city has grown until it touches the fringe of the woods, but just there the ax has been stayed and the natural treasure preserved, and reverent care has kept the Fernbank tract just as it was fifty years ago when Mr. Harrison acquired it.

Fernbank is not a country place as much as it is a wildwoods place and the house might well be called the "House-in-the-woods." From the front veranda in the summer time one looks into seemingly impenetrable depths of forest greenness and shy wood things like ferns, Jack-in-the-Pulpits and trilliums come boldly up to the very doorstep.

In the rear of the house are open, sunny spaces for lawn, garden and orchard, but to the north and east the forest which stretches away for sixty acres or more is entered by wood paths that beckon alluringly. These paths lead to the brook, the spring, the lake, and the place of the big trees, trees that are really giants. There are beeches, tulip poplars, hickories, pines, oaks, sweetgums,

Woodland Stream at Fernbank Photo by F. E. Lee

maples, and many other kinds. The State Forester, B. M. Lufburrow, who is well acquainted with the property, has said: "The Fernbank tract is absolutely unique, not only because of its situation so near to the city, but because of the age and beauty and great variety of the trees. I know of nothing comparable to it."

As there is a variety of trees, so likewise is there an infinite variety of wild flowers. Not only the lovely things common to Georgia woods like dogwood and azalea are found here in profusion, but shyer things—Lady Slipper orchids, Solomon's Seals, Pussy Toes, Turtle-heads and Indian Pipes—the very names have an unfamiliar sound, for these plants are denizens of the deep woods and must be sought in their forest retreats. From the earliest hepaticas, bloodroots and anemones of the springtime to the cardinal flowers and gentians of summer and fall, the forest is a wild garden of nature's sowing with something always in bloom for one who knows where to look.

Together with its trees and flowers the forest harbors a great variety of birds: bluebirds, cardinals, scarlet tanagers, robins, woodpeckers, thrashers and mocking birds, while in its inner depths are oven-birds, towhees, warblers, and thrushes. But this style of cataloging trees, flowers and birds conveys little of the living, infinite beauty of the woodland. Prompted by the feeling that such wealth of beauty should be widely shared, Mr. Harrison has extended the hospitality of the Fernbank woods to the Atlanta Bird Club and the Atlanta Girl Scouts. Each organization has now its camp house within the wood's precincts. Their members are forest rangers and forest conservationists. Thus the Fernbank forest has become a bird, tree and wild flower sanctuary, and the happy hunting ground of bird lovers and children.

Azalea and Dogwood at Fernbank Photo by F. E. Lee

Deodars and Pink Dogwood Along Driveway at Villa Clare

Photo by Reeves

Athos Menaboni

Villa Clare

James J. Haverty

Atlanta

THE entrance to Villa Clare is a winding driveway where stately old deodars make a background for beautiful spreading pink dogwoods. The rolling lawn is bordered with a deep planting of ivy, and near the house clumps of Clara Butt tulips and iris Queen of May, brighten the foundation planting of broad-leaf evergreens. Two crouching lions guard the entrance to the Italian house whose steps and open terrace are outlined with luxuriant panels of ivy.

Curving around the left wing of the house, the driveway at the back merges into a broad flagstone path which leads down to the natural terraces of the lower gardens where the retaining walls are garlanded with Silver Moon and pink Killarney rose vines.

At some distance from the house, the walkway crosses a white bridge and mounting again farther on skirts the edge of the deep and secluded ravine of the Quarry Garden. There are seven acres of woodland surrounding Villa Clare and the natural growth has been little disturbed. Here are honeysuckle, oak-leaf hydrangeas, sweet shrubs as tall as trees, "Grancy Greybeard," and great drifts of pink and white native azaleas. The woodsy trail follows closely the outer wall of the ravine and terminates at the head of the quarry steps. The children of the family built their own shrine here in honor of the Madonna, and the Della Robia plaque gives the color note for flowers of blue and white. There are snowdrops in early spring, muscari, single white and blue hyacinths, violets, valley lilies, candytuft, and vinca trails blue-starred evergreen vines over the moss-covered steps.

Athos Menaboni

In the quiet of this peaceful rock-walled garden it is hard to imagine the harrowing scenes that were once enacted here. For these smooth green-clad terraces were Confederate breastworks during the siege of Atlanta and on the hill above was stationed Captain Evan P. Howell's Battery. Over yonder, across Peachtree Creek, was Federal Hill, ably defended in 1864 by Benj. P. Harrison. To this ravine garden, twenty years ago, came a visitor from the North, this time on a peaceful pilgrimage. From Valparaiso, Indiana, an aged traveler had come back South to visit once more the scenes of the War Between the States. And it was on these grounds that he found the old stone quarry he had remembered all these years. It was a thrilling tale he told of the young Federal soldier boy that was himself, being sent to reconnoiter close up to the Confederate lines and having to seek refuge among the boulders and tangled undergrowth of the quarry until darkness should cloak his perilous return to the Union encampment.

Now a marble Pan is guardian of the old quarry where ivy and honeysuckle hang a curtain of dark green over grey granite walls. Rhododendron, mountain laurel, and wild azalea have been naturalized against the rugged rocks and the floor is covered with a carpet of moss, relieved here and there with patches of bluets and sprinklings of trilliums and anemones.

Photo by F. E. Lee

Mrs. William P. Hill
Atlanta

TODAY the traffic of mid-town streets has surrounded the old Hallman home and Mrs. Hill's flower garden, which in the nineties made a suburban beauty spot. Fortunately, the shade trees and shrubbery plantings grew as fast as the encroaching commerce and now give perfect seclusion to the garden—a hidden town-garden—which, once the tall green hedges are passed, offers a peaceful charm rarely to be encountered so near the city's din.

Completely cut off from the street by a dense screen of evergreen and flowering shrubs—January jasmine, forsythia, flowering almonds, lilacs and spireas for spring, crepe myrtle, gardenias, and altheas for summer—lies a garden of perennials amazingly full of color and bloom ten months of the year. Its inner walls of green are thickened by climbing roses, eleagnus, English laurel, and hardy privets, which also conceal the cutting gardens and rose beds behind them.

The garden, which adjoins the house on one side and on the other three sides is shut in by tall shrubs, has a very simple plan. Flagstone paths are laid between wide herbaceous borders which extend the length of both sides of an oblong stretch of lawn. Clipped biotas accent the two openings onto the lawn. At the far end are old iron benches "for the cool of the evening" and at the other end are the steps to the veranda of the house where the outlook on the garden is framed in tangles of wistaria hanging from an old cherry tree.

The wide borders are so generously planted that the procession of flowers never halts. Starting with the earliest daffodils, spring brings all the rainbow of the irises, with bright tinted tulips set in contrasting bands of blue phlox, pink thrift and spice pinks; then groupings of peonies and bleeding heart combine with early shasta daisies. June finds tall spires of hollyhocks near the sweet-scented masses of white, pink, and mauve phlox, which give way in turn to many kinds of chrysanthemums and asters for fall. Crinum (Resurrection) lilies have

Summer in Mrs. Hill's Garden Photo by F. E. Lee

grown here so long their great clumps dominate the summer annuals which file in, while hemerocallis of many fine varieties add lemon or gold to almost every month's color scheme.

Surprising indeed to find this garden of old fashioned loveliness hidden away among city streets.

Pine Hill

Mr. and Mrs. Clark Howell

Atlanta

"THE main charm of our place is that its natural beauty has been accentuated." Mr. Howell thus sums up the development at Pine Hill. The twenty-acre tract comprises two beautifully wooded hills guarding a ravine of deep wildwood where a stream widens into a series of rock-bound pools and the wealth of native growth has been wisely conserved. In accordance with nature's planting scheme for this section the hills are crowned with groves of aromatic pines. White oaks and other hardwoods shade the higher slopes, while great silver gray beeches overhang the ravine, and a myriad sourwoods, blackgums, sweetgums and maples give the autumn scene the rich coloring of a Paisley shawl. And even for this dogwood showered part of the world the profusion of fine dogwood trees is notable, and they combine with the red bud, wild cherry, crabapples, calycanthus and styrax to turn the ravine into a springtime carnival of bloom.

Set back among the pines of the hilltop and looking over its own woods to a view of Atlanta's skylines is the stucco house, its walls clothed in ivy and Virginia creeper, its foundation planting of evergreens and fig trees, old wistaria vines climb into the pines and reach out to the eaves of the house. From the high-road drives paved with pine needles wind uphill between thick hedges of unsheared abelia past a rock garden and pool guarded by a woodland figure, to approach the house where a row of small-leafed hollies is in formal outline and a dense planting of bamboo, dogwood, and flowering crabs screens the service court.

A flower garden lies on the hillside to the west, the slope terraced into arrangements of box-edged flower borders and rose beds. An abelia hedge and tall English laurel enclose the garden, and clipped conifers accent the design of the different levels. This cultivated garden, pleasantly colorful from iris time to the chrysanthemums of late fall,

Flower Garden Set Against Pine Woods, Pine Hill

Tea House and Swimming Pool at Pine Hill

is connected with the woodland by flagged paths and fieldstone stairways leading down to the ravine.

All through the ravine and the wild garden a lavish use of native rock—for bridges, draining, copings for the drives, rough-laid walls, stepping stones and tea house—is in character with the rugged beauty of woods and streams. Covered with mosses, liverworts and selaginella carpeting the borders, the rustic stone work is harmonious and vastly becoming to the natural pictures—of masses of flame or pinxter flowered azaleas, laurel, rhododendron, leucothoe and all the smaller flowers indigenous to woods such as these. Spring flowering bulbs have been naturalized among the blue smears of crowsfoot violets; a lily dell shelters many rare blossoms; little wild iris, wind-flowers and trillium are in natural drifts among the colonies of ferns. The main stream with its two tributaries has been dammed into a swimming pool, a lily pool, and a small fish pond, all bordered with outcroppings of the grayish stone. One particularly clever piece of construction is the placing of great boulders in cuts down the steepest slopes to turn heavy rainfall into sparkling cascades which empty into the stream below.

Swan House

Mrs. Edward H. Inman

Atlanta

Photo by F. E. Lee

IN a forty-five-acre stretch of woodland is set Mrs. Edward Inman's beautiful house which is early Georgian, with marked Italian influence. The architectural development between Andrews Drive and the house is altogether Italian villa in effect. From the entrance drive which is bordered by hedges of Citrus trifoliata, kept precisely cut, the formal area widens in circular fashion to an enclosing massive stone wall on each side, then rises in a series of five terraces to the west facade of the house where the high doorway is reached by a horse-shoe stairway with iron balustrades. The doorway is decorated with climbing rose vines that swing in curved lines against the walls and meet in a point above the pediment.

The first terrace, as long as the breadth of the house itself, is a boxwood court of great dignity. It resembles nothing so much as two massive circular rooms connected by a short straight hall lying between the straight line of the house and the head of the double stairway leading to the next terrace below. The outstanding feature of this development is a series of cascades like great lotus leaves which descend along the stairways bearing water plants on their mirror surfaces. The great difference in height of the two terraces is evident only from the lower one where the supporting wall comes into view, and here gardenias are the featured plant. All the terraces are covered with a grass carpet and the lower ones are reached by way of grass-covered ramps. The lowest is supported by a concave wall with ramps on either side and in this wall seven semi-circular niches filled with clipped ivy suggest entrances into possible grottos under the great hill.

The walls everywhere are draped with climbing rose vines. Many species appear but Lady Gay and American Pillar seem to determine the color scheme,

Vista Through Formal Garden to Pleached Allee of Judas Trees

Photo by Tebbs & Knell

while Paul's Scarlet Climbers twine the two obelisks that stand just where the ascent begins. Behind the ivy and rose-covered stone wall are lined mimosa trees with a background of native forest, and quantities of eleagnus are introduced above the walls.

A driveway leads east through the woods to the main entrance which is away from the road, and there is also a woodland approach to this entrance from Pace's Ferry Road. This facade of the house is early Georgian. The elliptical drive circles a shrub-enclosed grass court where, across the court from the doorway, is a high wall broken by five niches and two circular stairways ascending to a terrace above. The three inner niches are overgrown with closely clipped ivy, while the two outer ones hold immense urns, a characteristic decoration about the walls and garden.

South of the house is a walled formal garden adjoining the south porch. This garden is rectangular in shape and features box and gardenias. The central fountain basin has a petal-shaped outline that is repeated in the generous boxwood plantings of the formal beds. Against the walls are straight line beds for perennials and annuals and tall crepe myrtle trees on the inside and Magnolia grandiflora on the outside soften the lines of the walls. The garden is green most of the year but in early spring and again in late summer is full of color. On the wall at the far end of this enclosure is an imposing architectural feature copied from one found in Rome, as are the lava-trimmed urns marking the side entrances to the garden and decorating the walls wherever accent is needed.

From the formal garden a pleached allee of Judas trees shading wide bands of blue scillas leads down to a woodland retreat. Pines and bamboo thicken the background and many camassias and erythronium have been naturalized among the native wild flowers and shrubs.

Formal Garden from South Porch at Swan House Photo by F. E. Lee

Jasmine and Rose Covered Balustrades Along Grass Ramps at Swan House

Photo by F. E. Lee

Mrs. Richard W. Johnston

Atlanta

MRS. JOHNSTON'S garden is built on a hillside in a series of terraces and was designed by Robert Cridland in 1928. The principal feature is the boxwood, the hedges and the specimen plants having been collected from old Georgia gardens.

The first terrace is a formal green garden which adjoins the house. It is surrounded with hedges of dwarf box, occasional tree box, and other evergreens, and in the center is a small round pool bordered with ivy. From here the garden ascends through three levels to a semi-circle of grass enclosed by a tall planting of tree box, juniper, mimosa and dogwood, where an old Italian figure of Diana stands against the dark evergreens. All three terraces are bordered with wide beds of tulips and other spring bulbs combined with bleeding-heart and flowering almond; then lilies, phlox, platycodon, asters and helenium. One terrace specializes in Siberian iris in variety. There are outlines of dwarf box and liriope, and each terrace with its accents of specimen box has for a background the grass slope up to the next shrubbery.

From the Diana circle a winding box-bordered walk leads to the upper garden. Beds of lilies and Japanese iris are along this walk which is shaded by mimosa and acacia trees. The upper garden was designed and planted by W. C. Hunter of Atlanta in 1930. It also is composed of three terraces retained by walls of field stone planted with helianthemum, dianthus, saponaria, arabis, iberis, and nepeta mussini. The upper level is in German iris and bulbs with a fine background of tree box. Below the stone wall which bisects the garden here, runs a small canal full of aquatic plants and little fish, the water flowing from an old Verona marble basin which is overhung by a huge blackgum tree. On the second terrace is a rose garden, and the lowest level has rows of flowers for cutting—peonies, lilies, bulbs, and perennials, its low surrounding wall covered with Cherokee roses. Along the rises from each terrace rock gardens are laid, and to the east many southern wild flowers border the paths that lead into the woods.

Looking from Green Garden Toward Diana Circle, Johnston Garden

Photo by F. E. Lee

Photo by F. E. Lee

Rill with Aquatic Plants Against Fieldstone Wall, Johnston Garden

Knollwood

Mr. and Mrs. William H. Kiser

Atlanta

AT the entrance to the Kiser estate high walls of evergreens—abelia, English laurel and ligustrum—behind the hedge and bordering the drive, serve only as ornamental plantings and not to screen, for beyond them the land rises in a graceful sweep to the oak-shaded hill on which the house is placed, a lovely Georgian picture of mellow red brick with classic trim, set off by the green of tall trees and the massed box and gardenias across the front.

On the left of the entrance drive the lawns are bordered with thickets of bamboo and pampas grass, and there are groups of dogwoods, hawthorns, and cedars. To the right a long stretch of turf—Bermuda grass, bright green in summer, soft broom color in winter—spreads from the tangles of rosa bracteata at the hedge up to the rim of the woods where hundreds of sourwood have been introduced to make a scarlet fringe in autumn against the native pines.

Back of the north portico of the house lies the formal garden, designed about fifteen years ago by Norman C. Butts. In ideal arrangement for this climate the series of wide terraces are made on ground sloping to the north. A long panel of grass runs down the center of the garden, divided by the central walk and cut across by lateral walks on each level. In each of the resulting squares of green is an old boxwood while bordering the middle walk is a line of clipped junipers-Ashfordii, their gray green contrasting with the tall hedges of privet which bound the two sides of the garden and, on the lowest level, form a high clipped wind-break behind the tea-house.

Paired mimosa trees arch over the uppermost terrace which is kept all green, boxwood, January jasmine and berberis defining the entrance. At one side of the middle level stands a fine white oak and beneath it an opening is cut in the privet hedge for a path to the long rows of vegetables, small fruits, and flowers for cutting. The two flower terraces below the oak are planted in roses, the last retaining wall facing the tea house and a semi-circular plot of grass set with a small reflecting pool. The wall of lichen-covered stone is planted so thickly with creeping phlox, Siberian wall flowers, plumbago, tunica, alyssum saxatile and ajuga that the interwoven mats of bloom make a band of brilliant embroidered color between the garden proper and the tea house enclosure.

Color is the keynote of this garden, a fastidious selection of material resulting each year in new harmonies. The borders and formally cut beds on the terraces are faced down with thick plantings of low growing flowers—iberis, Longfellow daisies, phlox subulata, spice pinks or dwarf ageratum. Peonies, tulips, iris, lilies and chrysanthemums are ever present in a lovely profusion while around them skillful combinations of various annuals and perennials fill out the seasonal pictures.

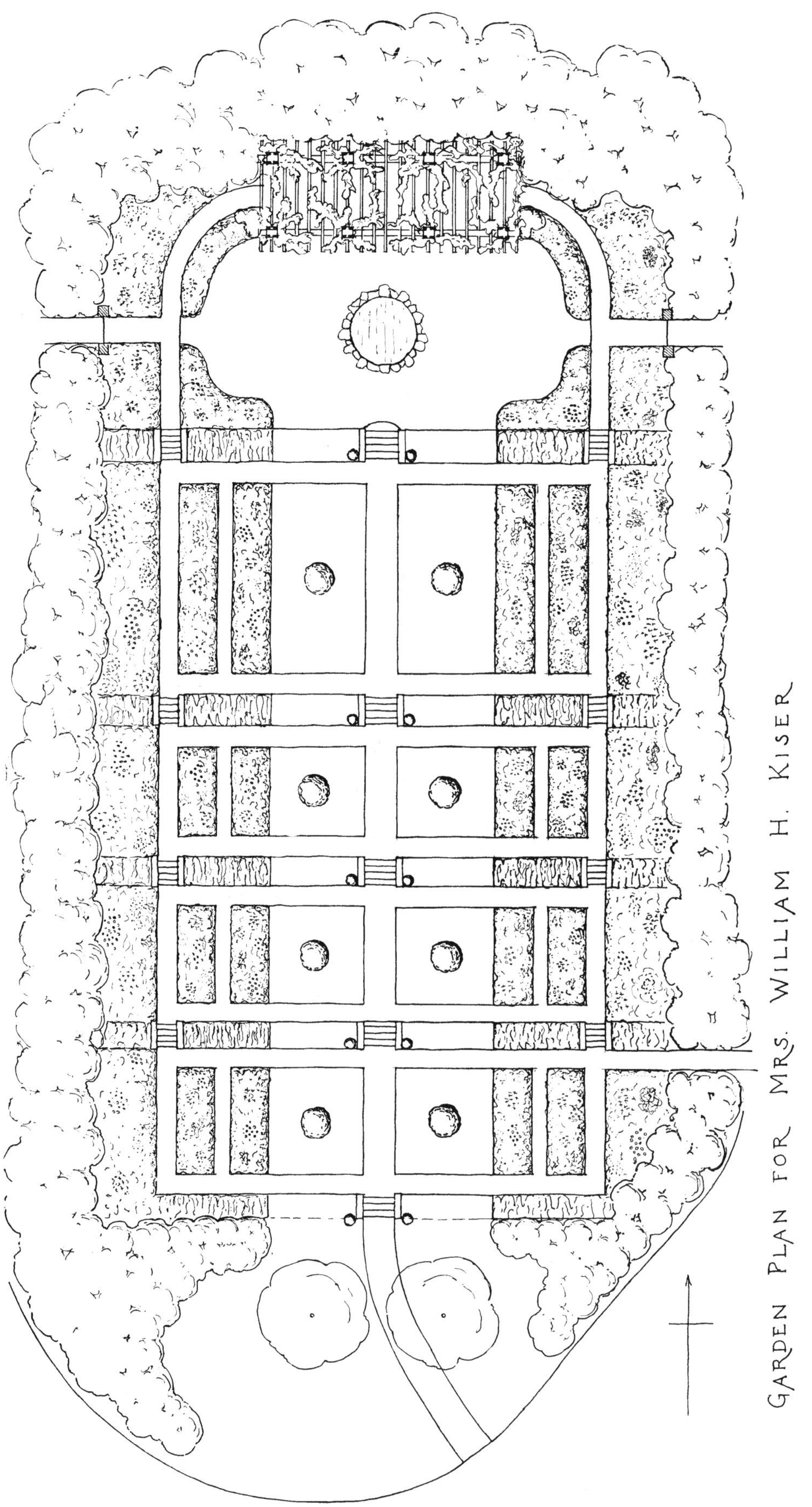
GARDEN PLAN FOR MRS. WILLIAM H. KISER

Terraced Formal Garden at Knollwood

Photo by F. E. Lee

Early Spring's Pastel Tints at Knollwood

Photo by F. E. Lee

Planted Wall on Lowest Terrace of Garden at Knollwood

Photo by F. E. Lee

Woodhaven

Mr. and Mrs. Robert F. Maddox

Atlanta

WOODHAVEN, the estate of Mr. and Mrs. Robert Foster Maddox, with its seventy-five acres of lawns, gardens and woodlands, has been planned entirely by the owners and in barely twenty years has acquired the mellowed air of a much older place. Originally the property consisted of a stretch of uneven but well-timbered woods ending in a deep ravine where corn and cotton straggled up the banks. In the ravine is now Mrs. Maddox's terraced sunken garden which was the first formal garden of any pretensions in Atlanta.

The big oaks of the forest were carefully preserved. Magnolias and other shade trees, flowering trees and shrubs, various conifers, boxwood and broad-leafed evergreens were added from year to year as one garden grew into another or one beautified section of the place called for further vistas. The "landscape" happened as the needs or taste of the owners required and the plan so evolved shows the art of adapting difficult conditions to use so naturally that the outcome is enduringly beautiful.

As an instance, the unsightly ravine adjacent to the ridge on which the house was built was terraced to prevent washing. After "a man and a mule" (Mrs. Maddox's only professional assistants) shaped the terraces evenly the great bowl was given a pool to hold the water which drained there and to reflect the color of the grass-bordered terraces. The steps which led from the old oaks down to the basin, were continued to the top of the opposite hillside and there a shelter for tea was built, whose pergola columns, swathed with roses and wistaria, now frame a lovely view. On the terraces low hedges of box hold in the massed bloom of peonies, iris, lilies and larkspur. The pool is emphasized by tall clipped biotas and against their dusky green stand Italian marble figures of the four seasons.

Woodhaven from the Air

Tea Terrace Under Great Oaks at Woodhaven

Photo by F. E. Lee

View of Bowl Garden at Woodhaven

Photo by F. E. Lee

These four ladies have aged gracefully in their Georgia setting and when the bowl is used as a theatre they are ornamental additions to the stage design, as well as to the garden symmetry. The path to the pergola is bordered by huge trimmed retinosporas, plumosa variety, which contrast with the more golden green of the biotas around the pool.

The Pace's Ferry road boundary of Woodhaven has clipped privet hedges and behind them a row of spaced deodars. The sloping lawn is shaded by oak trees through which glimpses can be seen of the English brick and plaster house set back on an elevation and overlooking the sunken garden from its western terrace. The entrance drive winds towards the house between heavy plantings of abelia, spireas, hardy hydrangeas and massed conifers tall enough to screen from view the vegetable gardens, cold frames, garage and servants' quarters. After passing the playhouse the drive circles the house, continues through a park-like woodland to the pergola tea-house with its vista of the formal garden, descends through plantings of rhododendron and laurel to cross a stream bordered by bamboo and native ferns.

The planting at Woodhaven is of great diversity but the material has been used in such quantities that the result is effectively structural. A succession of bloom has been planned in flowers, shrubs and trees. For spring there is the color of the naturalized small bulbs, many sorts of tulips, and iris of every nationality, along with the flowering shrubs. Summer brings various lilies: giganteum, auratum, and speciosum, with magnolias, crepe myrtles and hydrangeas. And roses—from April to November—are in fragrant profusion. In the formally-designed rose garden the paths are bordered by the ever-blooming little Marie Pavie and each of the twenty-four beds has a standard pink Radiance to give height to the pattern. The colors range through pink and rose shades to pale yellow and deep gold.

Autumn finds Michaelmas daisies, dahlias and chrysanthemums blending with the turning foliage, while in winter the shrubberies are enriched by purple and red barberry, mahonia, the blue-berried evergreen ligustrums, red fruited pyracanthas and nandina, and variegated aucubas. Woodhaven faithfully lives up to the promise of the ladies of the bowl garden in its offering of four seasons of beauty.

Photo by F. E. Lee

Mr. and Mrs. Edgar P. McBurney

Atlanta

MR. AND MRS. McBURNEY'S garden was planted about thirty years ago. It may fittingly be called a composite garden, and a cosmopolitan garden, as so many different elements have been combined to add interest to the concordant whole. Owned and planned by a flower-loving family there are mingled here traditions and echoes of their older gardens in other states—Virginia, Massachusetts, and New Jersey. And from Italy, France and Spain have come many of the garden ornaments and furnishings, while Holland has supplied the inspiration for one of the charming tulip gardens.

In the formal garden nearest the house the central flower beds are edged with dwarf box, a member of the garden family for nearly a century. Around this hale and hearty little old "grandmother of the garden" are grouped her taller kindred of other varieties of box, gathered here for memories of the earlier gardens as well as for its beauty of size. A semi-circular marble bench set against the tall box, and the sundial in the central bed came from Italy, while the graven bronze dial on the pedestal came from the old New Jersey garden.

Leaving the formal garden a path wanders along borders of evergreens and azaleas to the pool and Tempio d'amore. The classic white architectural features in a setting of green lawns and trees are picturesque by day, but particularly so by night when the fountain sprays are illuminated by an ingenious under-water lighting device which gives rainbow tints to the high jets of water. There is diffused lighting to produce moonlight effects on

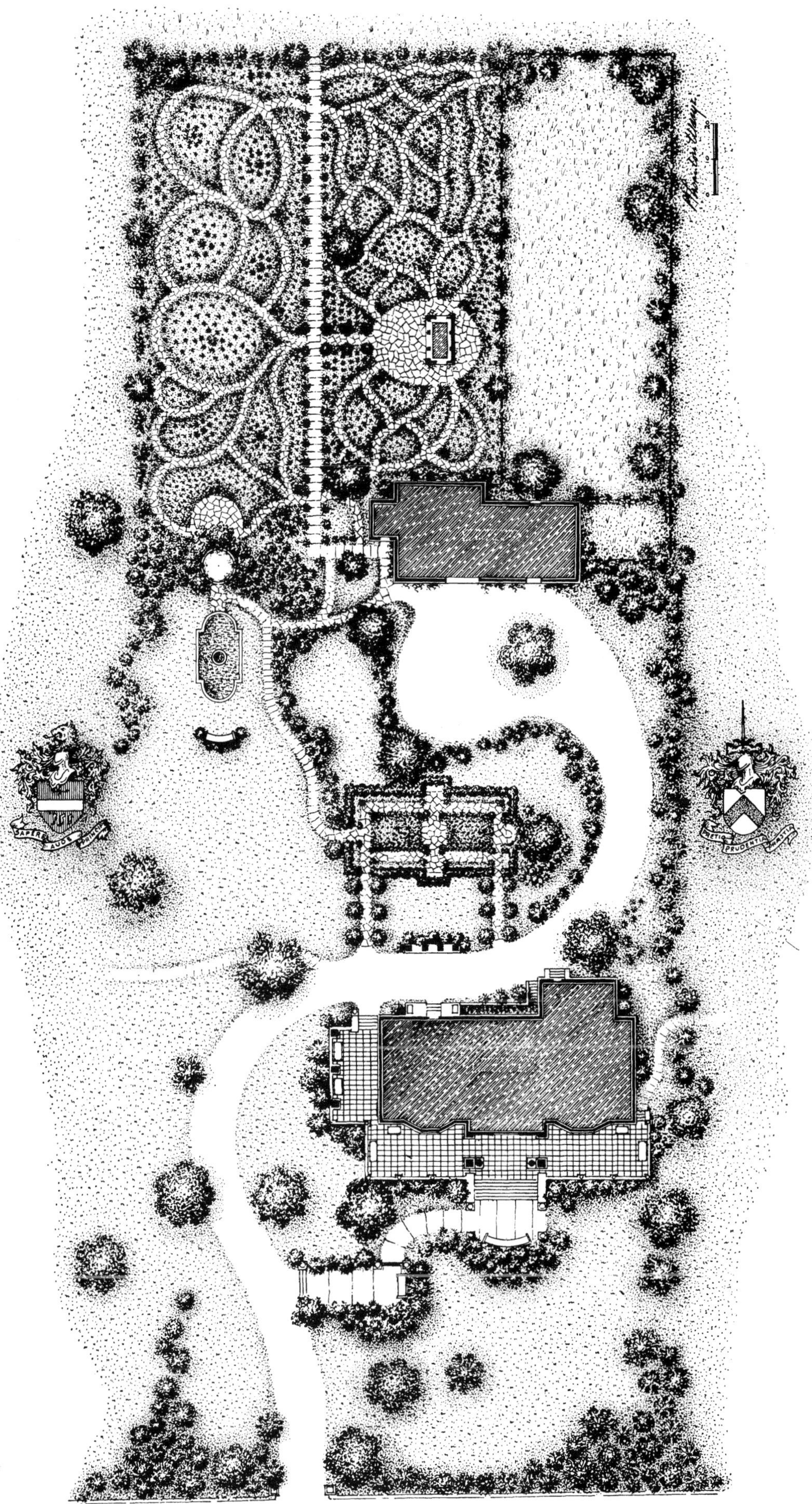

Boxwood Guards the Entrance to the McBurney Tulip Garden

the fine old trees and on the sculptured pieces and the mystical effect of white columns and changing iridescent spray against the deeper shadows of the garden is enchanting indeed.

Beyond the Tempio d'amore and completely hidden from it by thickly planted evergreens is an informal Dutch garden. Emerging from the shade of a gnarled old wistaria which curtains the evergreen entrance comes the surprise of this gay little garden, the youngest of the series. Here grass paths meander between closely set irregular beds of flowers and there are two shaded platforms with garden furniture and pleasant vistas—one looking across the arabesque of flower beds and ornamental bird baths, the other facing the sunset. The gardener's house to one side is a small Dutch cottage covered with vines and heavenly blue morning glories, their blue repeating the dominant note of the color scheme used in house and garden.

Shrubs and flowers of various seasons are in the different planting schemes about the grounds, but mid-April finds the gardens in full beauty with the tulips which are the specialty of the place. Mr. and Mrs. McBurney have given great consideration for many years to the choice of bulbs—for quality, period of bloom, length of stem and perfection of color. Darwins, breeders, cottage and May flowering tulips which do best in the South and bloom at approximately the same time, are planted each year by the many thousands and much thought is given to the color combinations which vary each season. Many of the old favorites are always used but new and rare varieties are tried out to make perfect the blended harmonies of the carefully worked out plantings.

The gardens for some years have been open to the public at tulip time and one day as many as seven thousand visitors shared the beauty of the superb display. According to Mrs. McBurney "not a leaf was disturbed at the end of the day, as these visitors were truly flower lovers and returned our hospitality with heart-warming courtesy and appreciation."

Boxwood House

Dr. and Mrs. Floyd W. McRae

Atlanta

"BOXWOOD HOUSE" presents an unusually interesting development of grounds and gardens in relation to the house. At the entrance gate one is immediately impressed with the effective use of a wall, well placed shrubbery and a few trees. Between the boxwood plantings on the right of the driveway, a stone walk leads to the main entrance of the broad gabled house of stucco with stone quoins, essentially English in character. Here the walk widens out into a terrace bordered by low boxwood. Beyond this, the lawn slopes away under native trees of oak, pine and sourwood to dense borders of shrubbery, evergreen and flowering, which extend entirely around the grounds and insure privacy. The lawn continues around the far end of the house, and here, under flowering crabs, one approaches the garden front which is pictured.

Small Pools Connected by Canals Planted with Water Iris Photo by Reeves

View from Terrace into Formal Garden

Photo by Reeves

The garden is so keenly in keeping with the atmosphere of the house that it seems an integral part of it. A low rock wall in the background is balanced on the opposite side by the loggia, while the stone terrace of the house is continued into the garden walk. Of particular interest here, as well as on the front and side wings, is the use of vines and climbing roses. Gnarled old grape vines can be seen against the house, with Lady Ashton roses on the balustrade. Wistaria and Euonymus radicans are used effectively on the loggia wing. On the left of the picture, opposite the broad steps, an old English stone and lead fountain, dated 1769, is set into a nook which is almost hidden by crabapples and lilacs and filled with shade-loving flowers. The four corner beds are planted for a succession of bloom; the low border around the garden just above the grass level is a brilliant mat of color in early spring; pseudacorus and Japanese iris grow at the ends of the rectangular pools where water lilies bloom all summer; and potted plants are changed with the seasons. Of simple design and in an appropriate setting, this garden is completely satisfying. Steps on either side of the fountain recess curve down to the rose garden.

In contrast to the open garden above, this one is charmingly secluded. It is designed on an ellipse, with walks of warm buff-colored stone, pansies border the rose beds and Cape jasmine is used against the wall, with Rugosa roses almost covering the curved iron railings. At the foot of the stairs a figure stands guard, and on the other side of the garden is a semi-circle of pear trees, whose overlapping branches can be seen in the foreground. Paths lead away through shrubbery borders and across the lawn and a turn brings one back again to the garden front.

On entering the loggia, with its rows of pot plants, a last backward glance reveals a view of the garden and in the distance a glimpse into a wooded recess.

Rose Garden at Boxwood House Photo by Reeves

Boxwood

Mr. and Mrs. Charles Veazey Rainwater
Atlanta

Photo by F. E. Lee

THE superb boxwood which gives its name to the home of Mr. and Mrs. Rainwater has been collected over a period of seventeen years. From deserted farm houses or old places whose owners were neglectful and unappreciative of its beauty, this treasure of boxwood has been transplanted to become the principal motif in a series of intimate gardens which surround the house. Three acres are laid out in an intricate and original plan in which box of all sizes and varieties is used as the basis of design.

The house lies hidden from the street by a hedge of arbor vitae growing above an ivy-covered bank and in this is set the delicately-designed white wooden entrance gate. Virginia red cedars and deodars increase the depth of the evergreen screen. Five-foot hedges of boxwood line the path to the white brick house, old box trees flank the entrance steps, and English box borders the lawns where white and pink dogwoods bloom against the deep green of magnolias.

Adjoining the house to the rear is a rectangular walled green garden used as an outdoor living-room and dining-room. Across the narrow ivy-bordered pool in the lawn is a garden figure set in a niche of the wall and shadowed by two tall cedars. Mahonia, abelia, osmanthus and English laurel afford varying foliage contrasts to the heavy clumps of English box against the side walls and the corner trees of Buxus arborescens.

Steps lead up from this garden to a semi-circle of lawn under big ivy-wrapped oak trees. The lateral hedges are of ten-foot Buxus sempervirens and two huge rounded specimens accent a vista to

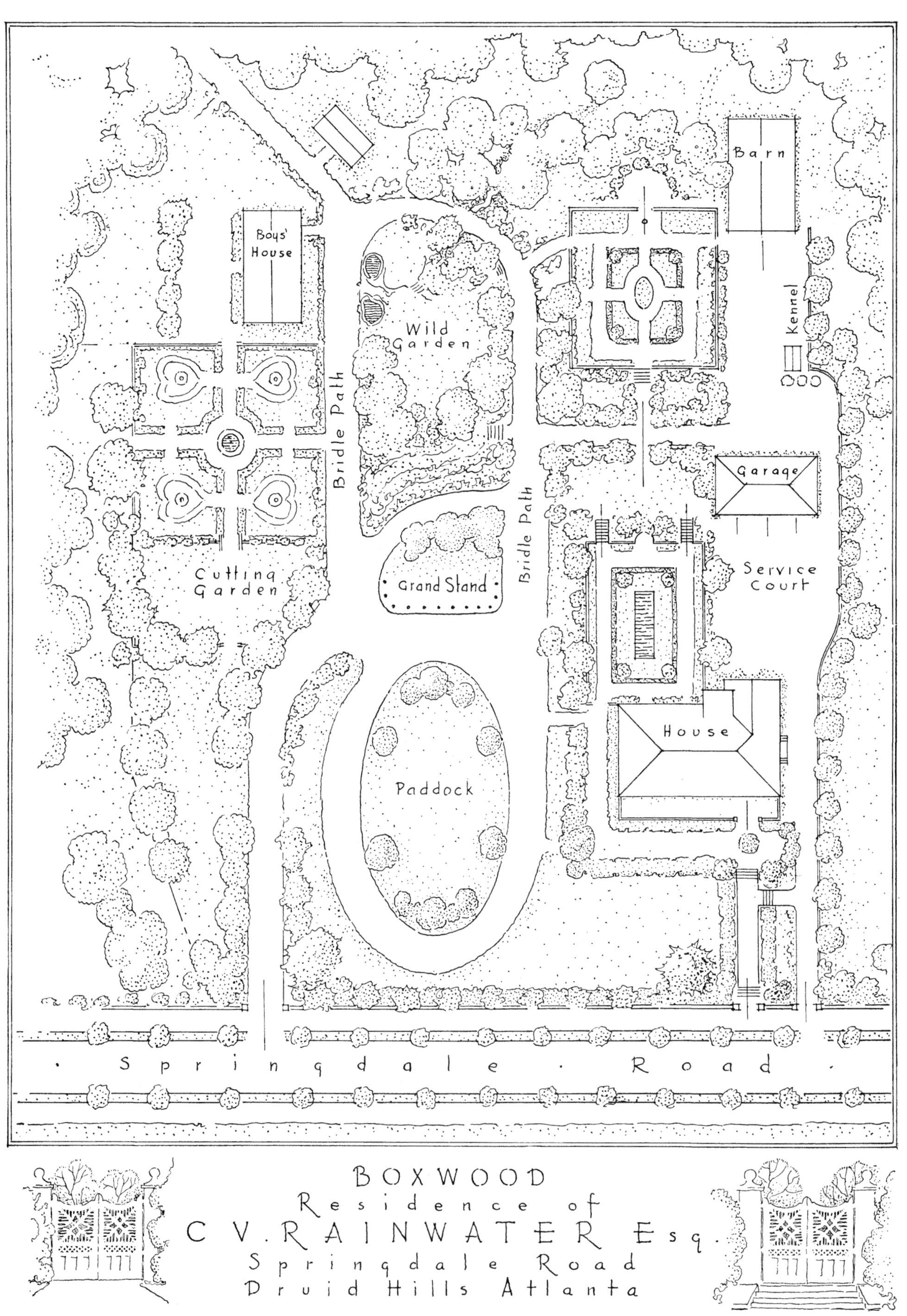

BOXWOOD
Residence of
C. V. RAINWATER Esq.
Springdale Road
Druid Hills Atlanta

Shadow and Sunlight, Boxwood

Photo by F. E. Lee

the rose garden on a still higher level. Buxus suffruticosa borders the path here and the formally-patterned rose beds are outlined by low dwarf edgings. A dense allee of flowering plum, pear, crabapple and peach trees with an under planting of native azalea separates the rose garden from the woodland path of the wild garden. In this shady spot, thick with rhododendron and kalmia, are rock-bordered pools and bird feeding stations and many native ferns and wild flowers.

The bridle path which circles the tree-screened knoll of the wild garden continues in a figure-eight loop around an oval space of lawn where a green mound, rising above a wall of ivy and boxwood, constitutes itself a "judge's stand" for the boy's horse shows. Along the oval "paddock" are big irregular masses of English box and a row of magnolias in the background hides the entrance drive.

The boy's Club House, with its early American architecture and furnishings, suggests a long gone day. In front, a tiny lawn has a picket fence and gate with an old farm bell. At the back is a border of herbs edged by conch shells, and, to one side, hedged in by tall boxwood, is an old-fashioned garden with four heart-shaped beds set around an ivy-covered stone wall. The beds are outlined in wide dwarf box and in each of the heart-shaped pavings is a millstone. Enormous Cape jasmine bushes are in the four corners and against the clipped arborvitae hedge which separates this garden from the cutting garden.

Roses, iris, peonies and many old-fashioned flowers grow here. These, with the spring-blooming fruit trees and dogwoods, and the summer wealth of crepe myrtle, magnolias and Cape jasmine give seasonal color among the many evergreens. But throughout the year, with or without the adjunct of bloom, it is the priceless collection of old boxwood which gives these gardens their distinction and great charm.

Early American Club House, Boxwood Photo by F. E. Lee

Broadlands

Mr. and Mrs. Hugh Richardson

Atlanta

"BROADLANDS," the country estate of Mr. and Mrs. Hugh Richardson, consists of a two hundred fifty acre tract of wooded hillsides, shaded valleys, and cleared farmlands. In the woodland are many native trees, white oaks, Loblolly pines, hickories, and tulip poplars predominating, though thirty or more species mix in goodly number and add beauty and interest to the grove. A vigorous native undergrowth of dogwood, red bud, hawthorn, crabapple, buck-eye and sumac has been increased in numbers by the introduction of thousands of these same kinds and other thousands of rhododendrons, kalmias, Japanese maples, Ligustrum—Japonica and lucidum—crepe myrtle, horse chestnut, oak-leaf hydrangeas, English laurels, Magnolia grandiflora, cherry laurel, euonymous, junipers, abelia, barberry and various blossoming shrubs.

The house, a charming combination of two periods of early American architecture, was planned by Aymar Embury II of New York. Its location is on the pinnacle of the highest hill of the tract. That the owner of these grounds is a lover and collector of boxwoods is everywhere evident for, though the house is but ten years old, boxwoods of

Openwork stone balustrades with lines of massed boxwood define the terraces and garden levels at Broadlands.

Sunken Garden, Broadlands Photo by F. E. Lee

Old Boxwood at Entrance, Broadlands

Photo by Richard Smith, N. Y.

fifty, in some cases a hundred years of age, soften the lines of the house, enclose the terraces, and outline the drive as far as it is in view from the doorway. The house with its Georgian porch fronts toward the distant valley in which flows Nancy's Creek, and toward the pine-covered hills beyond; and also immediately upon a series of grass-covered, box-enclosed terraces, each of which is a decorative unit within itself. The upper terrace is flush with the Georgian porch where flower boxes add color both to the porch and to the terrace. The lowest terrace forms a sunken garden against the strong retaining wall of the highest. A quilt of small-leaf ivy covering this wall is surpassed in beauty only by the magnificent wall of boxwoods that forms the outer edge of the terrace.

From the entrance on Pace's Ferry Road a woodland drive winds into a valley through deep shade and out into the sunshine again where climbing roses in great profusion make splashes of color against the banks. At one spot a dahlia bed, at another a garden for cut flowers, then into the shadow again, it zigzags its way up the hill in great curves till it reaches the doorway to form a loop for car exit. The outer edge of the loop is partly enclosed by a curved decorative fence in white, against which are planted boxwoods and behind which grow a great variety of broad-leaf evergreens.

A second entrance is on North Side Drive where the gates are of the same white wood lace-work as the circular fence near the house. Along this drive the cut-down banks have been planted attractively with rock garden plants and many low-growing junipers have been introduced. Enclosing the grounds on both fronts is a dry-laid rock wall, gradually growing green as plants spread themselves from its crevices.

The woodland stream at Broadlands cascades under the bridge and widens into pools near the rock gardens.

Photo by Tebbs and Knell, N. Y.

Llwyn

Mr. and Mrs. G. W. Rowbotham

Atlanta

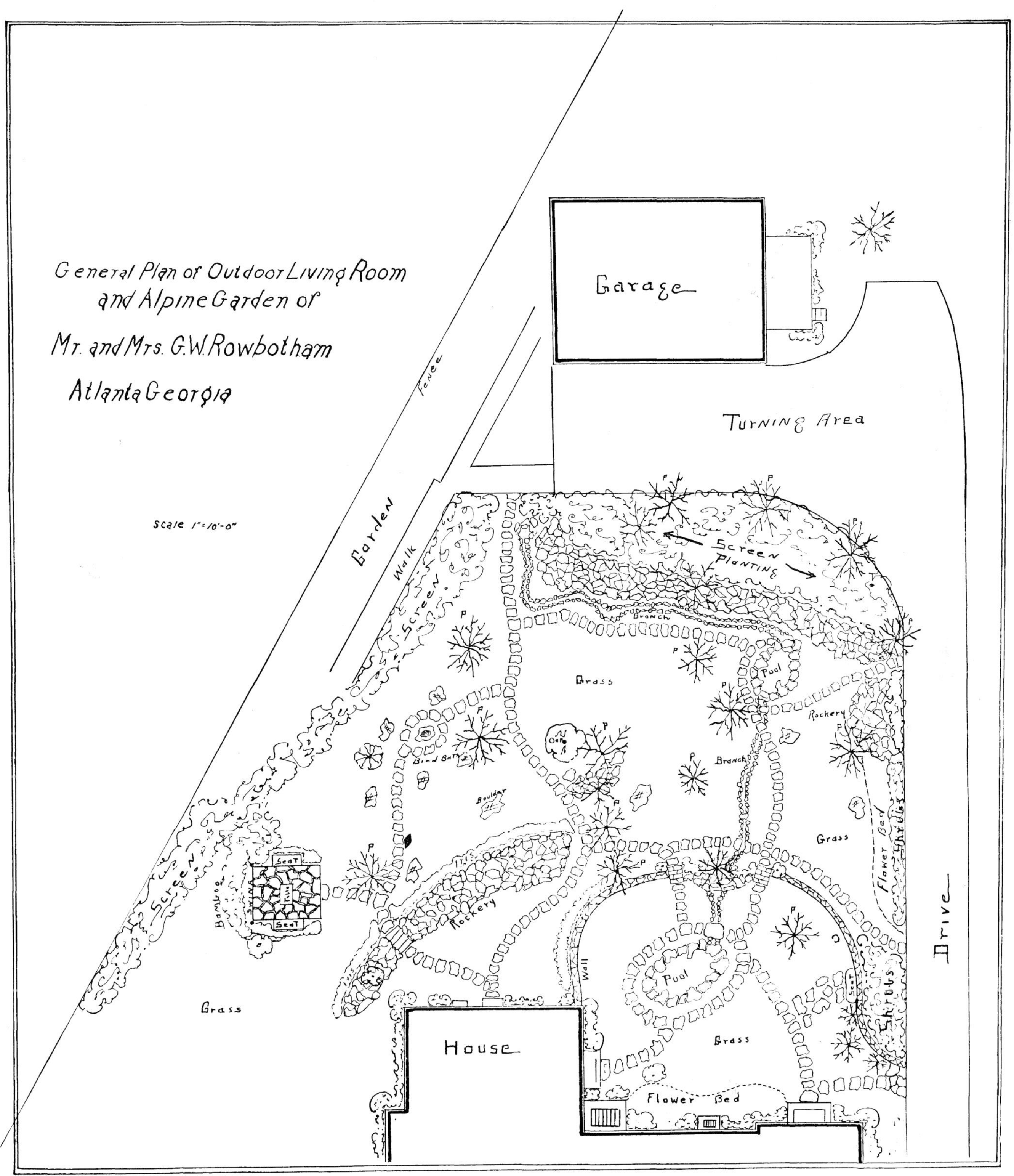

Pines and Rock Planting, Llwyn

Photo by F. E. Lee

"LLWYN," which in Welsh means "grove," is the name given by Mr. and Mrs. Rowbotham to their English-type residence situated atop a rolling hill in a pine grove and overlooking the golf course and lake of the Brookhaven Country Club. A lawn, with groupings of many kinds of shrubs and deciduous trees, surrounds the house. The grounds at Llwyn were laid out by W. L. Monroe of Atlanta.

The fact that the garden is on rising terraces makes it possible to enjoy some part of it from every window in the house, and the open door of the sunroom frames a section of the rock garden. Here is convincing proof of the fallacy of the belief that it is impossible to have a satisfactory garden beneath our Georgia pines. The carpet of grass and creeping plants, ferns, perennials, and broad-leaved evergreens, together present a picture of luxuriant growth seldom equalled by a garden in full sun. Amid all this green the first crocus is followed closely by the golden waves of narcissi—planted in different varieties for a long period of bloom—then come pansies, tulips, and columbines. Beyond a group of flowering cherry trees the vivid colors of azaleas show against a background of rhododendron and mountain laurel.

A woodland setting frames a tea garden with table and benches hewn out of stone, and a stream trickles down from the brow of the hill to ripple over rocks and into pools at lower levels. Lichen-covered rocks and portions of old walls have been deftly used to impart an air of age to the garden. A playground with shuffle-board court and rustic swings is shaded by pine trees in which wistaria and yellow jessamine grow. There is a background planting of wild azaleas, and the pungent odor of pine-straw arises from paths which lead back into a woodland garden abounding in calycanthus, azaleas, crabapples, redbuds, and dogwoods.

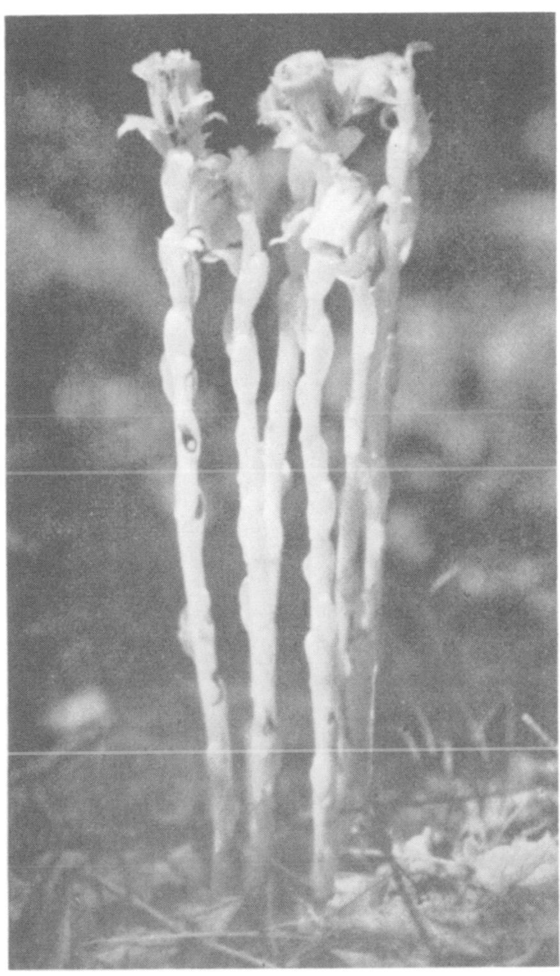

Indian Pipes Photo by F. E. Lee

Wingfield

Governor and Mrs. John M. Slaton

Atlanta

AT Wingfield on Peachtree Road is the estate of former Governor and Mrs. John M. Slaton, the property consisting of an extensive tract of open woodland surrounding the house with its shadowed lawn and formal gardens.

The house is connected with the garden by a brick walk and a broad-tread horse-shoe stairway outlined in low clipped hedges. At the garden level is a curved love-seat of flat stones surrounded by a planting of junipers and vinca, and the floor of each of the two garden terraces is woven of the same mellow red brick as the walk and the stairs. Centering the upper level lies a circular fountain pool where lilies, palms and cattails grow; and in each of the four large divisions is a particularly fine specimen of English laurel against which crepe myrtle blooms. Strips of grass separate the shrubs from the flower borders of annuals and perennials which complete the planting and furnish a display of brilliant color characteristic of summer gardens in Atlanta.

Beyond a tall clipped hedge of privet wide brick steps continue to the second terrace with its ivy-wrapped sun-dial, where tiny precise edgings enclose parterres filled with roses, six hundred strong, and in each of the four corner parterres is a big gardenia bush for accent.

The entire garden is enclosed by a privet hedge of twenty-five years' standing, the pride of a gardener of equal years of service. Broad-leafed evergreens and flowering shrubs are planted as windbreaks on the north and west, while three very large perfectly-shaped post oaks stand near three corners of the enclosure. The pattern of this garden was designed by R. B. Cridland of Philadelphia.

Photo by Reeves

To keep a forest and have a lawn too is a difficult task but it has been successfully accomplished at Wingfield. For many years selected native trees have been allowed all the space needed for perfect growth. The result is many handsome specimens, largely oaks: white, water, southern red, and post. Along the driveway there have been introduced many deodars, magnolias, crepe myrtles and mimosas. A hedge and a screen planting of broad-leafed evergreens across the long frontage shut out the street view and protect the spreading lawns which merge into a quiet forest where winding roads and bridle paths lead to the west gates, a half mile away on Andrews Drive.

Fountain in Formal Garden at Wingfield

Photo by Reeves

Mr. and Mrs. J. T. Selman
Atlanta

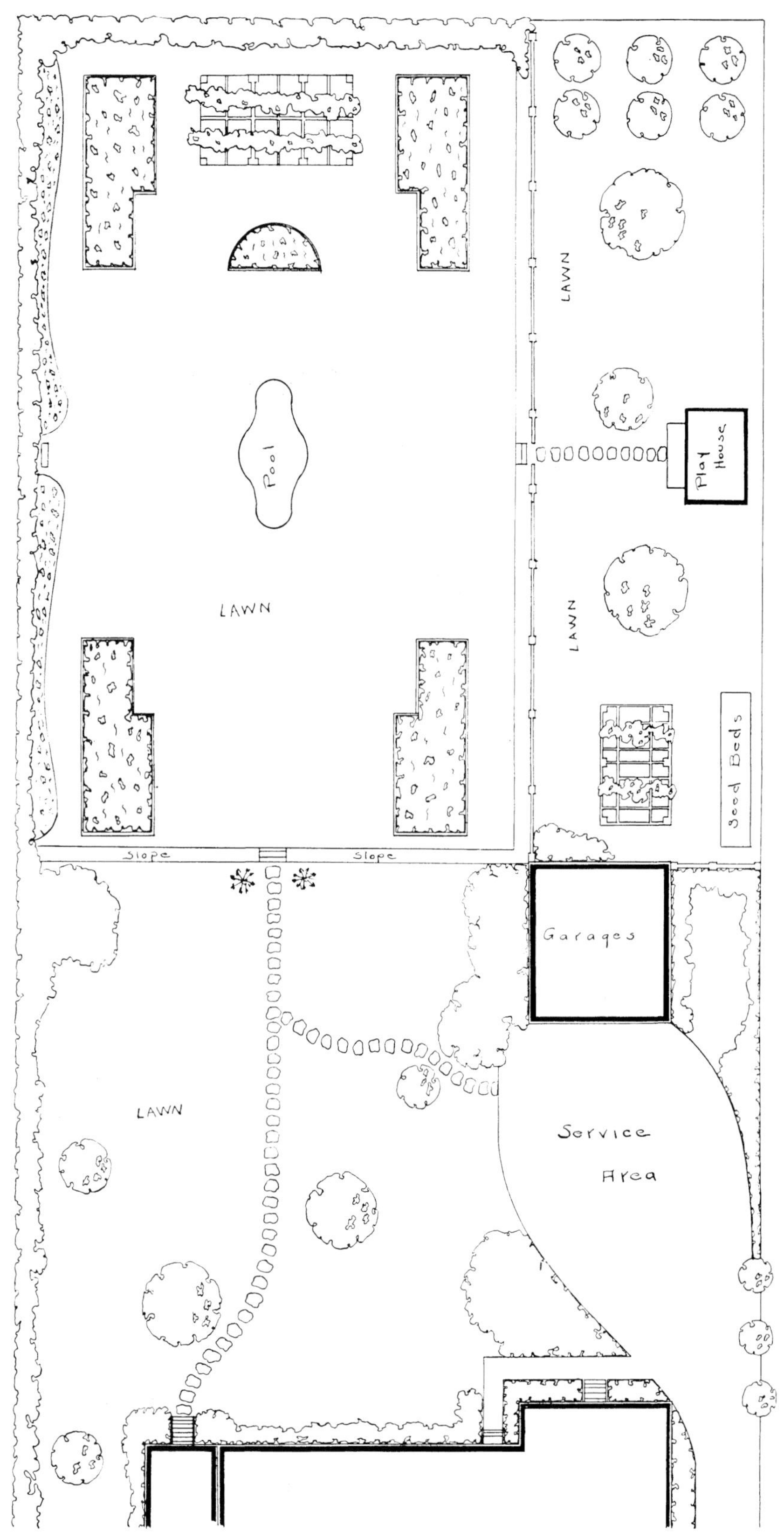

GARDENS are built for many purposes and to give expression to various ideals, but a garden built to be lived in invariably achieves a special charm. Mrs. Selman's secluded small garden which opens from the rear terrace of the house is planned and carried out on simple lines and with a selection of sturdy ornamental plants to furnish a succession of color around the central lawn.

From two big pine trees on the upper level where groups of moss-covered boulders are planted in many varieties of low creeping flowers, a path of weather-beaten flagstones leads across the grass towards a small rock-bound pool holding a fountain figure. The pool, in full sunshine, displays a wealth of water lilies and along its rim grow clumps of Japanese iris. Mimosa trees are in the background and beyond the pool a white-columned pergola living-room supports vines of wistaria, roses, Heavenly Blue morning glories and moon flowers—a combination to give succeeding bloom for all the outdoor months. In the four corners of the rectangular lawn are L-shaped beds of roses edged with wide strips of pansies which are replaced in summer by Rose of Heaven petunias. Borders of German and Spanish iris show against the ligustrum hedge which is the far boundary of the garden and along the white picket fence which separates the service yard and the seed and testing beds.

In the shrubbery which has grown high enough to give the garden complete privacy, there are many evergreens in front of a row of Lombardy poplars, while the summer background has the color of watermelon pink crepe myrtles contrasted with white altheas and hydrangeas.

Beyond the rose-hung picket fence, stepping-stones go past a scuppernong arbor and a row of fig bushes to a small log cabin stocked with garden gadgets, fertilizers, spraying machines and tools. And then, most important of all, comes the compost heap, a full-fledged soil factory, screened by shrubbery. This particular spot is the pride of the owner who believes the success of any garden may be measured by the efficiency of this adjunct.

The garden plans were made by W. L. Monroe.

Mr. and Mrs. W. H. Stephenson
Atlanta

Photo by Reeves

THE formal gardens of Mrs. W. H. Stephenson, which were designed by W. C. Pauley, lie hidden from the street by the red brick Georgian house. Matched pairs of boxwoods are used in the foundation plantings and to the right of the driveway stands a long line of splendid old tulip poplars, probably set there in the past as a land line. About the grounds are many dogwood and fine oak trees, while a lavish use of various white flowering shrubs creates a quiet, dignified background for the house and the colorful gardens.

From the driveway, a wide flag-stone walk gives on to the box-bordered brick terrace across the back of the house, and from here may be had the first full view of the formal gardens graduating upward from the lowest level. Two flights of steps ascend to a brick wall bordering a wide panel of grass, which is centered by a reflecting pool. A box hedge, trimmed low, finishes off this panel at either end, and beyond the walkways, to right and left, are thickly planted perennial borders. A massed effect in each corner is of azalea—Indica alba, Hemerocallis gold dust, columbine, Maid Marian phlox, bronze snapdragons, and stokesia.

Above the pool level is the upper garden of perennials where phlox-Von Lassburg, Iris-Lord of June, heuchera, and hardy candytuft are used in profusion. Standard roses—Sensation and Etoile de Hollande—spaced at regular intervals on either side, point the way to a summer-house of ornamental iron work, where a stone slab in the floor shows the points of the compass and informs the visitor that the exact elevation on which he stands is 1007.4 feet above sea level. A dense planting of shrubbery makes this a cool, inviting spot, and quantities of lilies of many different varieties furnish a succession of bloom throughout the summer months.

Beyond the perennial garden lie two semi-circular rose gardens, themselves enclosing grass panels, and screened by twin hedges of Rugosa roses.

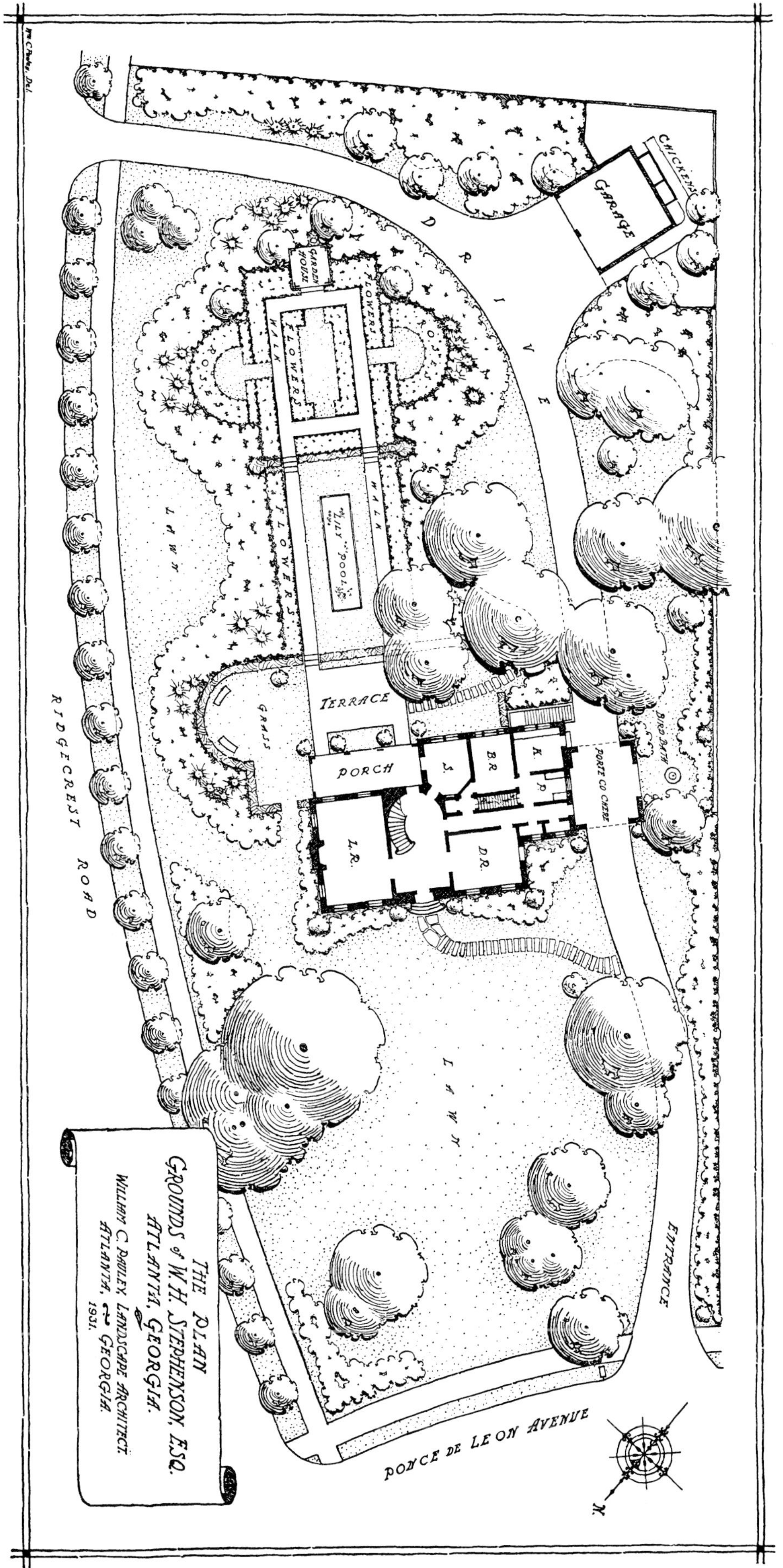
THE PLAN
GROUNDS of W.H. STEPHENSON, ESQ.
ATLANTA, GEORGIA.
WILLIAM C. PAULEY, LANDSCAPE ARCHITECT.
ATLANTA, GEORGIA.
1931.
DRIVE
GARAGE
CHICKENS
GARDEN HOUSE
FLOWERS
WALK
ROSES
LILY POOL
LAWN
TERRACE
GRASS
PORCH
L.R.
D.R.
S.
BR
K
P
PORTE CO CHERE
BIRD BATH
RIDGECREST ROAD
PONCE DE LEON AVENUE
ENTRANCE
N.

Summer House and Reflecting Pool, Stephenson Garden Photo by Reeves

Mr. and Mrs. Henry B. Tompkins

Atlanta

THIS garden was planned by Neel Reid when he planned the house, and their relation is so close that each seems a part of the other. The land rises at the back, so that in order to have the garden flat the hill was cut into, and the garden enclosed on three sides by stone walls thirteen feet in height. The fourth wall is that of the rear of the house, and the library opens through a doorway, hung with white clematis, upon the small rectangular garden which is formal and very simple in plan.

In the center of a tapis vert is a square pool. On each side of this are two box-bordered flower beds between which are walks of old brick, laid in sand. At the back of the garden rise two curved flights of steps leading to the garage which has a rose vine clambering over its classic portico. In the semicircle between the stone stairways is a fine old Italian statue. The garden walls are completely covered with English ivy, and the planting above the walls consists of alternating roses, Silver Moon and Doctor Van Fleet, which hang over the wall. The bloom in June is profuse and the clouds of pale pink and white are very lovely against the sombre green of the ivy. Between the roses above the wall are planted flowering shrubs; forsythia, January jasmine, spirea, syringa, crepe myrtle and gardenia bushes. Beyond is a row of mimosa trees which make a background of feathery green, and their bloom is like a rosy haze. So much for the outer edge of the little walled garden.

The garden itself is charming the year round, because in winter its ivy and box hedges are green and the January jasmine tumbles over the wall in a cascade of sunny yellow.

In the flower beds are planted the things which give a succession of bloom, from the tulips, scillas, phlox, narcissi and iris of spring, through the larkspur, peonies and gay annuals of summer, to the chrysanthemums of fall. Against the house are ligustrum, wistaria, funkia, and ginger lilies, lilies of the valley, white azalea, white iris and white peonies, while water hyacinths, lotus, and pink, blue and yellow water lilies give color to the pool.

The garden is lived in through many daytime hours and on moonlit nights it is a lovely spot, heavy with the fragrance of tuberoses, nicotiana, moon flowers and jasmine.

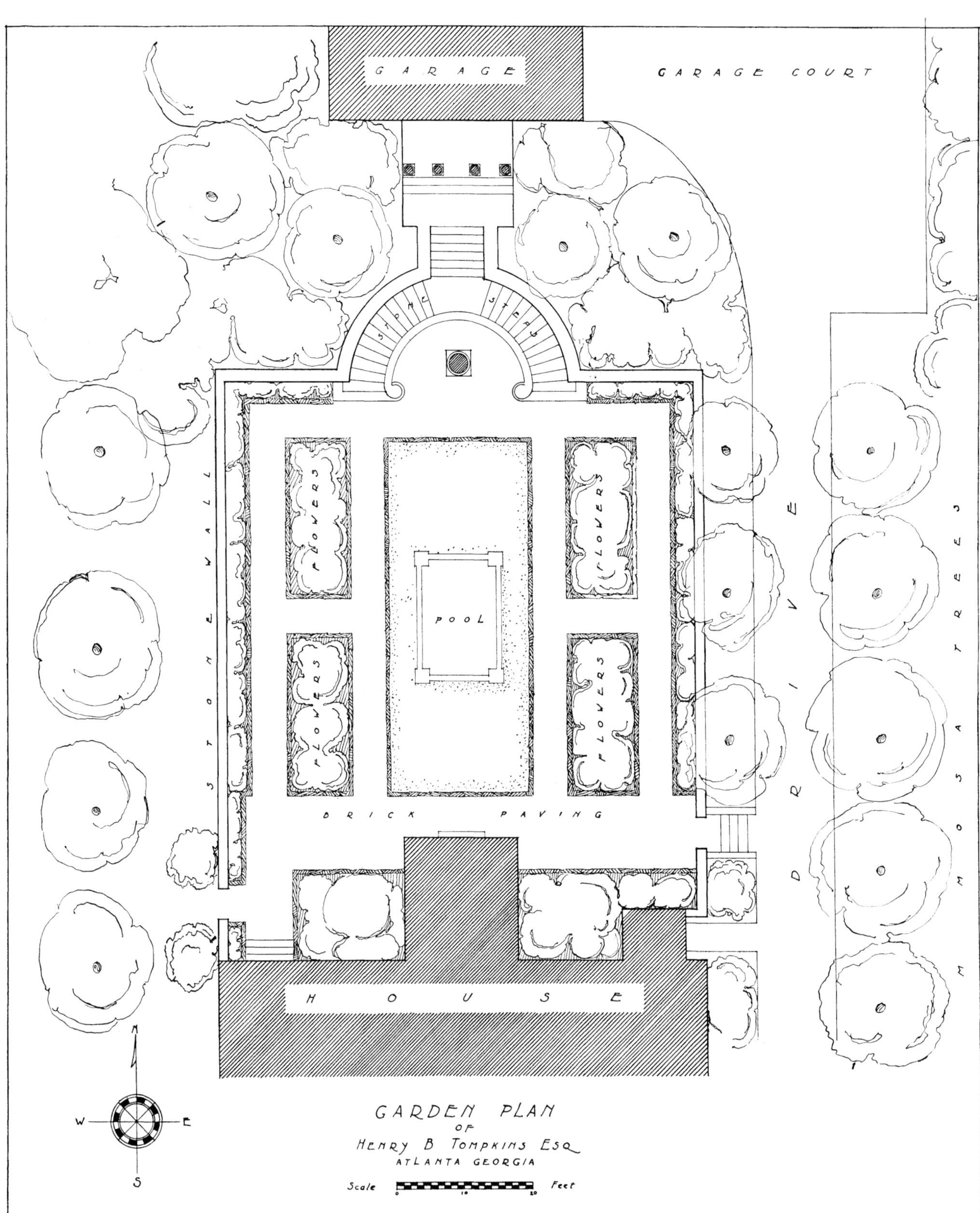
GARAGE
GARAGE COURT
STONE STEPS
STONE WALL
FLOWERS
FLOWERS
POOL
FLOWERS
FLOWERS
BRICK PAVING
DRIVE
MIMOSA TREES
HOUSE
N
W
E
S
GARDEN PLAN
OF
HENRY B TOMPKINS ESQ
ATLANTA GEORGIA
Scale
0
10
20
Feet

Ivy Bound Pool and Rose Hung Walls in Tompkins Garden

Woodland

Mrs. Arthur Tufts

Atlanta

Photo by Reeves

"WOODLAND," the estate of Mrs. Arthur Tufts, is a tract of twenty-five or more acres near Emory University, a suburb of Atlanta. The site was chosen because of the large trees, wild azaleas, stream, and dense woodland, and the name was given to accent the sanctuary idea, for here not only birds but the little wild animals, lizards, squirrels and chipmunks were to be left unmolested.

The passer-by sees no house but a long avenue of hackberry—locally called sugar berry—trees, a strip of grass bordered by sweet scented honeysuckle kept in bounds by shears; two hedges of

Iris Time at Woodland

Photo by Reeves

Van Houttei Spirea, a hundred or more feet long which are waterfalls of white blossoms in early spring; and ivy-clad pink gate posts at two entrances some five hundred feet apart and connected by a stretch of grass where specimen trees grow. The lawns between the gateways slope up to a hedge of flowering quince, Spirea thunbergii and purple iris, with a background of rambler roses against a dark forest of trees made vivid by many red-leaved Japanese maples, wistarias reaching to tops of pines or oaks, and hundreds of dogwoods and sourwood.

Paths lead through the woods where jonquils are naturalized and in June the effect is repeated with thousands of tawny lilies. In early spring wild oxalis, rue anemones and ferns grow under the trees and along the stream, the air is perfumed with thousands of sweet shrubs (calacanthus) and the woods are aglow with bright azaleas, while rhododendrons bloom in the cooler spots.

The roadway, bordered in Cherokee roses and perennial peas, forms a horseshoe following the contour of the land high above the little stream in the ravine and leads to the house which is built of pink plaster, along Spanish lines. A living-porch reaches out into the woods like the prow of a ship. The soft color of the plaster sets off the wistaria that drapes the house, and tones in with the autumn leaves in the fall. The house was planned by Henry Hornbostle of New York.

The garden is everywhere,—but what might be called the garden proper rambles in an informal manner in the sunshine near the tennis court, play grounds and kitchen garden, and uses the orchard, which is grassed, as a background. A yellow and blue garden is reached by way of a scuppernong arbor and a grass path bordered by forget-me-nots, ranunculus and valley lilies. Another garden is in pastel shades and still another in red and white. The main garden is a perpetual garden but is loveliest when the fifteen year old wall of roses: Silver Moon, Dr. Van Fleet, Caroline Testout, Christine Wright and Climbing Killarney, blend with hundreds of iris, painted daisies and Madonna Lilies.

Beyond a fence of Paul Scarlet climber, clematis, and hollyhocks is a field of poppies, larkspur and coreopsis bordering a rose garden.

The background for the rose garden is the woodland, where birds and the small wild animals rear their young without fear, and pay for their lodging with song and friendly approach.

Photo by Reeves

Jacqueland

Mr. Cator Woolford

Atlanta

THE gardens at Jacqueland are not old, as gardens go, having been laid out only twelve years ago by Robert B. Cridland of Philadelphia.

On a beautifully timbered hill which rises from a woodland area traversed by bold streams, the house was built to command views of the surrounding terrain. The varied character of the topography gave opportunity for gardens of different types: first and foremost the wild plantings which border the twisting bridle paths along streams and dogwood-shadowed slopes; then in open view from the portico of the house on the hill, the sunken formal gardens, one built around the clubhouse, the other laid beyond a rose hung tennis court. Informal gardens for the cutting rows, vegetable gardens and orchards are on the hillside across the stream which circles the two formal gardens, and on the hilltop close to the house are elaborate rockeries and a small walled court garden.

Mr. Woolford's intention in creating his gardens was not only the enjoyment of flowers and shrubs as such, but also to place in the beautiful setting offered by the estate, various types of recreation. With this in mind the tennis courts, swimming pool, the club house with dancing terrace and a miniature golf course were built, all with the advantage of the fine native trees and the planned gardens as background.

Around the larger formal garden are many big pink and white dogwoods which in early spring, against the evergreen of the tall cherry laurel trees and pines at the woodland's edge, give a bouquet effect to the set design of the flower beds. At the two entrances to the garden are wide curved beds

Entrance, Jacqueland Photo by Reeves

Specimen Conifers, Jacqueland

Photos by Reeves

of azalea Hinodegiri of notable size, one of the first attempts in the state to grow this type of azalea out of doors. The paths are bordered by lavender German iris interplanted with hyacinths and narcissi, and centering each formal bed is a huge specimen of clipped juniper Ashfordii around which Madonna lilies, delphinium and varicolored peonies are massed. In the shadier beds towards the woods are Japanese and Siberian Iris, fragrant pink viburnum carlesi, lilies of the valley and violas. Dwarf boxwood is used to hedge the inner paths and miscellaneous perennials and annuals furnish color almost the year around, but the supreme days of the garden occur in early April.

The tennis courts between this garden and the club house, which is Italian in architecture, are enclosed by a colonnade with pergola top over which pink and white Cherokee roses clamber and against the columns are tall plantings of sweet bay trees. Around the terrazzo dancing terrace the lawns are enclosed by low privet hedges, the only color furnished by narrow borders of spring bulbs which are replaced by ageratum and petunias for summer.

Hugging the balustrades of the long flight of steps leading up to the house are thick lines of nandina and juniper pfitzeriana. Azaleas and tulips border a flagstone walk to the rock garden on the upper level where many wild flowers are tucked in among the rhododendron, laurel and leucothoe. Centering the rock garden is a pool for water lilies and gold fish where the fountain spray is tinted by rainbow colored hidden lights.

In the woodsy sections of the grounds, along the streams and bridle paths, the native growth has been augmented by plantations of smoke tree, euonymous, viburnums and English laurels; ivy wraps the bridges of native stone, and clematis hangs from the trees.

The latest addition at Jacqueland is the junior guest house, a tiny early American cottage, set in its own trim garden, a picturesque playground.

Photo by Reeves

Mr. and Mrs. Kenyon B. Zahner

Atlanta

IN the historic "Battle of Peachtree Creek" section of Atlanta is the garden of Mr. and Mrs. Kenyon B. Zahner, begun in 1928 and built by the owners without professional assistance.

Foundation plantings of large boxwood are in character with the architecture of the Georgian house, and an atmosphere of age has been achieved in the gardens by the use of weathered rock, old brick, boxwood, and antique wrought iron gates and grill work. The garden walls are dry-laid, and moss and woods plants have settled comfortably in the crevices of the rock steps and paths.

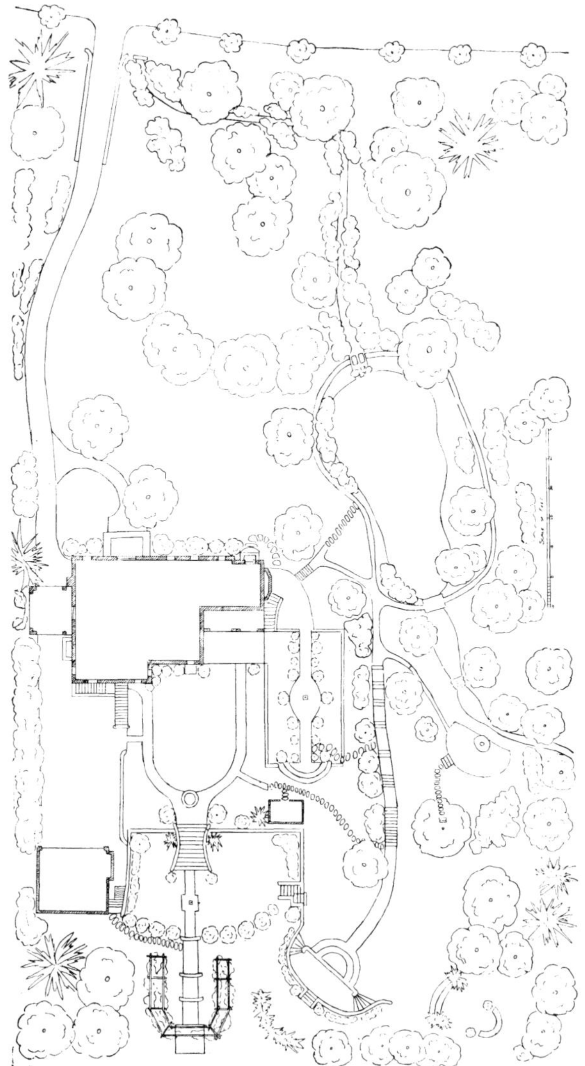

Balance and formality characterize the "horseshoe" garden which opens from the house. Roses are trained over a pair of arbors with grill gates beneath, and two perennial borders follow the horse-shoe curve, and give changing color and interest as the seasons pass. A wide flight of steps leaves this box-enclosed garden and goes past roses trained on poles and massed flowering shrubs against the gray stone wall to reach the next terrace. Here the planting is almost entirely of evergreens and berried shrubs around a Georgian sundial set in a flagged area. Leaving this green garden, the pathway leads under an arbor of roses, jasmine, and grape vines where at each post are groups of blue delphinium and Madonna lilies. Outlining the curved back of the arbor is a hedge the height of the arbor itself, clipped into an architectural niche, the dense shrubbery serving as a shadow box for espaliered fruit trees. Straight beds filled with iris, lemon lilies, peonies and violets border the path to the paved center of the arbor, a delightful outdoor sitting room with garden furniture and ornamental old oil jars.

A pleasing contrast exists between the more formally treated areas and the spring garden where sunlight and shelter promote early growth. The winding flower borders have a background of woodland trees beyond the retaining walls of field stones. The upper level, reached by curving stone steps, is planted with spring bulbs, and early roses

The Zahner Garden in Woodland Setting

are looped on chains against a dense growth of cedars and junipers. Wistaria climbs the tall pines behind these plantings, and masses of yellow primroses with Virginia cowslip and bleeding heart, followed later by pink heuchera, bloom beneath the flowering crabs.

From this garden a flagstone walk leads in a sweeping curve to a half-moon pool which reflects a weeping cherry and the lavender wistaria hanging from the wall above.

On the south the garden merges into the woods. A long flight of dry-laid steps leads down through an azalea trail to a pond where the children love to angle for the bream that hide under the water-lily pads and among the native swamp iris and cat-tails.

Walled Garden Near House

AUGUSTA

Mrs. Harry Albright

Augusta

THE gardens of Mrs. Albright, on "The Hill," show not only the touch of a skilled hand, but the beauty of elemental things—an appreciation the Saracens of old so keenly felt and the value of which the landscape architects of today recognize. Laid out by Herbert, Pray and White of Boston, in 1911, the gardens have gained in charm with the passing years.

When Mr. Francis H. Hardy of Chicago, former owner of the Albright home, built the gardens, he had countless loads of swamp soil transported on flat cars to the Hill and then carried by trucks to the place. In this loam were planted hundreds of large azaleas which soon made the gardens notable. A formal rose garden with box-bordered beds radiating from a silver gazing globe as an axis, has a planting of Pink Radiance, Killarney and Devoniensis, copper and gold Etoile de Lyon, Francesca Kruger, Kaiserin Augusta Victoria and Frau Karl Druschki, the handsomest of all white roses. In the tulip garden a bronze fountain is surrounded by formal beds of Pride of Haarlem and Clara Butt tulips bordered with pansies of varied hues.

Entering the main garden from the terrace which opens out from the flower room of the house, one looks across a spacious lawn shaded with magnificent trees and ornamented with a lotus lily pool which mirrors slender willows, pink, blue and white hyacinths, and purple and yellow iris. Beyond is a high brick wall set after the fashion of English gardens, with a tea house at either end garlanded with climbing roses and star jasmine and canopied with purple wistaria.

Among the favorite evergreen shrubs of the garden is the Assam tea plant (Thea bohea) peculiarly adapted to southern gardens. The petals, pearly white, are like orange blossoms in texture, but larger, with masses of yellow anthers in the center. One revels in the beauty of the azaleas—for there are hundreds of them—many rare ones showing colors as gorgeous as a Pagan's fancy; and in a great Ginkgo biloba, one of the choicest of ornamental trees. Along the winding paths, one comes unexpectedly on a bit of statuary or a garden seat in the shade of a tulip tree or a pink dogwood. And in spring, narcissi in long drifts of white and gold, grape hyacinths set like tiny jewels in the green of a sheltered nook, or a group of wild tulips swaying with the grace of gypsy flowers that have stolen into the garden—all these make exquisite pictures.

Reflected Color of Azaleas, Spirea and Lady Banksia Roses, Earliest Spring, Albright Garden

Morningside

Mrs. Alfred S. Bourne

Augusta

OPPOSITE the grounds of the Country Club, on a slope of the Hill above Augusta, is Morningside. The rambling wooden house, with no pretentions to any particular style of architecture, is screened almost completely from the road by dense trees and shrubs. Nor is there from the road any indication of the beautiful, hidden pleasure grounds where formal enclosures and architectural features contrast with groves of stately evergreens and flowering trees encouraged to grow wild. When Mr. and Mrs. F. H. Denny acquired the property many years ago, its chief attraction was the woodland, including tall native pines, picturesque oaks and other deciduous trees. The Dennys built the present dwelling, planted evergreens to insure its privacy, and laid out a pleasance behind the house as well as a sunken garden, thus adding delightful outdoor living rooms to those within.

In 1920, Mr. Alfred S. Bourne of New York bought the estate of six acres from Mrs. Denny. While preserving the original house and gardens, Mr. Bourne has made various alterations and additions too numerous for detailed description here. A general scheme for beautifying not merely this purchase, but ten more acres added recently, has been devised by Miss Rose Standish Nichols, and is gradually being carried out under her supervision.

For a stroll through the many paths leading from one interesting spot to another, the visitor would require at least an hour and might greatly overestimate the extent of the property. The secret of its apparent size lies in the diversity of its treatment and the contrast between the more formal lay-out and the sections where nature has been free to run nearly wild; between open spaces bathed in sunlight and stretches of woodland always veiled with shadows; between the dark, dense foliage of the long-lived evergreens and the brilliant hues of the transient flowers. Certain portions remain quite concealed from the rest and arouse that sensation of surprise so dear to "Capability Brown" and other landscape-architects early in the nineteenth century. Certainly, as the scene unfolds, it is anything but monotonous.

In logical sequence, the rear sun-parlor opens upon a cement terrace comfortably furnished with easy chairs, tables and rugs, an inviting place to spend an idle morning. From this vantage point, there is a charming view of an adjoining garden framed in masses of greenery. Water rising from a buff marble basin upheld on a fluted tripod, overflows into a rectangular pool which marks the center of a grass plot. Biotas clipped into columns guard the pool and add dignity to the tranquil enclosure. Outside the square of turf the border is thick with azaleas bearing blossoms of white and rosy-lavender.

From this intimate outdoor living-room a brick path, walled by privet hedges and heightened by rows of slender Italian cypresses, shortly leads to an old-fashioned wooden arbor overhung with purple wistaria. Below lies a small sunken garden, divided by walks of bluestone flagging into four grass panels, each enclosed by flower borders accented by Carolina cherry laurel clipped to resemble the little round-headed laurels so often seen in Italy, and rising above a carpet of pansies. The outside border of the entire rectangle is gay in spring with tulips of soft rosy-salmon and slaty-blue shades combining with lemon-yellow pansies. In the center of the garden a lead dolphin throws a spout of water above a circular pool set in a ring of tall cypresses which form a background for four eighteenth century English lead figures—Winter, Summer, Spring and Autumn—standing near the fountain. At the further end is a semicircular bench on a raised brick platform. Looking upward from the arbour, a cypress alley is seen ascending the steep hillside to a miniature temple, its simple white wooden columns festooned with trailing ivy, sheltered beneath a giant oak. In early spring, the sombre green of the cypresses contrasts with brilliant salmon Kurume azaleas blooming at their feet.

At the temple is the parting of several ways to wander through the remainder of the grounds. On one, the visitor can follow a grassy path defined by clumps of flaming azaleas and shaded by tall native pines. Beneath the trees, the greensward

The Temple, Amid Cypresses and Azaleas, Bourne Garden

Bands of Pansies and Iris Against a Diversity of Evergreens, Bourne Garden

affords space for various wild plants and is spangled with starry daffodils. Next comes a straight walk between rows of clipped arborvitae and German iris leading directly to a semi-circular arbor which conceals a gateway opening upon the road. Another connecting path winds between high hedges and flower-borders back to the house.

Close by, within the limits of the newly acquired territory, another cypress alley, set in a grove of pines, lines each side of a water-stairway suggestive of one laid out centuries ago at the Villa Cicogna in Northern Italy. The cascade falls into a pool at one side of a large grass oval and around the oval grows dwarf box of strange shapes, over fifty years old and about two feet high. From the spacious platform on the hillside is a view of a characteristic landscape of wide spreading fields merged in the misty horizon, outlined by a great semi-circle of trees and shrubs which conceal winding paths as well as the lower boundary of the pleasure-grounds.

Azalea Indica and Tulips, Bourne Garden

Mr. and Mrs. Harry Chafee

Augusta

I STROLLED through this lovely and ancient garden. The sweet scent of its flowers enveloped me and, like a magic cloak, wafted me back to its beginning. The return journey through time and flora culture was so entrancing that I must relate the story.

Peter Carnes, influential Tory, was granted a vast tract of hilly land in St. Paul's Parish. These sandy hills overlooked Augusta from the west. On the slope of one of them, he built a quaint little house in the manner of the time. It faced the setting sun. The basement was brick, the first and second stories of clapboards. The kitchen was properly placed fifty feet from the house, for baking, stewing, frying and roasting must not offend the olfactory sensibilities of the household, especially the feminine portion. In the eighteenth and nineteenth centuries, woman was still of a delicacy. She was prone to swoon, and dependent on sal volatile.

In 1784, Peter sold his cozy home and considerable acres to Mistress Howard, the great, great grandmother of the chatelaine of today. My magic mantle places me beside Hannah Howard, a stately matron in bouffant skirt and kerchief, as she lays out the formal garden. By her orders, the necessary trees have already been felled. She paces off with tiny feet the proper length and breadth. Now I sit beside this dear gardener on an iron bench. A swarm of darkies from the quarter level and shape the beds, sift the soil. A beaming black boy attends us. At our feet is a huge rush basket, filled with bulbs. A haughty but friendly Cherokee brave has placed it there. His squaw has dug them from Keowee to New Savannah, and the musket he so proudly fingers is his reward. They are blue bells, —and the first photograph clearly shows them and their prolific progeny bordering today's exotic bulbs of England and Spain, of Holland and Japan.

Hannah was wrapped up in her garden and in her

Daffodils and Hyacinths in the Old Bulb Garden

Rose Hung Veranda of Chafee House Looks over the Garden

The Lawn with Camellias and Informal Iris Planting

fourteen children, but alas! she was called to her reward. The house and garden passed to Louisa, wife of John. Borders were planted. Dogwoods, wild olives, Grand-daddy grey-beards, crabapples, Judas trees, wild azaleas, mountain laurel, woodbine, jasmines and the Cherokee rose were guarded and nurtured by this lady from Virginia.

It was she who encouraged Maum Sally and Maum Beccy to vie with one another in the rooting of cuttings. Maum Beccy was the first to succeed with the oleander bush Marse John had got in Darien from "dat Cap'n o' de slave ship." Maum Sally used "cunjer" on rose and geranium slips.

Louisa's experiments spread abroad, and Uncle Ignatius Few, who loved her "despite the errors of her faith," sent by stage coach from Mt. Carmel a plant he had got in Charleston. It was an odorless rose from Japan. Thus came the first Camellia to this garden. In the nomenclature of a day when ladies knew belles-lettres, to sew a fine seam, and the gentle arts, this garden now blossoms single and double "Japonicas," pink, white and red, as well as the flecked varieties. Lady gardeners today are botanically erudite, but the period of transition was fraught with disasters. One charming radical of her day is said to have written the first "Landscape Gardener" for advice as to bordering a walk. He suggested an evergreen of the Cinchonaceous family, Gardenidae. The lady promptly ordered and prepared for the planting. In her enthusiasm, she discarded ten Cape jasmines six feet tall. The story goes that, going forth to view the replanting, the good lady wrung her hands and was even heard to moan.

But I have dropped my magic wrap! Again I am with Louisa. She has found a daily rose. The rose of the horse shoe tea-nook in the picture. It is pink, and yields a most pervasive sweetness, shattering quickly. Verily it

"Opens to the morning sky,
But ere the shades of evening close
Is scattered on the ground to die."

In the evenings, by candle light, Louisa and her children delight in Paxton's Flowere Books. They are enthusiastic about the birds and flowers in the beautiful books of Mister Audubon. Louisa adds a wing to the house. She subscribes to a new magazine, "The Ladies' Book." The guest of today, walking in from this fairy like spot may smile back at her girlhood portrait by Gilbert Stuart, in appreciation of her contribution.

She, too, is called home. And, for a while, the garden is somewhat neglected, for troublesome times have come to the South. When the guns are silent, when the swords and uniforms have been packed away, we find Emeline Howard Thomas mistress. Weeds grow here and there, fences are not as well mended, servants are fewer. She sees bewildered post-bellum gentlemen shake their heads over their juleps in a corner of the garden. She hears them wonder if the depression will ever end. She begins shaping things, and finally 'twas she who planted the hedges around the place. Dying, she left her house and garden to a tiny granddaughter of seven summers, Maisie. The young heart was filled with pride. In a dimity pinafore, she watched her mother plant the rose which sprays the east entrance from the very roof. It was brought from the hedges of the Sand Bar Ferry Road. Alas! Signs have replaced the roses and Chinaberry trees of the past. It is Maisie herself who now truly lives in this garden. She has preserved its old landmarks and developed every feature of the place. You may follow the flagstones to a lily pond, a ferny dell. You may let them take you in another direction through azaleas riotous in color. You may encircle a quaint little house dripping purple and gold—wistaria and Lady Banksia. This little house is still the kitchen.

There are tulip trees and tulips, Iris of every color and nationality, There are roses red and violets blue, bridal wreath and matrimony, pansies and daisies, columbines and Madonna lilies. Thrift and boxwood etch the coat-of-arms, and over all is the witchery of "quilted sunshine and leaf shade".

Highgate

Mrs. Henry C. Cohen
Augusta

THIS property was first acquired by John Course on September 1, 1808. Here, nearly a century and a half ago, came a bride and groom to make this fair spot their home. They did not, as was the custom with the early settlers, scoop out a spring; for this was on the Sand Hills. They dug a deep well and built a comfortable, substantial house that endures as such to this far distant day. Slaves drew water from the well, hewed the timbers, and sawed the wide boards, while slow-moving carpenters put them together with square pegs and hand-wrought nails. And to this day, the heads of those same nails shine, like so many diamonds, on the polished floors of Highgate.

Broad front steps lead to the hospitable doorway; narrow, tortuous ones to the second floor. There are doors you must enter side-wise, and doors that were meant for a barn; spacious rooms and cell-like chambers; window-panes barely adequate for one eye; and fireplaces in which might roar the good logs of Algidue. For Highgate was not built with a plan borrowed from some distant clime; it was true to the time, in accord with the place. It spoke of the worthy families who lived about it, and the folks who lived within.

Seventy years later one of the great judges of the Supreme Court, Justice Starnes, became the owner and made a handsome addition, which likewise reflected the trend of his day and time. But it was an addition only, for he saved and cherished the old.

And so it has been with the trees and shrubs and flowers that nature, careless-handed, bestowed. Tough old post oaks, water oaks, live oaks, red oaks (some of them five feet through), big and little leaf hickories, a magnolia sixty feet high, China-berries, and mulberries, have spread their branches to shelter generations through sunny days and stormy. And each of these succeeding generations has left its plantings behind, bequeathing a

Entrance to Home of Mrs. Henry Cohen

A Secluded Bower, Mrs. Henry Cohen's Garden

rich legacy to those who follow them. No one sought to destroy or substitute. When a great tree fell, another was planted in its stead. Even the wild, tangled spots are kept intact for the sake of the wild life sheltered there.

Highgate's present owner came a decade ago, —came with appraising eye, skilled and tender hand. Choice shrubs and flowers from distant climes flourish side by side with native specimens. Camellias, Bamboos, azaleas, boxwood, tea olives, wild olive, dogwood, iris, lilies,—all are here.

An interesting feature of the garden is the old summer-house, octagonal in form. Paved with brick, it has brick pillars supporting a tin roof, and is draped about with an ivy-vine as large in diameter as a ship's rope.

Crystal and globe-bearing quartz rocks are strewn about, varying in size from a goose-egg to a large boulder, and here and there are grindstones that sharpened the axes that felled the forests. There are many millstones, too; some from near-by streams, others from Eusopas, New York, and burr-stones from the west coast of France. On these stones was ground the bread of the first settlers.

A charming part of this place is the old wrought-iron fence and brick wall, with its very high gates, from which the property takes its name.

Sandy Acres

Mr. and Mrs. Rodney S. Cohen

Augusta

DRIVING west on Battle Row, up the "Hill" and to the left—almost at the end of the Row—you come upon Sandy Acres, the home of Mr. and Mrs. Rodney S. Cohen.

The street itself seems to boast no proud heritage. One might imagine the name "Battle Row" was given in commemoration of the skirmishes fought there during Revolutionary days, but such is not the case. Instead, it got its name from a series of street brawls that used to take place day and night at the foot of the "Hill" in the vicinity of a general store where everything, including fire and brimstone, was sold during the early days of Augusta's history. Here, countrymen journeying to town over the old Tobacco Road would pause to refresh themselves the first thing on arriving and the last thing upon departing; hence the battles. A deed of the early 1800's speaks of the Gardiner property as being bounded on the north by Battle Row Road.

Sandy Acres is enclosed by a white picket fence, a copy of the one around the walled garden at Mt. Vernon. Its symmetrical scallops, following the natural curve of the roadway around the Hill, show against a background of evergreen shrubs. The house itself is surrounded by beautiful trees—magnolias, oaks and elms—and is of the cottage colonial type of architecture. Nobody seems to know just when it was built, but from its "creaking doors and uneven floors," wide old clapboards and hand-blown window panes, the impression is that it must have been constructed more than a century ago.

It is not possible to enumerate all the different owners during a period of so many years. The place was purchased from the late Mr. Thomas W. Loyless, in 1921. Some time before that it was owned by a Dr. Barry, whose "Antidote" was a household word over all the southern states. Mrs. Barry loved the garden and during her regime it was beautiful and fragrant with old-fashioned flowers and shrubs. Perhaps many of the fine old spirea bushes, tea olives, lilacs and banana shrubs that now give so much pleasure were planted and tended by her.

The Loyless family made many improvements to the interior of the house as well as to the grounds. A vast amount of planting has been done in recent years, but the general plan of the garden and grounds, as developed by them, has not been altered. The present owners, Mr. and Mrs. Rodney Cohen, have added an outdoor living room with an open fireplace, which is a joy on cool days, as well as for picnics and barbecues. Leading off from this inviting spot is the path to the sunken garden. This was formerly an old clay tennis court; now thousands of specimens of dwarf boxwood—all rooted and grown by Mrs. Cohen—border the paths and march in and out among the flower beds, in formal and informal patterns.

To the right, and screened by a wall of jasmine and honeysuckle, is the water garden, where five pools built on different levels present an ever-changing panorama. Both the water garden and the sunken garden open on to the rose garden. Here, in three box-bordered beds grouped about a sundial, hundreds of roses of old and new varieties find congenial soil and receive careful attention from the master of the house.

Along the eastern boundary a path known as the Long Walk carries the visitor almost the entire length of the property. Gigantic China-berry trees, festooned with jasmine and wistaria vines, furnish ample protection from the sun; a dense hedge of mock-orange secludes this charming pathway from the road, and here in the springtime hawthorn, dogwood and scented crabapple are prodigal of their loveliness.

Sunken Garden Patterned in Boxwood, Mrs. Rodney Cohen

Spring Blossoms in Mrs. Rodney Cohen's Garden

Green Court

Mr. H. P. Crowell

Augusta

THE Crowell garden might be termed an intimate garden despite its spaciousness. From the gate on Johns Road, a perfectly straight pathway leads the whole depth of the garden, about three hundred feet. On the right, tall evergreen shrubs form a screen which shuts off the neighboring grounds, while to the left is the flower garden, where choice annuals and perennials are carefully blended into a charming picture. The colorful blossoms show to advantage against a background of shrubs not too closely planted to prevent an occasional glimpse of a wide green lawn beyond, which boasts trees of a century's growth, with now and then a dash of vivid color in the distance from azaleas massed along the boundary walk. The objective of the straight path is a rose pergola where many varieties of climbers make a canopy of bloom and strike a happy color note against the screen of green.

Directly back of the house itself lies the sunken garden laid out in formal fashion. Four large divisions on different levels enclosed by high privet hedges and carpeted with winter grass are each centered by a pool, fountain or flower bed, and have corner plantings of roses, tulips and hyacinths. Dwarf flowering fruit trees form striking features here, growing in graceful fashion and lending a delicate lacework of shadow to the beds below. These secluded gardens are reached progressively through evergreen archways above steps of turf. A few bits of garden statuary and several comfortable seats are placed here and there among groups of shrubbery. A walk, ending in a circular bench, is laid between tall rows of clipped Arbor vitae, whose pyramidal form and sombre hue are effectively etched against a southern sky. Birds are attracted by the fountains and baths and the many berried shrubs about the gardens.

Twining in an old tree against the square, antebellum house, which has been kept to a neutral tone as a foil for nature's colors, there grows a Lady Banksia rose of great age, almost as high as the house itself. Its great arching branches of glossy foliage are weighted down in blossom season with thousands of delicate yellow blossoms.

A winding pathway follows the outer boundary of the estate. Hundreds of azaleas, in separate color masses, are grouped along its way, interspersed with rare and beautiful shrubs accented each spring with beds of narcissus, tulip, and iris. A fine old wistaria hangs like a purple cloud against the trees in the distance. The boundary walk not far from the high iron fence is so sheltered and protected that one feels quite shut off from the distractions of the near-by street, and enjoys a sense of privacy and seclusion. The main gate is guarded by a pair of venerable Magnolia grandiflora of great size and perfection of form.

Beautiful Formality Characterizes the Crowell Gardens at Green Court

Stately Italian Cypresses in the Garden, Green Court

Salubrity Hall

Mr. and Mrs. John W. Herbert

Augusta

MR. AND MRS. HERBERT'S home, which is of early English architecture, is one of the most interesting on the Sand Hills. It derives its name from Mont Salubrity, a school for girls, which was established on this site in years gone by. The property was purchased by Lord Sandwich in 1799 from the original owner who held title under a grant from the British Crown. When Mrs. Herbert acquired it and built the present home she used a part of the house which was then standing, and much of the old timber. One of the earliest sidewalks in Augusta was moved and the old brick laid into a terrace, and the exterior of the house was treated to give it an appearance of age.

There are four distinct gardens, all of them planned according to Mrs. Herbert's ideas.

On the west of the residence is the formal garden, with an ornamental fountain and a weeping willow drooping over a semi-circular marble seat. To the south is a terrace with a rose-covered pergola of antique columns. The back of the pergola is of weather-beaten brick, with a niche for a leaden figure of a boy holding a tray of flowers. This feature is flanked by old iron grille work. The balustrade on the north side looks down on a bronze dragon-fly fountain built of irregular stone, which is cleverly screened on two sides by a graduated planting of junipers and yews. In this garden is a large collection of iris.

From the formal garden brick steps descend between two large camellias to a box-bordered walk leading to a well head which is backed by fine old English boxwood.

From the well head to the east is a rose-covered

Liriope Bordered Pool, Salubrity Hall

Arabesque Garden at Salubrity Hall Planted in Spring Flowering Bulbs

pergola leading to the rose garden, in the center of which is a Swedish porcelain fountain. At its base are low-growing junipers interplanted with blue hyacinths harmonizing in tone. Separated by an informal planting of broad-leaf evergreens is the bulb and pansy garden. Here on two sides stand rows of flowering crabs, which frame the garden effectively. Two arabesques planted with bulbs and perennials run north and south. The marginal planting around the bulb garden contains many varieties of narcissi, tulips and various kinds of iris and perennials.

The wild garden is approached through woodsy paths bordered with cassena, Carolina cherry laurel and other native shrubs. Masses of Indian and Kurume azaleas are grouped along the paths and around the attractive English tea house. On the east boundary is a walk of grass steps bordered with kalmia and flame azaleas. Various bulbs are naturalized throughout the woods, while wistarias, yellow jasmine and woodbine grow up into the trees.

Rare and unusual plants are cultivated around the house and in different parts of the grounds and in secluded corners against evergreen backgrounds are many pieces of beautiful statuary. Camellias, which attain great beauty in Augusta, grow in this garden in interesting variety.

Azaleas Surround the Tea House, Salubrity Hall

Goshen Plantation

Mr. and Mrs. Joseph McK. Speer

Augusta

GOSHEN PLANTATION is ten miles from Augusta, on the old Savannah Road. The house, situated on the highest point in Richmond County, is two miles from the gate, and is reached by a winding road which crosses Spirit Creek, the historic spot where Eli Whitney made some of the experiments for his cotton gin. Leaving the creek bed, the road leads past level fields of grain relieved by an occasional barn and cabin; and so up to the house through a shady lane covered with pine needles, white with dogwood and fragrant with yellow jessamine, wistaria, and honeysuckle.

Goshen House is a low white clapboard building, with a box-bordered entrance walk, and a splendid old Banksia rose framing the hospitable doorway.

A pierced brick wall extends from one side of the house and, passing through its gateway, one enters upon the spacious terrace at the back, where the view spreads out across the Savannah Valley to the low hills of South Carolina in the distance. Centering this terrace is an old sun-dial copied from one at Hampton Court. A colorful border runs around the low wall, filled with iris, old-fashioned single hyacinths, and early narcissus.

The garden itself is arranged on two levels, reached by steps from the terrace. On the first level is the box garden. Here on either side of a sunken mill-stone, are two perfect roses, with blossom, foliage and stem embroidered on the turf in matched specimens of dwarf boxwood. The heart of each rose is planted with yellow pansies.

Leading from this to the lower garden is a double set of steps, concealed by a white balustrade garlanded with pink Cherokee roses. This makes a background for the planting of tulips in shades

Entrance Drive, Goshen Plantation

The Formal Garden at Goshen, with a Quaint Pattern of Two Cherokee Roses Outlined in Dwarf Boxwood

of purple and lavender below. A high brick wall covered with climbing roses encloses this garden on three sides, while the wall to the south is low, affording another view of the far-away hills. This wall is ivy-covered and it is relieved by a planting of azaleas.

The center of this lower garden is occupied by two oblong pools, bordered with Kurume azaleas and iris, one of them being sheltered by a picturesque mimosa tree, and the other by a fragrant tea olive and medlar.

In the west wall is a fountain, while in the corresponding position on the east side is an arched gateway leading back to the terrace and to a window shaped in the hedge which overlooks a four-acre slope studded with daffodils.

A short flight of steps in the south wall leads up to the iron gates which open on a path through a small woods, planted with native shrubs and trees, with a pool and rock garden surrounded with Atamasco lilies, dwarf iris and gentian. And if the visitor to Goshen happens on a certain shady lane in this quarter of the Plantation, he may be fortunate enough to come upon a most intriguing tool house and potting shed, which will prove to be intensely interesting, particularly if he is a real dirt gardener.

Le Manoir Fleuri

Mrs. Robert G. Reese
Augusta

Old Iron Grilles at Entrance to Garden

THE gardens of Mrs. Reese, on Meigs Street, were developed on the tract of land given by the State in 1802 to George Walton, signer of the Declaration of Independence.

In a setting of gnarled trees, enormous tea olives, crepe myrtles and mimosas, three gardens have been placed. Facing the house, on the Hickman Road side, is a rock-rimmed pool, backed by a semi-circle of tall evergreens, and having for its center ornament a bronze figure of Pan, the work of a well-known French sculptor. Fronting it are borders filled with camellias and azaleas.

Lying to the south side of the house is an oblong garden with fore-court and wide central path of flag stones, which leads to a fountain set in a high wall. This fountain, which stands between two unusually perfect specimens of boxwood, is of white and yellow marble, and is a copy of the fountain in the garden of the renowned Capuchin monastery in Amalfi. In the wall there are unusual panels of filagree tile brought from Italy.

Opening from this garden is another one on a lower level, with formal beds outlined with boxwood and surrounded on all sides with tall evergreens and flowering shrubs. At the end of the main axis is a semi-circular seat made of brick.

A particularly beautiful marble fountain that came from Italy is in the entrance court. It is backed by a planting of yuccas. Several fine camellias near by, and perpendicular accents in the form of Italian cypresses, make it seem very much at home.

Evergreen Accents of Boxwood, Cypress and Yucca, Le Manoir Fleuri

Mr. and Mrs. William B. White

Augusta

THE garden of Mr. and Mrs. White, on Milledge Road, The Hill, was laid out and planted according to the owners' ideas. It is a garden of many gardens and one of perpetual bloom, specializing in camellias, azaleas, roses and bulbs. There are seven gardens, each with its distinctive features, and all together comprise several acres. Over thirty-five varieties of rare camellias are to be found about these gardens, and azaleas too numerous to mention.

At the front entrance of the grounds are stone steps leading to a walk bordered by pink camellias with broad-leaf evergreens as a background. It is an appropriate entrance to the house, the architecture of which is Italian Renaissance. To the right of the house is a large planting of Herme and Chandleri Elegans camellias. Near these are some fine specimens of Cedrus deodara, and a little further on is an old cedar, festooned with Cherokee roses.

The formal box garden has as its special feature a fountain of old lead which is a copy of DeLagon's dancing girl and piping boy. Around the fountain is a bed bordered with boxwood, in which are planted Lady Derby, Enchantress hyacinths and Clara Butt tulips. Seven other box-edged beds are planted in daffodils, tulips and hyacinths. Behind the fountain is an Italian pergola covered with pink Cherokee roses. Here are camellias with buds and blooms from October until April, Chandleri elegans, Professor Sargent, Lady Campbell, alba plena, Debutante, Colette, Noblissima, Henry Gaore, Sacco and Wilderi. Azaleas shade from Fielder's White to Azalea Austrina and Hinodegiri.

Old Crepe Myrtle and Spring Flowering Shrubs on Path to Woodland Garden, White Garden

Next comes the Hanging Garden (in its infancy). Wistaria, ivy, yellow jessamine and Banksia roses overhang the Indica and Kurume azaleas (Coral Bell and Pink Pearl).

In the "Unmolested Garden" there is a century-old cedar covered with Spanish moss, which stands guard over a rocky pool where two large frogs spout water. Only pastel shades of flowers are used here, with a background of the lovely pink azaleas known as Croemina. Hidden away and enclosed in its green frame is "My Sanctuary," a charming and restful spot. Here are planted flowering peach, pussy willows and an old cedar entwined with roses and wistaria, while beneath are daffodils, tulips, scillas, candy tuft and pansies. There is a nook called "Thirty-four" in honor of the owners' thirty-fourth wedding anniversary, which has a lead bird-feeding station surrounded by white azaleas and pale pink camellias.

A little further on a garden is named in honor of the visit of the Garden Club of America in 1932, called "G. C. A.," which has Herme camellias alternating with Fielder's white azaleas, and Sir Watkin daffodils in the spring, Marechal Foch gladiolus in July. A path bordered with ophiopogon winds between beds of larkspur and plantings of camellias, flowering almonds, iris and violets, to the "Formosa Nook," where this lovely azalea is featured, from the dwarf variety to specimen plants several feet in height.

There is an "Herbaceous Garden," a large plot of grass surrounded by wide serpentine flower beds, bordered with solid yellow pansies. In these beds are lavender and rosemary; Regal, Madonna and Butterfly lilies, Dutch, Spanish and German iris; forsythia and spirea; stocks, snapdragons, phlox, tube roses, and violets. On a wistaria-covered rustic tea house Marie Henriette roses run riot and hanging baskets made of rhododendron roots are filled with gay petunias.

A picturesque path leads into a woodland garden. Tall old crepe myrtle trees are covered with Spanish moss, and rustic arches frame vistas of spring flowering shrubs and wistaria. Beyond this is the rose garden. Roses of every hue grow here in the beds that surround a sun dial of old English lead which is guarded by four tall standard roses.

Camelrest

Mr. and Mrs. Robt. Campbell

Cedartown

DESERTED for many years, this century-old place has been faithfully restored by a son of the family so that once again it reflects the quaint charm of the old South.

The gardens lie to the west of the house, in close relationship with it, and look out to the distant landscape of rolling pasture lands and tall cedars massed against a turquoise sky. In the foreground are groups of fine old trees. In early springtime thousands of bulbs blossom under their leafy canopy; daffodils, scillas, snowdrops, little blue hyacinths, and camassias.

The perennial gardens are slightly terraced in formal design, and are built in three sections. Besides the herbaceous borders, there are a German iris garden and a rose garden containing both new and old varieties. The several sections of the garden are divided by flowering shrubs. Among them are dense plantings of lilacs—some old varieties as well as the lovely French hybrids—kerria, cydonia, deutzias, Japanese crabs, and buddleias. These make coves for naturalizing small bulbs. Pride of Haarlem tulips and snowflakes are here below the lilacs. Cedars planted at cross sections and as focal points add depth to the design.

Near by, large boulders flecked with jade and

coral have eased themselves into positions of natural beauty. An old man of the hills, a naturalist by heritage, upon a visit to this garden remarked as he looked about him, "It's prettier than I heered or dreamed, but you'll never make me believe them rocks ain't growed there!" The garden is at its loveliest in early spring when the odor of the lilacs mingles with the aromatic boxwood. Spirea and almond are in flower, hundreds of columbines nod from their ferny beds, and the rocky cliff is gay with Alpine bloom.

A stone stairway goes up to a little path, brilliant with wild flowers, which leads over hillocks and among wooded spots and then out again into the open, where a rustic bench overlooks a V-shaped pool. The pool holds pale water lilies and its water spills down into cascades beneath masses of pink and white laurel. From a grotto, half hidden by fragile maiden-hair fern and misty white thalictrum and meadowsweet, the water trickles on down to feed the bog garden below where primroses of China, marsh marigolds, and grass of Parnassus thrive. From here a second stairway leads back again to the garden paths, past spring and pool, then on to reach the paved courtyard of the house.

Sunset Terrace

Mr. and Mrs. W. C. Bradley

Columbus

THE Bradley home stands at the top of a hill, facing west. A magnificent view from the wide terrace, of the sun going down behind the far Alabama hills, has given it the name Sunset Terrace. More than twenty years ago Mr. B. S. Miller, the former owner of these fifteen acres, built the house and made the formal garden. Nine years ago an informal garden was added, designed by the Olmstead Brothers of Philadelphia for the present owners.

Aside from the terraced rose gardens there are three features of interest at Sunset Terrace, the Fish Pond, the Swimming Pool, and the Ravine. The fish pond gets its water supply from a spring on the hillside which, summer and winter, continuously pours forth over thirty thousand gallons a day. Between the spring and the fish pond are ten little cascades twinkling over huge water-washed boulders brought from an old dam on the Chattahoochee river and each cascade empties into a pool set about with large rocks and surrounded by woodland flowers, ferns and shrubs. The swimming pool in the glade is bordered with hundreds of flowering shrubs and Japanese iris, and shaded by pine trees. The most interesting offering here is the walk from the pool which winds among tall pines and is bordered on either side by thickets of dogwood, azaleas, camellias, Japanese yew, viburnum, and pittosporum, with a ground cover of ivy.

In the Ravine the water is piped from the spring to a grotto on the hillside. There it gushes forth from under the big rocks as though from a natural spring, and winds its way down the valley. On its way to the fish pond at the bottom of the hill the stream is overhung by water oaks, sweet gum, sycamore, and dogwood trees, and in their shade grow camellias, euonymous, ligustrum, nandina, abelia and gallberry. Forget-me-nots and many sorts of wild flowers grow along the water's edge with clumps of liriope and native ferns.

Sunset Terrace

Ravine Garden and Waterfall, Sunset Terrace

Green Island Ranch

Mr. and Mrs. R. C. Jordan

Columbus

IN 1905, after a long day of quail hunting along the rich bottom lands of the old General Benning plantation, the late G. Gunby Jordan stopped to rest at Uncle Tom Narramore's cabin, on a ridge top on the River Road. The November sunset colored an unbroken view northward to Pine Mountain Ridge and the distant hills of Alabama. In the foreground shone Green Island, set in the tumbling waters of the Chattahoochee. The site and the view were so beautiful that Mr. Jordan shortly afterwards bought this property for his future home. The former owner was Uncle Tom Narramore, who had been overseer during and after the Civil War for General H. L. Benning—known as "Old Rock"—for whom Fort Benning is named. The enthusiastic new owner completed in 1907 a comfortable country home of English half-timber design, its lower story of massive Georgia granite.

The house faces northward to the view and is surrounded by extensive well-planned gardens. The obstinate hillside has been converted into terraces for the numerous garden plots and the stiff red Georgia clay has been "tamed" by hundreds of loads of loam and sand. The gardens, formal in design, are located on three terraces parallel with the house. A wide sweep of lawn with the original oak trees, separates the house from the gardens and stepping stones lead from the terrace porch along an ivy-covered wall to the central walk and a small fountain. Other walks lead from this center through the three terraces to circular plots in which tall urns holding clinging vines are placed. Each of the terraces is divided by clipped privet hedges into three parts, the western and middle portions devoted to annuals, and the eastern section to roses. The lower terrace, given over to native and other kinds of shrubbery, blends naturally into the hillside.

Green Island Ranch, now the home of Mr. R. C. Jordan, a son of the original owner and builder, is located six miles north of Columbus on the River Road.

Flower Garden, Green Island Ranch

Mrs. J. W. McKinnon and Miss Alsobrook
Columbus

THE McKinnon home is surrounded by colorful gardens. A walk leading to the entrance is bordered with tulips and Spanish iris, fringed with vari-colored pansies and forget-me-nots, which later on are replaced by green foliaged plants, marguerites and ageratum. The lawns and gardens are all hedged about with groups of evergreens and other shrubs. Azaleas, red, pink, lavender, and white, lend brilliant color to the foliage background in spring, while in summer red dahlias are massed against the shrubbery. For fragrance there are banana shrub, sweet shrub, tea olive, and trees of lemon verbena. Against the house the plantings of shrubbery are edged with bright blue pansies, which bloom in great profusion among pink and white azaleas.

To the south lies the sunny garden, its beds all bordered with blue pansies. Here are several rose-covered trellises, and in the center a sun-dial rests on an old mill stone. From this garden a tiny path leads under tall ligustrums to the rear of the house, and a secluded out-door living room. This shady garden holds a mirror lily pool set in grass among cool shadows, a quiet spot walled in by evergreen shrubbery, beneath which grow many shade-loving plants and early flowering bulbs.

The pathway to the right leads on to a delightful small formal garden, with grass walks and beds aglow with color. A crystal globe centrally placed reflects the varied pictures as the seasons come and go.

Outdoor Living-Room Under Big Oaks

Woodcrest

Mr. and Mrs. J. W. Woodruff
Columbus

A THICK growth of live oaks like a small evergreen forest covers the slope of the hill on which the house and gardens of Mr. and Mrs. Woodruff are built. On the shaded level hill top an English house looks out on spreading lawns and groves of fine native trees.

The gardens at Woodcrest are reached from the terrace of the house by way of a broad paved walk which curves past a tremendous old pear tree, its branches sweeping the lawn, laden each springtime with a snowdrift of bloom. Close by the picturesque old tree of a generation ago are great camellia bushes in all their shiny beauty, their colorful blossoms waning as the pear tree reaches its flowering zenith.

The limestone walk shortly loses its trim formality as it leaves the open lawn to enter the shady area of the rock garden. Here under deep hanging live oaks are plantations of many native wild flowers combined with woodland shrubs and ferns; and moss covered stones bind the pools of a tiny wandering stream where water poppies, forget-me-nots and little bog flowers thrive.

Further on, past the swimming pool, a panel of grass between two rows of square clipped columns of laurel, leads to the entrance of the formal gar-

Rock Garden at Woodcrest

den. In front of the lines of laurel are deep curving borders of choice iris and perennials, and flanking the path are rounded specimens of boxwood. A soft green hedge of sheared Spirea thunbergii bounds three sides of the garden while silvery gray junipers mark the openings onto the wide grass paths. Around a circle of turf, box bordered flower beds are designed in a simple and charming geometrical pattern, the soft color of spring bulbs and perennials skillfully replaced by masses of brilliant annuals for summer.

Set in the spirea hedge on one side is a rose hung gate, with roof of English tile, which opens into a long paneled rose garden. Roses of lovely quality are coaxed into nearly ten months of bloom at Woodcrest.

The formal garden and the rose garden are both fortunate in their backgrounds of mimosas, tamarix, live oaks, ailanthus, native pines and red cedars. About the grounds many specimen shrubs preserved from an earlier garden of the Woodruff family are still flourishing and lend their dignity of age. And here is also an aged scuppernong arbor of surpassing vigor and size—an old time adjunct of delight added to the charms of these beautifully cared for modern gardens.

Oneonta

Mrs. M. E. Judd
Dalton

ONLY a few years ago the property now known as Oneonta was an undeveloped rough stretch of land. Since it has been owned by Mrs. M. E. Judd a transformation has taken place, for under her direction avenues of trees have been planted, driveways engineered, walls and drainage laid in, an out-door theatre constructed and extensive gardens made.

On the gentle rise of a hill and surrounded by fine trees the house overlooks a series of gardens. Wide steps, at either side of a dry wall full of rock plants, descend towards the upper garden. A natural spring is at the base of the wall and benches are placed near by. The upper garden is a succession of terraces held by walls of field stone, and paths of the same material are laid between the flower beds. A formal use of evergreens brings out the structural lines of the plan. Tiny creeping plants soften the path stones and a succession of perennials and annuals gives a continuous display of color in the borders. From this level, one path leads to a playhouse with a miniature lily pool, another to the greenhouse where rare plants are propagated.

The lower garden with its retaining wall of stone is girdled by a swift mountain stream which flows

Rows of Arbor Vitae and Fieldstone Wall Along the Garden's Edge, Oneonta

Rose Walk, Oneonta

through the lower reaches of the property. The flower beds here are bordered with dwarf box while taller box is used for accents. Near by a picturesque tea house, in a setting of evergreens and crabapple trees, looks off to the pine woods across the stream. Along the banks of the stream are groupings of dogwood, flowering peach, pear, and cherry, judas and willow trees.

Leaving the gardens a walk through heavy plantings of native evergreens and azaleas winds back to the house. From the sun room, which houses a collection of Indian relics dug from the hills near Dalton, another path goes through thickets of rhododendron and laurel to yet another spring and not far off is the lake set amid forest trees.

Aside from specializing in primroses, peonies, and regale lilies Mrs. Judd is famous for her daffodils. In memory of Dalton's poet, Robert Loveman, millions of these bulbs have been spread over his beloved hills of Whitfield.

At Oneonta native material has been used with exceptional understanding. Trees, shrubs and flowers, peculiar to this section, grow here in the secure luxuriance only "at home" conditions give. Also, in the garden construction—for tea house, walls, paths and furniture—slabs of the local stone have been utilized. The stone, which is deeply veined and streaked with dull purple, green and Indian red, ties in the finished gardens with the rugged landscape in a natural harmony.

Oneonta makes evident the feeling for natural beauty and the wise use of the material at hand which have characterized Mrs. Judd's notable work for conservation and reforestation in the State.

Tucked-In

Mr. and Mrs. Bruce Hall

Decatur

Photo by Reeves

AN English cottage set in a nest of trees is "Tucked-In," the home of Mr. and Mrs. Bruce Hall. In spring the low white house and picket fence are garlanded with climbing roses, and a gnarled old mimosa tree casts its shadows across entrance gate and flagged path beyond. A big tree left at the garden entrance is the focal point of the garden, and its shade gives an ideal situation to the digitalis, white sweet william, and yellow columbine flourishing here. A wistaria vine climbs up the mossy gray trunk and a little white gate near by swings wide in welcome. A slightly lower level has a retaining wall of stones, its base planting of periwinkle providing a rich green background for daffodils, and other early flowering bulbs.

The more formal garden, which is about fifty by fifty feet, is enclosed by a white picket fence, and a rustic arbor is at the far end. Climbing roses—Gardenia and Silver-moon—and Clematis paniculata grow on the fence and embower the arbor. In the garden, now eight years old, are many well considered color compositions. Pleasant combinations in the flower beds are sulphur-colored marigolds with Salvia farinacea, white nicotiana, so fragrant at dusk, snapdragons, blue lace flower and the airy graceful little annual phlox. The borders are filled with perennials of fine quality and substance; colors, soft-toned and deep, are mingled in harmony. From the old home in the hills of Tennessee came such treasures as white lilacs, spireas, flowering almond, mock orange, dainty single blue hyacinths, and a very old Harrison yellow rose. Little border plants spill over the edges of the walkways, weaving gay patterns on the grass.

From the rustic arbor a path bordered with English daisies and forget-me-nots leads to the small out-door dining nook which is a delightful spot, shaded by trees and shrubs and canopied by climbing roses.

Spring Bloom in Garden of Mrs. Bruce Hall

Photo by Reeves

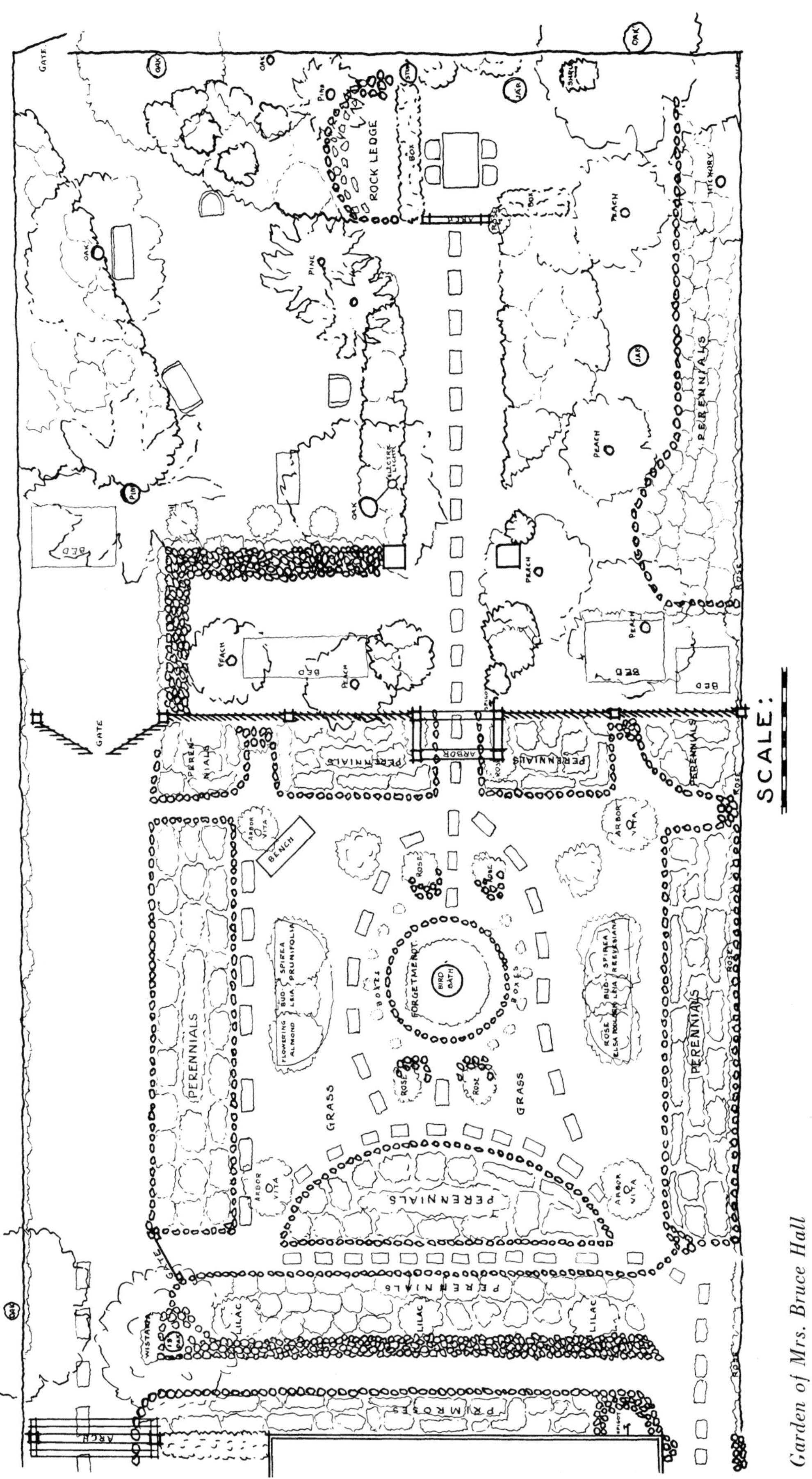

Garden of Mrs. Bruce Hall

Lazyknoll

Mr. and Mrs. William Nichols

Decatur

A TYPICAL example of the small southern blossom garden is that of Mrs. William M. Nichols at Lazyknoll—where no one has time to be lazy! The white frame house stands on the apex of a knoll overlooking a rolling lawn and the shrub-enclosed flower garden. Hidden by a screen of conifers, this garden adds to its other charms that of surprise for the approaching visitor. A rock and fern garden with flagstone court and path lies next the house under a canopy formed by an apple tree and a narrow rose arbor. Separated from the formal garden by a low rose-twined fence and an ornamental white gate, the court still commands a full view of the garden's luxuriant color.

A sturdy uncut hedge of abelia, cherry laurel, spirea, plums, figs, and elder gives the garden the appearance of great security and offers green in winter, blossoms in spring, and ripening fruit in summer and autumn as background for the border of flowers that faces it down in bands of striking color, changing with the seasons. The garden, planned by W. L. Monroe, is centered by an ivy-covered sun dial on a pedestal moulded by the owner. Two large rose squares are surrounded by smaller beds laden with low-growing masses of bloom to give the effect of a bright-colored mosaic. The entire enclosure is bordered with tiny box plants underlain with ivy and vinca, the box having been rooted by this indefatigable gardener from cuttings from the home of the Van Buren family in Virginia.

Photos by F. E. Lee

A Fern-bordered Shady Walk Leads to the Sunny Open Garden at Lazyknoll

Hills and Dales[+]

Mrs. Fuller E. Callaway

LaGrange

WITH fine feeling and admirable restraint there have been made at "Hills and Dales" several modern additions to the five acres of exquisite old formal boxwood gardens which were laid out nearly a hundred years ago by Sarah Coleman Ferrell.

Surrounded by the gardens and a vast area of natural woodland—the estate comprises three thousand acres—the mansion, which is Italo-Georgian in architecture, was erected in 1916 on the site of the old homestead. South of it lie the famous Ferrell gardens intact and almost exactly as their first mistress left them, only an occasional boxwood having, of necessity, been replaced by the present owner, Mrs. Fuller E. Callaway. Just outside the breakfast room on the south side of the house, a section of the old formal garden has been entirely renewed. Here in two semi-circles, around a great ivy-twined urn, have been worked out in dwarf box two mottoes, "Ora Pro Mi," and "St. Callaway," both after inscriptions in the little church of St. Neots in Cornwall, the original home of the Callaways in England. Another modern addition to the old section is the rock garden, designed and planted by Mrs. Callaway, in a shady ravine at the end of the old "Lovers' Lane" just below the first terrace.

Leaving the south side of the grounds, the wind-

Clipped Box Outlines the Pattern and Accents the Garden at Hills and Dales

* See Early Gardens.

Glimpse into the Cutting Garden from the Cedar Shaded Well, Hills and Dales

ing driveway proceeds in a westerly direction towards the formal gardens, the conservatory, and the greenhouses, which are separated from Sarah Coleman Ferrell's quaint gardens by a dense screen of century-old box. Here are five successive terraces, each hedged about pleasant vistas down long, green-arched aisles. On the second level is the interesting Florida garden with its masses of pink and blue hydrangeas, papaya, orange and lemon trees, and blossoming oleanders. On the last level a walkway leads off at right angles through a rose-covered trellis to the extensive plucking garden where are grown row after row of roses, dahlias, iris, peonies, and other perennials in season. This area is screened effectively from the new formal garden, by a clipped cedar hedge. Placed about these modern sections of the grounds are fine specimens of old boxwood and waxen-leaved camellias, and there are a few well-chosen bits of statuary. Great drifts of valley lilies, vinca and ivy are in the leafy shadows beneath the tall trees.

To the north the terrain slopes away from the house and, following the gently curving driveway over grassed hills and dales, one approaches the rolling orchards and wooded sections beyond. Gradually the descent is made to a cool grotto where weeping willows sway idly over the placid surface of a natural lily pool. The driveway encircles this charming water garden and leads on to the picnic grounds where massive tables and chairs of native cedar are spread invitingly under giant oaks and poplars. Here, too, is a bubbling spring and cascade with its surrounding rock garden and a fine backdrop of rhododendron, laurel, and azaleas. Great ropes of wistaria climb to the treetops and in early spring hang curtains of lavender against the white of dogwood and spirea.

Photo by Reeves

Magnolias Bloom Above Serried Ranks of Fragrant Box at Hills and Dales

Porterfield

Mr. and Mrs. James H. Porter

Macon

TWENTY-FIVE acres in extent, Porterfield, the country estate of Mr. and Mrs. James H. Porter, is located on the Perry Road, about seven miles southwest of Macon.

Along a winding driveway, outlined with luxuriant shrubbery plantings, one approaches the spacious buildings done in cream-washed brick with rough-hewn beams and stucco trim and brown Brittany roof tiles. A symbolic weather-vane tops the turret of this rambling Normandy farm-house; a busy gardener—pipe in mouth—with wisps of smoke curling over his shoulder, bends low over a blossoming rose. Just a silhouette, he "shows the way the wind blows" at Porterfield, where the most extensive trial rose gardens in the South are maintained.

The rose acres were the inspiration and creation of two life-long friends, Mr. James H. Porter and Mr. J. D. Crump (a Vice President of the American Rose Society). Together these two plan and plant and experiment and, incidentally, have a thoroughly good time, trying out new and old roses under varying conditions to determine their exact value for the southern garden. Thousands of highly recommended varieties are tested out each year, but the experimenters feel amply repaid if one rose out of fifty proves sufficiently satisfactory to receive the stamp of their approval.

Ornamental tree roses primly mark the path leading to the white-latticed rose pavilion in the heart of the formally planted section. This pavilion, which houses perhaps two hundred bushes, was constructed to establish the exact number of sunshine hours necessary for the best possible rose development in this section. Exactly 33 1/3 per cent. of the sunlight has been screened out by treillage. One enters the pavilion to find row after row of bushes on both sides of a broad white-chained walkway—and roses that rival the painted beauties of the catalogs. Not a sign of mildew or blackspot anywhere about these bushes of Duchess of Wellington, Madame Butterfly, Mrs. Aaron Ward, Lady Hillingdon, and the members of the Radiance family. The conclusions have been that

for the southern garden the ideal situation for roses has an eastern exposure, sheltered as much as possible from western winds, where no more than half or at most three-quarters of possible sunshine is received.

Leaving the cool, semi-shade of the pavilion, one finds the most beautiful sight of all in the vast expanse of the out-door rose garden, enclosed by a hedge of Frau Karl Druschki roses. There are perhaps a hundred blocks in each plot, every block containing about twenty-five rose bushes of the variety to be tested. Four-foot grass walks run between sections and narrower ones separate the blocks. The whole field is equipped with an extensive sprinkler system.

Visitors are welcomed at Porterfield from early morning until the great iron gates swing shut at sunset.

Tomotava

Mr. and Mrs. T. J. Stewart

Macon

A FEW miles from Macon, in Jones County, stands Tomotava, the country home of Mr. and Mrs. T. J. Stewart, on a tract of land which has been in the possession of the family since 1808. In the past ten years the owners have restored the old house which was built by Mr. Stewart's grandfather in 1865, and have laid out about it extensive lawns, shrubberies and gardens.

The house, facing west, stands on a high egg-shaped hill which drops about two hundred and fifty feet, and, thus overlooking two valleys, commands a panoramic view in all directions. The house is in the style of old Mobile houses. Giving the impression, from the front, of a one-story white wooden house, it is in reality two stories; the ground floor, beneath the main floor, is built of stone cut in three-foot blocks, quarried on the place. Shrub plantings soften the lines of the house and

Old Iron Fountain in Garden at Tomotava

blend it in with the site. The front lawn, sloping down to a grove about a quarter of a mile distant, is shaded by a giant oak standing just in line with the front door. In the rear of the house the lawn is centered by an old well, covered with wistaria. Several old barns and outhouses belonging to the original building and now utilized for garages and tool houses are screened by shrubbery and mulberry trees. On the left side of the house the lawn stretches into four wide terraces built up with field stone. On the bottom slope is an iris garden bordered with boxwood.

There are five distinct gardens that extend somewhat in the shape of a horseshoe around the sides of the rear lawn. On the northwest side lies the formal garden, typically colonial, with the small beds bordered in boxwood. This hillside garden is cut down about six feet and the incline is made into a rock garden studded with many rock-loving plants. Stone steps descend through the middle of the rockery and in the center of the garden is an old iron fountain. English junipers make accent points and the beds are kept ever blooming, filled with a succession of flowers. At one end stands a weeping willow, and at the opposite end an arch is cut in the hedge which encloses the perennial garden. Back of this garden, completely hidden by shrubbery, is a cutting garden and nursery where most of the shrubs for the place have been propagated.

The rose garden, which is Mr. Stewart's special pride, extends across the back of the spacious grounds and is separated from them by a hedge of broad-leaf evergreens and flowering shrubs which add seasonal color. Growing here are more than one hundred and sixty varieties of roses. Besides hybrid teas, there are many old teas, Chinas and Bourbons. All the beds are bordered with polyanthus roses, and climbing roses are festooned between cedar posts.

The grounds present a different picture every month as the flowers and shrubs bloom in their seasons. Forsythia, spirea, redbud, dogwood, iris and narcissi welcome the spring; crepe myrtle, mimosa, althea and gardenias come with the roses and summer flowers, and in the fall nandina and pyracantha with their brilliant berries make a great display along with the old pomegranate and fruit-laden pear trees.

With the restoration of both house and grounds the place has lost none of its old-time charm.

Mr. and Mrs. Morgan McNeel

Marietta

THE Marietta home of Mr. and Mrs. Morgan McNeel has been occupied by four generations of her family and the gardens show the imprint of each generation. A grove of fine old pecan trees near the house—one of the earliest pecan plantings in Georgia—was set out by Mr. E. S. Barrows, the first of the family to live here. Two generations ago the gardens were many acres in extent but at a later period part of the tract was converted into a residential section. Near the close of the Civil War General Sherman established his cavalry headquarters on the McNeel place during the occupation of Marietta and on the walls of the buildings are still faint traces of mottoes—and other marks—made by the soldiers. An old brick slave house still standing in the shade of the pecan trees has been converted into a quaint playhouse in the section of the gardens given over to the grandchildren. Possibly the oldest construction on the place is a retaining wall of weathered home-made brick which

Kennesaw Mountain Shows Beyond the McNeel Garden

A Giant Pecan Tree Leans Over the Garden

binds the drive and the upper garden, but a row of lilac trees, lovely today, was planted nearly a hundred years ago.

The house, surrounded by sloping green lawns, stands on a pleasant elevation in a grove of old oaks. Directly back of the house is a sizeable kitchen garden, to the west lie the flower gardens, the pecan grove and the playgrounds. The formal gardens are laid on two levels. An arch of roses is over the entrance to the upper garden which is bound on one side by the ivy-covered brick wall and on the other by low-clipped hedges. Here are carefully planned borders, arranged for a succession of bloom. Jonquils and tulips of early spring give way to iris, fox glove, larkspur, poppies and phlox, then later perennials and annuals furnish color till frost. The garden on the lower level has a white marble pool holding goldfish and vari-colored water lilies. To the right and left of the pool are box-bordered rose beds.

Beyond this level, in a setting of shrubs and dwarf trees, is an old-fashioned summer-house covered with climbing roses and from here the view looks out toward battle-torn Kennesaw Mountain in the near distance.

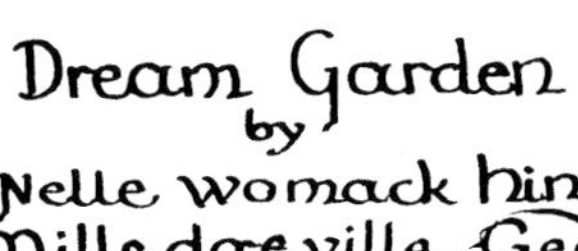

Dream Garden

by
Nelle Womack Hines
Milledgeville, Georgia

Growing in my garden
There must be a rose,
For she blooms in beauty
Everybody knows.
There must be a little place
Where pansy faces smile,
And saucy yellow daffodils
Are dancing all the while.
There must be a little seat
Beside a quiet pool
Where wee star-eyed forget-me-nots
Are taught the golden rule;
Where I may rest and dream I see
The tiny heartease grow,
And pray to learn the secrets
That only flowers know.

Somewhere in my garden
Coral bells should ring,
Tinkling out a tune
For buttercups to sing.
There must be some violets
All nestled on a mound,
And yellow winged butterflies
All fluttering around.
There must be some four o'clocks
So all the flowers may see
Just the time for evening prayer;
A bird must sing to me
From swaying boughs of lilacs
White as drifts of perfumed snow;
Maybe they'd tell me secrets
That only flowers know.

F.E.S.

Greenacre

Judge and Mrs. E. R. Hines

Milledgeville

THE rock garden at Greenacre, viewed of a morning in early spring, is a picture to be remembered. Strolling leisurely down the "Old Road" there comes a sense of nature's perfection in the hush of the new day. On either side are great masses of blossoms—low ones—spilling over the rocks—English daisies, dwarf tulips, wild iris, and pansy faces, still wet with dew. From the "Old Road" there branches off a woodland pathway leading on to a flagstone terrace, and, from the old mill-stone imbedded there, a lovely view opens on the various rock gardens and terraces that merge and blend into a colorful whole.

In the language of the owner and builder of the garden, "The planning, construction and planting of the rock gardens at Greenacre was a labor of love, main strength and pure ignorance. After great trials and tribulations the rocks and boulders were collected from a branch down in the pasture at the end of the 'Old Road' where the two boys of the family had waded and fished, with bent pins for hooks, when they were very, very young. Every rock was moved at least three times, and some could count to six! The entire rock garden at Greenacre was built around a reflecting pool, and it was a red letter day when the 'spring' was first turned on. The woods around had furnished ferns and shrubs, and it really was astonishing what the wearing out of several pairs of shoes had accomplished towards the making of a most satisfactory collection of native wild flowers."

In the evolution of this garden, there have been many changes, and still more upheavals, but its owner found great joy in the arduous task, and she sends greetings to all gardening enthusiasts, and bids them welcome to Greenacre.

Dappled Shadow in the Rock Garden at Greenacre

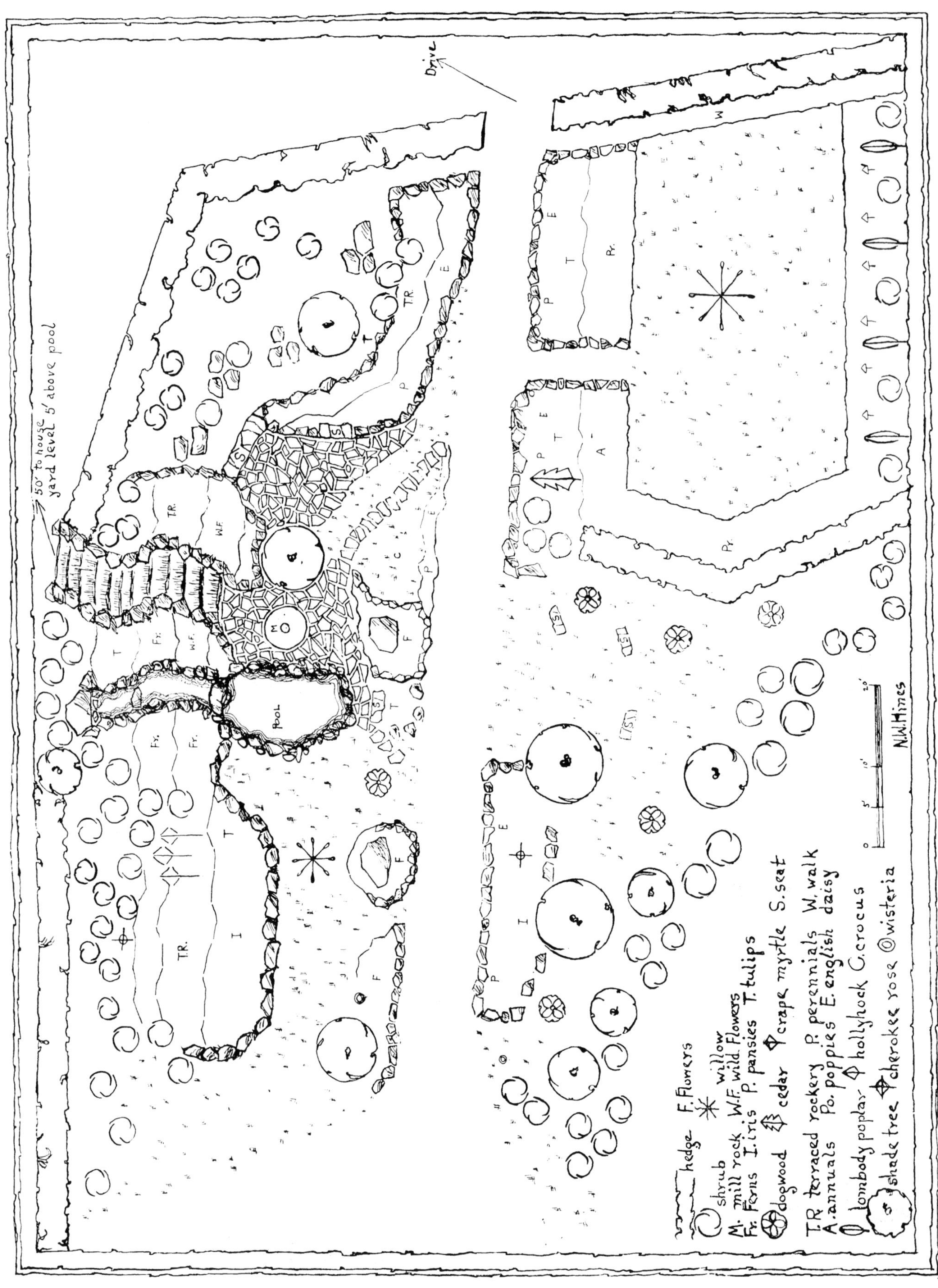

Drive
50' to house
yard level 5' above pool
POOL
hedge F. Flowers
shrub willow
M. mill rock W.F. wild flowers
Fr. Ferns I. iris P. pansies T. tulips
dogwood cedar crape myrtle S. seat
T.R. terraced rockery P. perennials W. walk
A. annuals Po. poppies E. english daisy
lombody poplar hollyhock C. crocus
shade tree cherokee rose wisteria
N.W. Hines

Looking Toward the Sunrise, Reflecting Pool, Greenacre

The Old Road, Greenacre

Plan of Garden of Mr. and Mrs. Miller S. Bell
Milledgeville

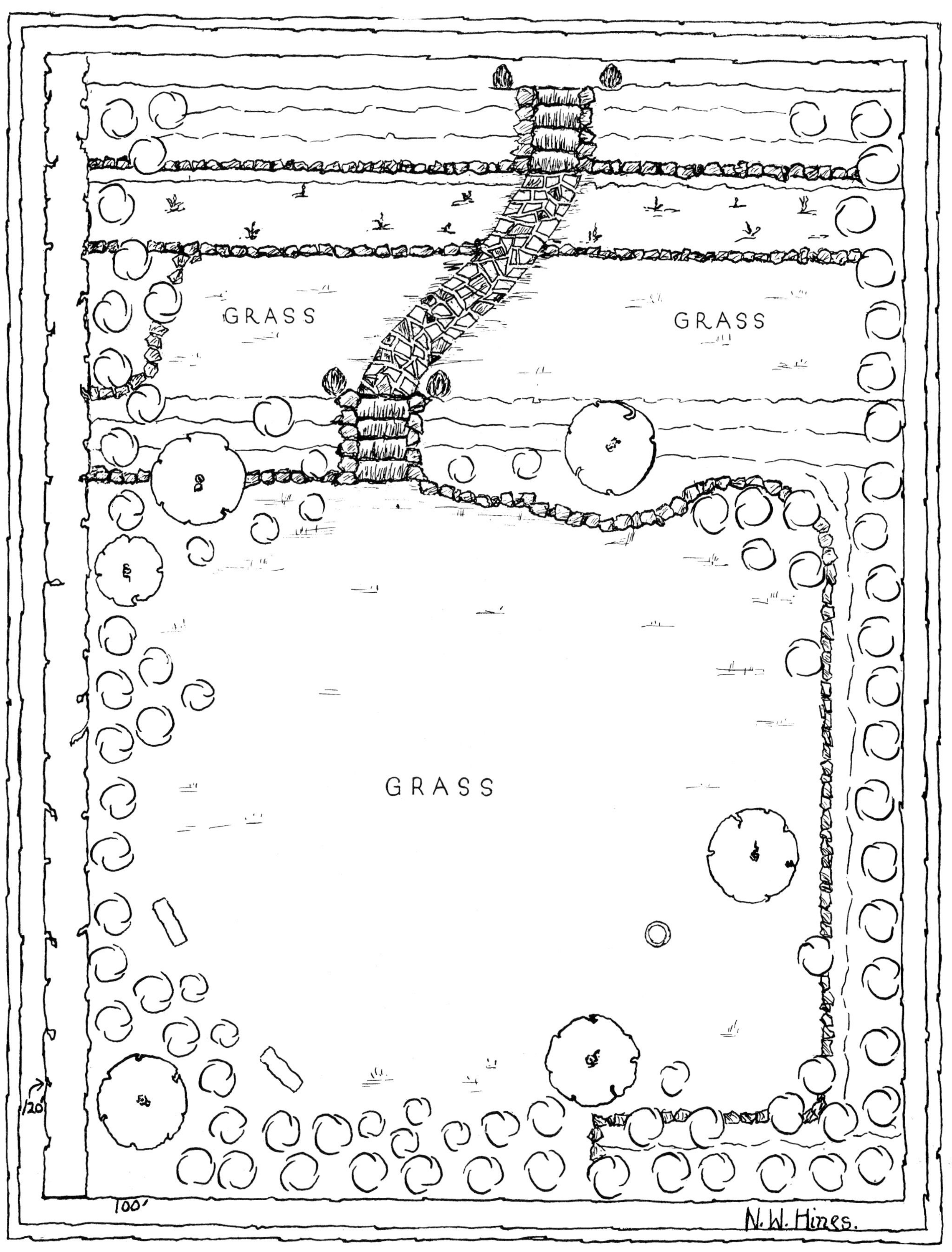

Grass Walk in Springtime, Bell Garden

THE sunken garden on the property of Mr. and Mrs. Miller S. Bell was planned with great care under the direct supervision of its owners. The garden is at its best in springtime when iris and tulips and many dainty rock plants in the crannies of the walls are all in bloom. A generous planting of shrubs of varied heights and shapes encloses the entire property and gives it a delightful seclusion from the world outside.

Descending the stone steps which flank the sides of the first rocked terrace, one passes between two long borders where iris, perennial phlox, daisies, Madonna lilies, Oriental poppies, hollyhocks, and larkspur are grouped harmoniously, while interplanted with them are achillea, armeria, and petunias dotted about for small spots of color. In still another bed below the last terrace are day lilies, physostegia, daisies and iris. The rock terraces are lovely when pansies bloom against a background of ivy and lippia, armeria and dwarf iris. Here, too, are tulips in gay colors. A bird bath is set in a panel of grass and benches under the big tree tempt one to linger in this pleasant spot.

Blue Bonnet Lodge

Mr. and Mrs. Wayne P. Sewell

Newnan

BLUE BONNET LODGE, on the Sewell plantation, is six miles from Newnan, just off the Franklin D. Roosevelt Highway. A long winding road, its banks planted with Paul's Scarlet roses, approaches the Lodge with its surrounding gardens, twenty acres enclosed by a rustic cedar fence.

The "Wishing-Well" at Blue Bonnet Lodge.

Photo by F. E. Lee

The garden has been planned to take advantage of many rugged outcroppings of rocks and boulders—one of them, "Little Stone Mountain," covering half an acre. In carrying out the development Mrs. Sewell has had professional assistance, from Mr. Cagle of the Monroe Nurseries, and from Mrs. Fletcher Pearson Crown, but the original idea and the individual planting details are her own.

Rustic trellises on the front and sides of the lodge are covered with Marechal Niel and Mary Wallace roses, while evergreen hedges and flowering shrubs, with groups of dogwoods and native cedars add to the setting. Two massive oaks are noteworthy; one near the shrubbery, another at the southwest corner of the house. The lodge is an ancient structure, having been put together slowly and painstakingly about a century ago. An old peach tree grows through the floor boards of the rear porch. The view from the porch is a spreading panorama of hills and stream-fed valleys surrounding fields of corn and cotton and acres of red poppies. From the porch, steps lead to the outdoor living room, paved with flagstones around the trunk of a huge oak which is said to be several hundred years old. This area is raised four feet above the garden proper, thus affording a view of the whole.

The sunken garden has been made against a background of rugged beauty, where a cascade dances over mossy boulders. The stream winds its way through the garden and forms three lily pools farther on. There are seven such springs on the property; and centering the sunken garden is an old-fashioned "wishing well."

To the north of the lodge lies the formal rose garden, and still farther, at the bottom of a deep ravine is a woodland garden with its many bird houses and feeding stations. A bridge spanning the little stream leads towards a rustic pergola and a tea house where the treatment is informally charming.

Near the lodge an old barn has been converted into a small theatre for amateur theatricals and Saturday night barn dances for the neighborhood. Here, too, entertainment is often furnished by the colored folks from the plantation, the pickaninnies singing and dancing to the rhythm of "pat of the foot and clap of the hand."

Outdoor Sitting-Room at Blue Bonnet Lodge Photo by F. E. Lee

Rock-bordered Pools, Blue Bonnet Lodge Photo by F. E. Lee

Ossabaw Island

Dr. and Mrs. H. N. Torrey

ON historic Ossabaw Island, one of the "Golden Isles of Georgia," Dr. and Mrs. H. N. Torrey, of Detroit, have built their winter residence. Hard white beaches washed by a rolling surf, forests of moss-hung live oaks leading down towards the Sound, lush tropical vegetation along stretches of golden marshes—all offered a bewildering variety of settings for the house. To insure the health and happiness of flower gardens, however, a site was chosen away from the ocean winds, and at the north end of the island, a thick woods commanding picturesque views of the Sound. Here, in 1924, shortly after the purchase of Ossabaw, the dwelling was erected. It is a long rambling plaster house of Spanish ranch-house type, an architecture appropriate not only to the native growth of palmettos and yuccas but to the historical associations here of sixteenth century Spanish occupation.

The first garden made was a patio garden, designed by Ellen Shipman. The later gardens have been planned by Mrs. Torrey.

Bermuda pink walls surround three sides of the patio which is the important feature of the garden side of the house. The pavement is of dark terra cotta tiles and at the centre, supported on two hexagonal stone steps is an aquarium, fifteen feet in

Peter Pan in the Glade of the Wild Garden, Ossabaw

Live Oaks, Camellias and Azaleas, Ossabaw

Colorful Tile Fountain and Luxuriant Blossoms in One of the Twin Gardens, Ossabaw

circumference, where gold and silver fish gleam among the water plants. At one corner an iron staircase winds up to the second story of the house and iron rings at each step hold gay Spanish pots planted with yellow oxalis or vari-colored petunias. On the west wall is a tangle of roses, Reve d'or, and white and yellow Banksias, against a background of viburnum, eleagnus, and camphor trees.

The east wall, with its arched entrance to the forecourt, is covered with ivy and cat's claw-vine (Bignonia unguis cati) which escapes from the wall to the house, and mingles its large, golden-yellow trumpets with the lavender ones of the Bignonia Speciosa that completely covers the patio side of the house. Flanking these walls, a set of twin gardens, with an old brick walk between, terminate in twin tile fountains of a lovely blue and green color, the water spouting from the mouth of green lion heads. Here the planting is confined to flowers that give bloom in winter and early spring. In January, the patio gardens are full of stock, snapdragon, calendula, nemesia and wall flowers. A little later the bulbs—hyacinths, narcissi, scillas, iris and sparaxis—push their way through the nodding bloom and completely change the aspect of the gardens from day to day.

Broad steps lead to the green sward where the camellia garden begins and then wanders under old live-oaks in one large plantation. Here are many choice varieties but no large trees, the average being about six feet. A little further on is the spring walk, of rolled turf, ten feet wide and two hundred and seventy feet long, leading to the wild garden. Large semi-circular beds of Azalea Indica mark the entrance to the path and it continues between wide, irregular borders, which in spring are a riot of color. Their edging is of large flowered pink and lavender oxalis, forming a solid mat. Flowering fruit trees and Kurume azaleas are staggered through the center and the intervening spaces filled with drifts of solid color pansies, spring bulbs and tall growing, pink and yellow oxalis. The lower end of the walk

The Azalea Walk, Ossabaw

terminates in semi-circular beds of wild Azaleas; and, at a turn to the left, is the wild garden.

A driveway runs through this section and on the right are clumps of wild azaleas with a carpet-planting of naturalized narcissi and snowdrops. From a mound on the left, surmounted by a stone figure of Peter Pan, a stream flows over rocky ledges forming two pools, and a connecting rocky spillway of the water garden. Here is a collection of violets, blue, white, yellow, the Confederate gray, crowfoot and several varieties of Johnny-jump-ups. Thousands of wild Zephyranthes or Fairy lilies, as they are known in the South, raise their heads from beds of fern and wild oxalis in delightful effect in March, while the white Cherokee rose festoons many of the surrounding trees.

Circling the ponds, the return to the house is by way of a path, bordered with alternate clumps of spring bulbs and small azaleas, which leads to the rose garden. This is informal, and very lovely when the tall arches are hung with the garlands of the climbers, each one a different variety.

Water Garden at Ossabaw

Rock City

Mr. and Mrs. Garnett Carter

Walker County

THOUGH located on Lookout Mountain, in Tennessee, the gardens of Mr. and Mrs. Garnett Carter are on the side of the mountain that is part of Georgia. Hence Rock City is rightfully included in Georgia gardens, and is presented as a unique rock garden. A strange formation of lichen-covered sandstone, it is of interest to geologists, artists, horticulturists and others. The sand formation covers an area of ten acres. The fissures or crevices in the rocks vary in depth, some being one hundred and twenty feet from the surface to the trail below. For countless years this great extent of rock had rested undisturbed, and, until Mr. and Mrs. Carter in 1932 built their Enchanted Trail, it was impossible to pass through the many narrow tunnels and devious windings.

At the entrance to Rock City is a weathered stone Norman tower, built for the use of the gatekeeper and to house a little service shop. The Enchanted Trail begins near the gate-house and winds in and above, through and below Rock City for three thousand feet. The Trail, a path four feet wide, leads through tunnels and over bridges bordered with gray rocks and surfaced with pine needles and moss, and makes accessible every cranny and crevice in the entire ten acres. Stone stairways have been built to provide ease and comfort for the long trail. Pulpit Rock, Fat Man's Squeeze, the Needle's Eye and Grand Corridor, Shelter Rock, Lover's Leap, Tortoise Shell Rock, Pedestal Rock and the Lion's Den are some of the named features, each one a garden in itself. In the dainty Fairy-ring, down deep in a cavern, are soft whispers of elves and fairies. We pass Galoochee, the old stone witch, and reach the Ship Rock, moss covered and gray with lichens.

Many little figures add to the charm, the mystery and the interest of the place. On a wide platform under an overhanging rock an orchestra of gnomes stands ready to play fairy music. Others serve as

Old Indian Signal Rock Looking Far Out into Tennessee

The Enchanted Trail at Rock City

Stairway Through Rocks as Nature Plants Them

guides, standing at points of interest along the Trail to show the different locations. On a shadowy slope within the cavern sits Rip Van Winkle, awakened from his nap of twenty years, watching, in dazed fashion, the gnomes as they roll their ten pins down the hill. In a barberry thicket Red Riding Hood and the Wolf delight the children who visit the garden.

Down deep in the caverns the Enchanted Trail winds through the Grand Corridor where shrubs and plants, including many galax and trillium, wild iris and mosses, border the path. A double stone bridge has been built over an unusual cross-crevice, which is said to be a rare trick of nature.

The chasms are spanned by three cable bridges, the shortest twenty-five feet long; the longest, one hundred and eighty feet, swings out over the Cave of the Winds, reaching from one high bluff to another. It affords a close-up of the rock formation and a spectacular view of the Chattanooga Valley below. Two tunnels have been made, one thirty and the other sixty feet in length, through which can be seen interesting vistas beyond.

On the side of the mountain, close by the rocks, the forest is dense, lofty and over-reaching. Pine and hemlock, sweetgum, maple, birch, wild crab, oak, hickory, dogwood, ash, serviceberry, elderberry, holly and scores of other trees grow on the mountain slope near the rock garden. Bird houses have been placed in the trees and nooks, and bird families dwell there in sanctuary. A small enclosed park shelters a small herd of deer. The rock reservation of ten acres is enclosed by a weathered rock wall, rustic in design and in harmony with the surroundings. A broad, irregular border of wide-leafed shrubs, have been planted to separate the Carter home from Rock City.

Of peculiar interest is the rare coral moss carpeting surfaces of the rock in patches of delicate blossoms. Wild baby's breath, spiderwort, liatris, butterfly weed, trillium, trailing arbutus, partridge berry, galax, laurel, azaleas, and rhododendron flourish in this wonder garden. One of its fairest flowers is called for a nymph, the white goddess, "Leucothoe," and its curved racemes of tiny white bells are worthy emblems of the charming name. Many other flowers transplanted to the rock garden are growing luxuriantly in the rich leaf-mold deposited there throughout the ages. Late trees, like the white oak and ash abound. Twisted, stunted, windblown pines, hemlocks and dogwood add a picturesque note, while in more sheltered places the trees are symmetrical and luxuriant.

The result of the development is to afford access to a natural rock garden unequaled in beauty, and to protect and preserve one of nature's most remarkable formations. Mrs. Carter received the 1933 Garden Club of America's horticultural bronze medal of distinction for her efforts in preserving and making accessible to all this strange and impressive spectacle of nature.

Seven Oaks

Mr. and Mrs. Thomas Berry

Rome

SEVEN OAKS, the home of Mr. and Mrs. Thomas Berry, stands in the shade of fine old trees on the summit of a little knoll just outside of Rome and its seven hills. From the level site of the house a view spreads out northward towards Lavender Mountain and a range of other low lying hills whose changing tints of blue and lavender make a poetic back drop for the gardens.

Against the nothwest side of the house is a tiny cloister garden enclosed in an ivy-hung rock wall. The intricately patterned beds are bordered with dwarf boxwood and the dominant color note in the planting is blue, but over the walls Van Fleet roses bloom in a shower of pale pink, and regale lilies are massed in the four wall corners.

From the little garden a flagstone path goes out to a wide lawn and a tree-shaded swimming pool. Down a few steps from this level the path continues to the rose garden which is bounded by a high privet hedge. The inner hedges are of boxwood and the beds are laid out in formal design. The center beds hold white, yellow and pale pink roses, the next circle pink Radiance, while the outer beds are full of Purple Prince petunias through which rise standard red roses.

Long grass paths between borders of old shrubs lead to the rows of fruit trees, fig trees and vegetable gardens. The tennis court is hidden by a trellis of Jacotte roses. Across the far end of the lawn and at the edge of the slope is a dry wall planted in herbs and creeping plants, an effective line of color between Seven Oaks and the view of the misty hills.

Garden at Seven Oaks, Rome

Sun Dial in Rose Garden, Seven Oaks, Rome

Mimosa Hall[+]

Mrs. John Reid

Roswell

ON a quest for a place where "friendship, contentment, nature, simplicity, and beauty would combine to bring about a kind of Paradise" came Roswell King about 1789 and with a few friends, established a summer colony. He so loved his adopted country that he persuaded twelve of his friends to join him in building permanent homes and the town of Roswell was begun. About 1830 an architect from Boston was summoned, and among the builders of the fine old mansions was John Dunwoodie who built Phoenix Hall. It was later owned by General Hansell and long afterwards acquired by the late Neel Reid, architect, who restored and improved it with the rare appreciation and feeling of the true artist. The gardens as they are now at Mimosa Hall, a name applied by Mrs. Hansell, are largely the work of this last owner and the result is charming in its simple perfection. Much of the old planting was destroyed by fire in the sixties, but it is difficult to realize today that a modern has had any part in the planting.

There is a twenty-foot driveway to an ample court, paved with huge granite blocks. The house of old plaster, laid in courses, is white with four tall columns of Greek Revival type. Brick steps lead to a brick porch, at the right of which is a large chaste tree overhung with Banksia roses. In pots are Bird of Paradise bushes that reach larger growth in the garden beyond.

There are many fine old trees, cedars and oaks with a quantity of tree-box, but through and over all are the predominating Mimosas for which the place is called.

Mimosa Hall

* See Early Gardens.

Formal Box Garden with Accents of English Laurel, Mimosa Hall

The formal garden is entered by a flight of steps flanked by a sweeping curved hedge of graceful line. On the steps, potted plants are used, as one season follows another. The beds are box-bordered and the paths of swept earth so often used in old gardens lead to a flat inlaid pool in the center of which is an old water jar. The path to the north ends in a gate covered over with a fine Harrison's yellow rose, and opens on a wide horizon of meadow and sky.

Adjoining is another garden with borders of clove-scented pinks, clipped and coaxed into a profusion of spicy bloom with iris and Hemerocallis in fine variety. A long narrow pool, an integral feature of the plan, reflects the rarer iris. A survival of old roses and a replanting now and then shows the chinquapin, Harrison's yellow, Gold of Ophir, Seven Sisters, Cloth of Gold and La Duchesse, and within a long arbor vitae hedge are the small old-fashioned red roses known and loved in our grandmother's gardens. In a place apart and with the dark background they are effectively vivid.

To the right is the vegetable garden, which serves as a cutting and kitchen garden, with herbs and aromatics that are attractive as well as utilitarian.

From the higher levels the various sections of the gardens can be surveyed, and everywhere are hauntingly sweet reminders of earlier gardeners.

Old Red Roses Within a Hedge of Arbor Vitae, Mimosa Hall

Clipped Ivy and Hedges Border the Iris Pool at Mimosa Hall.

Sapelo Island

Mr. Howard Coffin

THE house at Sapelo opens on a loggia, its classic columns extending through two stories, and a tiled terrace which extends across the front commands a lovely view of the main garden and the surrounding woodland. Potted tropical plants and gay colored urns are placed in the terrace corners and along the coping, while ficus vines form a delicate tracery of green against the oyster white tabby walls. At each end of the terrace date and cocos palms are planted and azaleas and camellias are banked along the retaining wall.

Broad steps descend to the level of the main garden which is rectangular in shape, extending the full length of the house, and raised about two feet above the level of the surrounding woodland. The garden, in a grove of two hundred year old live oaks draped with Spanish moss, is simple in design, except for the ornate detail of the pool. On the main axis, the wide oyster shell walk terminates in a flight of steps leading to the path which winds through the woodland toward the green houses and pool garden, and at either end of the cross walk are pieces of Italian statuary. The central architectural feature is a large pool in the form of a Byzantine cross and surrounded by a shell walk and low tabby walls of the same contour as the pool. A Florentine marble figure stands on a pedestal in the center of the pool in whose depths are mirrored reflections of the house and the overhanging trees.

In the planting of the garden everything has been subordinated to the beautiful old trees with their twisted moss-covered branches which cast an ever changing pattern of light and shade on the open lawn. Arbor vitaes are used as accents along the walks and around the pool. Azaleas and camellias are in the outer borders, while yellow jessamine, white and pink Cherokee roses and wistaria vines climb up the tree trunks and add brilliant color in the spring in contrast to the sombre gray of the moss and the olive green of the live oaks.

The great lawn on the opposite side of the house merges into the surrounding woodland, and on both sides of the lawn are flat, circular lily pools.

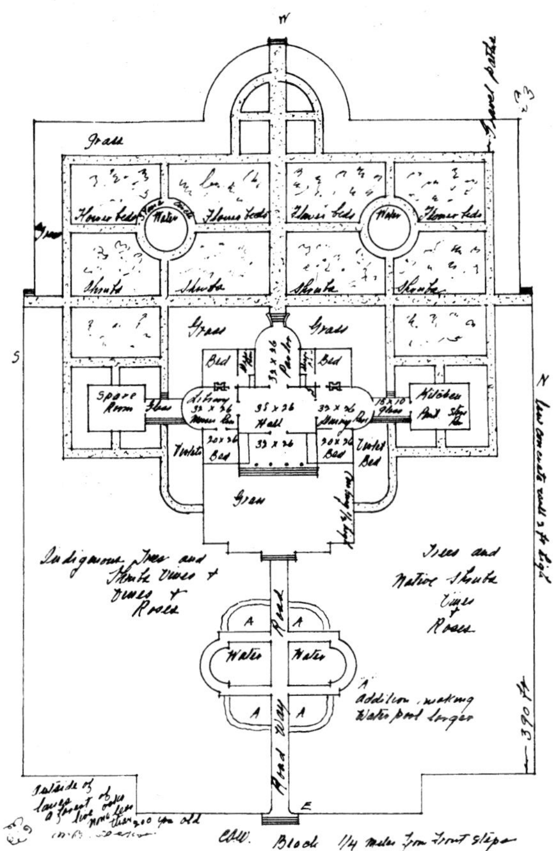

Groupings of palms, camellias, orange trees, oleanders and other semi-tropical shrubs supplement the natural woodland growth. One vista from the greensward looks toward a statue placed in the end bay of the glassed-in swimming pool. Paths lead through the woods to the tennis court, the administrative and farm buildings and the elaborate duck ponds and to the water gardens which may be seen from the terrace. Not far away is the largest green house which comprises a palm room, a rose bay, water lily propagating pools and vegetable beds in addition to the usual flower benches. There are several acres of orchards and vegetable gardens which surround the fruit house where oranges, grapefruit, figs, pomegranates, and other fruits are grown.

Age-old Live Oaks Frame the House at Sapelo

A Modern Evocation of a Romantic Past, Sapelo

Savannah

Notes from W. W. DeRenne Library

by Augusta Floyd DeRenne

THE principal industry for the Georgia Colonists was to be the raising of silk and wine, and therefore one of the first acts of the Trustees was to establish a public garden.

We have the following account from the Colonial Records: "From the Ninth of June 1733 to Nine of June 1734."

"Besides the several Works on which the People were employed at Savannah, as palisading the Town, clearing the Place of Pine-trees, etc. and building of House, some other Works were carried on; viz a publik Garden was laid out, which was designed as a Nursery, in order to supply the People for their several Plantations with White Mulberry trees, Vines, Oranges, Olives, and other necessary Plants; a Gardener was appointed for the Care of it, and to be paid by the Trustees."

Mr. William Houstoun was appointed Botanist for the garden Oct. 3, 1732, to serve three years and was ordered, "to take his passage in the first ship that shall Sail from the River for Jamaica, by way of Madera to inform himself of the Manner of cultivating the vineyards and making the wines there," and to procure "cuttings of their best sorts of Vines and Seeds, Roots of any other useful plants he shall meet with on that Island, which are wanting in our American Colonies." Four different voyages besides that to Madera and Jamaica were intended but Mr. Houstoun died while in Jamaica before his first year was quite over and Mr. Robt. Millar was appointed to succeed him for "the remaining two-years and forty-six days."

Mr. Millar proved to be very unsatisfactory; he was not reappointed and in August 1736 Mr. Hugh Anderson was appointed "Inspector of the public Gardens and Mulberry Plantations in Georgia." He served three years and was removed by General Oglethorpe because of long illness and to save expenses and moved to Charlestown where he read lectures in botany. The Trustees were not very fortunate in their botanists for the gardens, as the first one died while searching for plants, the second one added nothing and the third one became ill and moved away.

Plants in great variety were sent over and we find in June 1733 an order "That Mr. Brownjohn do buy Sage, Mint, and other Plants for the next Imbarkation," that Mr. Christopher Tower contributed, "Two Gallons of Lucerne Seed in two Kegs Sent on board the Georgia Pink," by Capt. Danbuz; that Mr. Phillip Miller of Chelsea contributed, "Some white Mulberry Seeds from Italy Sent on board the James," by Capt. Yaokley; Mr. Robt. More gave "Three Olive Trees in Baskets"; Mr. Phillip Miller of Chelsea, "Two Papers of Egyptian Kali or Pot Ash seed, a Paper of Cotton seed, a Tub of White Mulberry Plants and Burgundy Vines."

In 1735, "Fifty Caper Plants" were given by Mr. Thomas Hyam; also "Ten Olive Trees from Venice, Sent to the Physick-Gardens at Chelsea to be preserved, till proper for them to be sent to Georgia." Mr. Miller was the botanist in charge of the Physick Gardens at Chelsea. He sent at another time, "A tub of Madder Roots for the use of the Colony," probably to be used for dye. Mr. Solomon Merret gave, "A Bag of Barilla seed from Spain"—and there were, "Three large tubs of bamboo from the East Indies," and "Some Neapolitan Chestnuts for sowing in Georgia."

So much for the plants of which the above are just a few samples.

That the Trust supplied the labor for the gardens is shown by the following:

In 1738, 116 German servants were sent over for General Oglethorpe to distribute and "four Heads to be employed in the publick Gardens under the care of Joseph Fitz Walker." I find in the accounts money spent for the "fencing in and making a large garden to supply the Colony with Mulberry plants etc," which shows it was probably enclosed. The earliest records do not describe the exact location of the Gardens but from Wm. De Brahm—"His Majesty's Serveyer General for the Southern District of North America" —in 1764 is found the following:

"The City consists of 400 Houses—a church, and independent Meeting-House, a Council House, a Court House, and a Filatur. The Plane of the City is at the highest Place 30 feet above the Surface of the Stream, or rather—above the Springs under the Quick Sand, and the whole Depth is a meer Sand down to the General Springs in the Quick Sand.

"The City is since increased by two Suburbs, the one is the West, called Iamacraw (sic), a name reserved from the Indian Town formerly at this Place, of which the famous Thamachaychee (sic) was the last King. Another Suburb is to the East called the Trustees Gardens, a Place where the Trustees had a famous Garden laid out in order to make Experiments before they were advised to be accounted Objects profitable to be introduced in that Climate; both these Suburbs are increasing since 1760 extremely fast, so that above 160 Houses are by these Suburbs added to the Number of the Houses in the City.

"Between the City and the Trustees Garden is an artificial Hill upon the Bay, part of which in 1760 was dug through (:to open a Communication with this Suburb and the City:) whereby a stratum was opened near the Plane of the City filled with human bones; this confirmed the History of this Mount, which had traduced it to be an ancient Indian burying ground, on which (:as Thamachaychee (sic) the last Iamacraw (sic) King related to General Oglethorpe at his Arrival:) one of the Iamacraw (sic) Kings had had entertained a great white Man with a red Beard, who had entered the Port of Savannah Stream with a very large Vessel, and himself came up in his Barge to Iamacraw (sic), and had expressed great Affection to the Indians, from which he Hath had the Return of as Much. The white Man with his red Beard intending to present the King with a Piece of Curiosity (:he had on board of his Vessel:) for which he desired some Indians might go down to receive it from his Lieutenant on board, to whom he wrote a Note, which he signified the Indians would deliver to this Officer, who (:pursuant to the order in the Note:) delivered, what was demanded, and the Indians brought it up to Iamacraw, at which their King was greatly surprised, but more so, that this white Man could send his thoughts to so great a Distance upon a white Leaf, which surpassing their Conception, they were ready to believe this white to be more than a Man, as the Indians have no other way to express times passed or to come than by rising and setting of the Sun, by New Moons, by sprouting of the Trees and the Number of their ancestors; the General by the nearest Computation, and comparing History with Chronology, concluded the person to have been Admiral Sir Walter Raleigh, who probably entered the Savannah Port in 1584, when on his Navigation upon this Coast.

"The Gardens in Savannah are productive of all manner of Shrubs, Fruit Trees and Pot Herbs. The many experiments which are made there will as inexceptionable evidences testify to the Truth of these Facts. The author could alledge many, which were successfully made before his Arrival in Georgia by those who had the Care of the famous Trustees Gardens: But the useful undertaking had been for some years abandoned when the author came to Savannah who, however met with two large Olive Trees, some Sevel Orange, Apple, Plumb, Peach, Mulberry, Honey Locust, one Apricok (sic) and one Amerel Cherry Tree as Testimonies of the laborious Experiments and good Successes."

References:

1. *History of the Province of Georgia:* with Maps of Original Surveys by John Gerar William de Brahm, His Majesty's Surveyor-General for the Southern District of North America.
2. Now First Printed — *Wormsloe* 1849 (George Wymberley Jones.)
3. Colonial Records.
4. Stephens' Journal.
5. Egmont's Journal.

Wormsloe[+]

Mr. and Mrs. W. W. DeRenne

Savannah

SINCE the early days of this historic place, more formal areas have been developed, the plans fitting in with the original design as closely as possible. The present owners, Wymberley W. DeRenne, and his wife, Augusta Floyd DeRenne, have contributed so much to the garden interest of Georgia that the additions they have made at Wormsloe deserve full description.

The first section of the formal gardens is a walled rectangle, with a recess to the east and a flagged walk on the west side. In the recess a grille panel is used in the center of which is a medallion of Storey, the southern writer. Over the recess is a cedar arbor planted to roses, scuppernong vines, and Clematis paniculata. Four old Italian marbles from Spalding House on Sapelo Island have been used in this garden after the Pompeian manner.

In planning the additions, walls of old brick have been employed to lend charm and seclusion to the enclosed gardens. The hand-made bricks laid in the walls are from the old slave quarters, and the flagstones of the walkways were brought over from England in Colonial days as ship ballast. One section, the sunken garden, is directly west of the flagged terrace, and the other, the Gnome Garden, is south of the western garden. These plots are contiguous and form an "L". Directly opposite the steps, which lead down into the sunken garden, is a solid cypress door set between two brick pillars supporting a brick panel on a slate lintel.

* See Early Gardens.

The Perfection of Azaleas and Moss-hung Live Oaks

Bronzes by Lucy Currier Richards lend distinction to the gardens, one particularly noteworthy is the "Sundial,"—the figure of a girl plucking a waterlily, the stem casting a shadow on the face of the dial. Centering another plot is a well-head supported by a circular base of square cobbles from the streets of old Savannah. On the well-head, which is from an old abandoned plantation, is a bronze figure of a girl pouring water from a pitcher. There is also a radiant figure of Browning's Pippa and another of a maid in pensive mood.

The walls are six feet high around three sides of the sunken gardens, leaving an open side between this and the older development. In the south wall is a grille of lacework design, affording a glimpse of the Gnome Garden. There is a fountain here and surrounding it are potted yellow callas interspersed with ancient Spanish jugs. A dovecote stands just outside the garden, and tumblers and fan-tails add gaiety. Blue larkspur, pale pink arctotis, and valerian are used extensively at Wormsloe, and the native yuccas and palms lend a tropical flavor.

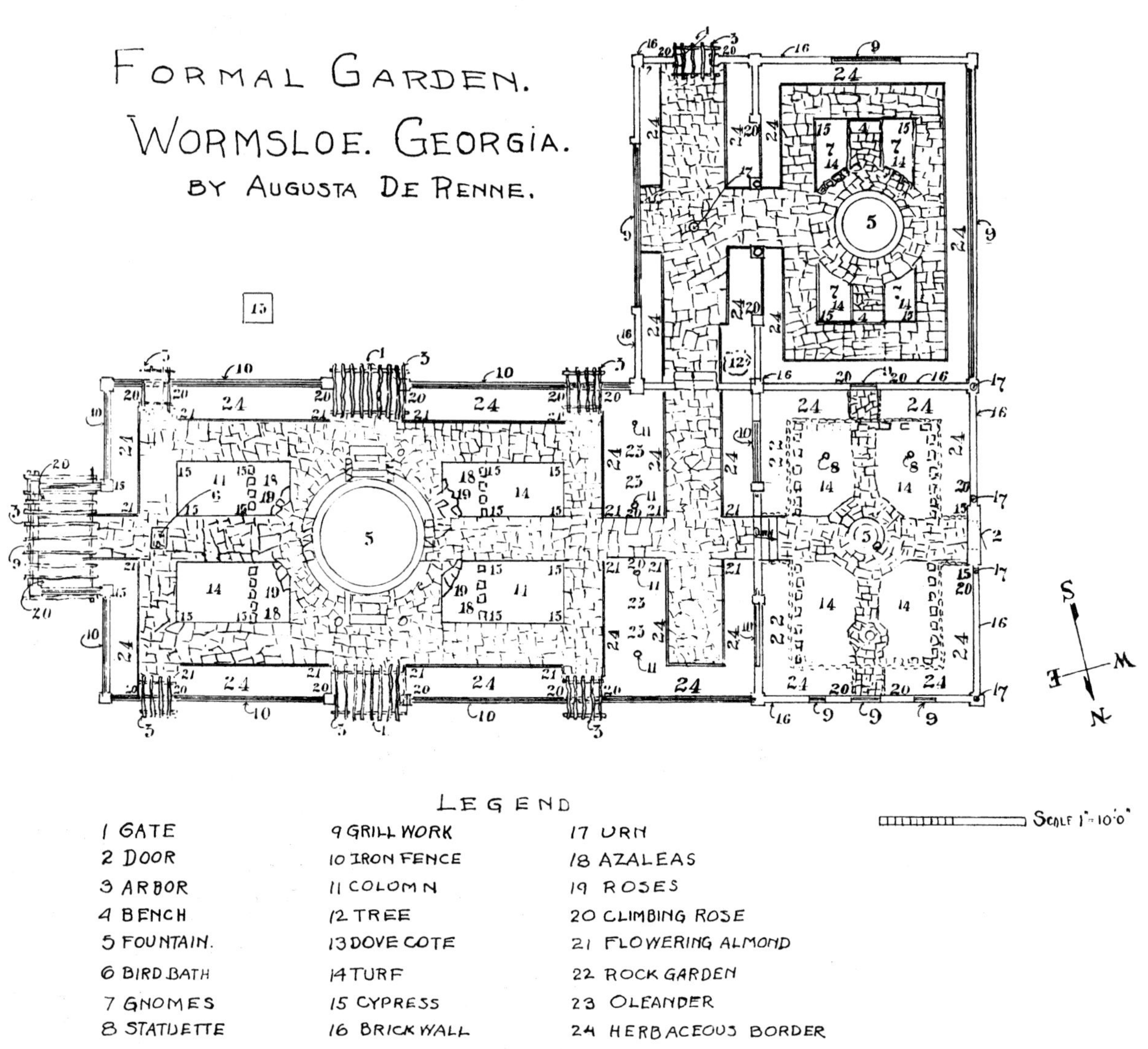

Two Views of Walled Garden at Wormsloe

Mrs. Thomas Hilton
Savannah

MRS. HILTON'S garden has been placed in a sheltered spot to the southeast of the L-shaped house. A rose arbor on one side and a ligustrum and bamboo hedge on the other, complete the enclosure which gives it a delightful seclusion. On the arbor grow a succession of roses, the bloom starting in February with the Pink Cherokee, then followed by Yellow Banksia, White Cherokee, Silver Moon, and American Pillar. Twined among the roses and adding to their fragrance are yellow jessamine and Confederate jasmine (Rhynchospermum jasminoides). In earliest spring masses of white and red azaleas make splotches of color against the evergreen background of three large camphor trees.

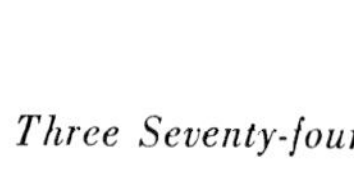

Near the arbor is a naturalistic planting of wild ferns and native iris, while beyond lie the rose gardens and the cutting garden, shut off by a tall hedge and a row of long-leaf pine trees.

Rural Felicity

Mr. and Mrs. Malcolm Maclean

Savannah

"RURAL FELICITY," the home of Mrs. Malcolm Maclean, stands on a bluff over-looking Grimball's Creek, one of the several arms of the sea, surrounding the Isle-of-Hope. Across the broad salt marsh lies Dutch Island and in the far distance the yellow banks of Skidaway outline the passage of the inland waterway. To the south are the old Confederate embankments which command that approach to Savannah.

Originally the home of General White, of Revolutionary fame, the place passed through several families before it was bought and remodeled about 1914 by Mr. Joseph Hull. He developed it as a summer home and model farm. After his death it was purchased by the present owner. Of flower garden there was then no sign except two magnificent fig trees and several crape myrtles with lovely spreading branches, which in summer wave plumes of pink flowers. The need for an intimate garden near the house was very great. The constant sea breeze blowing across the marsh was too chilling to permit enjoyment of the bright winter sun, and too destructive of tender flowers. The side of the grounds near the road was chosen, and planting was begun in 1927. First of all privacy had to be obtained, and the iron fence was planted with Algerian ivy, known locally as "Wormsloe" ivy. This has a very large leaf, and is a rapid grower, so rapid that the fence is now completely covered. Cassena berry (Ilex cassine) alternating with kumquat trees were planted under the tall native palms (Sabal palmetto), bordering it.

A background being established, the space was divided into three gardens, separated by high trellises, the center garden to be enclosed in shrubs, the other two to be planted in relation to the spreading fig trees. The planting was done in such a way as to keep open a view of the marsh, so gold in winter, so green in summer. The center garden

Oleanders and Lady Banksia Roses at Rural Felicity

Waving Banners of Spanish Moss, Rural Felicity

is entered from the left side by a path leading between a bed of Anthony Waterer spirea, edged with euonymous, and one of figs, which in winter shows a trunk as gray as the Spanish moss waving pennant-like from the great live oak towering above it. This garden has become the outdoor living room so essential in a mild climate. Jade green furniture is placed between the shrubbery and the beds surrounding a little pool. In the winter these beds are filled with pansies, in the summer with pink straw flowers and the pool with pink lotus. January is perhaps the most delightful month in this sheltered spot, for the warm sun brings out the fragrance of the winter honeysuckle (Lonicera fragrantissima) and the Buddleia officinallis, and attracts varieties of migratory birds, bees and the little yellow winter butterfly.

To fulfill the shade requirements of azaleas and camellias, such rapid growers as oleanders and Buddleia officinallis are used in quantities. Both are evergreen and blooming shrubs. The dark green of the oleander is a delightful contrast to the gray green of the buddleia; its season for bloom is May and June, that of the buddleia January into February. Pittosporum—spring blooming—banked against cherry laurel (Prunus caroliniana), the best of all native evergreens to clip and feature, viburnum,—February bloom,—Eleagnus pungens —September bloom,—and varieties of arbor vitae and clipped native cedars are used to shade the green of the background. At the foot of these are beds of small azaleas and camellias, bordered by freesias and violets. These afford masses of color throughout late winter and spring as annuals are planted with them.

The trellises are covered by Cherokee roses,—evergreen and with occasional bloom in winter, a mass of white in spring. Climbing lilies grow in and over the arches, draping their clusters of vari-colored monks' caps across the flanking oleanders. In "Beautiful Gardens in America" Louise Shelton writes that "after April, on account of the climate, gardens are not attempted in the states of the far South." If that was ever true it is not now, for at "Rural Felicity" as in many other Savannah gardens, the beds are filled all summer with a succession of annuals, lilies, and roses, in the fall with chrysanthemums, and the shrubbery is lighted with "tree" dahlias and poinsettias.

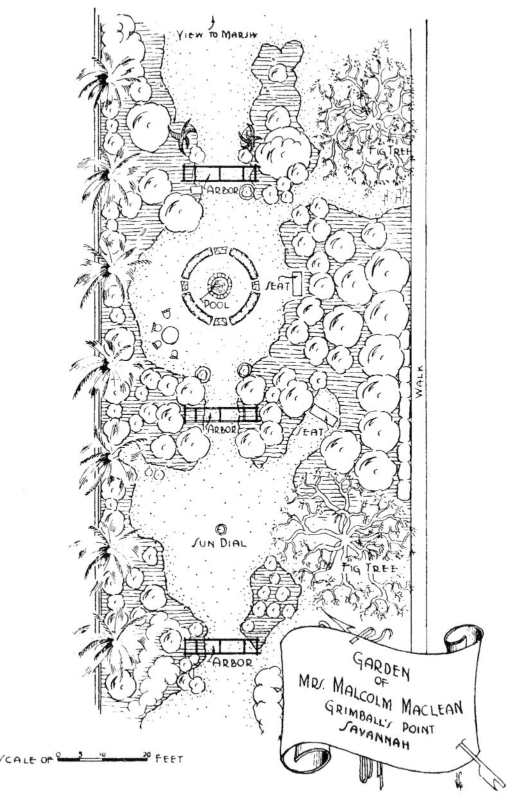

Miss Lucy B. Trosdal
Savannah

THE gardens of Miss Lucy Trosdal were made three years ago on sand mounds which had to be painstakingly transformed into good garden soil. Growth is so rapid and vigorous in Savannah's climate that these few years have already produced a seasoned and finished garden effect.

There are two gardens, both walled. One is a small patio garden 30 x 40 feet, opening from the dining room on the north side of the house. To the west side lies the larger garden, 90 x 120 feet. The plans are simple and in keeping with the architecture of the house. Walled gardens for privacy distinguish Savannah and add much to its old world atmosphere. A lavish use of the evergreen, camellias, azaleas, and other plant material of this section,—the design tied in with the house by means of the characteristic walls achieves for Miss Trosdal's gardens a distinct charm.

Iron work and old jars harmonize with semi-tropical planting in the Patio Garden

Two Views of Walled Garden of Miss Lucy Trosdal

Hamilton Plantation

Mr. and Mrs. Eugene B. Lewis

St. Simons Island

PASSING between a long double line of live oaks, one enters the gateway built of old ballast rock and white palings. A few hundred feet to the right stands the Glebe House, an old church restored and furnished as a recreation room. Its old bell still hangs in the belfry, its architecture is unchanged, but its foundation is now obscured by plantings of broad-leaf evergreens and two fine arbor vitae, one at each side of its green painted, heavy hinged door.

Up the winding driveway under moss hung live oaks, to the left is seen the sand-trapped putting green of a tiny golf course. Beyond, ancient cedars stand on the banks of the Frederica River and the golden "Marshes of Glynn" spread away in the distance. Close to the bank of the river with a full view of its sweep, stands a little tabby cabin, the only one left of a row of slave cabins built about a hundred and twenty-five years ago. Its interior, restored with old beams and pecky cypress walls, is furnished in primitive American style and the outer walls form a background for English ivy, yellow bignonia, yucca, azaleas, bottle-brush and climbing verbena. A matching crude pergola paved in old hand made brick and covered with purple wistaria and white Cherokee roses, stands on the bank of the broad Frederica. To the right, shaded by moss hung oaks, is the house, the winter home of the owners. An old frame farm house that has been added to and extended to meet the needs of the present day keeps in its green shuttered white walls the picture of the past. It was built about 1875 and its Victorian embellishment of front porches and scroll work has been removed and the architecture simplified.

Hamilton is one of the oldest plantations of Coastal Georgia. A huge map that hangs over the fireplace of the Glebe House, carries this brief legend of its history: "Favorite spot of the Indians. Landing of Spanish Missionaries 1560. Oglethorpe landed here with his settlers in 1736, convoyed by Captain Gascoine's sloop of war 'Hawk'. Captain Gascoine was the first owner. It was given him by a grant of King George II. All the plantation buildings were destroyed by the Spaniards in 1742. Prior to 1790, Hamilton was owned by Major Alexander Bissett, who raised the first Sea Island cotton in this country. It was next the property of John Dillworth. The next owner was William Oakman who sold it to Richard Leake. In 1795 John Titus Morgan purchased Hamilton, Ledbetter, and Hawkins Island for five hundred guineas. James Hamilton and John Couper bought it in 1798. Hamilton made it his residence and it became known as Hamilton Plantation, one of the most important plantations on the coast. In 1874 Dodge Meigs built and operated the third largest lumber mill in the United States. Later it became the property of the Hilton Dodge Company until 1896. There were several other owners until December, 1926, when it was bought by Eugene B. Lewis."

Through the three months of each of the six winters that its owners have spent on the plantation, they have labored indefatigably to build its present gardens,—wrought from bare fields, ditches and dense undergrowth, planned, staked out, and planted by them without the help of other than plantation labor.

The swimming pool garden just east of the house, was made the first year. Completely surrounded by a heavy planting of tall evergreens and bamboo that form a wind-break for the swimmers, its borders and beds are filled with low growing flowers.

From the swimming pool garden, one enters between tall arbor vitae the Green Terrace overlooking the Rose Garden. The wall and steps were built of old English brick found on the plantation and coarse heavy mortar, giving a lovely texture that the English ivy and Ficus repens are not permitted to completely hide. The semi-circular back planting of the terrace is in long sweeping curves of cedar, oleander, and arbor vitae, faced down to the velvet green turf (Bermuda for summer, Italian Rye and Red Top for winter), by creeping juniper. Not a blossom nor spot of color breaks the restful green. Only a white bench, one of the pews from the old church, stands opposite the steps leading down into the Rose Garden. On the back of this bench is carved "Not wholly in the busy world not quite beyond it blooms the garden that I love." Sunk in the turf in front of the bench is an old grindstone from Butler Plantation, the home of Fanny Kemble, on which has been carved a compass that points the north, probably to remind its owners of their northern home.

Native Material Used in Rock Planting and Pool Garden, Hamilton Plantation

The Rose Garden was planned with the same thought of broad restful sweep of green, the beds planted each in a separate color like small jewels set in a green mounting. At the season of the year when the roses are not in their best dress, the garden is still lovely with its tall thick hedge of oleanders surrounding three sides and broken by four white arches covered with pink and white Cherokees, and the four corners with plantings of cedar, ligustrum, and arbor vitae, edged down with annuals.

The pool in the center was built from old ballast rock found on the plantation river bank, and rose, purple, and white nympheas and little yellow water-poppies float in the reflection of the blue of Georgia skies. The arch at the end of the Rose Garden leads to the Rock Garden, which was originally a low boggy piece of ground. Water from an artesian well was piped to flow down the rocks and under a small stone bridge. The rocks are all old ballast brought from the river bank, where they had been dropped by ships in the early days coming from all parts of the world to get cotton and lumber.

The overflow from the pool in the Rose Garden forms another little stream tumbling over rocks at the left of the picture. All the evergreen material of the background was brought from the woods and marshes of the plantation. Among the rocks are masses of bloom of every hue. Azaleas, yellow daffodils, purple, white and yellow Spanish iris, white ornithogalum, little orange and bronze ixias, purple violets, blue periwinkle, lilac alyssum, yellow hemerocallis, pink oxalis, rose and white English daisies, blue dwarf ageratum, yellow ranunculus, blue ajuga, leucojum, amaryllis, and masses of rose verbena trailing to the water's edge, and in the pool, purple and blue nympheas and water hyacinth, with native blue flags on the margins.

The water from the pool cascades again over rocks and forms a wandering streamlet banked by palms and azaleas until it flows under a rustic bridge and disappears into a little jungle that will, if the owners' plans carry through, become a sunken azalea garden next year. Running the full length of the gardens but completely screened by the tall planting is the cutting garden, green house, slat house, and tool house, making the work of replanting and care of all the gardens an easy task because of accessibility.

On the north stretch fields, marshes and woodlands through which have been cut miles of bridle trails. Causeways have been built to Hawkin's Island and Ledbetter Island and on the banks of Ledbetter Creek rustic tables, benches and an oven of old bricks make a picnic ground on a glamorous spot shaded by moss hung live oaks.

THOMASVILLE

Elsoma

Mrs. Charles Merrill Chapin

Thomasville

ORIGINALLY a part of the property of Col. A. T. McIntyre, one of the first settlers in the Thomasville section, the Elsoma plantation was given by Col. McIntyre to his son, Thomas, at the time of his marriage. A home of Southern Colonial type was built, which was purchased about forty years ago by Mrs. J. Wyman Jones of New Jersey, and her son, Mr. Charles Merrill Chapin, and is now occupied during the winter seasons by Mr. and Mrs. Chapin. The old house was destroyed by fire in 1922. The new one built in 1925 is English in type and of whitewashed brick.

Elsoma is situated on the beautiful highway leading from Thomasville to Tallahassee, Florida, about two miles from Thomasville. At the entrance gates there is an attractive grouping of native shrubbery,—Spanish bayonet, wild azalea, and wistaria. The approach to the house is by a broad, winding driveway through a growth of tall pines, bordered on either side by magnificent magnolias and oaks. To reach the house one enters a large circular court formed by a hedge of pittosporum, against which are narrow beds of vinca bordered with liriope. Adorning the front of the house are two large magnolia trees planted flat against the two wings and trained to make almost a complete covering for the walls. This idea was taken by Mrs. Chapin from Cobham Hall in England.

From the open bricked terrace at the southern end of the living room, one gets a view of the old-fashioned flower garden enclosed by a tall hedge of arbor vitae, with its rose garden and formal beds of all the sweet old-timey flowers. Mrs. Chapin

Old Fashioned Rose Garden, Elsoma

Fragrant Masses of Bloom at Elsoma

specializes in flowers that bloom during the winter months, and in these beds are found narcissi, jonquils, violets, primroses, thrift, verbena, daisies, snowdrops, and literally millions of pansies; besides such shrubs as camellias, azaleas and tea olives. The central feature of the garden is a bronze statuette,—a small boy riding a dragon fly.

The dining porch at the northeastern corner of the house looks out over a broad lawn with groups of shrubbery, — Spanish bayonet, Christmas honeysuckle, viburnum. Separating the stretch of green from the garage is a high brick wall banked with various evergreens and flowering shrubs. To the rear, and cutting the lawn off from the old servants' quarters, is a French fence covered with ivy and festooned with the native fragrant yellow jessamine. To the rear of the house, on the western side, is the living porch, opening on to the fruit garden. On the right is an arbor of wistaria, its interlaced boughs forming an arch overhead while to the left is a similar arbor of Lady Banksia roses. In this enclosure are many handsome specimens of camellias and shadowing the garden are various tall trees, draped in lavender wistaria.

Like most of the places in this vicinity, Elsoma has a background of many acres of stately pine forest, whose spicy resinous odor mingles with the fragrance of the garden flowers.

Inwood Plantation

Mr. and Mrs. J. Morse Ely

Thomasville

INWOOD PLANTATION, the home of Mr. and Mrs. J. Morse Ely, is situated two miles out on Pinetree Boulevard which encircles the City of Thomasville. This immense tract of pineland was acquired by Mr. and Mrs. J. C. Morse of Cleveland, Ohio, about thirty years ago, and is now owned by their nephew, J. Morse Ely, and Mrs. Ely. The name "Inwood" is most appropriate since this home is set in the midst of a vast pine wood.

At each of the entrance gates to the plantation there are massed plantings of native shrubbery such as wild azalea, Spanish bayonet, honeysuckle, yellow jessamine, as well as magnolia, dogwood, redbud, and crabapple trees. Beginning at the main gateway the winding drive is bordered with a clipped hedge, followed by a uniform line of dogwood trees and at all intersections of the plantation roads there are groups of native evergreens and flowering shrubs. The driveway describes a circle up to the doorway of the low, wide-spreading house of stucco where the foundation planting is of choice evergreens shaded by splendid specimens of deodar cedar. Just across from the doorway is an immense crescent-shaped bed of Formosa azaleas, which makes a brilliant splash of color in the springtime.

At the eastern end of the house are the rose gardens, heavily bordered with liriope. An entire section is devoted to yellow roses which are particularly fine in variety and color.

The broad, open terrace across the south side of the house is banked with a planting of tea olive (Osmanthus fragrans), about ten feet in width. This is permitted to grow to the height of about three feet at its outer edge. In blossom nearly the entire year, the tiny white florets of these evergreen shrubs diffuse a fragrance that is delightful beyond compare. Over against the right wing of the house is a planting of banana shrub (Michelia fuscata), which wafts its own subtle sweetness. The terrace looks out over the formal flower garden which is bordered with a clipped abelia hedge. Here are beds of various annuals and perennials, and a number of very handsome specimens of boxwood and camellia. In the distance one glimpses a formal arrangement of rose beds and bulb garden. Beyond this rises a hedge of yaupon (Ilex cassine), separating the floral section from the greensward which stretches away to a pine woods undergrown with redbud, dogwood, crabapple and azalea.

At the western end of the flower gardens is a circular bricked tea garden with gay striped umbrellas and refreshment tables.

Bright Spears of Yucca Against the Blue Green of Pines, Inwood Gardens

Melrose Plantation

Howard M. Hanna

Thomasville

MELROSE PLANTATION, situated five miles from Thomasville on the Dixie Highway leading to Florida, was originally owned by Dr. Samuel J. Jones, who sold to Mr. Charles Merrill Chapin, who in turn sold the place, about forty years ago, to Mr. Melville Hanna, of Ohio, father of the present owner.

The original house forms the central unit of the present dwelling but broad wings added on each side give the whole a spacious and rambling effect. The old portion of the building is constructed of pine logs cut from the place and covered with broad clapboards, painted buff with white trimming. To the west of the house, Mr. and Mrs. Hanna have built for their daughter a lovely red brick house with white columns and trimming. The old servants' quarters have been replaced by a colony of neat white cottages and these with the large modern brick barns for the Jersey cattle, the garages, and other outbuildings, are grouped as were the ante-bellum plantation settlements.

As a sort of community house, the Hannas have constructed a small theatre which they call "The Show Boat." Built to represent one of the old Mississippi steamboats, the approach to the Boat is by gangway over a made pool, which further carries out the idea. In the theater, picture shows are given each week for the pleasure of the family and their friends, as well as the employees on the place—both black and white.

The approach to the house from the highway is by a broad grassed walk bordered with a luxuriant tea hedge. To right and left are spread many acres of velvety lawn with groups of ancient oaks and magnolias and such flowering trees as Japanese magnolia, flowering peach, redbud, dogwood, kumquat, crepe myrtle, and wild azalea. The fence bordering the estate is covered with Cherokee roses and native yellow jessamine vines, and just inside is a hedge of Madame Lombard roses. Clambering over the house, fences and trees are lavender wistaria vines and on the grounds are many wistaria

Vista Through Hedge of Pittosporum, Melrose

Azaleas Against Banks of Evergreens, Pine Forest in the Distance, Melrose

trees. East of the house and beyond the flower gardens is the riding field, a stretch of smooth turf at the edge of a forest of pines and dogwood trees.

Indoors the deep bay of the living room, which is paneled in native pine tinted to the shade of the trunks of crepe myrtle trees, looks out over a white garden. This sunken garden is grass-carpeted and bordered with a hedge of pittosporum, and against the green background are masses of white azalea, white camellia, beds of snowdrops and white pansies. From the white garden, steps of snowy marble lead up to the pink garden with its pink camellias, azaleas and roses—a lovely contrast.

West of the house lies the main rose garden laid out in formal beds and containing hundreds of roses of all varieties. Around it a clipped hedge of Louis Phillippe roses blooms practically all the year.

Not far away on the property is the old Jones cemetery, ivy grown and enclosed by a brick wall banked with shrubbery. This memorial spot is beautifully cared for by Mr. and Mrs. Hanna.

Pebble Hill Plantation

Mrs. Perry W. Harvey

Thomasville

PEBBLE HILL PLANTATION is situated about six miles south of Thomasville on the Dixie Highway. The estate was an original grant from the State of Georgia to James Johnson, passing from him to his son—Thomas Jefferson Johnson—whose daughter, Julia Ann, married John W. H. Mitchell. The place remained in the Mitchell family until about thirty-five years ago when it was bought by Mr. H. Melville Hanna of Cleveland, Ohio, and given by him to his daughter, Mrs.

Wistaria at Pebble Hill

Harvey. Mrs. Harvey and the late Col. Harvey have spent a great deal of time at Pebble Hill and have made it not only beautiful but productive, giving employment to a host of workers both black and white. They still maintain for their colored servants what used to be called the "Negro Quarters" in ante-bellum days, and Mrs. Harvey takes a personal interest in the negroes and looks after their welfare as the owners did in the days before the Civil War. The comfortable modernized "Quarters," possibly not as picturesque as the cabins of slavery days, are grouped to form a quadrangle, hedges marking the individual boundary lines of each cabin yard, where flowers and fruit trees are grown.

The fences along the highway are covered with jessamine vine and Cherokee roses, and in addition to the natural growth already there, Mrs. Harvey has planted an irregular border—in some places as wide as thirty feet—of native evergreen and flowering shrubs, and trees taken from the woods of the plantation;—dogwood, redbud, sparkleberry, wild azalea, crabapple, greybeard, and various haws. The entrance drive from the highway is bordered with magnolias and Azalea indica and the original "Front Garden" of the old plantation dwelling is defined at its corners by splendid old magnolia trees. Two others mark the path which leads to the house, forming an archway overhead.

The house is white, low and rambling, with the deep eaves of Southern Colonial architecture. The central portion is the old house, with paneled ceiling and heavy old-fashioned mouldings and casings. Wings have been added from time to time—all in keeping with the original type. At the extreme end of the east wing the drawing room opens on to a flower garden in all shades of blue, lavender and purple,—violets, violas, pansies, stocks, larkspur, and little tree wistarias. Around this garden is a hedge of Spiraea thunbergii. An opening in the hedge, flanked by tall Italian cypresses gives a view of the swimming pool which is enclosed by a low vine-covered wall, with stone seats and garden furniture at each of the four corners. From the pool to the east stretches a well kept lawn, with a wide view through the pine woods beyond.

Another opening from the East Garden leads through a grassed crabapple walk to a tea house in the wood, the doorway framed by two enormous pine trees. Still another opening leads to the "Maze", planted in camphor wood, which is the delight of all children. The Maze and the Front Garden are connected by a path of abelia trained over an arched iron trellis, which makes a pleasant shady walk on hot summer days.

Along the northern side of the east wing of the house extends a grass enclosed loggia, which shelters tender flowering plants during the winter months and overlooks a formal rose garden, bordered with boxwood. Winter plantings of English daisies and vari-colored pansies keep this garden gay until the roses bloom each early spring.

There are other gardens to be discovered; the Terrace Garden, at the foot of which is seen the old well house and the ancient sugar boiling kettle and press, whose shelter is buried in wistaria; the Camellia Garden with many varieties of japonicas, some of them very large and handsome; the walled-in vegetable garden with its border of annuals, where the gardener makes a specialty of sweet peas; the Wild Garden, whose flowers and shrubs are all native to this section of Georgia.

Not far from the house is the old family burying ground, enclosed by a tall brick wall with a wrought iron gate. The wall is covered with vines, among them the white flowered Confederate jasmine.

The drives through the fields and woods of the plantation show the varied character of the woodland growth. Here are hammocks of hard wood trees—one of them a lovely "Beech Hammock" with vistas through beech covered hillsides rising gently from a winding stream bed. There are cypress swamps, the trees hung with grey moss; pine woods of the higher lands with brown carpets of long-leafed pine needles; and tenant fields and cottages with flowering dooryards and neatly fenced kitchen gardens.

Pebble Hill is also the home of the famous "Pebble Hill Herd" of prize Jersey cattle. The barns and dairy are a group of buildings constructed of native red brick, with white Colonial columns and doorways. The courtyard where the cattle are shown is a large grass plot with a double row of liveoak trees, enclosed by a serpentine wall over which wistaria is trained. Other planting is of white flowering shrubs, cape jasmine of the old South, the star jasmine vine with its delicate white blossom, and magnolia stellata.

One's impression of Pebble Hill is that in developing the vast grounds such close harmony with nature has been preserved that "There is an art which doth mend nature, change it rather, but the art itself is nature."

Hedges, Picket Fence, and Live Oaks at Winnstead

Winnstead

Mrs. Coburn Haskell
Thomasville

TRULY typical of the Old South is the spacious and hospitable winter home of Mrs. Coburn Haskell of Cleveland, Ohio. The house of Colonial architecture with wide-spreading wings stands at the head of an avenue about a quarter-mile long, cut through a grove of pines and bordered on either side with a line of magnolia and dogwood trees.

Before entering the grounds proper the main driveway sends a branch off to the right leading to the home of the manager of the estate. Just at this curve is an immense bed of Formosa azaleas against a background of palms and other evergreen trees and shrubs. To the left of the road is another bed of azaleas in various shades of pink and white. Scattered throughout the pine woods on either side of the driveway are hundreds of dogwood trees, and the effect of the green and white in spring is very lovely.

Architecturally in keeping with the house is the white picket fence set inside a closely clipped hedge of privet. The gateway is between two huge magnolia trees and opens onto a broad brick walk which carries further the spacious feeling of the driveway, and leads directly to the doorway. On either side of the walkway is a border of handsome boxwood, clipped to uniform size, and beyond the border is an unusual planting, consisting of a line

Rose Garden at Winnstead

of alternating Arbor vitae, kumquat, and banana shrub, the latter about ten feet in height and clipped to a smooth, round ball. Against this line of evergreens are the rose beds, each containing a different variety.

To the left of the walk is a narrow path, bordered on either side with a planting of kumquat, leading to an arbor covered with Marie van Houtte roses, while beyond is an arbor of Lady Banksias. To the left of the main walk another arbor is covered with native yellow jessamine vine. The doorway is flanked by large palms rising from a base planting of vari-colored pansies.

tance and dotted with old oaks and spreading magnolia trees. Underneath many of the larger trees are garden seats, and several groups of flowering trees have been introduced into the picture.

Across the western wing of the house a long glassed loggia with its great tubs of orange trees overlooks a court filled with masses of azaleas of every variety. The living room at the extreme end of this wing looks out over another rose garden which is Mrs. Haskell's particular pride. This is laid out in formal beds around a central sundial—each bed exhibiting a different kind of rose —and the whole garden bordered with a low

Evergreen Reflections at Winnstead

In the main flower garden there are many beds of annuals of various kinds, as well as rose beds bordered with violets. Beyond the flower garden on either side are well kept lawns hedged with tall thick privet, and grouped about the lawns are rare and exotic trees and shrubs, among them olive, Australian silk oak, Italian hawthorn, Dalmatian holly, Irish yew, and red tea olive.

To the south of the flower garden is the tennis court, the wire fencing covered with roses at one end and sweet peas at the other, with a background planting of kumquats. Beyond are great open stretches of lawn leading to the woods in the dis-

clipped hedge of Louis Phillippe roses. Everywhere there are roses covering trellises, bordering driveways, garlanding fences.

Winnstead is one of the historic places of the County, having been an original grant to the Winn family and remaining in their possession until about thirty years ago, when it was purchased by Mr. Melville Hanna and given by him to his daughter, Mrs. Coburn Haskell. Mrs. Haskell has rebuilt and restored the place, and while adding many modern comforts and improvements has carefully preserved its ante-bellum flavor of hospitality, dignity and charm.

Bay Tree Farms

Mr. and Mrs. M. L. Lively

Thomasville

A SUCCESSFUL combination of the useful and the beautiful is Bay Tree Farms, a pecan plantation of some four hundred acres, stretching from the Dixie Highway on the east to the Lone Star Trail on the west. Situated on a high hill about two miles out from the City of Thomasville, the house commands a spreading view of the surrounding country. The boundary fences of the plantation are all covered with climbing roses—crimson rambler, Dorothy Perkins, American Pillar, American beauty, and white rambler, while the many gateways are garlanded with the old-fashioned Malmaison rose. On the Lone Star Trail the Cherokee rose, Georgia's State flower, grows in luxuriant masses and inside the fences are large groups of magnolias and crape myrtle trees.

The plantings in the grounds surrounding the house include such sweet scented shrubs and trees as the tea olive, banana shrub, sweet shrub, mimosa, syringa, Cape jasmine, Christmas honeysuckle, magnolia, bay, mock orange, kumquat, and azalea. Various members of the lily family also thrive here in the semi-shade, among them Easter lilies, Madonna, butterfly, and several sorts of lemon lilies. Nearer the house are particularly fine specimens of the favorite ornamental shrubs of this region, azaleas and camellias.

On the south porch of the house a trellis is covered with red and white roses, while the arbor on the west side presents a charming color harmony with the dainty yellow of the Lady Banksia roses and the lavender of wistaria. A conspicuous bed of poinsettia against the south porch grows to a great height and is very showy in the autumn.

Across the lawn and cutting it off from the pecan groves runs a broad, irregular bed of flowering

Rose-bordered Road at Bay Tree Farms

shrubs and roses serving as a background for the annual and perennial borders. And beyond, the wide expanse of lawn slopes down to a meadow which is centered by a large, clear pool, a natural mirror, reflecting the tall, majestic pines in the distance.

The meadow has a colorful rim, a deep irregular border of evergreens and flowering shrubs combined with hundreds of such sweet, old-timey tea roses as the Duchess de Brabant, Madame Lombard, Papa Gontier, and Louis Phillippe, as well as many of the newer varieties. Below these are groups of various annuals and perennials in harmonizing colors, and edging them are low-growing bulbs in profusion.

The pecan grove is itself a flower garden when, in spring, the ground is covered with Austrian peas and vetch, in myriad purple and lavender blossom.

Pecan Trees at Bay Tree Farms

Millpond Plantation

J. H. Wade Family

Thomasville

MILLPOND PLANTATION, the winter home of the late Mr. J. H. Wade of Cleveland, Ohio, is now owned by his sons, Mr. Jeptha H. Wade, and Mr. Garretson Wade, and a daughter, Mrs. E. B. Greene—all of Cleveland.

The estate consists of about ten thousand acres, mostly virgin pine, and within it are fifty miles of winding drives penetrating splendid forests of pine, magnolia, oak, dogwood, redbud, with a thick undergrowth of other beautiful shrubs and wild flowers indigenous to the deep South.

About thirty years ago Mr. Wade purchased the tract containing the old millpond from which the plantation takes its name. This portion of the estate was long ago the site of Linton's Mill, the original owner having been Mr. John L. Linton.

In an unusually picturesque setting Mr. Wade built a spacious home. Spanish in type, it is built around a patio about a hundred feet square where a tropical atmosphere has been created by the use of palms, tree ferns and other exotic plants grouped about pool and fountain.

The house is thickly hung with great ropes of purple wistaria and is shaded by magnificent live oaks. To the south is the Palm Garden with an infinite variety of palms grouped around a rectangular greensward, the whole bordered with liriope. At the extreme end is a lovely reflecting pool to mirror the fronds of the palms on its clear green surface.

Toward the west is the Camellia Garden, containing a remarkably fine collection of these ever prized blossoms. Through the gate to this garden one catches a glimpse of an alluring pleached walk beyond, which leads to a tea house in the distance. From the tea house, like so many spokes of a wheel, radiate seven pleached alleys, each bordered with a different variety of fruit tree, the interlacing boughs forming the green archways overhead. When in early spring the fruit walks are in flower, their beauty and sweetness are indescribable.

To the east stretches a smooth lawn of many acres, where tall pine and oak trees are hung with "the tattered banners" of gray Spanish moss. This lawn leads down to the old millpond in the distance.

Last comes the rose gardens where are grown hundreds of specimens of roses in almost endless variety. (Much of the beauty of the Thomasville Rose Shows derives from this garden). Here, too, is the famous Rose Walk, a long avenue bordered on each side with massed combination plantings of roses. Nearest the walk are the dainty polyanthas, next them the bush roses, and then the garland posts over which are trained climbing roses of every color.

Nature is kind, particularly to roses, in this section. At Thomasville the display of bloom starts with the Banksia in early March and continues through ten months of the year. The roses at Millpond Plantation and the pleached alleys are possibly the most notable features, but the other garden pictures on this vast estate are as varied in beauty as the contrasting natural landscape.

Live Oaks, Magnolias and Wistaria at Millpond Plantation

A Venerable Live Oak Casts Lacy Shadows on Millpond's Camellias

Palm Garden at Millpond Plantation

Greenwood+

Mrs. Payne Whitney

Thomasville

THOUGH Greenwood is included in the Early Gardens section, in which it clearly belongs, no modern garden book would be complete without depicting its later additions. An estate of twenty thousand acres it presents a finished and alluring picture from the driveway, set thickly with Cherokee roses and showing woodlands framed with azaleas, to the stately palm garden and classic garden of Italian type, planned and executed by the late Stanford White. When the property came into possession of Mr. and Mrs. Payne Whitney of New York, that eminent architect was consulted and arrived at Greenwood to consider alterations and additions. He declined to alter the house, so excellent did he consider it in design, and concentrated on the importation of antiques from Pompeii with which to enhance the beauty of green sweeps of lawn and shrub planting already at Greenwood. Among the treasures is an old fountain and there are balustrades and figures so placed that for an effect of extent and dignity, the garden is unique in Georgia.

Camellias, magnolias and azaleas are proper color accents for a palm garden which includes all varieties that thrive in that locality and in the rectangular beds are carpet plantings of small and colorful flowers.

It is a justly famous place, and its perfect maintenance from field to parterre is as impressive in the consciousness of those who visit Greenwood as is its architecture and landscape beauty.

* See Early Gardens.

Walk Through Tropical Evergreens Leading to Avenue of Palms

Aloes in Garden Designed by Stanford White at Greenwood

Natural Gardens of Georgia

Woolford B. Baker

Stone Mountain

IN North Georgia there occur many unique areas of botanical interest to the student of Nature. One of the most interesting, in many respects, is the Stone Mountain granite region located in DeKalb County, 16 miles east of Atlanta. Here is found a mass of exposed granite rock rising 686 feet above the surrounding lowland plane, 1686 feet above sea level. It measures seven miles in circumference at the base and includes about 563 acres of exposed surface.

The general shape of the mountain is elliptical with an abrupt face on its northern side. On the southern and western faces it slopes gradually to the level of the surrounding territory. On the southern side is a creek fed throughout the year by springs and during the rainy season by the water which falls on the mountain side or seeps from the many crevices on the slope. Along the creek banks may be found the vegetation characteristic of such a moist locality: ferns, Jack-in-the-Pulpits, (Arisaema triphyllum and A. acuminatum), liverworts, and mosses. From this locality where the soil is fairly deep and moist, one may climb the gradual slope and encounter typical mesophytic vegetation which gives away in turn to that found in extremely dry areas.

Here and there along the slope are crevices in the granite, in which sufficient soil has collected to give a foot hold for pines, junipers, small shrubs and a few vines. In the main, however, various xerophytic species of lichens and mosses constitute the most abundant vegetation.

The type of formation of the mountain is known as exfoliaceous granite, which means that the rock breaks away in extensive flat sheets several feet in thickness. Underneath these sheets, the decaying lichens and mosses have formed the nucleus of a soil layer which remains fairly moist throughout the year. At the edge of such sheets there may be found extensive beds of Polystichum, together with Dryopteris marginale (Marginal Shield Fern), Cheilanthea tomentosa (Wooly Lip Fern), and a few herbaceous plants of characteristic type. Occasionally a scrubby pine or juniper gains a foot hold and furnishes a lodging place for the accumulation of a small area of soil of sufficient depth for a variety of plants to become established.

The dominant vegetation of the mountain changes quite noticeably during the course of the season. In the early spring the creek area shows Jack-in-the-Pulpit in abundance with Erythronium (Dog's tooth Violet), various species of Viola, and an occasional Medeola (Indian Cucumber-Root), scattered about. Later in the season the ferns become dominant and present a beautiful picture. The tall and stately Osmundas, O. regalis or Royal Fern, and O. cinnamomea or Cinnamon Fern, may be seen surrounded by the coarse chain fern (Woodwardia areolata), the lacy Lady Fern, (Asplenium filix-fœmina) and the New York Fern (Dryopteris noveboraceanæ). Rising from this type of undergrowth are Sweet Gums, Tulip Trees, Giant-Leaved Magnolias, Sycamores, and Red Maples. A few low shrubs such as Calycanthus or Sweetshrub, Maple-leaved Viburnum, and various azaleas are to be found.

Leading from the creek area up the southern slope are water channels, which through the years have become ravine-like in places. Along these channels are deeper pools hollowed out in the underlying granite, where water usually stands throughout the year. In these may be found beds of Sphagnum associated with other types of mosses. Along the banks of the ravines are masses of Mountain Laurel (Kalmia latifolia), which in the early summer is covered with a profusion of blossoms.

Following the slope upward one finds small forests of Pines (Pinus taeda), with an occasional oak and hickory. At the edge of the pines are various grasses, clumps of Brake Ferns (Pteria aquilina), Yellow jessamine (Gelsemium sempervirens), Greenbrier (Smilax), Blackberries and Virginia Creeper (Ampelopsis quinquefolia).

On the exposed areas beyond the pines are encountered various xerophytes and upland mesophytes. The most abundant of these in the early spring are Diamorpha cyamosa, a reddish succulent-leafed plant related to the Sedums; Alsinopsis brevifolia, a small, delicate, white flowered member of the pink family; and a small Saxifrage, Micranthea virginiensis. On the larger patches of soil in the exposed area, are found Oxytria coreca, a lily-like plant with a loose spike of small yellow flowers, Commelina saxicola or Day Flower, Tradescantia hirsuticaulis and T. reflexa. Here and there occur specimens of Yucca and Opuntia. The ground cover consists of a few species of mosses and lichens together with a member of the Juncaceae, Juncus Georgianus.

In the mid-summer a species of coreopsis together with a few mints, particularly Kœllia verticillata, and evening Primrose, Oenothera fruticosa, Talinum teretifolim, a member of the Family Portulacaceae; and Sarothra or Pine Weed, are particularly abundant.

In the late fall a species of the Sun Flower Family, Gymnolomia porteri, almost completely covers each soil area and gives to the entire mountain a golden color.

On the summit of the mountain are found several shallow pools hollowed out by weathering to a depth of from two to six inches and containing coarse soil one to three inches deep. During the rainy season these fill with water and furnish a suitable habitat for certain rare plants which have not yet been described from any other locality. Two of these are especially interesting, though quite insignificant looking. The first, Isœtes melanospora, belongs to the quillworts, a division of the Fern group. The plant consists of a cluster of quill-like leaves grouped around a very short stem, which grows to a height of three to four inches. Each leaf bears at its base a special container or sporangium in which are produced the reproductive cells or spores. These, because of their dark color when mature, give the species name to the plant.

The other plant, Amphianthus pusillus, belongs to the family, Scrophulariaceae, or Figworts. It consists of a cluster of submersed leaves, borne on a very short stem, and a single long filamentous stalk which grows to the surface of the water where it is buoyed up by two small floating leaves. Between these leaves a single small, white flower is produced which in turn matures a capsule-like fruit. In addition a cluster of submersed flowers and fruits are produced in clusters on the short stem.

So far as has been found neither of these plants has migrated to other spots on the mountain, even though what would seem to be more favorable environments might be encountered farther down the slope.

Naturalists from all parts of America visit Stone Mountain from time to time in order to study the unique associations of flora. To most Georgians the very proximity of the area tends to make it commonplace but as a matter of fact, it is all the more to be appreciated as one becomes more familiar with it.

Okefenokee Swamp

PRESENTING a sharp contrast to the Stone Mountain area is the Okefenokee Swamp region in the southeastern corner of the State, lying principally in Charlton, Ware and Clinch counties. The swamp is approximately sixty miles long by eighteen to thirty miles wide, and contains between 500,000 and 700,000 acres. During the rainy season a good portion of the interior is under water with the exception of some twenty-one principal islands and numerous small tree-covered areas known locally as "houses." The latter have been built up by the accumulation of vegetable humus and are completely water soaked. They appear as floating masses of vegetable matter and debris upon which trees such as bays, hollies and the like have become established. The name "quivering earth" is quite appropriate since the soil seems to shake to its very foundations as one walks over it. On such "houses" the collectors, hunters and fishermen set up camp as a center for their explorations.

Surrounding the inundated portion of the swamp are forests of long leaf pine (Pinus palustris) and slash pine (Pinus caribaea), with an undergrowth of saw palmetto (Serenoa serrulata), gall berries (Ilex glabra), myrtles and huckleberries. Scattered among these are found various herbaceous plants such as Eriocaulon (Pipewort), Polygala (Milkwort), and partridge peas.

Upon entering the swamp from the eastern side at Folkston, one is struck by the abundance of vegetation characteristic of marsh-swamp habitat. Running into the interior of the inundated portion is a large canal known as "Jackson's Folly" begun in 1891 and continued until it was found that drainage of the swamp into St. Mary's River was not practical. This is now used for bringing out timber from the interior by motor boats.

Along the banks of the canal are bay trees, Cyrilla racemiflora, Ilex Cassine and I. vomitoria, with an occasional black gum and an abundance of Leucothœ racemosa drooping over the water. Here and there are luxuriant clumps of golden club (Crontium aquaticum) with leaves, flowers and seeds much larger than those found in the swamp proper. Unusually tall specimens of iris versicolor are also found.

On each side of the canal lie inundated areas called "prairies" by the guides. They are covered by from one to three feet of water and when viewed from a distance appear as level stretches of vegetation of approximately equal height. The water lilies, golden clubs and saw grass almost completely cover the water giving the general appearance of the typical prairies of the west, hence the name. The only means of transportation over these marshes, which often extend for several miles, is by boats propelled by poles operated by a man standing in the stern. The thick vegetation makes the use of oars impossible.

Dotted here and there over the prairies are the so-called "houses." Around each "house" are found a typical fern, Anchistea Virginiana, associated with Pontederia Sagittaria, water lilies and golden clubs. On the "quivering earth" of the "houses" occur a few trees, usually bays, hollies, and an occasional cypress. These are covered with a dense growth of Smilax laurifolia, Tillandsia or Spanish moss, and muscadine vines. In the deep swamp many representatives of the orchid family furnish a profuse color-scheme against the background of grey and green. In order to pitch a camp one must cut a space from this thick undergrowth. The moss incidentally makes excellent bedding for the camp.

On the larger islands may be found forests of Cypress, much of which have not been cut over. These with their low hanging moss, their yellow green, feathery foliage and their grey trunks, make a never to be forgotten picture. In addition to the cypress are stands of slash pine, the trees in many instances measuring two to three feet in diameter at the base and growing seventy or eighty feet before the first limbs are encountered. Around the foot of the pines are extensive areas covered with tall growths of broom sedge.

As one explores the prairies many "gator runs" are to be found leading to open stretches of water called "gator holes" or in some cases lakes. Bordering both the runs and the holes are found sagittaria, often growing six feet in height, several species of Lyris or yellow grass, scirpus or bull rush, and pontederia. It is not uncommon to find the bodies of large alligators which have been killed by hunters, lying on the "houses" around the holes. That an abundance of "gators" inhabit the holes is evidenced by the bellowing one hears at night while in camp in the swamp.

Many scientific expeditions from various institutions and museums have visited the swamp to study the flora and fauna, but as yet the area has by no means been completely studied. It is hoped that either the State or the Federal Government will make arrangements for this unique natural history region to be set aside as a preserve for wild life and that those interested in the development of science in Georgia will make every effort to complete the surveys of the flora and fauna found there.

Part Three

GARDEN CLUB PROJECTS

INSTITUTIONAL GARDENS

SCHOOL GARDENS AND CAMPUSES

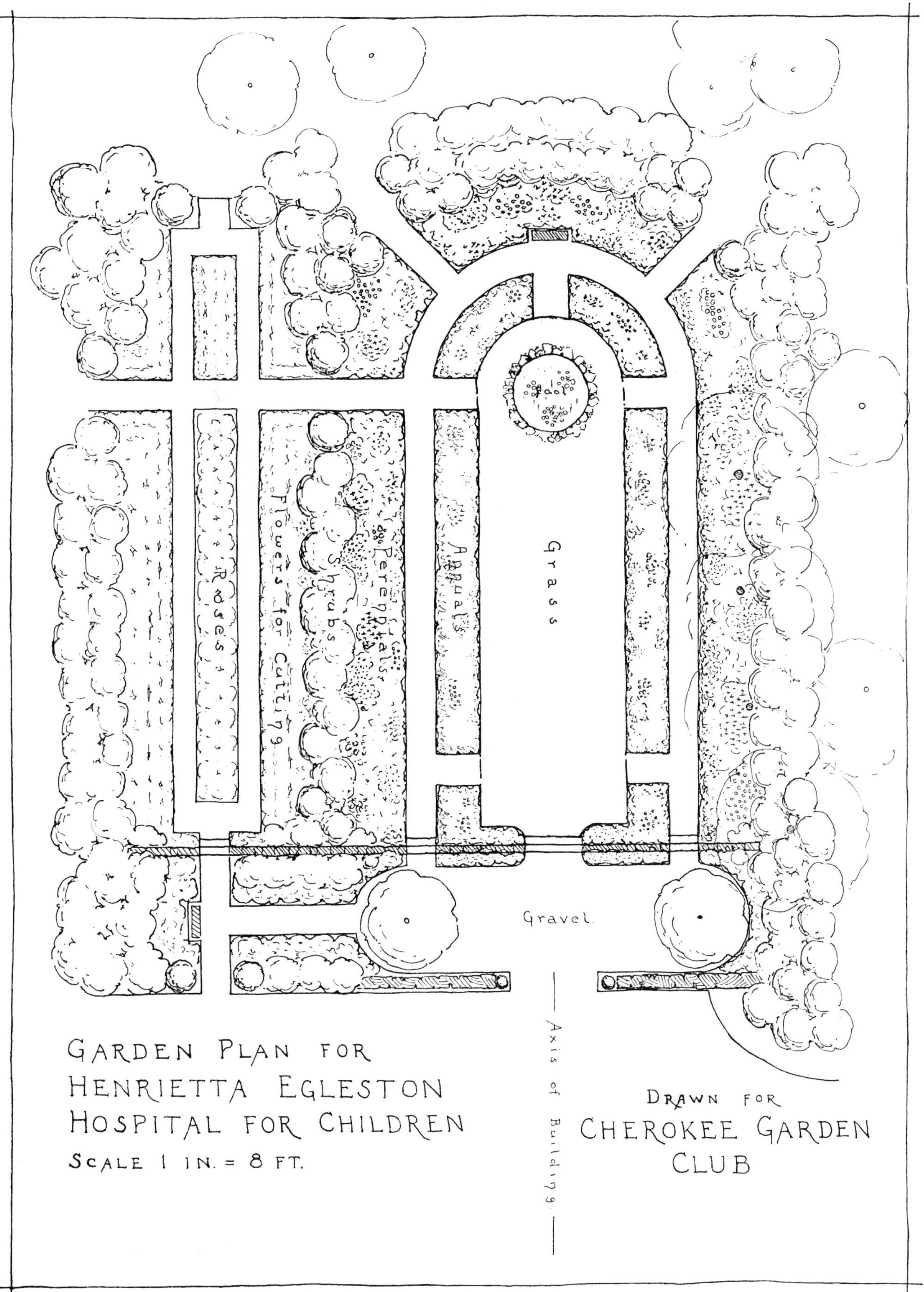
Pool
Grass
Annuals
Perennials
Shrubs
Flowers for Cutting
Roses
Gravel
Axis of Building
GARDEN PLAN FOR
HENRIETTA EGLESTON
HOSPITAL FOR CHILDREN
SCALE 1 IN. = 8 FT.
DRAWN FOR
CHEROKEE GARDEN
CLUB

Dolly Blalock Black Memorial Garden, Egleston Hospital for Children, Atlanta

THE memorial garden at Egleston Hospital for Children was planned by Norman C. Butts for the Cherokee Garden Club.

A driveway planted with forty-two mimosa trees (in memory of the late Neel Reid, owner of Mimosa Hall) leads around the main hospital building and widens out across the back to provide an approach to the garden. A ligustrum hedge separates it from the driveway, with two tall cedars guarding the entrance, directly in line with the main axis of the building. The garden was purposely placed near the hospital, that patients and visitors might enjoy it from the windows and long balcony. A natural grove of oaks and locusts forms the setting and provides a welcome shade through the day. Beyond the trees, the lawn slopes away on two sides while on the third a path winds under the trees from the rose garden to the Nurses' Club House.

The garden itself is formal in design and informal in planting. The gravel terrace at the entrance, sheltered by the hedge and balanced at either end by mimosa trees, is broad enough to accommodate chairs and tables. From this level, rock steps lead directly on to the broad grass panel, circular at the far end to provide interesting detail to the design and an appropriate setting for a charming rock pool. From the low stone retaining wall of the terrace, the grass panel is bordered with narrow flower beds, broken at intervals by short paths which connect with one encircling path. Beyond this, wide borders of perennials and shrubbery give background and depth to the garden. At the far end, beyond the pool, and on a direct line with it, a low marble bench commands a view down the garden to the hospital.

The shrubbery planting is particularly effective. A few conifers are placed for accent while broadleaf evergreens lend interest to the winter scene. Flowering shrubs are used in mass so that from January Jasmine and the earliest Spirea thunbergii, through all the spring and summer flowering shrubs, to the late buddleia and crape myrtle, there is color in the background. This color effect is continued into the hardy perennials—hollyhocks, lilies, foxglove, phlox, daisies, coreopsis, boltonia, asters, and chrysanthemums down to candytuft, ranunculus, primroses, forget-me-nots, and old fashioned pinks. In the long narrow beds the tulips, pansies, Longfellow daisies, and irises of early spring are followed by drought resisting petunias, verbenas, ageratum and heliotrope which are colorful far into the fall. The selection of plants each season depends somewhat on the generosity of friends and the excess output from seed beds of the garden club members, for the idea of the most effective garden for a minimum upkeep has to be considered. The personal work of the club and the active interest of the resident staff has made this possible.

The plan of the building as well as the natural setting of the trees provided a location for a rose and cutting garden and in this garden, entered by connecting paths under rose arches, the same effective use of shrubs is continued.

IN MEMORIAM

In May, 1932, this garden was dedicated to Dolly Blalock Black, a charter member of the Cherokee Garden Club, and a bronze memorial tablet was set in the edge of the rock pool.

The story of the making of this garden is one of devotion. Friends and relatives have shared in it, with gifts of many plants, the pool, the bench, and a bird bath. Sometimes a special corner is planted as a memorial. In this spirit the garden was begun, and in this spirit it shall always remain a friendship garden.

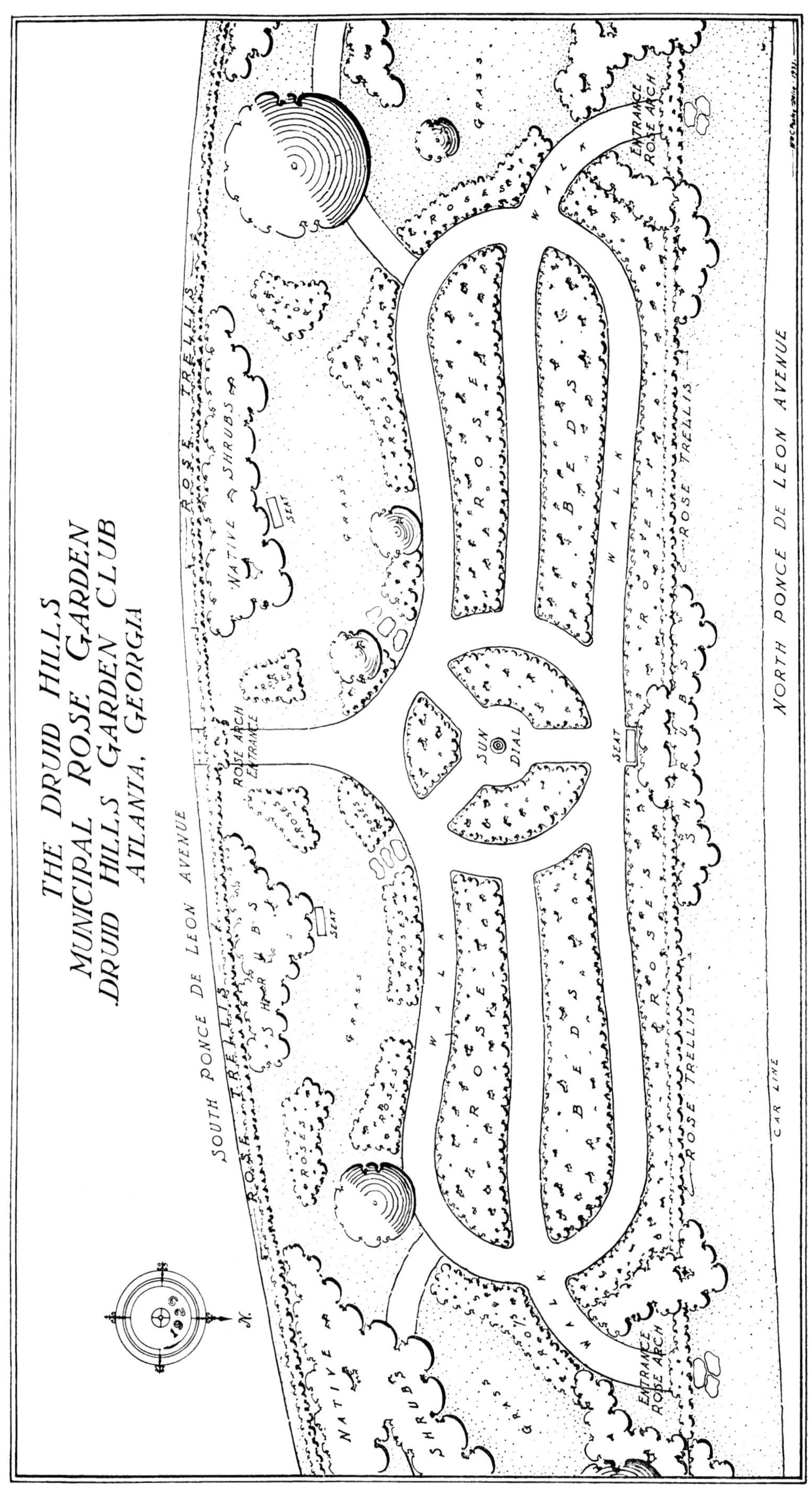
THE DRUID HILLS
MUNICIPAL ROSE GARDEN
DRUID HILLS GARDEN CLUB
ATLANTA, GEORGIA
SOUTH PONCE DE LEON AVENUE
NORTH PONCE DE LEON AVENUE
ROSE TRELLIS
NATIVE SHRUBS
SHRUBS
GRASS
ROSES
ROSE BEDS
WALK
SEAT
SUN DIAL
ENTRANCE ROSE ARCH
CAR LINE
N.

Municipal Rose Garden

Druid Hills Garden Club

Atlanta

SHORTLY after its organization five years ago the Druid Hills Garden Club had the inspiration that led to the making of their Municipal Rose Garden. Today hundreds of Atlantans as well as visitors from other sections, pause on their way out Ponce de Leon Avenue to study the colorful rose display. Here a thousand roses blossom against a background of crabapple and dogwood trees, and blend their sweetness with the exotic perfume of the Cape jasmines planted near by.

The Rose Garden, seventy-five by three hundred feet in size, occupies a tract of land between North and South Ponce de Leon Avenue, extending from Oakdale to Lullwater Road, which has been designated by the authorities as a city park.

William C. Pauley designed the garden, which charmingly combines the informal with the conventional. This property was at one time landscaped by an English gardener, and the remaining evergreens, trees, and shrubs have been kept as a background for the new plantings. Surrounding the entire tract is a garland fence and the three entrances are marked by wrought-iron gates, topped with graceful rose-arches.

The center garden has been so designed that the eye catches a veritable shower of gold from plantings composed of Ville de Paris, Rev. Page Roberts, Mrs. E. Pembroke Thom, and Sunburst. Then the coloring shades off to the golden pink of Pres. Hoover, Talisman, and Chas. P. Kilham; then again to the deeper tones of Betty Uprichard and Etoile de Hollande.

Members of the club have made an exhaustive study of roses, their habits, needs and diseases, and plant only those which promise hardy blooms over the longest period. Work in the rose garden goes forward practically every month in the year. In February, when the daffodils and golden forsythia brighten all the landscape, spraying begins, and in early March the hybrid teas are pruned to two or three canes. The climbing roses are left to give early bloom, and are pruned after blossoming to keep them within definite bounds. Hundreds of new roses of various colors and kinds are being tested out in the garden and careful records of their behavior kept, and it is believed that this data will prove invaluable to Southern rose lovers. For the forty members composing the Druid Hills Garden Club, the work of developing the Rose Garden has been a labor of love.

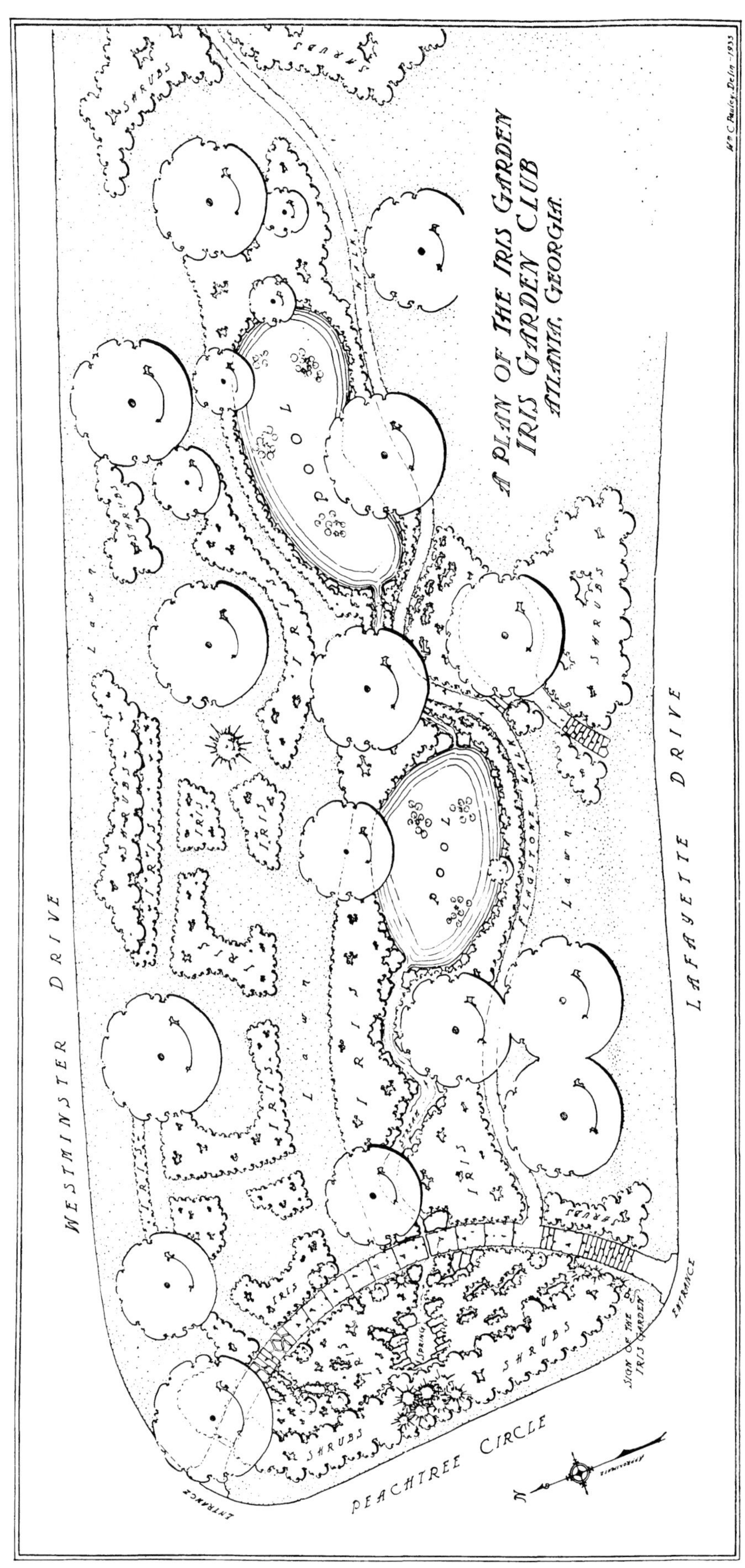
A PLAN OF THE IRIS GARDEN
IRIS GARDEN CLUB
ATLANTA, GEORGIA
WESTMINSTER DRIVE
LAFAYETTE DRIVE
PEACHTREE CIRCLE
POOL
POOL
IRIS
SHRUBS
Lawn
ENTRANCE
ENTRANCE
SIGN OF THE IRIS GARDEN

The Iris Garden

Iris Garden Club

Atlanta

LOCATED in a small triangular park bounded by Peachtree Circle, Lafayette Drive and Westminster Drive in Ansley Park, is The Iris Garden, an eminently successful conservation project of the Iris Garden Club. Work on the project was started in April, 1930, on a piece of land which was mainly a deep red clay ravine, falling away from the street to a depth of about twenty feet. The length is about two city blocks, varying in width from fifty to three hundred feet. There were many good-sized trees growing on the tract and they have been carefully preserved.

Now, by standing at the upper end of the garden, one may see at the head of the ravine a delightful little waterfall which comes dancing down over moss covered boulders to fall into a small pool. On each side of the waterfall and pool are wide plantings of iris of every color, ranging from the rarest pink to the most delicate blues which in turn shade through deep blues to royal purples; here too are all the yellows, from the pale canary hues to the oriental golds.

Interspersed with the iris are bleeding heart and columbine, and pink and blue forget-me-nots spread among the clumps of low-growing thrift, candytuft, yellow primroses and blue phlox.

The rippling water from the pool at the foot of the falls flows between grassy banks into a larger pool where there are tall lotus and low-growing lilies whose rich green leaves support frail blossoms of pink, blue, yellow and purple. From the second pool a sparkling brook wends its way among moss covered rocks into a third pool, possibly the most interesting, for around it are grouped fern, trillium, anemone, lady slipper, and many varieties of wild flowers.

Photo by F. E. Lee

The Iris Garden, Ansley Park, Atlanta

Photo by F. E. Lee

Not only the small flowers of the woods have found their way into the garden, but many wild azaleas, dogwoods, sweet shrubs, red bud, crab-apples, rhododendron, and mountain laurel have been transplanted here. The unsightly red clay slopes have been laid in colorful rock gardens where thousands of bulbs, rock plants and perennials are set out. Flowering shrubs and evergreens form backgrounds for the borders, while masses of azaleas are near enough to be reflected in each of the pools.

Markers for the various trees, shrubs, and plants have been placed throughout the garden to add interest and instruction, while flagstone walks, tables, and benches lure the passers-by to stop and enjoy the beauty of this carefully tended spot.

In the garden are now growing thousands of German iris of a hundred and fifty fine named varieties. In addition to these there are hundreds of Japanese, Siberian, Spanish, and Dutch iris. Violas and pansies border all the beds.

On March 13, 1932, the magazine, Better Homes and Gardens, announced the award to the Iris Garden Club of the third prize in their national "More Beautiful America" contest. The pleasure of receiving the award—as well as the substantial aid it gave towards the beautification of their project—served to augment the vital interest already shown by the thirty members of the Club in their Iris culture. And the garden itself has become a permanent beauty spot and a matter of prideful interest to the community.

Conservation Project

Lullwater Garden Club

Atlanta

ALONG Lullwater Creek in Druid Hills lies a beautiful stretch of natural woodland, irregular oblong in shape, between Lullwater Road and Lullwater Parkway. Growing here in splendid profusion are specimens of nearly all of Georgia's native trees: pine, beech, maple, sycamore, hickory, ash, elm, willow, wild cherry, poplar, and oak. And when the first warm days of early spring encourage the opening of crabapple blossoms, wild azaleas and dogwoods along the banks of the ravines, it is a spot of exquisite loveliness. No less beautiful is the scene in late autumn when every tree and shrub shows splashes of brilliant color; when the gold of the hickory and the wine-red of the maple afford a striking contrast against the russets and warm browns of oak, elm and beech, and the ever-restful green of Georgia pines.

About two years ago the Lullwater Garden Club had the inspiration to make of this wooded section a conservation garden and bird sanctuary and permission for this project was granted by the Druid Hills Land Company. Here it is planned to accumulate specimens of all of our native trees and shrubs, flowers and ferns, and to mark each of them permanently with both the botanical and common name.

The accompanying sketch shows a plot plan, an entrance, and a vista of Lullwater Creek and one of the bridges.

The extent of the tract can be best realized by the following figures: the perimeter or total road frontage is nearly one half mile; the completed walkways will measure eighteen hundred fifty linear feet, or nearly one-third mile. Thus it may be seen that this development is a major undertaking and cannot be accomplished all at once. The entire tract is below the road level, and although the extreme length of the plot is more than eleven hundred feet, its average width is less than two hundred feet, thereby affording a full view of the scenic development from the roads and adjoining properties as well as from the interior itself.

At Lullwater Road and Lullwater Parkway a pylon entrance of rustic stone will be constructed. To the front of this and on either side of the walks a formal planting of shrubbery will make a gradual transition from the residential atmosphere to that of the woodland. Foot bridges of appropriate rustic design have been built and all the further constructions will be in harmony with the spirit of this deep-tangled wildwood. The tract, with its sparkling brook, is already a bird sanctuary, but the erection of bird houses of rustic design can but increase the feathered population. In addition to planting berried shrubs, grain will be distributed during the winter months, as a recompense for "each golden note of music that greets the listening leaves."

Plans and drawings for the project were made by Eugene C. Wachendorff, of Atlanta.

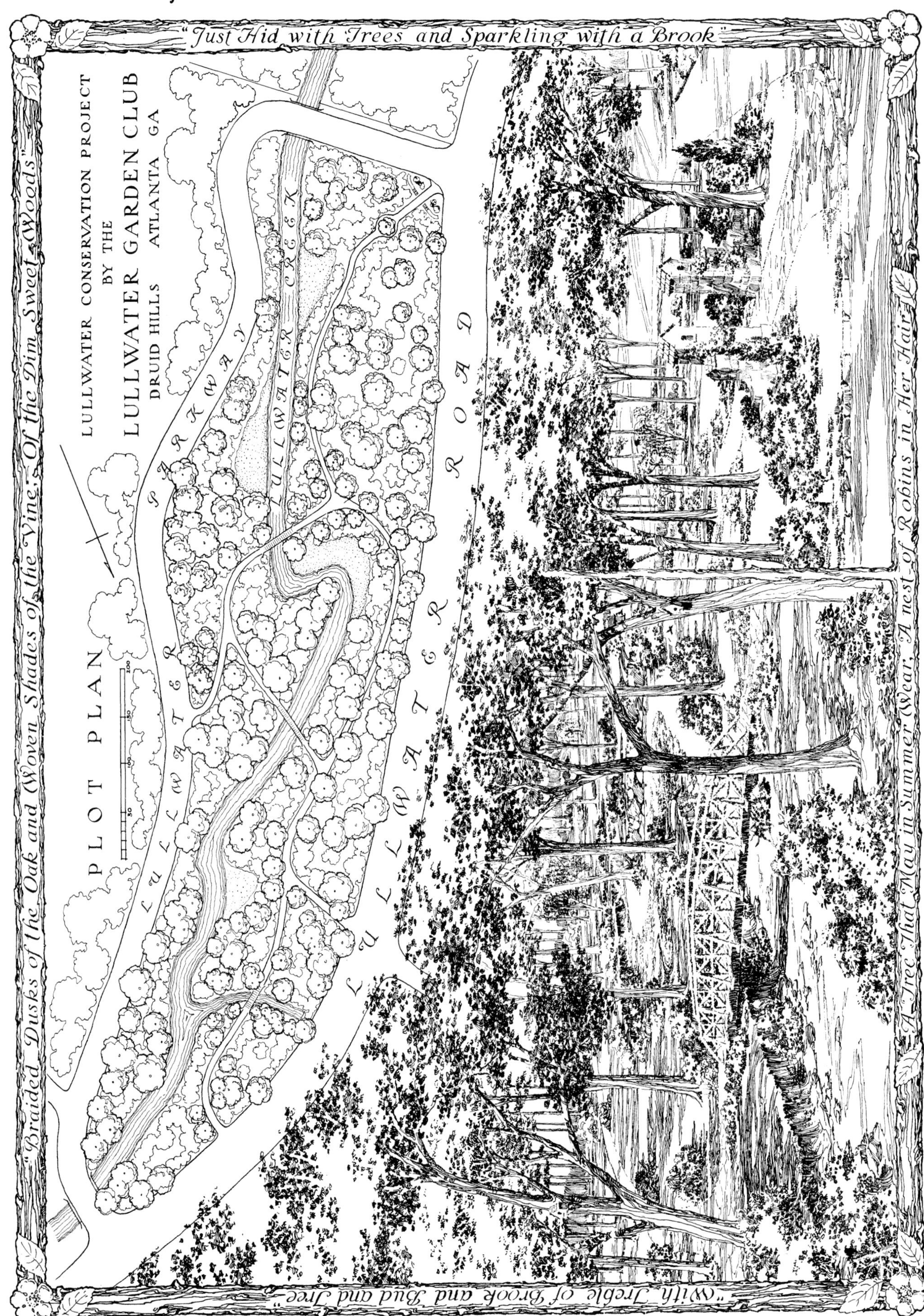
"Just Hid with Trees and Sparkling with a Brook"
"Braided Dusks of the Oak and Woven Shades of the Vine; Of the Dim Sweet Woods"
A Tree That May in Summer Wear, A nest of Robins in Her Hair
"With Treble of Brook and Bud and Tree"
PLOT PLAN
LULLWATER CONSERVATION PROJECT
BY THE
LULLWATER GARDEN CLUB
DRUID HILLS ATLANTA GA
LULLWATER PARKWAY
LULLWATER CREEK
LULLWATER ROAD

Old Medical College

Sand Hills Garden Club

Augusta

"SIMPLE—Erect—Severe—Austere—Sublime," a pure type of Greek Revival architecture, the old Medical Building was erected in 1835. Here was Georgia's first medical college until, as the Medical Department of the University of Georgia, it was moved into the present building on University Place. Later the old building housed the technical school of the Richmond Academy until 1926.

At present it is in process of restoration by The Sand Hills Garden Club, who, with the Trustees of the Academy, have built a wall around the entire property—using brick from the old City Hospital which adjoined it, and which was condemned two years ago. The wall is an exact copy of the one section of the old wall left standing at the east end. Iron gates add beauty and protection, while on either side of the broad entrance walk, a memorial avenue of camellias leads to the front of the building.

Already much has been accomplished. And today happy ghosts may wander under century-old trees, along box-bordered paths, over a carpet of clover and blue grass where occasional splashes of color delight the eye and the fragrance of tea olives and jessamine vines awaken memories. They may pause before grim cypress trees or linger to read the Latin inscription that marks the grave of its founder, Dr. Milton Antony, who fell a victim to the yellow fever scourge in 1839.

On the west side, through an iron gate one enters a little walled-in boxwood garden where the initials S. H. G. C. and the date 1930 have been outlined in box. Here a sun-dial marks the hours.

On the east is the nucleus of what will some day be as fine a collection of camellias as one may see in this part of the country. Fifty or more plants of different and choice varieties have recently been set out. These will be augmented from time to time as new ones are developed or introduced. There are many plans. The Old Building is "much too beautiful to pass" and the Sand Hills Garden Club has visions of making it "A Temple and a Shrine."

Designed in the initials of the Sand Hills Garden Club, the garden at the old medical college spreads like an Oriental rug.

Savannah Female Orphans Home

Junior League Garden

Savannah

THE Orphans Home occupies what was once one of the most beautiful old mansions in Savannah, the lofty rooms with their curved white marble mantels still giving evidence of its past grandeurs. Externally the house is interesting because of the second story balconies whose cast iron balustrades are ornamented with stamped medallions of famous poets, musicians and writers.

At the rear of the house the garden has been made in an area enclosed in a high brick and tabby wall. While clearing this yard the workers discovered the original pattern of an old flower bed and this inspired further exploration until a complete plan was disclosed: the plan showing a formal design, a quaint heart shaped bed at the center, and paths of old brick laid in herring bone pattern. All the planting has been worked out to conform with that of old fashioned gardens in this locality, and the flowers and shrubs were selected accordingly. In the narrow beds along the walls are Camellia japonica, Pyrus japonica, crape myrtle, tea olive, oppoponax, eleagnus, strawberry and banana shrubs in massed effect, while yellow and blue bignonias and ficus vines grow against the walls. Spanish bayonets lend a tropical air, and against the house and clambering up the iron railings of the lower balcony are Lady Banksia roses, for early bloom.

All the flower beds are outlined in English ivy or violets and in the heart-shaped central bed are pansies with a border of snowdrops for early spring, then zinnias and petunias for summer. In a circular bed a dogwood tree blooms above a carpet of periwinkle. Spireas, dogwoods and Silver Moon roses add white blossoms, while verbenas, creeping lantana, plumbago, zephyr lilies, daisies, and hollyhocks give seasonal color.

To cut off the garden from the children's playground, a new, low wall has been built of old bricks, with a graceful wrought iron gate adding much to the picturesqueness of the garden and against the wall are planted Wistaria and Paul's Scarlet Climber.

The whole idea of the garden is to encourage an appreciation of beauty and to stimulate an interest in flowers among the girls at the Home. Two members of the club are appointed each month to supervise the garden, but the girls themselves are taught to do most of the actual work in caring for the flowers.

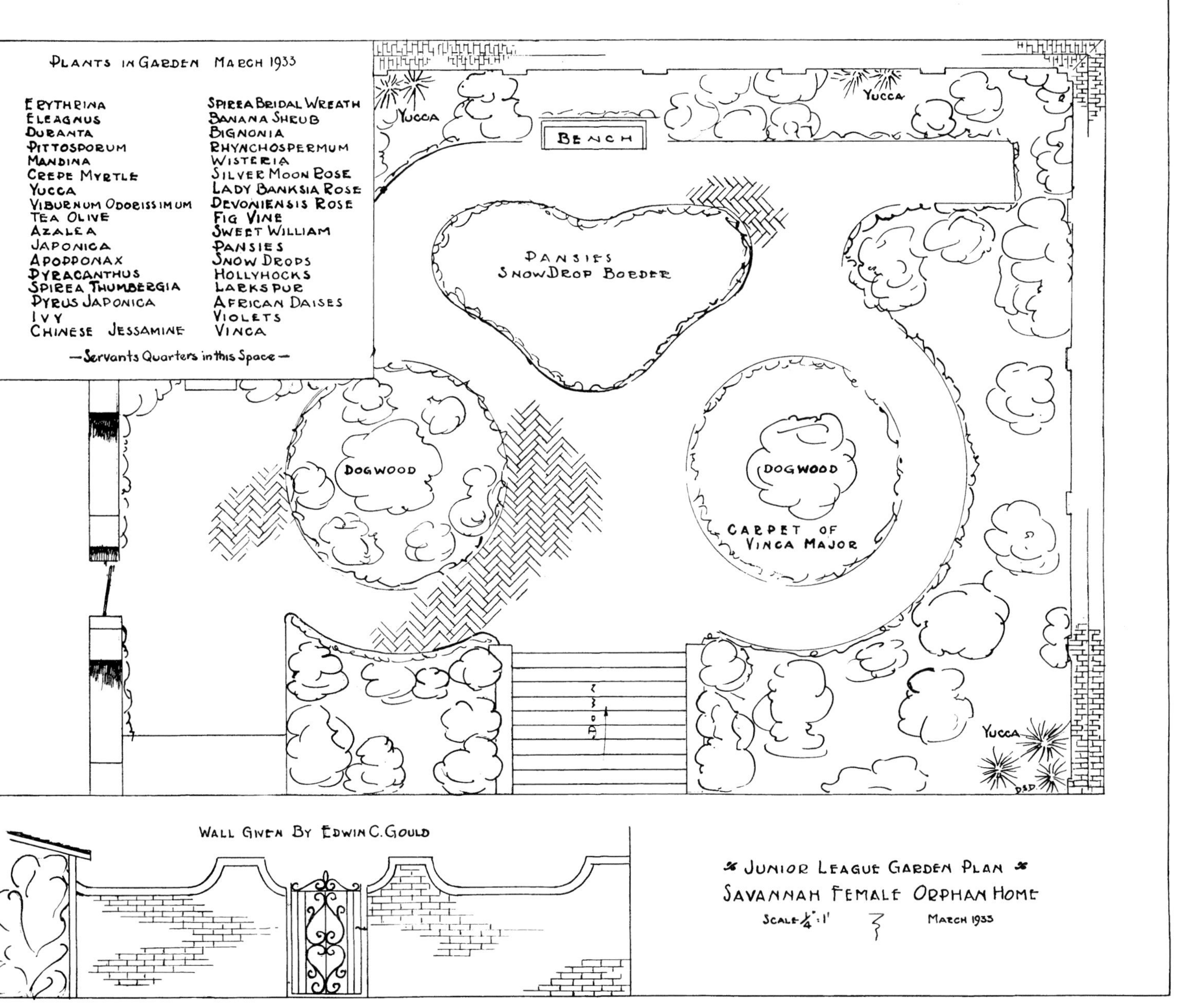

Sandersville Library Garden

Transylvania Garden Club

Sandersville

THE garden made for the Sandersville Library by the Transylvania Garden Club is consistent in character with the historic charm of the library building. Old brick from the court house that Sherman burned in 1865 were salvaged after the war and used in the construction of the quaint building now housing the library, which has wooden gables and—more recently applied—rough stucco walls. The old brick, large but not uniform in size, had been made by hand by slave labor from local clay which dried in the sun to a lovely soft brown color. In building the garden similar brown brick from the ruins of the old Masonic Temple were used—to hold the grass terrace at the rear of the library and for the gate posts and paths. A sun-dial whose pedestal is carved out of a beam of wood from the home of the first ordinary of Washington County adds another touch of local history. In front the entrance gate has columns of the old brick set in a picket fence copied from an old Charleston pattern and stained a soft weathered brown.

The picturesque library is situated in the business center of Sandersville, so the garden plot is practically enclosed on three sides by the walls of buildings. Ivy, ficus, and Virginia creeper clothe the walls with greenery and on the fourth side is a fence covered with Georgia's State flower, the Cherokee rose. The garden, of formal design, is developed in an informal way. Around an open lawn—a pleasant place for meetings and parties—are plantings of evergreen and flowering shrubs and there are thick borders of bulbs and seasonal flowers to furnish continuous color.

A salient feature of the garden plan is a fine specimen of native juniperus Virginiana planted in honor of Washington's bicentennial. This lovely memorial cedar enhances the privacy of the rear garden, almost screening it from the street, yet allowing the passer-by an alluring glimpse of the blossoming enclosure within. The path from the street to the Washington tree is bordered with dwarf boxwood and the flagstones here and at the small entrance are being assembled—each from an historic spot in Georgia.

When the library observes national book day on Washington's birthday, the garden proudly wears the national colors, in red flowering crab, white narcissus and blue violets. Later on, long spikes of creamy white hyacinths are enhanced by the golden notes of yellow daffodils, followed by pink tulips and purple iris, while valley lilies form a dainty trim in a protected nook. Pink, lavender and white azaleas claim the garden still later, then Coreopsis and larkspur in blue and gold strike the next color scheme which fades into rose and blue as pink hollyhocks and cornflowers gradually open. Easter lilies announce the arrival of summer, followed by gladioli and shasta daisies. Then perennial phlox are joined by hazy pink and gold zinnias, petunia and verbena, accented by gaillardias, and as summer begins to wane, physostegias, lupines, Michaelmas daisies and chrysanthemums furnish color preceding the autumn leaves.

The magazine, Better Homes and Gardens, awarded first honorable mention in its "More Beautiful America" contest to the Transylvania Garden Club for their Sandersville Library Garden work.

Bonaventure

Savannah

BONAVENTURE, the Colonial estate of an English gentleman, Josiah Tatnall, and his wife, Mary Mulryne, on the Savannah River, three miles below Savannah, though now used as a cemetery, was once the scene of life and gaiety. Whether it was due to the efforts of the grant landowners around Savannah to make their baronial domains vie with those of the Mother Country or whether the instinct of gardening was inborn in them, is not known. It is a fact, however, that Mr. Tatnall sent over to England for landscape gardeners to come to Georgia and expend their efforts on his broad and fertile acres. They began by planting wonderful avenues of live-oaks, that guard the dead today, in the form of a great monogram combining the letters "M" and "T." Imagine the effect now—these century-old trees, their arms interlacing and draped with Spanish moss, leading one in and out among monuments of brick and stone with here and there a vista through which one catches a glimpse of the sea. All along the way azaleas and camellias are planted, and in the early spring, wistaria vines festoon themselves into garlands overhead. There are many fine old cypress trees, while, in private sections, individuals have planted extensively Cape jasmines, tea olives, azaleas and camellias—now enormous in size.

Wistaria, Bonaventure

Moss-hung Live Oaks, Bonaventure, Savannah

Spring Hill

H. M. Patterson & Son

Atlanta

Rock Garden, Spring Hill, Atlanta Photo by Reeves

BEGUN in 1928, the original plans for the gardens at Spring Hill were made by Mr. and Mrs. Patterson, the planting effects and color harmonies later worked out by J. D. Shannon. The rambling style of the white building and the topography of the land afforded opportunity for variety in landscaping.

A wide driveway leads to the formal North Garden where the entrance is marked by large matched specimens of boxwood and two iron grey hounds. The flower borders are laid in conventional design about panels of grass intersected by gravel walks. Dwarf box has been used to outline the beds, and bleeding heart, blue phlox, iris, hardy phlox, various lilies, and standard roses are in the plantings. A field stone wall bounding this sunken area displays pocket-plantings of dianthus deltoides, creeping sedums, and similar dwarf material. Nearest the building, the wall is topped with a clipped hedge of Spirea thunbergii, and directly across in the opposite wall is a semi-circular lily pool. Two flights of steps leading to the higher level are finished with balustrades of iron grille work.

South of the building lie the rock gardens where flowering fruit trees are used with good effect and in the background are dogwood, azaleas and other shrubs. The overflow of a rockbound spring cascades over mossy boulders down to the drip pool below. There is much color in the rock plants and low-growing perennials along the stone-paved paths.

Two secluded court gardens, which are entered from the main vestibule of the building, are centered by pools set in box-edged rectangles of turf. There are foundation plantings of evergreen shrubs and a delicate tracery of vines against the white walls, while in each pool is a fountain figure. Japanese iris grow about the pool's flat rims and wrought iron vases hold trailing ivy.

Formal Sunken Garden, Spring Hill, Atlanta

Photo by Reeves

West View

Atlanta

Entrance Drive, West View, Atlanta Photo by Reeves

ON a tract of five hundred acres of rolling, beautifully wooded land—fought over during the Battle of Atlanta—West View Cemetery was founded about fifty years ago. There is unusual horticultural interest in the hundred acres which have since been developed, for here can be found probably the finest and most varied collection of plant material in the State. The landscaping of this park-like cemetery has been in the charge of two expert gardeners—both Englishmen—(the first one, in 1896, giving his name "Burford" to a handsome variety of Ilex aquifolia which originated here). More recent planting has been designed by Constance Draper.

When the drives and sections were originally planned the best of the forest trees were carefully left to attain their present fine dimensions. Today the avenues of water oaks, willow oaks, deodars, and magnolias planted at that time are almost as impressive as the big oaks, pines, elms, maples, gums, ashes, poplars and beeches of the native groves. Other trees, little used then in this part of the world, were set out—such as camperdown elm, copper beech, American and European lindens, ginkgo, koelreuteria, mossy cup oak, sophora, Schwendler's maple, cedrela and the deciduous cypress.

Coniferous trees are well represented by the

three true cedars: deodara, Atlantica, and Lebanon; Virginia red cedar, hemlocks, spruces, junipers, retinosporas, cryptomerias and cunninghamias, of considerable size—and of the pine family there are white pines, Austrian, Scotch and Himalayan as well as groves of the Georgia pine in its several varieties.

Flowering trees have been added to the native dogwood, Judas and crabapples. Prunus pissardi comes first, followed by Japanese magnolias, flowering crabs and cherries, pink dogwood, white and pink hawthorn, locusts, paulownia, smoke tree, horse chestnuts, styrax, chinaberry and mimosas.

Broad-leafed evergreens peculiarly southern in their luxuriance are used in massed plantings and are backgrounds for the various flowering shrubs which give color to almost every month in the year. Noticeably fine are the isolated specimens of osmanthus fortunei, the huge clipped globes of eleagnus pungens, English laurel and Carolina cherry laurel twenty feet wide at the base, and the rare beautiful smooth-leafed English holly in great rounded bushes thirty feet in diameter. (A seedling of this holly is the Ilex burfordii furnished by a southern nurseryman.)

In the shade of a wooded hillside is a superb collection of hybrid and American rhododendrons. Kurume azaleas bloom with the wistaria while along the grassy slopes narcissi of many types have been naturalized. Forty thousand Darwin and Cottage tulips make a brilliant display against the shrubberies and a lake is framed in wide borders of German and Siberian iris. Crepe myrtle in all colors, hardy hydrangea, tamarix, clethra, and vitex are summer featured shrubs.

In winter the cone-bearing trees and shrubs are unusually interesting, the orange globes of citrus trifoliata, the fruits of evergreen and deciduous eleagnus, cornus, and euonymous are conspicuous, while many showy berries are borne on nandinas, berberis, the ligustrums, aucuba, loniceras, pyracanthas and several varieties of ilex—verticillata, cassine and glabra, as well as the American and English hollies.

Wistaria at West View, Atlanta Photo by F. E. Lee

Showing Central Feature of English Avenue School Garden in Larkspur Time. Kindergarten Children

Public Schools

Atlanta

THE public schools of Atlanta turned to gardening in earnest when conditions during the World War made it advisable to form a school garden army into which children should be enlisted—for the purpose of conserving and supplying food and also in the interest of morale.

In 1917 the school gardens were vegetable gardens. These and an increasing number of home gardens developed under the impetus and scientific direction given by traveling supervisors in the Government service. Agricultural methods were taught to the teachers in service, and to the teachers in training as well as to the children.

Financed at first by private subscription, the work was later taken over by the Board of Education and successfully carried on under the direction of Mr. D. A. Russell, a graduate of the Tennessee Agricultural College. He was succeeded by Miss May Hardin, an Atlanta teacher, and upon her retirement in 1922 Miss Hattie Rainwater, the present supervisor, became head of nature study and gardening for the whole public school system.

With the cessation of war-time conditions the school vegetable plots gradually changed into flower gardens. Lessons in garden design and placing were added to the program, and each school garden became a law unto itself as regards structure and plan.

The Nature Study Course began in the kindergarten with lessons about the bees and butterflies, the birds and frogs. In low first grade the "Three R's" are all concerned with stories of life "down on the farm," while in high first grade the study is based on community life—the sidewalk trees, flowers in the park, and other civic plantings.

The school garden report at the close of the spring term of 1933 shows at the forty-three schools (white) a total of one hundred ten gardens, with several new ones in the making, and at each of the eleven colored schools some form of garden activity going forward regularly. These gardens are of various types—formal, informal, borders, sidewalk strips, lily pools, rose and rock gardens.

The school gardens are laboratories. Here the children experiment, test soils, learn the needs of different plants, how to improve drainage, etc.—all with the basic idea of having each child carry back to his own home the desire to build a garden, plus

Iris and Dogwood Time in the Faith School Garden, Atlanta

Third Annual Tulip Show, Atlanta Elementary Schools, Held at the W. F. Slaton School, April, 1932. Show Sponsored by Slaton Pupils

the requisite information and experience. As a direct result, during 1931-32 more than fifteen thousand home gardens were made by Atlanta school children under the supervision of teachers and classroom visiting committees.

Of great assistance in making and maintaining the children's home gardens has been the plant "pass-on" custom of the school gardens. Each spring at all the schools many flower seeds are sown and, naturally, hundreds of volunteer seedlings appear. When word is sent around by means of the "School Garden News" requests are received and filled, the pupils' home gardens being given preference, and after that, the gardens at other schools. Finally, requests for plants from anyone residing in the community are attended to, without charge.

Many other adventures in gardening have grown out of the nature study program in the Atlanta schools. The children are keenly interested in the study of flower arrangement and flower names, and in the growing of bulbs for beautifying both home and classroom. They enjoy building dish gardens and old-fashioned American gardens in miniature. Intensive bird and insect study goes on throughout the school year and into the vacation projects. Reforestation and tree planting for shade and beauty are encouraged, with emphasis on the planting and protecting of our native dogwood.

The latest and most ambitious planting project of the Public School children is the Georgia Bicentennial Memorial Forest in Peachtree Memorial Park in honor of the men and women who have notably contributed to the progress of Georgia.

In their school and home gardens the children are taught to grow all of the well-known annuals and many perennials and shrubs, and they never fail to point out to their visitors with special pride the tulip beds and chrysanthemum borders in their home gardens. There's a reason. Each April the thirty-five thousand elementary school children of Atlanta stage a Tulip Show at one of their auditoriums, when, as special prizes for the outstanding exhibits, dozens of chrysanthemum plants are given. Tulip time past, the young gardeners begin at once to concentrate upon the Chrysanthemum Show scheduled for the fall. They persevere through the summer months with digging, disbudding and spraying, and the result is a chrysanthemum show each autumn that would reflect credit upon grown-up gardeners. This time the special prizes are tulip bulbs.

With the depression, again came the need for vegetable growing. Home vegetable gardens were encouraged and Example Gardens were started on vacant lots by some of the schools in the spring of 1932. The produce was used for free lunches in the school cafeterias, and distributed in the homes of the unemployed. The "Community Gardens" work is carried on largely by unemployed fathers and emergency relief workmen, though the children help also.

Forty-three elementary and nine high schools scattered over the city of Atlanta, with the aid of their P.-T. A.'s, and the emergency relief workmen, have planted shrubbery against the school buildings and are keeping green lawns in condition the year round. These grounds have stimulated the communities in which the schools are located and many attractive home grounds have resulted.

A brief description follows of some of the elementary school gardens—planned and developed by the children themselves.

Fourth Annual Chrysanthemum Show, Held by Atlanta Elementary Schools in November, 1932, at Anne West School

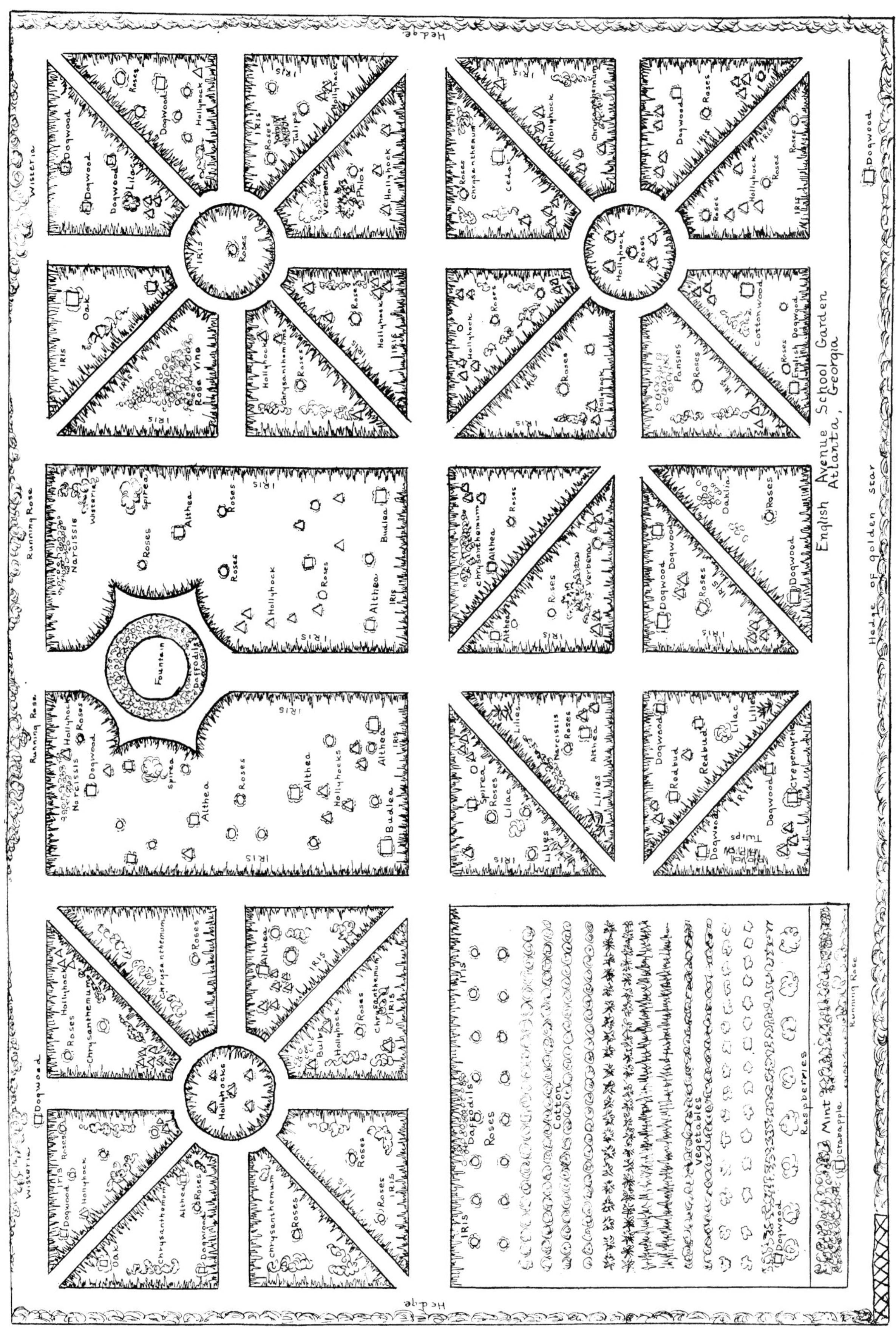
English Avenue School Garden
Atlanta, Georgia
Hedge
Hedge of golden star
Running Rose
Wisteria
Fountain
Daffodils
Vegetables
Cotton
Raspberries
Mint
Crabapple

The English Avenue School Garden, the largest and oldest of Atlanta school gardens, began in the spring of 1927, and was laid out in thirty-two divisions in order that each of the thirty-two grades might have its own small gardening space (see diagram).

Much time and thought went into working out a scheme of planting for every grade so that each season the garden presents a finished picture. There are many flowers, and in the background are dogwood and redbud trees, a young white oak, scion of the Athens tree that owns itself, and one germinated from an acorn of President Roosevelt's oaks at Warm Springs.

From its very beginning English Avenue Garden has been sort of a plant depot. Here school children throughout the entire system come each spring and avail themselves of the opportunity to stock their home gardens from the over-supply, and hundreds of seedlings find their way into numerous small backyard gardens in the community.

One section of the garden is given over to Georgia farm products. Cotton, peanuts and sweet potatoes grow in rows almost as ornamental as the flower plots, and many cotton bolls have gone from this garden into other, sometimes far distant, states. Another vegetable garden supplies vegetables for the school cafeteria and for canning.

A little garden all to itself, of which English Avenue is inordinately proud, is planned and planted by the children of the ungraded classes.

The Whitefoord School garden can be called a conservation garden—for the life of a great white oak was saved by building the garden in such close proximity to the tree that its roots could be fed and watered by the overflow from a pool which is the garden's most cherished feature. The pool is shaped like a butterfly, the wings green with parrots' feather and other aquatic plants, the spots of color being furnished by poppies, hyacinths and water lilies of many hues.

There are colorful rock gardens here, shrub plantings, rose gardens, and rose-hung picket fences, while across the street is the community vegetable garden laid off in circular rows.

The sixth grade children of the East Lake School

A Section of the Rock Garden at Whitefoord School

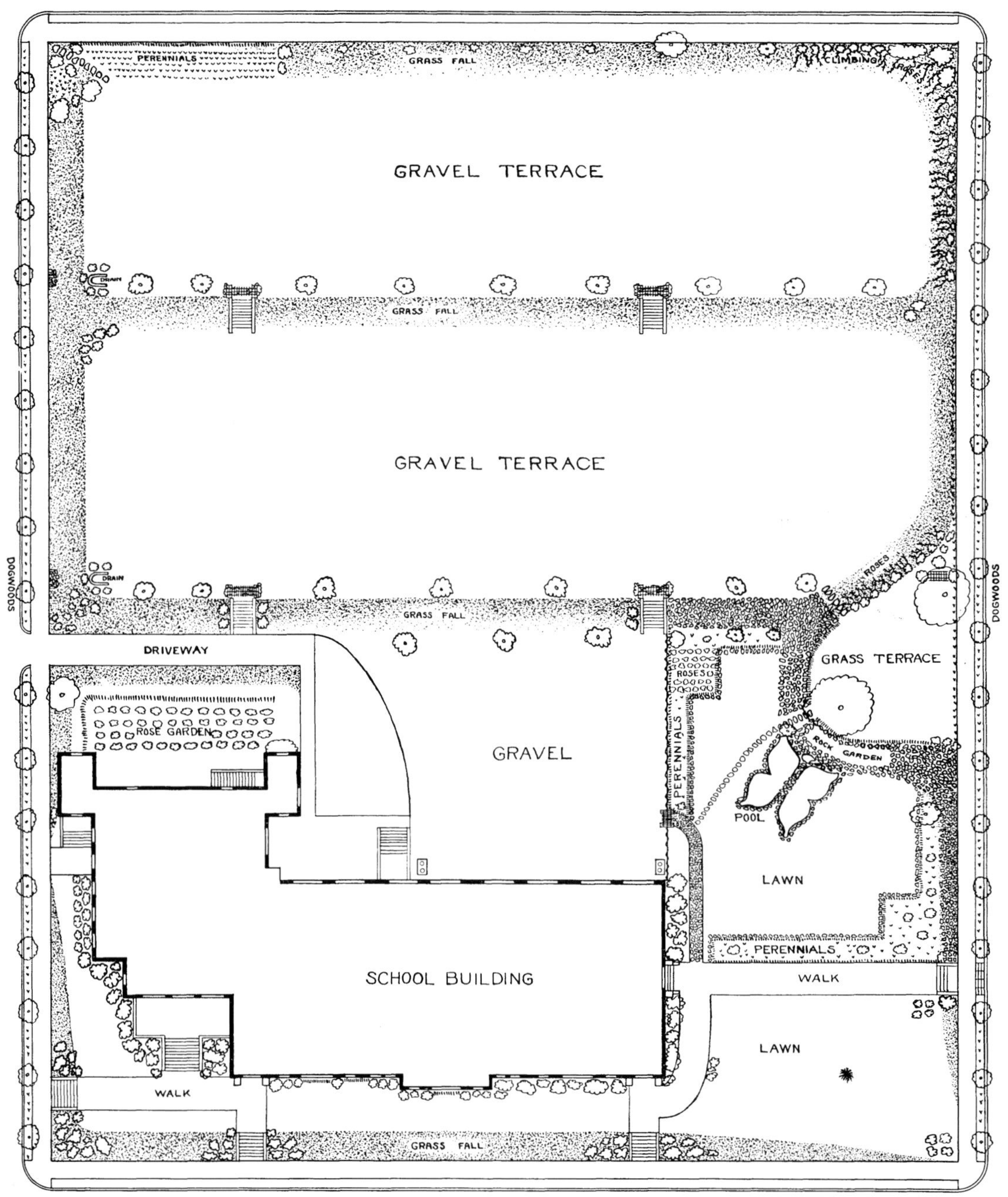

Plan of Whitefoord School Grounds, Showing Garden and Butterfly Pool

performed a notable feat of garden engineering by converting part of a narrow ravine adjacent to the playground into an interesting garden. Miracles of grading, trenching and drainage were accomplished by their own hands in making rock gardens on the steep clay banks and in laying out formally designed flower beds on the level floor of the ravine. Lovely quartz rocks were available for edging the beds and holding the planting of the banks; two pieces of cement were ingeniously made into a bird bath, and every boy and girl contributed to the "rock shower" and the "plant shower" that followed.

So successful was this venture that the other grades followed suit and soon completed the beautification of the whole strip of land. First was added another similar garden with a pool and cold frame, then rustic bridges and trellises were built, and the formal garden plots continued the length of the ravine.

Morningside School Rock Garden

A Section of East Lake School Garden

The "Beauty Spot" at Formwalt School, Gardeners from Every Grade

Faced with a situation somewhat like the one at East Lake were the children at Faith, Harris, and Tenth Street Schools. At all of these buildings an ugly red clay bank had been exposed in cutting out an area-way to admit light to basement rooms. Here the children have developed sunken gardens and Alpine gardens that are truly remarkable in the face of the adverse conditions they have had to overcome. Faith has also made extensive sidewalk gardens, and a community vegetable garden of economic usefulness. At the W. F. Slaton School is a formally laid out tulip garden and a rose square in which they take great pride.

The Moses W. Formwalt School gave a fine demonstration of soil building when, in 1929, their garden was perforce constructed on a level of hard red clay from which the top soil had been graded. Alternating crops of peas and rye were dug under, and a carefully manufactured compost heap contributed its share to the "better soil" program.

Eventually the garden was so successful that the children dubbed it the "Beauty Spot." Tulips, hardy annuals and perennials are grown in the well-planned beds, and trellises, garden seats and a bird bath were added the second year. More pretentious planting schemes are indulged in year by year, the results constituting a fine example of garden making under extreme difficulties.

At the Frank L. Stanton School all the children have had a hand in the making of their series of rock gardens. The big stones dug from the hill on which the school was built were fortunately dumped in a huge semi-circle on the banks above the playground. Enthusiastically taking charge of this unused material the children constructed steps, flagstone paths, garden seats, and even chiseled from one big stone a bird bath. Soil was brought in to make flower pockets, and many creepers and rock-loving plants were set out. One class made a terrace with flagstones and flower beds, another built a garden above the rock banks on the edge of the playground, and each class has contributed a rock garden—the resulting whole an effective series of colorful gardens made from what was regarded as waste material.

Many kinds of gardening activities go on at Adair School. Good lawns are kept up, shrubs and tulip and iris beds are under the windows of the school rooms, successive rock gardens have been laid on each side of the drive and at one corner of the lot, and, most important of all, a formally laid out flower garden has been made. Separated from the lawns by a low hedge and furnished with a background of evergreen and flowering shrubs, the generously planted flower beds are designed around a fountain of quartz rocks which sends its waters into a pool below.

Successful efforts at the high schools are the rock garden wall and curving twin stairways at the Girls' High School, and the terracing and planting of neglected slopes to the rear of the school. Attractive rock work and a pool add to the beauty of O'Keefe Junior High School's lawn; a rock garden improves the clay bank at Murphy Junior High, while the Maddox Junior High School students have built a flower garden which adds much to the beauty of their grounds. The rose garden at Maddox is their special pride.

The pupils at each of the schools are tremendously proud of the results they have achieved, and well they may be for a great deal of ingenuity and hard work have gone into the making of these gardens.

Frank L. Stanton School. One of the Many Natural Rock Gardens

Public Schools

Chatham County

SAVANNAH, Georgia's first capital, and the county seat, is situated at the very end of the eastern part of the State, in the Tidewater section, on the Savannah River, eighteen miles from the Atlantic. Nature has abundantly clothed Chatham with immense trees, shrubs and wild flowers of rare beauty.

School gardens in this county have varied horticultural histories. County schools often are close to long stretches of marshes. The fact that most of the city schools face on parks or squares, or are adjacent to them, causes one to think that the founders when selecting the site were not unmindful of the teachings of the great educator, Hermes, who maintained that "a garden should be connected with every school so that children can, at times, gaze leisurely on trees, flowers and herbs and be taught to enjoy them."

Records reveal that the first school in Georgia was Chatham Academy. It opened to pupils on January 3, 1813. The first record of garden work by pupils dates from 1919, when this Academy became a Junior High School. Miss Ruby Rahn, science teacher, sponsored the first Junior Garden Club Garden and it has functioned through each semester. Pittosporum, oleander, arbor-vitae and ivy form its background; a twin holly (gift of two pupils) is a choir loft for birds, while azaleas, spring blooming bulbs and fragrant annuals make a colorful setting for a bird bath.

The Senior High School adjoins the Junior High School, facing Bull Street with no garden other than its foundation planting of pittosporum and ivy creeping on the walls. The greensward to the edge of the pavement is adorned with various colored azaleas. These two schools, with the elementary schools in this section of the city, adopted Oglethorpe Avenue as their garden project under the combined Arbor Day program of the Garden Club of Savannah and the Park and Tree Commission. In the center of this avenue is a stretch of lawn shaded by live oaks and under these trees, on each side, the pupils planted azaleas, camellias and tea olives. This same program was repeated by pupils in the eastern section of the city, planting Henry Street for four blocks with azaleas and tea olives.

Thirty-fifth Junior High was opened in 1920. Adjoining the science rooms is a conservatory

Shrub Planting, Port Wentworth School, Savannah

where pupils may experiment in seed germination and plant propagation. The garden clubs, started this first semester, assumed responsibility and care of all school yard planting. Each year the club members care for flower boxes on the windows and the boys help in preparing soil and re-seeding the grass. On the southeastern corner is a bird bath, a gift of the 1929 class, and here in the early spring are daffodils, pansies and hyacinths, replaced later by old-fashioned annuals.

Montgomery School's Garden and Bird Club work is a garden enclosed by a high brick wall. The President of the Bird Club, a fifth grade boy, broadcasted the following over the Savannah Radio: "As President of the 'Birds' Friends Club' of Montgomery Street School, I ask the boys and girls of the city of Savannah to help us protect our bird friends. Our city is noted for its trees. Many people come to see the 'Forest City' as Savannah is called. Birds have protected trees that Oglethorpe planted long, long ago and have kept them alive to this day. I ask you to protect the birds of this city."

County school gardens are natural arboretums. Bethel, the oldest, is about fifteen miles south of Savannah and east of the Ogeechee Road. Plants from the Experimental Station, "Bamboo Farm," with magnolias and tea olives, have been planted here. On the side of the school an ugly ditch has been transformed into a charming water garden where cardinals, towhees, and brown thrashers take daily baths.

About ten miles from Savannah, just off the above mentioned highway, is the garden of the Pooler School, which has been created in the last six years in place of an ugly, barren spot. Brick walks lead from the hedge at the front to the side entrances where old-fashioned Louis Phillippe and Cherokee roses are planted. Other roses, azaleas and spireas grow in the side beds, and around the building are native evergreens. Verbenas, nasturtiums, and other annuals are near the bird bath, a gift of the pupils, while pansies which border the fish pool in winter are replaced by petunias for spring and summer. To the rear hang Uncle Remus' favorite bird houses, gourds, which are eagerly sought by purple martins when they arrive in early spring.

On the road to Carolina, about seven miles from Savannah, are the gardens of Port Wentworth School, begun in 1927. Each fall additions of evergreens, flowering shrubs and roses are made, euonymus, pittosporum, ligustrum, abelia, spirea and oleander, palmettos and live oaks, dogwoods and tea olives making this limited area a place of beauty. Annuals and perennials for spring and summer are cared for by the children, and in the lily pool a lotus bloomed on Christmas Day last

Continuation of View on Opposite Page

year. A rock garden, sun dial and bird bath are gifts of the pupils.

Isle of Hope School records show that its first garden was started in 1914 with a planting of rambler roses and annuals. This garden now covers about two acres of ground. The County Commissioners gave labor and material; fertilizer came from Ossabaw; English ivy from Wormsloe, azaleas from the Solomon gardens, and friends in the community sent hydrangeas. Wistaria and woodbine brought by the pupils twine with the Cherokee roses round the trunks of live oaks which are a hundred or more years old. Ivy makes a green wrap on other trees, around whose base there is always a mass of bloom and in their shade a bird bath and feeding stand are placed. The pupils place bits from their own lunch on the stand for the birds, who in return gather insects from the fifty-two species of plant life in this garden.

Montgomery Rural School is about eleven miles from Savannah. Its garden bears the name of "Beck Park." When the school was built in 1917, one-tenth of an acre was separated from the two-acre tract of the school grounds. The land was cleared and leveled by the County Commissioners; the pupils on hands and knees cleared the soil of rubbish, roots and other obstacles to gardening. Mr. Everett, custodian of schools and grounds, planned and laid out the plot, carefully protecting the oaks, pines, gums, dogwood, redbud and holly trees on the site. Abelias and spirea are in the foundation planting; crepe myrtle and altheas are grouped about the grounds, and azaleas border the driveway. A rose garden features many colors and kinds of roses, and the walks are bordered with beds of perennials and annuals. A granite bird bath, martin box and feeding shelf were gifts, but other boxes and food shelters are the workmanship of the boys.

Thunderbolt School gardens are about five miles from Savannah, facing Victory Drive. The first school building was erected in 1917, and at that time the children planted wistaria and yellow jessamine to run on fence and trees. On the grounds are the original live oak trees. In 1927 a more ambitious garden was commenced. Through a greensward of goose grass goes an entrance walk bordered with pansies, violets and dwarf boxwood. Arbor vitae mark the entrance on the street where magenta azaleas under dogwood trees tie in the garden with the azalea and Palmetto Highway leading to the ocean. Ivy, wistaria and woodbine climb the live oaks, where there are bird houses made by the boys. A garden of bush roses is enclosed by a fence of Cherokee roses which also serves as a trellis for perennial sweet peas. The Park and Tree Commission, Savannah Garden Club and numbers of interested friends assisted the gardeners in supplying abelias, spireas and roses.

Old Oglethorpe University

Milledgeville

SEVERAL miles from Milledgeville at Midway, on the site of old Oglethorpe University, Dr. and Mrs. H. D. Allen have built a rock garden, a memorial to the old institution which in 1860 gave its life, in giving its student body en masse to the Confederate cause. The large rocks used in the construction of the garden and the pool had been the foundation stones of the main University building. The pool is now placed on the spot from which the cornerstone of the main building was dug after the fire which destroyed it many years ago, and the cornerstone itself has been incorporated in a marker within the confines of the garden. The marker was set up by the Daughters of the American Revolution in commemoration of the University (see engraving). A picture of Oglethorpe and many valuable papers were found in the cornerstone, some of the papers were presented by Dr. and Mrs. Allen to Dr. Thornwell Jacobs, president of new Oglethorpe University, while others may be seen in the Sidney Lanier room in Thalian Hall, the only one left of the original buildings of the old University.

Memorial Rock Garden, Old Oglethorpe, Milledgeville

New Oglethorpe University

Atlanta

FROM Old Oglethorpe University yard and its memorial garden interest turns naturally to New Oglethorpe University and the beauty of its grounds. Six hundred acres of native woodland surrounding an eighty-two-acre lake and fronting on Peachtree Road comprise the campus of New Oglethorpe. This woodland is rich in the tree, shrub and small plant life characteristic of North Georgia, and springtime brings each year its wealth of bloom: dogwood, wild crab, redbud, azaleas, hawthorns, viburnums and millions of small flowering plants. Nature has been especially generous to the Oglethorpe woods in her gift of wild flower variety, and a careful study is sure to disclose one or two species not found in other woodlands about Atlanta. The entire six hundred acres is kept as a bird refuge—the combined presence of water and woodland making the situation ideal for bird life. It is the plan of the University to border Silver Lake with Japanese cherry trees and already, for about a thousand feet, the double boulevard known as Lanier Avenue, leading from Peachtree Road to the lake, is divided by an old-fashioned hedge row of scores of flowering shrubs.

The college buildings are in a section of the campus near Peachtree Road and the grounds are being developed gradually. A quadrangle has been made into a yard by means of a studied planting of blossoming and broad-leaf evergreen shrubs on the outline and near the buildings, and at the front is a lawn on which specimen native oaks have been left and handsome maples have been planted. Between the buildings are borders of annuals to give a touch of summer color, while in spring the beds are filled with tulips, a gift direct from Holland. In the rear of the Administration building is a rose garden against a background of shrubs and native trees.

Of the six hundred acres comprising the campus of Oglethorpe University four hundred acres, including the eighty-two-acre Silver Lake, were given to the University by Mr. William Randolph Hearst.

Rome

Court Garden, Shorter College

High School
Rome

FOLLOWING the custom of several years the senior class at Rome High School in 1932 left a gift to the school. Always the seniors' gifts are to be kept and cherished by the lower classes, but this gift is to be kept and cherished with an even more precious care, for it consists of the start of a Shakespearian Garden, the first of its kind in the State.

In 1932, on Shakespeare's birthday, April 23rd, the garden was presented to the school by the president of the senior Scribblers' Club and received by the principal and the president of the Junior Scribblers with appropriate assurances that the succeeding classes would treasure always and endeavor to develop and enlarge this living heritage.

The garden is laid out on the lower terrace of

Shakespeare Garden, Rome High School

Shorter College
Rome

THE COURT is a formal garden and of a dignity not to be ruffled by the chatter of the girls as they laugh along its brick-lined walks for, though it is walled in on three sides by the ivy-covered red brick buildings, it looks out upon the northern hills and valleys in solemn contemplation.

Tall sugar-berry trees, to right and to left, afford the robins and the blue birds high perches on which to sing to southern skies; and on the laurels of hunter's green cardinals hint that summer soon shall come. Below in the center walk is a white marble sundial that not only shows the time of day, but also directs attention to that part of the garden which is most beautiful—the heart or center—the lily pool. The pool is bounded by a ring of spirea which touches the gravel walk and four stately cedar trees look into the crystal water where gold fish play among the white and yellow lilies and their green lily pads.

the school grounds and patterned after the Italian garden plans of the prevailing fashion in England in Shakespeare's day. Here are planted most of the ninety-nine flowers, herbs and shrubs mentioned in the plays, that will thrive in this climate. There are romantic nooks made by the high cut rock steps and vine hung corners. A tiny fish pond set in uneven stones holds pale water lilies and gold fish (named after characters in the plays!) A bath for the birds centers its garden and bird houses are set back in a near-by wistaria vine.

What keener inspiration could there be for a budding "Scribbler" than this glamorous spot—fragrant with violets and pansies, rosemary and herb-grace — in which to sit and dream on the "honied muse"?

Martha Berry Schools

Mount Berry

A GARDEN for a lovely home; a campus that is a garden for America's largest school estate; and a garden to God, where stately branches of lofty poplars are lifted against the rugged rocks and tower of the Lavender Range; these are the three gardens created in Georgia for her schools by Martha Berry, founder and director of the Berry Schools for boys and girls of the eleven southern states who were low in cash but high in character qualities.

Today the "Road of Opportunity," a wide grey-pebbled drive, between a line of stately elms and a second row of dogwood trees is a memorial to the efforts of the founder. Miss Berry walked through the woods, attaching white ribbons to likely young trees. Boys in the school followed, digging up the trees and bringing them to the drive. The boys in those days were not trained and were far from expert tree-planters, so some of the trees died and had to be replaced. Elms are of slow growth, and although they have already formed a lovely arch over the road, it will be a hundred years

The Gate of Opportunity, Martha Berry Schools

before their real zenith comes. But thirty years have passed and the elm-lined driveway has its place in the hearts of ten thousand boys and girls who have passed up and down its shaded walks.

When an entirely new campus was created from a corn field for a group of new stone buildings, long lanes of trees were moved and planted along the driveways. With the passing of years expert direction and better equipment had been acquired for transplanting, and tall pines that lifted their proud crests fifty feet from the ground were moved; elms thirty and forty feet high were started in new pastures. "Living in one place might get tiresome for a tree as well as for a person," says Martha Berry cheerily.

The entire thirty-thousand-acre campus of the Schools has been made a forest, fish and game preserve.

Air heavy with the scent of roses, jasmine, and honeysuckle, eyes dazzled with the splendor of acres of white and pink dogwood trees, canyons abloom with myriads of lavender and orchid azaleas, while hill slopes beyond gleam with daffodils and jonquils—these are among the delights which have been created at Berry. All winter nandina flaunts its scarlet berries in gorgeous clusters against the walls of grey stone buildings and the background of sedge fields that otherwise would be bleak and sere.

Sleepless nights were caused by the slough, swamp and mosquito-infested grounds back of the Girls' School. Drastic measures were necessary. It was decided to have the swamp cleaned of all trees and shrubs, a dam built, and a lake made. The result is Victory Lake, today a broad placid expanse of water where migrating ducks nestle in safety, and weeping willow trees form a background to waters that mirror the hazy Blue Ridge mountains in the distance.

At Oakhill, the birthplace and home of Martha Berry, stands the lovely old colonial house, a typical Georgian creation of the period when Greek architecture had become the standard of the South. At the front and back of the house are the classic white pillars that stretch from the lawn to the roof.

Naturally the first problem in planting around a period-type house is to create a garden that belongs. Long ago the boxwood-bordered walks were planted around Oakhill and dwarf box was set out against the base of the house. English ivy swirled over the brick steps in riotous profusion, aids in blending the house with the landscape.

Tall English hollies grow near the house on each side, the scarlet berries vivid in the green against the white woodwork. Red cedars point skyward, and Cape jasmine and splendid old magnolia trees are near the porticos. Walks radiating from the house go southward into the formal box garden, the rose garden, and the walled garden. Northward, a golden rose-arched pathway leads to a summer house two hundred yards away, at the edge of the bluffs overlooking the Oostanaula river valley. Directly in front of the house is a wide terrace and the great oak grove from which Oakhill derives its name. Behind the house is the brick paved piazza that merges into the terraced garden, by means of a broad, ivy-clad step leading onto the grass. A wall of old English box surrounds this terrace, where the white peacocks love to strut—beautiful silhouettes against the evergreens.

The old rose garden is surrounded with a hedge of smaller English box and purple violets that bloom all winter line every walk. Petunias, pansies, mignonette and heliotrope are mixed in borders along the paths, while farther back across a stretch of green turf is the circular rose garden, where several hundred rose bushes brighten the spring and summer air with fragrant blooms. Where a natural semi-circle occurs in the bluff, an iris garden has been made in a series of terraces. In the stone walks old millstones mark each corner and intersection. A rectangular reflecting pool centers the rose garden. Another pool, diamond-shaped, with a sparkling cascade tumbling from its fountain, centers the rock garden, where flowers of many types are transplanted by trained student gardeners for each changing season. Near the crossing of paths is a granite sun dial of which the old colored mammy, who lives close by, has her own idea—"Sun dial! Hm! It mought as well be keepin' Chinese time for all the good it do. What would a body use a sun dial for when the only time you wants to set the clock is nights when it's bein' wound—and then what-for good is the sun?"

Past Aunt Martha's tiny house the walk leads through roses and box bushes to a seat encircled by slender Lombardy poplars and cypresses. A pine-needle path wanders on down the bluffs into the shadows of giant oak and pine trees where a gurgling spring whispers over a large worn rock, drips into a fern bank and scurries down the slope towards the waiting river. Azalea, laurel, dogwood, and flowering bulbs of various kinds lend color to this forest garden.

Upward again the trail leads to the summer house at the north end of the gardens. Here the

Oakhill, Ancestral House and Garden of Martha Berry, Founder of the Martha Berry Schools

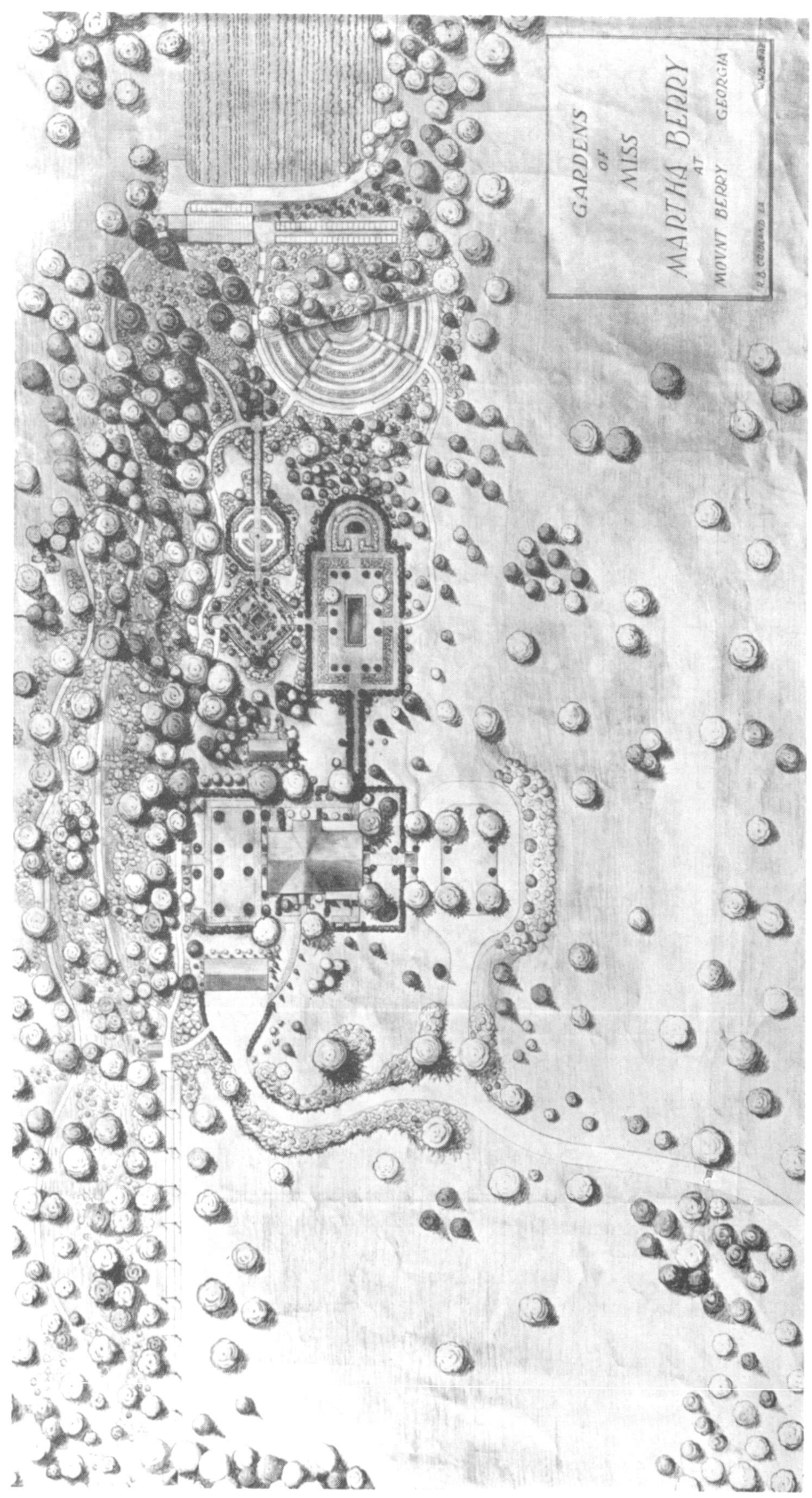
GARDENS
OF
MISS
MARTHA BERRY
AT
MOUNT BERRY GEORGIA

Martha Berry's House o' Dreams and Garden on Lavender Mountain

view looks down across a broad expanse of green to the cabin in which the Berry Schools were founded. Around the cabin is an atmosphere of another day, the grounds a carpet of bright wild flowers right up to the door, whereon a coon skin is tacked, looking as if it had been there twice thirty years.

Oakhill brings to mind the graciousness and spaciousness of life in the Old South, a cherished bit of memory living on with Martha Berry in modern days.

Scraping the top off a mountain is quite an effort, but that is what it took to begin the House o' Dreams garden, Martha Berry's retreat atop Lavender ridge, at the very heart of the Berry grounds.

Building a five-mile road that back-tracks and twists itself into dizziness on hill slopes five hundred to one thousand feet sheer, was a bit of the task in converting Mount Berry into a garden. Along the road is the natural beauty of a profusion of wild shrubs and there are many glorious views across wide valleys to far-off misty blue hills before the walled corner is turned which ends in a tulip-filled court beside the House o' Dreams.

The thick-walled ivy-covered stone house lifts its sturdy chimneys against the battling storms and winds of the mountain top. Inside are guest and rest rooms, and a sitting room the length of the building which is dwarfed by a huge fireplace "to sit by and re-make the far-away work-a-day world." From the top of Mount Berry on a clear day one can see Little Sand Mountain, twenty miles away in Alabama, Lookout Mountain, sixty miles away in Tennessee, and, farther still, the faint shimmering peaks of the Cohuttas, seventy-five miles away in North Carolina.

The terrace of the house is a partly closed-in bit of the surrounding garden, for house and garden live closely together in their seclusion on the mountain top. The various garden levels are held by thick rock walls, and flagstone paths connect the lawn (where a blue peacock spreads his brilliant fan) with the garden and the lily pool.

A wistaria-covered arbor offers shade from the bright sun and a frame for the panoramic view. Fragrant boxwood, lilacs and snowballs grow along the walls. A lower terrace is given over to peach trees, strawberries and raspberries. Hollyhocks, delphinium, dahlias, chrysanthemums, and the other flowers which flourish in the borders, seem stronger, sweeter and intensified in color in this garden against the sky.

Campuses

University of Georgia

Athens

THE University of Georgia bears the distinction of being the oldest chartered State University in the country. Its charter antedates the Constitution of the United States, as it was granted by the Legislative Assembly in 1785. At that time the site chosen for the institution was practically on the Indian frontier.

Lands on the banks of the Oconee River were set aside for the use of the University. On these lands, purchased largely from the University, the city of Athens grew up following the opening of the institution in 1801. Soon after 1900, expansion became imperative, and the University, with the assistance of the alumni and other friends, repurchased properties that had at one time belonged to it. Now the campus contains more than a thousand acres.

At this date there are three separate, yet intimately connected, portions of the institution: namely, the grounds around the original Franklin College which were begun in 1801; those about the Teachers College of the University which are on lands donated by the University to the State Normal School in 1892; and finally the campus of the Georgia State College of Agriculture, the development of which started in 1907. These properties were managed and planted separately until 1932 when they were combined into one institution under the Board of Regents.

The old campus was started in 1801. History does not relate that any plans were laid for its development. Numerous massive oaks and pines were left from the native growth and convenient walks and drives were constructed as may be seen from the picture of the campus in the forties. Several of the trees shown are still living and five of the buildings are in use. As with most old institutions, construction took place without regard to plan, "things just developed" and convenience in walks and roads predominated over beauty. Little or no money was expended on the campus itself, though during the early days of the institution there was a marked interest in plants and a large botanical garden was maintained along Tanyard Branch. This thrived for many years and in this section of the city of Athens numerous interesting and imported plants may yet be seen. This garden disappeared immediately following the War Between the States and the property was sold for residential purposes.

At one time there were many fine plantings on the campus itself, but these have fallen before the march of progress, the last specimen being removed in 1931. During the nineties the main quadrangle was planted by P. J. Berckmans, a noted horticulturist of the State, but the work was not continued nor maintained, and has now disappeared.

Tree and Old College of 1801, University of Georgia Campus

In 1906, with the establishment of the Georgia State College of Agriculture and with an extensive educational expansion just ahead, Mr. George Foster Peabody supplied funds for a planning of the campuses of the three institutions in Athens by Charles W. Leavett of New York. The plans were excellent but called for the moving of "Old

University of Georgia, 1830

College," the first building on the campus, and sentiment within the Board of Trustees prevented this; consequently the development was blocked. The last decade has developed renewed interest in landscaping, and at this time the grounds of Franklin College, commonly called the University, are in better condition than ever before.

In spite of its haphazard growth, this campus is well worth visiting. It is filled with traditions and mellowed with age. Its academic walk is flanked on one side by the classic columns of Greece and on the other by magnificent trees whose shadows lay a mosaic across the path that has been trod by Georgia's great since the days the Colony became a State. Its chapel, more than a century old, is one of the most satisfying examples of ante-bellum architecture in the South. It looks out upon a quadrangle most attractive in effect and just in front of it is a sundial, marking the spot of the historic Toombs oak. In the newer part of the campus is the new stadium filling a natural amphitheatre. This structure is excellent in design and planting. It is already notable and destined to become more so for few, if any, stadiums in America have a setting of such natural beauty. Broadleafed evergreens have been liberally used about it and large quantities of eleagnus perfume the southern autumn with its elusive and mystic sweetness, a rare atmosphere to pervade nationally famous gridiron struggles which are watched by cheering thousands.

In 1906, the Legislature established the Georgia State College of Agriculture and located it on nearly 1,000 acres of land purchased by the alumni of the University and contiguous to the University campus. Leavett's plan included the development of this new purchase and the main building, Conner Hall, and the roads about it were located in conformity with his plan. This campus has had more careful supervision than either of the other two. Building crowding has been avoided save in the instance of Governor Wilson Lumpkin's home which was built in 1830 and stands near the site of Conner Hall. Great open spaces feature the development which is now about twenty-five years old and when it is realized that the grounds have been created from open farm lands the present results are little less than marvelous. The future will mellow and mature it into one of the outstanding institutions of the State.

This campus is a combination of natural and planned gardening. There are walks and drives along the Oconee River; vast open areas, formal gardens and woods of natural growth, cleared just enough to make them attractive. On the grounds is an open-air theater, one of the largest in the

Grass-carpeted Stage, Outdoor Theatre, Agricultural College, University of Georgia, Athens

Air View of University of Georgia Campus (1933). Franklin College Buildings and Stadium in Upper Right. Outdoor Theatre in Center, Partly Surrounded by Agricultural College Buildings

Academic Walk, University of Georgia

country, capable of holding twenty thousand or more people. There are formal gardens and collections of plants well worth studying. A series of lakes gives opportunity for water plant culture and adds greatly to the beauty of the grounds. The atmosphere of this campus is entirely different from that of the old University. Its broad fields, sweeping roads, woods and open lawns proclaim the new ideas in gardening, yet it has kept enough of the classical feeling to accentuate the modern.

The campus of the State Teachers College is two miles from the other colleges of the University. This was organized in 1892 as the State Normal School. The University gave it forty acres of land and a building known as "The Rock College." With this as a beginning quite a remarkable institution was developed, though a rapid increase in student body and a comparatively small area of ground forced a crowding of buildings arranged on no particular plan. Not much was done until 1901, when an extensive planting of trees and walk construction greatly improved the grounds. In 1906, Leavett made a plan for the institution, but lack of money has prevented its development. Recently some new properties have been added and under the new organization rapid improvement is to be expected.

Many of the buildings are vine covered and several of the quadrangles have been made into formal gardens worthy of note. There are many attractive spots on the campus, including the plantings near Winnie Davis Hall and about the Library as well as around Gilmer Hall, the oldest building.